Loss and Grief:
Psychological Management
in Medical Practice

Loss and Grief:
Psychological Management
in Medical Practice

Edited by Bernard Schoenberg, Arthur C. Carr,
David Peretz, and Austin H. Kutscher

Columbia University Press / New York and London   1970

Copyright © 1970 Columbia University Press

ISBN: 0-231-03329-X

Library of Congress Catalog Card Number: 75-118356

Printed in the United States of America

Foreword

Man's long-standing inclination to deny the threat of death and illness has been reinforced in recent years by the very successes of medicine's application of science to its practice. The frequent and recurrent tragedy of early demise, maiming, and crippling for many is, in certain ways, less pressing now than in the past. At the same time, however, those protective social and psychological defenses against the pain of loss and grief, devised over the centuries to afford man relief from these overbearing emotional responses, are weakened by the omnipresent threat of nuclear holocaust, war, violence, and the diminished dependence on religious faith.

Perhaps the recognition of a necessity to understand and support man more adequately today in the face of threats to his existence has brought those in the health professions to address themselves so directly to the emotional struggles of patients and others confronted with potential death or impairing illness. Psychological and psychoanalytic theory until recently gave only limited attention to the response and adaptation of man to these threats. Freud was concerned largely with man's conflicts in regard to socially forbidden sexual, aggressive, and dependency drives. His interests were other than those experienced by his colleagues who practiced in the hospitals and clinics where men and women regularly faced immediate threats to their existence. Psychoanalytic theory left open the need for the emergence of existential philosophy and psychology with their concern for man's struggle to attain a sense of being and the consequences of loss of his adaptation.

The editors and contributors to this volume are to be commended for bringing together the wealth of information, theoretical and prac-

FOREWORD

tical, now available for the comprehension of man's struggles to cope with loss and its associated emotion, grief. This knowledge has immediate and valuable application to alleviate the suffering of our fellow men, whether they be ill or suffering as members of the family, friends or associates of the sick person. Too, the editors and contributors have sought through their efforts new information of the experiences of men derived from the direct subjective knowledge of those who have so suffered.

Whether physician, nurse, psychologist, social worker, clergyman, family member, or friend, the reader will find in this volume much of aid and value to assist others in the acceptance of loss that is necessary to the support of continuing health.

Lawrence C. Kolb

Preface

The preparation of this volume began with the editors' shared observation that present-day health education and practice, by and large, have overlooked the psychology of loss, grief, and bereavement, and the management of both the dying patient and the bereaved. The cure of disease and prolongation of life constitute the dominant priorities in medicine, while the psychophysiological and psychosocial effects of loss upon patients and families are generally neglected. During the past ten years, with the publication of excellent journal articles and specialized books on the subject, cracks in the barrier of denial and avoidance of these subjects have begun to appear. To our knowledge, however, there is no available volume which emphasizes the psychological management of the patient or family members who have sustained or anticipate serious loss.

Recent surveys of medical, nursing, and theological schools by the editors have indicated that the gap in this crucial area of education for practitioners remains largely unfilled. It is our hope that this book will, in some measure, bridge this gap for students of the health professions and for established practitioners who must remain students if they are to meet the needs of their patients and their own ideals of service.

From the beginning, the editors recognized that no single individual can any longer be expected to prepare an "authoritative" textbook, covering one, let alone several, entire disciplines. Thus, it was evident from the outset that if this book were to fulfill the objective of being truly authoritative, the editors would have to be dependent upon specialists in each of a number of specific fields. The contributors were carefully selected so as to obtain scholarly manuscripts. We have ac-

PREFACE

cepted some repetition of basic concepts in recognition that some will prefer to read only those chapters related to their own area of interest.

We are indebted to numerous individuals for their advice and aid in regard to the accuracy of textual material. Many of our colleagues at the College of Physicians and Surgeons of Columbia University and at the New York State Psychiatric Institute were most generous with help and criticism. The reference librarians of both institutions provided constant assistance.

The contributions of Miss Ann Calderwood and Mrs. Lillian G. Kutscher require special comment. Our warmest thanks are extended to them for their inestimable aid in reading and editing each manuscript.

Dr. Austin I. Mehrhof, Jr., Dr. Alan Rosell, and Dr. Geoffrey Robinson, while students, performed a great many of the details necessary to the compilation of the manuscript.

We are also grateful to the many secretaries who worked diligently with us, and especially do we extend our appreciation to Mrs. Roberta Scioscio, Mrs. Mary Lou Woods, Mrs. Joyce Rosso and Mrs. Kathleen Young.

Finally, we express our gratitude to the Foundation of Thanatology for financial support and encouragement in this endeavor.

The Editors

Contents

CONTENTS

Contents

HUMANISTIC AND BIOLOGIC CONCEPTS REGARDING
LOSS AND GRIEF

Loss and Grief:
Psychological Management
in Medical Practice

I

Psychological Concepts Central to Loss and Grief

1

Development, Object-Relationships, and Loss

David Peretz

Loss and the Health Personnel

Loss is an integral part of human experience which has profound consequences from birth to death. The physician and nurse face loss daily and must constantly deal with the diverse reactions to various forms of loss, including death. The physician and nurse must manage the loss itself, the reactions of patient and family to the loss, the responses of other medical personnel, and, eventually, the patient's family in its bereavement.

The meaning of loss and death to the physician, nurse, and other health personnel is woven into the fabric of their identity. For many, the core of their self-image is that of a "helping person." This legitimately provides gratification of pride and curiosity in seeking answers to problems of health and illness. On the other hand, many health personnel seek through their particular identities and social roles to regain childhood feelings of omnipotence. The very act of struggling against loss, pain, disability, and ultimately, death, enhances feelings of power and security. The patient's awe of the physician as possessor of special knowledge, secrets, and remedies may be a source of considerable pleasure. But the long-range problem this engenders is that each major loss sustained by a patient becomes a personal defeat for the physician and nurse. When to this is added grief over the anticipated loss of a patient with whom the individual has worked, it is easy to understand the frequent defensive maneuver of psychological isolation. At times, the physician may literally withdraw from the patient, spending less and less time with him or transferring his care to other medical personnel.

The physician and nurse are in a unique position with respect to death. While other individuals may be supported in their psychological denial of death by long periods without major loss, most physicians and nurses meet it frequently, if not daily, in their practice. From their first day of training they must cope with the reality of death. Indeed, in the anatomy room the harbingers of reactions to death can be seen almost in caricature. Some students become depressed; some display grisly humor; some displace their rage at death onto their partners at the table; some drop out of school; some let their partners do the work while they learn just enough to get by, studying the illustrated text and preferring the disembodied illustrations to the real thing.

The individual's response is determined by his previous experience with loss and death, by his methods of coping with the vicissitudes of pain, by cultural prescriptions available for handling the fact of death, and later by the structure of his professional identity.

The health professional must be prepared to recognize and manage his own anticipation of and reaction to loss as well as the reactions of the patient, the patient's family, and paramedical personnel who must serve the dying patient. Death and the treatment of the dying patient are rarely subjects of a health professional school curriculum; any such education usually has as its source major figures in the student's education who serve as role-models. Certain principles can serve to augment the understanding, prediction, and management of reactions to loss as they occur in medical practice.

Types of Loss

Loss may be defined as a state of being deprived of or being without something one has had. While certain losses are necessary concomitants of growth and are predictable, others are haphazard and unpre-

4

dictable. Losses may be sudden or gradual, traumatic or non-traumatic. As will become apparent in subsequent chapters of this book, loss may take many different forms.

1) Undoubtedly, the most profound loss experienced by individuals (and of which physicians are most generally aware) is the loss of a significant loved or valued person. The loss may be total or partial, permanent or temporary. Loss of a loved or valued person usually occurs through death, although it may also occur through divorce or separation. The incapacitation of a valued person through acute or chronic illness may result in loss of some aspect of that person, such as a special quality or attribute which provided gratification.

2) One may also lose some aspect of the "self." By self, we refer to the over-all mental representation or image each of us has of his body and of his person. This self-representation includes ideas and feelings about the self, its worth, attractiveness, lovability, special qualities and capacities. Loss of health, for example, is usually experienced as a change in some aspect of the self. It may be felt as loss of a positive feeling state replaced with vague malaise, weakness, pain, easy fatigability, or other symptoms. There may be partial or total loss of a body function, such as ease in breathing or regularity of bowel function. Visual acuity, hearing, memory, intellectual power, motor coordination, sensation, and strength may be lost to varying degrees. The individual may face loss of a body part due to trauma, amputation, mastectomy, or colectomy. Reduced bodily drives such as appetite and sexual interest are also experienced as loss. Loss of positive self-attitudes such as attractiveness, pride, esteem, independence, or control, as well as important ideals, can also have marked psychological and physiological consequences. Loss of self-definitions—social roles such as occupation, profession, position in the family, and the status associated with each—frequently has dramatic impact on a person's life. Even the loss of an old, familiar symptom as a result of medical intervention can result in unpleasant feeling states when the symptom has provided degrees of secondary gain and control over aspects of the environment.

3) A third form of loss is that of external objects. These can be loss of possessions such as money, treasures, home, or homeland.

4) A fourth form of loss is developmental loss, or that loss which occurs in the process of human growth and development. The child loses the breast or the bottle, his teeth and hair, and a host of grati-

5

fications associated with secured positions (for example, an only child is displaced from the center of attention with the birth of a sibling). Parallel with the growth of physical, psychological, and emotional capacities, loss of gratifications associated with more rudimentary abilities occurs. These gratifications may have been provided by others in the environment. As more equipment becomes available for mastery, these significant individuals expect more of the child who must renounce certain pleasures and techniques, at times before substitutes or alternatives are well established. While the newly acquired emotional and cognitive capacities aid in sustaining frustration and integrating the experience of loss, the quality and quantity of the loss as well as its meaning at the time may nevertheless create a negative and lasting impression upon the developing personality of the child.

Loss is simultaneously a real event and a perception by which the individual endows the event with personal or symbolic meaning. One may experience an event as a loss when another individual would not describe it as such. Loss of honor or "loss of face" are examples of this kind of loss. Symbolic loss or anticipated loss, just as actual loss, may produce intense and sometimes pathologic reactions.

Each loss carries with it the threat of additional or future loss. For example, serious loss of health may lead to loss of skills, loss of job, loss of role as a breadwinner, and real or anticipated loss of respect from others. There may be associated loss of pride as well.

Infancy and childhood are particularly vulnerable times for loss to occur. Old age, when defensive and adaptive skills are often diminished, is another time when loss which would otherwise prove surmountable may overwhelm the psychic apparatus, resulting in depression and/or symptoms of or predisposition to illness. At times losses that are necessary and expectable may prove traumatic to an individual because of his limited physical or emotional capacity to master the loss.

Because loss is a universal experience, it may easily be overlooked as an etiologic agent in the production of disease and dysfunction. There is increasing evidence which assigns to it a sometimes central, sometimes peripheral role in the pathogenesis and outcome of illness. The period of bereavement following loss of a loved or valued person is one of greater risk in terms of the precipitation of illness and death for the bereaved individual. Other findings (see Chapter 3) relate object-loss to the pathogenesis of certain symptoms and serious illnesses.

6

Development and Object-Relations

Birth itself constitutes a sudden loss of the relative security of intra-
uterine life. While the gain of neonatal life lies in its potential autonomy,
life is more dangerous for the newborn than it was in previous months
in utero. The human infant depends heavily on the good graces of other
persons for its survival. Although its cries and smiles evoke maternal
responses in the human object, the gratifications are not nearly so constant as in utero. Placental circulation and cushioning provide a more
even flow of metabolites, excretion, and temperature regulation than
life in the external world. If abandoned during the early years of its
life, the infant suffers extreme tension and discomfort as fundamental
needs go unmet, and will inevitably die. The reaction of young children to even brief separation from those who provide their primary
care suggests the degree of threat to survival they experience. As cognitive capacities gradually develop, the threat of separation or loss
appears to be experienced as the dreadful anticipation of uncomfortable feeling states associated with lack of the human object—the person who has provided a variety of life-sustaining, tension-reducing, or
pleasurable gratifications.

The earliest communication and hence relationship of the infant
with other humans is through the mouth and skin as well as hands and
fingers. Skin and body contact in the earliest months becomes one route
toward the definition of an autonomous self. The kinesthetic experiences of one's body in action is another aspect of the rudimentary
organization of self. Space is explored, at first accidentally, then repe-
titiously; when objects are grasped, the infant touches materials that
differ from himself and establishes an awareness of the external world.

Objects—human and nonhuman—from our earliest days have real
or symbolic representation and are associated, in the simplest sense, with
pleasant or unpleasant feelings. Objects may promote pleasurable feelings and cause or reduce discomfort. Later we begin to recognize that
they can have an effect on whether we feel good or bad. Objects develop value as signals as our power to anticipate, substitute, and symbolize develops.

By object relations we refer to the relations between an individual
and the "things" in his environment in which he vests emotional significance. Object-relations include relations between the individual and

7

other persons, the individual and himself (for example, his attitude toward his own body), and the individual and inanimate things (such as toys, money, food, job). The infant's body, as a source of feelings and stimuli, is an early object for him. Certain body areas come to be highly valued and emotionally charged (mouth, alimentary canal, genitals, muscles) at certain stages of development. These areas can be associated with pain, pleasure, or relief of tension.

Thus, food, money, social roles, a valued person, a body part, a sense of efficacy or desirability—all can be considered objects. Each object is accompanied by a history which includes the relationships to other objects originally associated with it. The relation to food, for example, is determined not only by the fundamental survival value of food but also by the early feeding patterns and emotional interactions between mother and child. Attitudes toward food and eating habits are related to earlier experiences with food and the feeding process. Severe deprivation or overstimulation by valued objects at critical periods can result in fixation. Fixation may be reflected in an overvaluation of an object (for example, one may intensely desire a particular type of person) or, may be reflected in a conscious denial of any value in a particular object while unconsciously experiencing a great yearning for it.

As development proceeds, the child's cognitive apparatus structures his relationships with objects through particular modes of thinking, perceiving, and feeling. Early in life magical thought predominates, resembling the world of the dream in which contradictions may coexist and drives may press for hallucinatory gratification. The very young child believes that wishing or feeling can make something come true. Gradually the child develops realistic thought. As adults, however, many of us display vestiges of magical thinking, especially at stressful times. For example, an experience of loss may be regarded as punishment for previous misdeeds, or it may be regarded as the fulfillment of earlier angry thoughts and feelings toward the deceased.

The child experiences disappointment and frustration and learns how to cope with them. He develops hope—the capacity to anticipate that even though one feels uncomfortable now, one may feel better later. While initially this is through the medium of trust in another human, the child also learns that his own efforts can lead to a change in his feeling state. At first the infant evokes a response by crying and smiling. Later

8

on he learns to verbalize what he wants, and eventually he learns that he can get certain things through other means.

The "primary objects"—mother, father, siblings, and peers, as well as other authorities—are used as models. They are needed, loved, envied, idealized, and at times hated or ambivalently experienced. By imitating and identifying with their traits, affects, defenses against anxiety, fears, and aspirations, the child grows more capable of dealing with himself and the world. These identifications become part of the child, and each carries with it an associated emotional state. When the identification is born of idealization and love, the emotional state will be positive and serve as a motivating force for behavior which results in increased self-esteem. In circumstances of fear and hostility, the identification will be associated with guilt or shame, and certain behavior will be inhibited, or if carried out, productive of decreased self-esteem. When loss occurs where idealization of the object has been the dominant element of identification, the feelings will be those associated with grief. When fearful or hostile elements are prominent in the identification with the object there will be guilt and anxiety associated with the loss.

Through object-relations, the individual learns about the nature of relationships—what one can anticipate, how one develops closeness, what is safe to invest in, and where the risks lie. These object-relations and early identifications contribute in a fundamental way to later object-choices and the kind of marriage he will make, the friendships he will enjoy, and the parent he will become.

Object-Loss and Adaptation

Object-loss refers to the loss of an object which has special value and emotional meaning to a person. Throughout life individuals will experience repeated losses. At times they may hardly be noticeable, yet they are reacted to intensely. There are numerous developmental losses: The baby is parted (intentionally or accidentally) from the breast, bottle, toys, and crib. Later, such incidents as graduation, marriage, childbirth, trips, and even vacations, confront one with separation and loss. The parturient loses a part of herself in giving birth to her baby and in addition may lose whatever special feeling, attention, or importance

9

was attached to pregnancy. An experience of loss may accompany change even where there is elation and excitement.

Early object-losses, gradual and anticipated or abrupt and unexpected, provide challenges which are ordinarily met by the development of adaptive techniques which eventually constitute a part of the individual's personality. When the loss is traumatic, however, the adaptational techniques may be fixated or there may be regression to earlier and more primitive methods of coping.

A loss may present a great threat to our psychologic economy. The more we have invested emotionally in the lost person, place, or aspect of our self, the more threatened we are likely to feel in anticipation of that loss. The threat of a major loss is unconsciously a basic threat to survival. The initial overwhelming sense of helplessness, experienced by most individuals, is usually transient. Others, however, may be overwhelmed by the loss and experience a persistent sense of helplessness until reassured that they will be cared for in the same way that the lost object had provided. The overwhelming feeling of loss may be related to realistic factors, the subjective meaning of the object to the bereaved, or the diminished capacity to adapt to the loss because of physical illness or concurrent losses.

When disruptive loss has occurred, the experience of various feelings, wishes, or impulses in reaction to the loss presents an additional threat with which the bereaved must cope. For example, sexual feelings, angry or competitive impulses, envy or yearning may threaten him insofar as their overt expression is linked with the fantasy of some further loss: loss of love, approval, respect, or with the fear of direct retaliation from others.

In order to guard against anxiety as well as to secure the gratification of achievement, various techniques are developed which are referred to as the psychological mechanisms of defense. They are more than defensive—they represent attempts to arrive at a compromise between repression of the desire and fulfillment of the desire. Common examples of these mechanisms are cited below, with special reference to the bereaved.

The basic and most primitive mechanism of defense is repression. It is an unconscious riddance phenomenon. If the repressive factor is dominant, the individual will be protected from his feelings and wishes, and hence will be spared shame or guilt. There are times when repression fails. This may occur because 1) the impulse, wish, or idea is too strong; 2) the defensive structure is too weak; or 3) because the environment stimulates and/or promotes expression of the wish. The psychic apparatus must then allow expression, or repress again with the aid of a different mechanism. Among the additional mechanisms are the following:

A beareaved individual may say that the wish or the feeling exists but that he is not responsible for it and that it does not belong to him. He may feel intense guilt because of hostility toward the lost loved or valued person, and may cope with this feeling by claiming negligence or indifference on the part of the physician and medical personnel. Minimal evidence can become the focus for the projection of these unacceptable internal feeling states. A variation of this mechanism is when the person denies a defect in himself and attributes the consequences of the defect to something external. For example, rather than acknowledge his decreased physical strength, the patient may blame faulty equipment or lack of cooperation from his associates.

The bereaved may express his feeling as an idea but isolate its emotional content. Intense yearning may be isolated and while the individual will acknowledge missing the deceased he expresses this in an aloof and unemotional manner. If the bereaved experiences guilt he may act apologetically, or in an expiatory manner, but without any awareness that he is doing it out of guilt.

A bereaved individual may allow a feeling to be expressed but displaces it to another object. He may be angry with the lost loved object, feeling deprived and abandoned, but express this toward relatives and friends, maintaining that they are not doing enough for him.

A bereaved individual may substitute another object for his original one. If his satisfaction was in being needed by his lost loved one, he may turn to his business and attempt to extract the same kind of response from colleagues or employees. He may quickly seek another spouse with whom to reestablish the same kind of relationship.

A bereaved individual may express his need but rationalize the motive for it, to make it more acceptable to his conscience or ideals. For example, he may decide to take a vacation but indicate that he is not doing it for pleasure and relaxation but because it is "essential to his health."

A bereaved individual may seek someone to tell him what to do (often what he wants to hear) to avoid being the initiator of an activity. Or he may maintain that he is doing certain activities to make another happy, and deny his own need for gratification.

11

CONCEPTS CENTRAL TO LOSS AND GRIEF

Other methods utilized to deny feared feelings and thoughts include acting out feelings and thoughts vis-a-vis substitute objects; anesthetizing oneself by use of alcohol and drugs; or literally fleeing from situations that evoke these unacceptable feelings.

Another mechanism may be that of denying the reality or possibility of loss. The person who needs to deny that a loss has occurred maintains his denial by avoiding scenes and settings that remind him of the lost object. Persons with loss of function often attempt to dissimulate to avoid facing their feelings about the loss. Confabulation is a variant of denial, probably with an organic base. It is important to recognize that in the bereaved denial may be supported by any number of the mechanisms mentioned above.

Everyone retains the memory of past ways of seeking gratification, and under stress may regress to them. Regression is not necessarily a pathologic phenomenon. There are benign forms of regression which are temporary and in the service of coping with severe stress. Normal grief, for example, may involve benign regression. In the event of loss, memories of childhood separations with accompanying bewilderment, confusion, and anxiety as well as associated aggressive impulses are stirred up. Regression can occur at the level of thought, feeling, defense, or activity as well as at the level of social relationships. A bereaved individual may regress in the form of relationship he seeks in substitution for loss. He may regress in the kinds of more primitive defenses he uses to cope with the feelings stirred by loss. Or regression may occur in the character of the conceptualization he uses to integrate the experience of loss. The degree of stress which provokes regressive behavior varies, of course, from individual to individual.

In summary—to integrate a loss means that one must come to terms with the feeling that one's survival and positive feeling states are threatened. One must also come to terms with the objective meaning of the loss. The bereaved may have lost his economic provider and must face the very real problems that this poses. Simultaneously, the bereaved must cope with the inner apprehension, fear, or anger that this new or exaggerated burden evokes. The lost loved object may have been a source of tenderness, comfort, support, sexual satisfaction, or pride. Conversely, the lost object may have been a painful burden and source of frustration; or a combination of these positive and negative aspects. Because of the

12

varied qualities and attributes which are lost, multiple and conflicting feelings are aroused, though often one in particular predominates.

The feelings and emotional states aroused by loss of a loved or valued object include mental pain, yearning, anguish, sorrow, dejection, sadness, depression, fear, anxiety, nervousness, agitation, panic, anger, disappointment, guilt, shame, helplessness, hopelessness, despair, disbelief, denial, shock, numbness, relief, emptiness, and lack of feeling. The conflict between feelings that an individual anticipated and can accept and those he did not expect and cannot accept generates secondary emotional reactions. The bereaved person may find himself struggling to cope with a mixture of sorrow, yearning, and anger toward the loved and lost object. Unable to accept being angry with someone he loved who has been lost, he may experience shame and guilt. He must deal ultimately with the painful feelings of shame and guilt as well as the original feelings associated with the loss.

The reaction to loss inevitably includes attempts to repair the real or anticipated disruption. For example, grief, the most common and presumably most adaptive reaction to serious loss, contains many positive elements. Grief, when expressed, usually involves a period of convalescence in which the ties to the object can gradually be withdrawn and energies reconstituted for the establishment of new ties. The person in grief may weep, wail, fail to eat, tear at his hair, and pace restlessly. The painful suffering is a stimulus for relatives, friends, and associates to offer assistance and to communicate the availability of other objects. The rituals of mourning also enforce emotional ties. Wakes, memorial services, the funeral, and periods of mourning during which the bereaved is to be visited, remind both the bereaved and others of the needs and responsibilities toward one who has suffered the loss of a loved or valued person.

Determinants of the Reaction to Loss

To understand and treat the bereaved, the physician must know in what specific ways the object was important to the individual; the typical coping patterns of the individual; his social and cultural milieu, and its attitudes toward loss and death; and the special resources or disabilities the individual and family possess for coping with loss.

13

CONCEPTS CENTRAL TO LOSS AND GRIEF

Individual personality characteristics and coping techniques vary tremendously. Each person has unique hereditary and constitutional components expressed in dispositions of temperament. These dispositions interact with specific familial environments which reflect not only the broad cultural matrix of Western civilization and its ethos, but also narrower subcultural characteristics. Each definition of self carries with it particular outlooks, attitudes, and expectations for behavior. Within this field of forces, each of us develops typical styles of perceiving, problem-solving, thinking, feeling, and acting toward others and ourselves. This enduring psychological style that we refer to as personality becomes a powerful determinant of the type of response elicited by loss. The psychological style has contributed to the kinds of object-ties constructed and to their special significance for us. In a like manner, the qualitative aspects of early object-relationships have fundamentally influenced the development of personality.

To appreciate in what way a person will grieve for another and for himself, we need to know whether the bereaved readily accepts his feelings related to loss. Most persons readily accept one kind of feeling but may be ashamed or guilty about another. Some individuals fear and mistrust any strong feelings. Others recognize and accept their feelings but do not wish friends or relatives to be aware of them. Still others express themselves dramatically and at times exaggeratedly. Acceptance of feelings may depend upon the object toward whom they are directed or about whom they are felt. A negative feeling toward someone important upon whom we depend may be held back and may more readily be expressed toward a less important object.

The physician must make several central judgments about the bereaved. Does he feel capable of managing his life without someone else playing a central role in it? Does he feel valuable and worthwhile as a person in his own right? Does he have trust and optimism about making a new relationship, or is he racked with mistrust, hopelessness, and pessimism? What is the character and extent of guilt feelings expressed by the bereaved in his grief?

The physician can often help the bereaved to grieve rather than substitute, displace, or suppress his despair. While we feel that it is better to express than to suppress grief, we must also recognize that some individuals cannot face their feelings directly. In these cases, the physician's role is to support some measure of grieving, to encourage

14

it (without provoking shame in those for whom it is so terrifying they must avoid it at all costs), and most importantly, to discourage markedly maladaptive modes of coping with loss (that is, substitutions of drugs, promiscuity, denial, etc.).

In order to provide maximal support, the physician must know something of the relationship between the individual and the lost loved or valued object. Unwarranted assumptions about the relationship to the lost object will lead to unwarranted expectations as to how the bereaved should feel or act. What is qualitatively most crucial in a relationship is its dynamic history and current meaning for the participants. We must understand in what way the bereaved depended upon the lost object. We all depend upon various objects in our environment for various gratifications. Relative autonomy refers to the capacity to derive considerable gratification from one's own efforts and to the ability to sustain the frustrations (whether physical, mental, or emotional) inevitably involved in living. Most of us seek appreciation, warmth, understanding, love, and sexual gratification from others. The relative capacity of a person to move from one object to another with trust and hope if the situation so demands is an indication of the independence of an individual.

Dependency has objective and subjective dimensions. We know that the child of two depends upon the parent for survival and finds it painful when separation occurs. He has centered his emotional life on the parent and has not yet developed the capacity to shift readily to another object. Cognitive and emotional development, if proceeding normally, permits the child of three or four to recognize that he will be relatively safe and protected by another person. He has gained trust in his earlier relationships and has added hopefulness to it. Without genuine trust there can be no genuine hope, and elements of bitterness, resentment, despair, and depression will be present. While any person can feel temporarily helpless under overwhelming circumstances, the problem of chronic helplessness often grows out of an underlying hopelessness. For this reason it is important, when dealing with the bereaved or bereaved-to-be, to evaluate the capacity for hope. Pseudo-hopelessness is not uncommon and can be seen in individuals with much guilt and fear. It serves as a magical defense against expected punishment. If one presents himself as without hope and therefore with no future, can anyone be worse off or further punished? The person's

15

history of object-relationships with prior evidence of true hopes and expectations provides indicators for distinguishing true hopelessness from pseudo-hopelessness.

In early developmental phases our own bodies provide gratification of certain physical and psychosocial needs. Later, we involve others as providers of these needs. For example, we come to need jobs and money to provide for food, shelter, and clothing. We depend on others to provide added sources of control when we doubt our own ability to control impulses which we fear will get us in trouble or produce guilt or shame. The death of a father may provide an adolescent son with enormous distress in that he loses a source of love, support, and care. In addition, the boy may experience anxiety because he has also lost a source of identification with a strong ideal or conscience. What is the adolescent to do with his burgeoning sexual impulses with no father to teach or control him? He may be anxious about his ability to control himself. In addition, he may feel inadequate to step into his father's roles, and yet may feel that he is being called upon to do so. The call may come from deep within him in his latent wish to be the man of the house, or may be stimulated by the reality that he is the oldest male of the house. His feeling of obligation may become intensified by his mother's appearance of helplessness and need. Therefore, guilt, shame, and a sense of inadequacy all may exist parallel to the grief over the loss of the father.

We depend upon our own bodies as sources of self-esteem, self-confidence, pride, and pleasure. Different parts of the body carry different degrees of valuation. In our society, a woman's breasts have value far beyond their function in childrearing. Prospective or actual mastectomy can, therefore, produce intense emotional reactions. Retirement because of age can be experienced as a serious loss if the job represents a person's predominant source of esteem, pride, and feeling of worth.

To summarize, the physician should attempt to determine both the form and content of the dependency relationship between the bereaved and the lost loved or valued object. He should learn whether the areas of dependency were acknowledged without shame, guilt, or resentment and if not, how they were expressed and resolved.

Each society has a prevailing system of values which includes implicit guides to human conduct. Early cultures prescribed worship and

16

propitiation of the dead as a means of avoiding vengeance of the spirit of the dead. Later cultures reintegrated these forms in terms of honoring, revering, and grieving for the dead. Some societies added the custom of maintaining affection for the dead and consolation of the living for the loss suffered.

Only in recent decades has the notion of social welfare become a central concern in our society. This nation, built on the themes of the vigorous extension of man's boundaries, acquisition, and competition, needed, in some ways, to deny loss and death. Currently, society provides minimal support for the bereaved. Grief, rather than being encouraged as adaptively essential, is viewed somewhat short-sightedly as inimical to the smooth workings of a highly technological society. Admiration is extended to those who appear strong and limit their expression of emotion, especially so in the case of the male in our society. In contrast, the bereaved in other, less "advanced" societies, is identified as a person with singular status and particular needs.

Social and religious rituals during bereavement, such as funerals, wakes, prescribed periods of mourning with written or group prayers for mourners, modes of dress, and condolence observances (visits by clergy, relatives and friends, condolence cards and indulgences), provide significant support for the mourner. They not only provide a clear role for the bereaved with definite expectations, timetables, and practices, but also actually encourage open expression of grief. Certain religious and ethnic groups still subscribe to these practices. This may be helpful for some individuals but create conflict for others. The bereaved may find himself at odds with the dominant culture or may elect to follow the dominant value and transgress against the culture of his family and subculture. It should be clear that there is no standard, culturally approved road to the successful working-through of a serious loss. But there are useful lessons from the subcultures which the pressure of social utility and the need to deny death cause us to forget.

The dominant social expectation of the bereaved is that he will quickly pick up the pattern of his life, return to work, family responsibilities, and socialization with the community and be quiet about his grief. With this ethos, the lack of support from family, friends, and neighbors will force the bereaved to abandon his grief prematurely. Family dispersal in our urban society may also contribute to the failure to grieve fully since there are fewer family members with whom to share one's grief.

There is a strong need in most of us to flee from the reality of death. Funeral practices in recent decades have moved increasingly toward the practice of presenting the deceased as if he were still alive. Cosmetics, mattresses and pillows, and euphemisms which suggest that the deceased is asleep rather than dead function to support denial of reality. Were the bereaved to wear black and to show grief for a prolonged period of time it would serve as a constant reminder of the reality of death and the pain of grief. The metaphors used to discuss death, our mourning practices, and our failure to educate children to the facts of death attest to the anxiety which death provokes.

Frequently, friends and relatives withdraw from the bereaved person just as they may have from the terminally ill or dying person. Withdrawal from the bereaved or seriously ill may occur because friends and relatives feel uncomfortable with the anxiety, pain, and sadness of grief, and do not know specifically how to "help." The idea of helping is often a euphemism for controlling the expression of strong feelings on one's own part and on the part of the bereaved. The need to escape these feelings often leads to the failure to realize that what the bereaved person needs may be presence alone, without words. The ambiguous responses that bereaved individuals give in answer to what they want makes it possible to select that with which the relative or friend is most comfortable. If help is offered it may take the form of encouragement of occupational therapies rather than of expression of grief. This leaves the bereaved isolated and alone at a time when the knowledge that there are those who care and are prepared to share painful feelings is crucial.

At times the bereaved person flees from his own painful feelings by selecting those aspects of social values or expectations which permit him prematurely to terminate the bereavement. In our society, symptoms of physical illness, being more acceptable, are frequently substituted for painful emotional states.

The field of medicine has its own special problem concerning loss and death. Death as a subject of serious scientific inquiry has only recently come within the medical purview. Prior efforts focused on understanding and delineating normal and pathological life processes for the purpose of extending life. Heroic efforts in most recent decades have been toward the maintenance of life. In this struggle, the experience of death, the meaning of death in the life cycle, and the management of death and bereavement have often been overlooked, obscured, or suppressed.

The physician and scientist understandably made their priorities those which would support their own need to deny and flee from death, rather than those which would increase their discomfort, frustration, and pain. Death represents the ultimate loss and therefore has a particular capacity to arouse powerful emotional states in each of us. Each time we confront death, we lose not only the loved or valued object but also suffer an eroding of our sense of immortality. Death is a cruel and recurrent reminder of the limits of our power—our power to save another or to save ourselves from the same fate.

2

Reaction To Loss

David Peretz

The purpose of this chapter is to describe specific reactions to loss. Reactions to loss will be referred to as bereavement states, bereavement referring to the state of thought, feeling, and activity, which is a consequence of the loss of a loved or valued object. The loss may be gradual, as in aging or chronic illness, or sudden, as with traumatic injury or sudden death. The bereavement state is the outcome of an interaction between the personal characteristics of the bereaved, the kind of relationship that existed between the bereaved and the lost loved or valued object, and social forces which may support certain bereavement states and discourage others.

Bereavement may be viewed as an illness since it represents a significant departure from the bereaved's usual state of feeling, thought, and behavior and is associated with physical and emotional symptoms. Recovery from bereavement, as in any illness, is achieved when the individual has no further symptoms or disabilities and when his capacity to deal with his feelings and his environment is no longer reduced. As with any illness, recovery may be total or partial. The bereaved's reaction to loss may be likened to a reaction to a wound or infection. For some, the wound or infection is minor, while for others it is major. For some, healing proceeds in a smooth, predictable way without complications, while for others healing leaves serious scars which later interfere with function or produce weakness in a system which is then predisposed to later failures in function.

Bereavement states are often limited in intensity and duration and require no specific medical advice or treatment. They run their course

with time, environmental support, and the natural resources of the bereaved. This type of bereavement state is known as grief.

Other bereavement states are more maladaptive. They are not
limited, do not run a direct course to recovery, and may last for many
months or for years. They are exaggerated and persistent, more crippling and disruptive to the bereaved, his family, and friends. Certain
bereavement states give the *appearance* of being adaptive. An example
would be the individual who shows no grief and proceeds to act as if
nothing had happened. If the lost loved or valued object was emotionally significant in the life of the bereaved, the absence of a grief
reaction or symptoms of bereavement suggests a prognosis of future
maladaptation.

Types of bereavement states include 1) "normal" grief; 2) anticipatory grief; 3) inhibited, delayed, and absent grief; 4) chronic grief
(perpetual mourning); 5) depression; 6) hypochondriasis and exacerbation of pre-existent somatic conditions; 7) development of medical
symptoms and illness; 8) psychophysiologic reactions; 9) acting-out
(psychopathic behavior, drugs, promiscuity); and 10) specific neurotic
and psychotic states.

Before we turn to these specific states, the state of the dying
patient must be noted. Because medical concern has so often directed
itself toward the struggle against the patient's death, the fact is often
overlooked that the dying patient, too, is experiencing some form of
bereavement. As he consciously or unconsciously anticipates death, he
anticipates and fears separation from and loss of the loved and valued
persons and things in his world.

The dying patient also faces loss of self, for he will lose, trau-
matically or gradually, various capacities and functions: cognitive
skills, motor skills, and capacity for pleasure.

The study of death-anxiety in children and adolescents indicates
that death is represented in the imagination as separation from those
who love and nurture; it is not oblivion but awareness of the pain of
being alone. At times, fantasies of punishment dominate the imagined
experience with painful ideas about the destruction of the body.

Patients need help in dying, just as they often do in living.
Families must be helped to meet death and bereavement. Each must be
given the support needed to face what must be faced. Each must be
given the understanding to live the life that remains in the best way

21

that it can be lived—not with illusion, but with a continuity that is not prematurely set aside.

"Normal" Grief

Grief is ordinarily characterized by intense mental suffering and distress, deep sorrow and painful regret. Initially, the bereaved experiences shock and numbness and denies that the loss has really happened. His incomprehension soon gives way to, or alternates with, bewilderment and weeping, despairing acknowledgment of the loss with constantly returning thoughts and memories of the deceased.

In addition to mental pain, the bereaved will usually exhibit physical reactions—dyspnea and deep sighing, "lumps" or tight sensations in the throat, weakness, feelings of emptiness, exhaustion, decreased appetite, and insomnia. Anxiety and tension are prominent symptoms in the early period following loss. There may be agitation and restlessness, hand-wringing and an appearance of confusion and puzzlement. There is a marked tendency for the emotional state to come in waves lasting up to an hour. These occur more frequently at the beginning of the period of bereavement and then less and less frequently. Mention of the loss may trigger these episodes of intense emotional suffering, and for this reason the bereaved may appear to reject discussion and comfort. He is, however, attempting to sustain denial and avoid the painful state that comes with recognition of the loss. If family members can be apprised of this, they will be less likely to withdraw from the bereaved and more likely to sit quietly with him to share the grief. Words at such a time are less important than supportive presence.

Painful yearning and loneliness for the lost object are also prominent. The bereaved may weep tearlessly and experience a sense of emptiness. When the waves of powerful emotion subside, there will be increasing periods in which the bereaved appears to be "himself." Sexual desire and the capacity for pleasure are usually diminished during the early period of bereavement.

Feelings of unreality about himself and others are frequently experienced in the acute stages of grief. Illusory phenomena may occur in which people appear vague or smaller than usual. Or the bereaved may believe, for example, that he hears the footsteps or the voice of the dead person. There may be momentary feeling and perception of the deceased's presence even though these are, at the same time, recognized as illusions. The mental image of the deceased preoccupies the bereaved. In some instances, it is as though the lost person were still present, and indeed, this preoccupation may function as a denial of loss. The bereaved may express fears of losing emotional control and mental faculties; many are frightened by the intensity of their own feelings. During the first days and weeks of bereavement, he may have terrifying nightmares. Later on he often has dreams of the dead person which are frequently described as comforting and in which the deceased may appear as younger than at the time of death.

Guilt feelings are frequently present in the acute stage of bereavement. The bereaved will recall ways in which he failed the deceased: quarrels, disappointments, infidelities in thought or deed, negligence, impatience, and anger. If the deceased had suffered a protracted and painful illness, his family may experience relief at his death but at the same time shame and guilt over this relief. At times, the focus of guilt on small, inconsequential facts of the relationship may serve as a screen for more profound guilt for being the survivor. The prospect of continued health, life, and ultimately pleasure in new relationships can be an additional source or impetus for guilt feelings. When the bereaved insists on seeing the loss as punishment, hidden guilt may be responsible.

Irrational anger at the dead person for not remaining alive, for leaving one burdened, or for withdrawal of gratification may be experienced. This is often difficult for the bereaved to accept in himself or to discuss with relatives or friends. Because most relationships are ambivalent to some degree, with disappointment and anger as well as love and affection, the seedbed of guilt is present in everyone. Normal guilt feelings in grief states may be reduced by reassurance. Depressive guilt, on the other hand, is persistent and not responsive to reassurance. Early and unresolved guilt feelings which have little to do with the relationship to the lost object can be activated by bereavement. Instead of overt self-reproach, one may see evidence of expiatory behavior without apparent feeling. Excessive religious devotion, ritual involvement, and compulsive behavior (cleaning, straightening up) in the bereavement state often indicate unconscious guilt.

In the first days or weeks following loss, the bereaved may appear irritable and may be misunderstood by those around him. These attitudes may represent the mobilization of hopelessness and bitter disappointment, but more likely are inconsistent attempts to ward off the closeness to others which might produce more intense suffering by serving as a reminder of the loss. The intimacy may also provoke guilt by reminding the bereaved that he is still living and has other relationships while his loved one is dead. Compassion and firm insistence upon the wish to be with the bereaved rather than withdrawal from him is usually required.

Depressive symptoms may occur in grief without necessarily indicating clinical depression requiring psychiatric treatment. Insomnia, anorexia, weight loss, inability to concentrate, restlessness, hypersensitivity, sadness, weeping, and self-reproach are, as has been indicated, common in normal grief. If they persist beyond several weeks, they must be regarded as possible indicators of more serious pathology. Their differential diagnosis and management will be discussed in the section on depression.

Feelings of numbness may reflect a deep identification with the dead person and for a brief period give the impression that the bereaved has experienced a total loss of feeling. He will, however, respond to people in the environment who reach out to him. Identification with the lost object may also be dramatically exhibited in unconscious imitations of certain gestures or habits of the deceased. Although it may appear bizarre, it can be considered a part of the normal grief state if it occurs early in the bereavement period and does not persist.

Helplessness may be expressed both in terms of not having been able to save the lost object and not being able to live without the loved one. Statements of the bereaved that he "would be better off dead" or that "it should have happened to me" also express both helplessness and guilt. He may wish for death as relief from the mental pain or the anticipated burdens. Fleeting suicidal thoughts such as these need not be confused with the more persistent suicidal ideation of the depressed person.

Some bereaved individuals tend to blame others for the loss as a way of coping with their own painful feeling state. They are usually amenable to reason when family or friends point out the inaccuracy of their belief. If other elements of grief are absent, however, and if the bereaved is not amenable to reason but persistently blames others, then paranoid features or other serious difficulties may be developing and should be investigated.

The duration of grief is variable and may range up to six months or a year. The acute phase should be over within one to two months. The progress of grief can be judged in terms of whether there is a gradual return to the level of functioning prior to the loss. It should be expected that when faced with reminders of the deceased (such as by pictures, songs, and old haunts) temporary upsurges of grief will occur even in later months. Another indication of recovery from grief includes whether new relationships are being established or interest expressed in them; particularly important for recovery from grief is the return of full capacity for pleasure without shame or guilt.

The first task in treating bereavement is to evaluate the nature of the bereavement state. Bereaved individuals will often seek, in the acute phase of grief, surcease from their mental pain and its physiological concomitants. They will not understand and may be frightened by their intense feelings, and will look to the physician and others to help them to control these feelings. It may be hard to resist the temptation to prescribe pharmacologic agents at such times but the physician must keep in mind that the grief work is necessary for maximal recovery. Within this framework he may prescribe mild daytime sedation and medication to encourage sleep. It is more important that he communicate to such patients his appreciation of their loss and his support of their grief. By explaining to the patient and the bereaved family that reactions of grief are normal and that to repress them is to deny the significance of the loss, he will encourage and enable them to sustain and express their feelings. Should the physician's differential diagnosis suggest pathologic bereavement states, psychiatric consultation will be necessary.

Anticipatory Grief

Grief frequently begins before loss actually occurs. The person faced with his own declining health, serious illness, or impending surgery may grieve for himself in much the same way he would grieve when an actual loss is sustained. In nearly all instances in which loss is imminent, those concerned experience the beginnings of grief. Anticipatory grief may range from quiet periods of sadness and tears to those symptoms

25

usually associated with grief over actual loss. Anticipatory grief may deprive both the dying patient and the bereaved-to-be of the possibilities still remaining in their relationship.

The manner in which the physician presents the prognosis will influence the character of grief. If the hopelessness of the case is emphasized, anticipatory grief will, of course, be more intense. The physician should emphasize both the patient's and family's needs and encourage expression of their thoughts and feelings. Medication in the form of mild sedation or tranquilizers may reduce the more intense symptoms of anticipatory grief and permit the relationships to continue in a positive way during the terminal period.

Individuals who express anticipatory grief when the probability of loss is low are likely to be psychologically predisposed to hopelessness and pessimism, and are often guilty and self-punitive. It is also likely that when actual loss does occur the individual will not show grief but some other bereavement behavior—most frequently, depression or one of its equivalents.

Absent, Delayed, and Inhibited Grief

The development of a specific bereavement state may not occur until days, weeks, or months after the loss has been experienced; in some instances such symptoms and signs may never become apparent. The absence of evidence of bereavement after loss is not always indicative of maladaptation. The relationship between the bereaved and the deceased may at one time have been intense but is no longer so because of increased independence, separation, or the establishment of and investment in new relationships. Similarly, where the relationship had been predominantly negative, a bereavement state may not be observed.

Absence of emotion immediately following loss may represent temporary shock, numbness or denial. Grief may be postponed until it can no longer be avoided, for example, at the funeral service or burial where it may then flood forth. This is most often observed in those bereaved who must attend to certain details surrounding the loss, or to more vulnerable bereaved persons. Responsibilities in business or as head of the family may combine with the individual's predisposition to appear "strong" and result in delayed or inhibited grief. These individuals should, however, ultimately reveal some evidence of a bereavement state.

Lastly, there is the individual who "hides" his grief publicly and grieves secretly in the privacy of home or room. This limits the degree to which he can express grief or receive support. Those individuals consciously control themselves in public or rationalize their loss by the fact that the deceased is now free from suffering. They are ashamed of feeling as deeply as they do about the dead loved person. There is frequently a need to deny the reality of the loss because of their close identification with the deceased. These people will be seen by others as strong but not cold; their sadness will be felt only by those close to them. Although their actions seem to belie their feelings, they often express these feelings by caring for others. Medical consultation may be sought for physical complaints by these bereaved. The family physician can encourage that the grief be expressed in his office or suggest that it be shared with a few close friends or relatives.

There are individuals who neither show nor are aware of feeling deeply grieved. Such a person commonly has experienced intense ambivalent feelings toward the lost object and is unconsciously afraid that in his grief he will reveal strong hostility as well as love. They are often accused by family and friends of being unfeeling and this only serves to exacerbate their unconscious guilt and shame. In response, they defensively isolate themselves—by compulsive busywork, involvement with details, cleaning up, or some form of ritualized activity. Apprehensions may be expressed about what should have been done for the deceased. These apprehensions usually have as their source guilt feelings about the deceased.

Individuals who delay grief become more vulnerable to what is referred to as "anniversary reactions"—the re-experiencing of loss on an important date associated with the deceased. This may be the anniversary of the death, a wedding date, or it may be a date at which the survivor reaches the age of the deceased at death. Subsequent losses, symbolic of the first loss, may also reactivate the remaining original feelings of loss. In the treatment of normal or pathologic grief, then, the physician should, as a matter of course, inquire into the bereaved's history of previous loss.

27

CONCEPTS CENTRAL TO LOSS AND GRIEF

Chronic Grief

The condition of chronic grief is one of persistent mourning. Some individuals arrange their environment after the loss to reflect no change in life pattern. It is as if the home and way of life were enshrined at the time of loss, and the return of the deceased is awaited. Such a response represents a denial of the reality of the loss, and aims to protect against the intense suffering its acknowledgment would engender. Thus, though it appears outwardly to be a prolongation of grief, it is actually a defense against grief. This state should be distinguished from chronic depression secondary to loss of a loved one. The chronic "mourner" is guarding against anticipated guilt and depression by utilizing certain behavior patterns which deny the loss. This response can be observed in parents whose child has died and who leave his room untouched for a long period of time. Parents of servicemen killed in the war occasionally reveal such behavior. It would seem that it may be especially difficult for a parent to accept the loss of a child, and particularly so for a mother to whom the child has represented the central function in her life.

Depression

While many of the signs and symptoms of acute grief are observed in depression, the two conditions differ qualitatively as well as quantitatively. Depression may occur as the dominant feature of the bereavement state. It may develop almost immediately in response to loss or anticipated loss, develop gradually during the weeks or months following the loss, or may appear even after apparent recovery from grief. Depression may occur after a prolonged period in which there have been no discernible or prominent signs of a bereavement state. It is important to distinguish transient depressive affects from the severe depressive reaction with aberration of mood, motor behavior, and thought processes. The latter should be recognized so that psychotherapy or antidepressant medication can be instituted to prevent prolonged morbidity and crippling disability, and to make it possible for grief to proceed with favorable adaptive consequences.

28

Depression as an emotional state is one in which sadness, tension, and a sense of depletion are prominent. The patient appears to be in a state of marked conservation: he moves more slowly than usual, features are fixed in a position of despair, and there is a subjective sense of a slowdown of mental processes. Anorexia with weight loss, bowel sluggishness, and markedly decreased sexual interest all suggest a turning inward. Verbal communication is diminished but its content is revealing, often characterized by self-reproach and criticism. The depressed person often sees himself as "bad" because he is depressed, rather than depressed because he feels he is "bad." This contrasts with guilty grief, in which case the self-reproach is directly related to failure to provide adequately for the lost object.

The grief-stricken person will, within a reasonably short period of time after the loss, show shifts of mood from sadness to a more normal state within the same day. He will usually be responsive to words of reassurance and support, and will be able, after a time, to laugh a little. In contrast, the depressed person will be more persistently downcast, gloomy, and pessimistic, although his depression may subside toward evening each day. While the grieving person may respond to warmth and reassurance, the mildly depressed person may respond to pressure, promises, and urging. The more severely depressed person will be relatively unresponsive to most stimuli and will sit huddled and downcast in gloom. Restriction of pleasure is markedly persistent in the depressed.

Some depressed individuals have difficulty weeping, although they often wish they could and express the conviction they would feel better if they did. Suicidal ideas and feelings may occur to the depressed, and constitute serious symptoms. This is especially true when the individual is still deeply depressed but may have recovered sufficiently from psychomotor retardation to have the will to act. He may also experience increased anxiety associated with the prospect of facing life once more.

In conversation, the depressed person will prove to be much more preoccupied with himself than with the deceased loved or valued one. This preoccupation is often in the form of negative, self-reproachful comments. He is likely to call himself names, and figuratively, if not literally, beat his breast about how he should be doing more, about how inadequate or worthless he is; feeling that he has no future, that he will never get better, and that he is hurting others. These ideas will be

29

variously interwoven with periods of irritability, criticism, and complaints directed toward others. Open anger or hostility will not be prominent in the depressed person.

Whereas the bereaved in a state of grief may feel that the world is empty and experience only brief periods of personal emptiness, the depressed individual tends to feel an inner emptiness more persistently and intensely. Among the complaints of the depressed will be lassitude, difficulty in starting something, lack of energy, difficulty concentrating and thinking clearly. Depressed people frequently experience physical complaints. They may suffer from severe insomnia, waking up at 5 or 6 A.M., unable to go back to sleep. They may waken frequently during the night. This contrasts with the insomnia pattern in tense, anxious individuals who have difficulty getting to sleep. Hypochondriasis is common in depressive states. More severe states may be associated with delusional elaboration of guilty or hypochondriacal themes.

One tends to feel sympathy for a bereaved person expressing feelings of grief, in contrast to growing irritation when one is with the depressed individual. When the person denies feeling depressed and focuses on physical complaints instead, the physician, family member, or friend may find themselves feeling irritated or depressed rather than sad when with the bereaved. The physician should use his own personal reactions to aid in the differential diagnosis. Distinguishing depression from grief in the bereaved individual permits early psychiatric consultation when necessary and treatment as indicated.

Psychotic depression, the depressive phase in persons with manic-depressive reaction, as well as psychotic reactions in the involutional phase of life can all be triggered by serious loss. Because their signs and symptoms are readily distinguishable from grief and neurotic depressive reactions, they will not be detailed. Their management usually requires psychiatric treatment.

Hypochondriasis

The hypochondriacal person will express considerable anxiety and tension around a physical concern rather than the loss and its consequences. Examination usually establishes no demonstrable basis for the presenting complaint. The bereaved person who becomes hypochondriacal may interpret symptoms of a tension headache as representative of a brain tumor and become agitated over that belief. Arthritic shoulder pain is often interpreted as heart disease; constipation and loss of appetite—common symptoms of grief and/or depression—become indicators of malignancy. Rather than reacting to a symptom in terms of its most probable cause, a remote possibility is given total credence.

Hypochondriasis may occur transiently in grief, may be an important symptom of depression, or may exist independently as an illness in its own right. The hypochondriacal disease may be an elaboration of a genuine symptom associated with either grief or depression. In some instances, the complaint is similar to or the same as that which caused the loss of the loved one. Medical consultation is necessary to 1) rule out the presence of serious illness; 2) treat whatever illness may be present; 3) clarify the emotional components of the state; and 4) attempt to resolve the underlying feelings. Consultation may, however, elicit 1) the emergence of underlying anxiety, guilt, grief, or depression; 2) a shift to another hypochondriacal complaint; 3) a persistent, worried conviction of illness and a conviction that the examination failed to reveal it or that the doctor was not sufficiently thorough.

The physician must understand that these patients are venting intense anxiety, hostility, and guilt through these symptoms. They are guilty over a variety of wishes and aggressive fantasies and tend to make their own body the victim in an attempt to both expiate for and gratify the unacceptable wish. They gain attention and physical care but pay an enormous price for it in the worry and agitation they feel. One must assume that to go through such elaborate symptomatic behavior the person must be defending against an enormous fantasied threat. The leading principle of management of these patients is "do no harm." The patient needs to be reassured that there is no evidence that he is suffering from the disease he believes he has. At the same time, the *symptoms* of the disease (headache, constipation, pain, weakness, tremor, etc.) need to be respected as genuine and scrupulously dealt with. To confront and reject the patient's anguish as "imaginary" is to invite him to pursue further medical opinion, shift to another symptom, or at times develop considerable depression. By dealing with the symptoms, which may screen anxiety, depression, or grief, we can help the patient to appreciate his use of bodily language to express emotional

31

distress. Often, in the diagnostic process, it becomes possible to explore the effect of the symptom or "illness" upon the patient's life. In so doing, what secondary gains the patient is making may become obvious and he can be helped to similar gains in a less costly manner. As the consultation progresses, it becomes possible to question the patient about his feelings related to the loss, and the hidden conflicts or tensions it may have generated. If the physician provides patience, understanding, reassurance, and interest in the patient's life, the bereaved patient may find it possible to reduce, if not eliminate, the hypochondriacal focus. He may then turn, with help if necessary, to face the real issues confronting him in the bereavement state.

Hypochondriacal complaints of the bereaved should not be confused with the increase in specific physical symptoms of pre-existing ailments. The gastrointestinal system, for example, is a common site of increased symptomatology during bereavement. Persons with hiatus hernia, ulcer, duodenitis, and colitis complain of increased discomfort (vomiting, nausea, pain, constipation, diarrhea). Previously quiescent conditions may be exacerbated. The overt sadness, mental pain, and suffering experienced in bereavement are frequently not focused on the loss, but are directed instead to physical illness. In contrast to hypochondriasis, the person with physical illness which appears intensified during bereavement does not demonstrate an increasing preoccupation with the belief that his exacerbated symptoms mean a new and terrible disease. He may tend to explain feelings of sadness, anxiety, or depression as secondary to physical symptoms, for example, "If only my stomach didn't hurt, everything would be fine." The statement denies the fact that the loss and feelings of grief would still have to be met.

The bereaved individual who experiences his grief through exacerbated physical symptoms may be of an exaggeratedly independent nature. He has difficulty in showing his feelings to others although he is well aware of them. He is commonly ashamed of accepting help from others. Physical symptoms appear to be a more acceptable route to both the expression of painful feelings and the acceptance of support.

When careful examination reveals no change in the actual physical condition, the physician may suggest that the "increased pain" is due to the "pain of the loss" and indicate that anxiety, tension, and yearning as well as depression can either aggravate symptoms of physical illness or cause excessive focus on pre-existing complaints. Such bereaved individuals may well "open-up" to the physician if he presents a sympathetic ear and encourages the expression of these emotions. Several visits may afford considerable relief and allow grief to proceed more directly.

Development of Psychophysiologic Reactions

There is increasing evidence that object-loss can result in the formation of physical symptoms in predisposed individuals. This is discussed more fully in Chapter 3, "Object-Loss and Somatic Symptom Formation." Symptoms which so appear have been described by some as "depressive equivalents," and indeed, depressive affects may appear when the symptoms are in remission, and disappear when symptoms are exacerbated.

Other investigators believe that the loss of a loved or valued object can contribute significantly to the onset of serious, at times life-threatening physical illness. It has been postulated that depression and/or marked feelings of helplessness lower resistance to infection and perhaps even reduce the body's immune defense against blood dyscrasias and neoplasm.

Psychophysiological reactions such as essential hypertension, ulcerative colitis, duodenal ulcer, and neurodermatitis have also been implicated as a response to loss, both in terms of pathogenesis and exacerbation. Research is needed in defining the relationship between the reaction to loss and physical or psychosomatic illness.

The treatment of these conditions is outlined in appropriate medical textbooks and will not be described here. It is sufficient to say that every medical history should include exploration of recent and past object-loss or anticipated loss.

Acting-Out

Some individuals deal with strong internal feeling states by action, and in bereavement they may throw themselves into activity rather than experience its pain. Instead of living with their yearning, loneliness, and sadness, they attempt to satisfy these feelings by flying into the arms of another person, by immediately finding a substitute for the dead loved or valued person. They may find a series of substitutes and behave pro-

33

miscuously, or find one substitute and rapidly remarry. Other individuals flee the bereavement state by denying the pain and yearning and by immersing themselves in their work, travel, or hobby. To all appearances, they have managed their grief in an acceptable manner.

By questioning the activity of the bereaved, the physician may slow him down sufficiently so that some of the feelings of grief come through. At times it is necessary for the physician to indicate his belief that the activity represents a frenetic attempt to avoid the pain of grief and that the individual would be better off facing and working through his loss. Though driven by the need to avoid feelings of loss, the bereaved person may nevertheless choose an appropriate object by which to satisfy his yearning and need. For this reason, careful exploration with the bereaved may permit him to pursue new relationships while at the same time acknowledging his feelings about the lost one.

Drug dependence may be a problem for some bereaved. They may substitute dependence on drugs for dependence on people. These drugs most frequently include tranquilizers, barbiturates, stimulants, or alcohol. Each has its place in the management of various stages of bereavement, but should not serve to obliterate feelings or memories. In these individuals, there will usually be a history of prior usage of drugs under stress. Such moderate usage may become excessive during bereavement. Sudden and unaccustomed usage of drugs may also occur. Persistent, unaccustomed patterns of drug or alcohol usage should alert those close to the bereaved that something is amiss and that emotional reactions to loss are becoming pathological.

Neurotic and Psychotic States

The various forms of neurotic and psychotic reactions may be precipitated or exacerbated by severe loss. Anxiety, phobic, hysterical, as well as depressive reactions may occur during or after bereavement. Similarly, schizophrenic reactions may appear acutely or recur in the context of loss. Detailed descriptions of these states appear in textbooks; their management will be that of the primary illness, although treatment will take into account the role of the loss and the possible adaptive steps open to the patient. Aged individuals with organic brain syndromes may also show exacerbation of symptoms associated with object-loss. This occurs, for example, when they lose their familiar environment and are moved to a nursing home or hospital. Similarly, the loss of central figures in their life will contribute to more severe signs and symptoms.

Summary

Bereavement states vary according to the personality of the bereaved, the relationship between the bereaved and the lost loved or valued object, and the values or institutions of the society of which the bereaved is a member. Any attempt to block or inhibit feelings and behavior related to bereavement may lead to serious maladaptation to future relationships and future losses. The expression of feelings of grief after loss is not only appropriate but is also to be encouraged. The development of certain bereavement states which clearly indicate the need for medical consultation and treatment include depression, hypochondriasis, exacerbation or exaggeration of symptoms of prior physical illness, psychophysiologic reactions, alcholism and drug dependence, neurotic and psychotic states, as well as certain cases of inhibited or absent grief. The physician must be increasingly aware of the importance of loss and bereavement for he is in a unique position to provide advice, support, and treatment where they appear indicated.

3

Object-Loss and Somatic Symptom Formation

Arthur C. Carr and Bernard Schoenberg

In recent years increasing interest and attention have been focused on the relationship between object-loss and the development of somatic illness. Recognition of the diverse manifestations of mourning has greatly expanded the range of so-called psychosomatic disorders and other physical illnesses which are influenced by emotional factors. While the role of hostility and anxiety in certain somatic reactions is generally taken for granted, the influence of separation and depression has more typically been considered to be related to psychiatric rather than to physical disorder.

The specific thesis arising from accumulating research and clinical evidence is that object loss (often the death of or separation from a loved person) is a factor in the development of a wide range of somatic disorders, including fatal illness. Evidence for this hypothesis is based primarily on the demonstrated temporal relationship between such loss and the onset of the physical illness or death.

The concept that bereavement is associated with increased mortality is supported by numerous studies. In what appears to be one of the better-controlled studies, for example, Rees and Lutkins (1) surveyed deaths occurring during a six-year period in a semirural area to determine whether bereavement produced increased mortality among bereaved close relatives (spouse, child, parent, or sibling). A group of close relatives of 371 deceased persons was compared to a control group composed of relatives of 371 people matched by age, sex, and marital status with the deceased. Bereaved relatives were found to have a much higher mortality rate during the first year of bereavement. Increased risk of mortality was greatest for widowed people. For example, during the first year of bereavement 12.2 per cent of widowed people died, compared with 1.2 per cent in the control group. A relation between the place at which a person dies and the subsequent mortality of bereaved relatives was also found. The risk of close relatives dying during the first year of bereavement was significantly greater when the death causing the bereavement had occurred some place other than at home.

In a study of the general effects of bereavement on both physical and mental health, Parkes (2) compared the medical records of widows during bereavement with the records on the same patients during the period prior to bereavement. The medical office consultation rate for all causes during the first six months after bereavement rose 63 per cent. The highest percentages of increase were for psychiatric and chronic somatic conditions (e.g., rheumatism, arthritis, etc.). Thereafter the rate decreased but still remained higher than for the pre–bereavement period. Consultation rates for nonpsychiatric symptoms increased by nearly a half in both older and younger widows. Higher rates for patients over 64 years of age supported the contention that aged patients, in particular, tend to express their reactions in terms of somatic symptoms.

In a study of hospitalized medical patients unselected except for age, Schmale (3) investigated the relationship of separation and depression to the onset of medical disease through interview of patient and family members. He inferred that forty-one of the forty-two patients experienced actual, threatened, or symbolic object-loss, as well as feelings of helplessness and hopelessness, immediately prior to the onset of the disease. For example, thirty-one of the patients developed the onset of their disease within a week after what was considered a significant change in object-relationship which elicited feelings of helplessness or hopelessness. The frequency of a symbolic loss preceding the illness suggested that the individual often had been unable to defend himself against reminders of significant early loss or threat of loss which was also frequently reported.

In addition to increased medical illness and mortality in general, a wide range of specific somatic disturbances has been related to pre-disease conditions involving separation and depression. The variety of physical disorders presented in the literature includes cancer, tuberculosis, ulcerative colitis, burning mouth, asthma, obesity, thyrotoxicosis, rheumatoid arthritis, congestive heart failure, leukemia and lymphoma, and diabetes mellitus. For purposes of this review, two disorders will be discussed briefly: 1) cancer and 2) burning mouth (idiopathic glossodynia).

Cancer

The idea that psychological phenomena are associated with cancer is not a new one (4), although it has recently again appeared in the literature. LeShan and Worthington (5) report that Galen believed melancholic women are more prone to cancer than those of sanguine temperament. Following the humoral theory, physicians of the eighteenth and nineteenth centuries were impressed with the apparent relationship between personality and neoplastic disease. Almost one hundred years ago, Paget (6) suggested that deep anxiety, deferred hope, and disappointment are quickly followed by the growth and increase of cancer so that ". . . we can hardly doubt that mental depression is a weighty addition to the other influences that favour the development of the cancerous constitution." In 1885, Parker (7), an American surgeon, singled out the emotion "grief" as being especially associated with cancer of the breast. Two years later, Cutter (8) reported that mental depression is "too often an element in cancerous cases to be overlooked," indicating that the depression "aids much in the tissue rot." In 1893 Snow (9) affirmed that the number of breast and uterine cancers following "immediately antecedent emotion of a depressing character" is greatly above chance expectations. In reputedly the first statistical study in this area, he reported that in over 60 per cent of a series of 50 cancer patients there had been "immediately antecedent trouble, often in the very poignant form as the loss of a near relative. . . ." Such observations were not fully integrated in the developing clinical psychiatry of the early twentieth century, probably because advances in surgery and radiation treatment focused attention on cancer as a local phenomenon and encouraged unwarranted optimism about eliminating cancer as a serious problem. While loss and separation were coming to be viewed as having an intimate relationship to the genesis and the precipitation of psychological disorders, most somatic illnesses were still treated as unpredictable conditions which randomly might afflict anyone, in spite of lip-service given to the concept of the holistic nature of the organism (10).

Support for the viewpoint that separation and depression precede the occurrence of cancer now comes from a number of recent investigations. Peller (11) demonstrated statistically that widows in all age groups had a higher cancer mortality rate than spinsters or married women. Part of the statistical procedure was to rule out genetic predisposition, reproductive accomplishment, and social class as factors in the obtained difference. It was hypothesized that diminished resistance in widowhood accelerates the appearance of, and death from, cancer. Dorn (12) similarly found a significantly greater number of cancer patients, as compared to controls, to have been either widowed, divorced, or separated.

In a study of twenty consecutive male patients with all types of leukemia and lymphoma, Greene (13) reported that in all cases the symptoms and the recognition of the disease occurred while the patient was adjusting to multiple stresses arising from multiple sources. In seventeen of the twenty patients, these stresses included separation from a significant person, usually the mother or mother-figure. This separation was more frequently due to death, but in some cases was due to desertion or rivalry caused by birth of a sibling. Frequently, separation occurred when there was no available replacement. Concurrently, in most cases there were other trauma, such as injury, operation, aging, retirement, and changes in work. In a related study of female subjects, Greene, Young, and Swisher (14) reported observations on thirty-two patients describing the occurrence of various types of losses, separations, or threats of separation prior to the apparent onset of the lymphoma or leukemia. Losses included that of a significant person such as a mother, father, husband, or child, as well as those occurring through menopause or the change of a home. One or more such losses occurred in thirty of the thirty-two women during the four-year period prior to the apparent onset of the disorder. Half of such losses occurred during one year prior to the apparent onset. In many, the onset occurred in an anniversary relationship to the loss. Greene and Miller (15) later reported observations on thirty-three children and adolescents with leukemia. In thirty-one of the patients there was evidence of prodromal events which could be interpreted as separations or losses, such as the birth of a new sibling, a change in home, beginning school, loss of father, of grandparents. Half of these separations or losses occurred during the six months prior to the apparent onset of the disease. The findings suggested that in children, as well as in adults, separation with resultant depression may be a necessary condition for the manifestation of leukemia.

In one of the few predictive studies in this area, Schmale and Iker (16) attempted to identify the presence or absence of uterine cervical cancer in women with atypical cytology. Psychological criteria for the identification were based on previous observations of cancer patients which revealed that many had experienced feelings of helplessness for varying lengths of time prior to the clinical appearance of the disease. The subjects were forty women who were hospitalized for diagnostic cone biopsy because of repeated Papanicolaou Class III changes in their cervical cytology. The diagnosis of cancer was predicted on the basis of the interview criteria of a high hopelessness potential and/or recent feelings of hopelessness. On the basis of these cirteria, thirty-one correct predictions were made on the forty women. In the psychological tests given, only the depression scale of the MMPI approached significance in discriminating between cancer and noncancer groups. In contrast to the high hopelessness potential for predicting the occurrence of cancer, other psychological factors suggested by some investigators (for example, dominant mother, rejection of the feminine role, infrequent orgasm), showed no relation with the disease.

LeShan (17) has independently characterized the basic psychological orientation associated with malignant disease as that of "despair," a state obviously quite similar to that described by Greene as "helplessness and hopelessness." LeShan has evaluated the emotional life histories of 400 adult cancer patients and has conducted intensive psychotherapy with numerous patients who have cancer. As part of a series of publications related to psychological status and neoplastic disease, he has recently hypothesized that the despair arises on the basis of the patient's early perception of the environment as dangerous. Sometime later in life—often in adolescence—a safe relationship is found in which the patient has a profound emotional investment. For some uncontrollable reason, this relationship is eventually lost through such events as death, separation, or retirement. When efforts to develop new but similar relationships are unsuccessful, feelings of despair are then re-experienced.

40

Summarizing data relevant to the hypothesis concerning separation and occurrence of cancer, LeShan cites age-equated mortality rates for cancer that are highest among the widowed, lower among the divorced, still lower among the married, and lowest for the unmarried group. He reports that no statistical studies were found which were not consistent with the hypothesis relating incidence of cancer to separation and loss.

To be sure, such evidence continues to be tentative, with many questions unanswered. The connecting links between psyche and cell are yet unknown. Similar emotional states have been found with other physical disorders; hence, the specificity of cancer either as to type or location is unclear. Attempts to relate location of cancer site to such variables as the patient's unconscious image of his body as measured by psychological tests have shown interesting correlations; unfortunately, such results are confounded by the uncertainty of whether the tests reflect pre-illness personality or merely current behavior reactions. Necessary controls including age at onset, type of cancer, location, and rate of growth have not yet been executed to allow for more definitive findings other than the striking temporal relationship existing between object-loss, the consequent mourning state, and the development of the disease.

Burning Mouth (Idiopathic Glossodynia)

Another disorder recently related to object-loss has been investigated by the present authors. Traditionally, the burning mouth (referred to as glossodynia, stomadynia, or glossopyrosis) has been described as a syndrome without specific organic etiology found in emotionally disturbed postmenopausal women. More recent observations indicate that the symptom occurs in men as well as in women and is not necessarily confined to the older age groups. Wide varieties of treatments have been described, including estrogen replacement, removal of all dissimilar metals, covering the teeth to prevent galvanism, ingestion of hydrochloric acid, liver injections, vitamins, x-ray, and local dental or surgical treatment.

In a preliminary report, Schoenberg (18) summarized clinical impressions on twenty-five patients who complained of the sensation of burning in the oral cavity and in whom complete examination and laboratory workup failed to reveal a physical basis for their complaints. Hospital charts were evaluated to discover the climate in which the symptom had developed. Chosen randomly from cases referred to a specialist in oral diagnosis, one out of every three patients was male. Ages ranged from 32 to 69, with an average of 54. The author concluded that the burning mouth is a symptom of depression and is the result of psychological stress, often related to loss and separation. Sixty-four per cent of the patients related the onset of symptoms to dental procedures such as injection, extraction, insertion of a bridge, or extensive mouth rehabilitation. In 24 per cent, the onset coincided with the death or threatened loss of a loved person. In 6 per cent, the onset was related to natural or surgical menopause. The remaining 6 per cent associated the onset of symptoms with retirement, overt depression, or multiple somatic complaints. Many of the patients complained of anorexia, gastrointestinal disorders, fears of having cancer, agitation, dejection, sadness, and multiple somatic complaints.

In a related investigation, Schoenberg, Carr, Kutscher, and Zegarelli (19) have interviewed a total of twenty-one additional cases. Patients were also administered the MMPI and the Buss-Durkee hostility questionnaires. Five patients have been carried in psychotherapy. These additional cases appear consistent with the original hypothesis about the prevalence of depression, although sometimes the patients appeared to deny being depressed while showing all the clinical manifestations of that state. With unusual frequency, the patients were easily moved to tears in the interview. Many had numerous and varied complaints about what doctors had done to them. For many patients the sensation of burning was precipitated by a dental procedure which was unconsciously experienced as an attack. Although all the patients appeared to have in common such experiences as loss, guilt, and depression (either overt or masked), they were different as to personality type or psychiatric diagnosis. At least two patients appeared to be overtly schizophrenic. In others, the burning mouth appeared as part of a whole series of hypochondriacal concerns about the functioning of the body. In some instances, the term "conversion" appeared to apply. What the patients appeared to have in common was preoccupation with a loss as well as the inability to accept or integrate the loss and the accompanying feelings about it.

N. A. was a 46-year-old woman who reported that following extensive mouth rehabilitation she suffered a sharp, excruciating, burning pain described as, "if my mouth would go up in flames," and "saliva seemed to stop." She found the pain agonizing and saw a second dentist, who worked on her for seven consecutive hours. Following this, her pain became worse and she received extensive treatment from dentists, oral surgeons, otolaryngologists, a psychiatrist, neurologists, internists, etc., with no alleviation of symptoms. Five years before, following the death of her mother, she had developed insomnia. She stated that she had never accepted her mother's death and had been in a state of continuous mourning. She was still unable to dispose of her mother's clothes and dreamed of her frequently. She compared her present state to the postpartum reaction after the birth of her first child, stating that she "was deathly ill for three years, depressed and neurasthenic." Following the interview, she started psychotherapy on a weekly basis, complaining of despair, guilt, and depression. She made frequent slips that her mother was not dead. She made constant reference to her mouth as "dirty, biting, rotten, lousy, vicious," and complained of her inability to accept the reality of death in any family member. Despite the interpretations of her therapist that her pain was psychogenic, she continued to seek a physical explanation for her symptoms. One day prior to the anniversary of her mother's death, she persuaded a dentist to extract another tooth, although "we both knew it was a perfectly healthy tooth." She described the persistent burning as "mother revenge." Following an unanticipated business failure by her husband and the failure to find relief promised by an oral surgeon through local injections, she committed suicide by ingesting large quantities of drugs that she had collected over a period of time.

U. O. was a 37-year-old married woman who had a history of extreme early loss and deprivation. She noted the onset of a burning, painful tongue and mouth following a visit to a dentist when she was told that extensive rehabilitation was required on her gums and teeth. Following this examination (without treatment), she developed a generalized feeling of pain on the right side of her mouth and jaw. About this time she was also told that her son (her only child) should go to a boarding school. Despite her protest that she would be unable to tolerate dental work at this time, treatment was started and she developed intolerable burning and pain. She was treated by a number of specialists with no alleviation of symptoms. When finally told that her symptoms were psychogenic, she experienced complete relief of symptoms for two weeks, although her symptoms then slowly returned. She indicated that she had been subject to somatic symptoms for the past twelve years and dated these specifically to separation from her son when he was two years old. At that time she was on an ocean voyage and developed anorexia, globus hystericus, nausea, vomiting, severe depression, headaches, and tearfulness. Following her return, she continued to have severe headaches and suffered an exacerbation of symptoms when separated from her husband. When her son returned to boarding school one year following the onset of her symptoms, she was surprised to discover that she had a total amnesia for his first admission to school, the previous year. She became depressed, was unable to cry (similar to her reaction to the death of her best friend), and experienced an exacerbation of oral pain the following day. In therapy she quickly associated her symptoms to her inability to express anger toward her husband, who she feared would die.

Discussion

It should be made explicit that none of the investigators maintains that separation and depression are the cause of the physical disorder. Rather, it is the belief that the emotional state is one of the conditions which allows the disease to appear. The general hypothesis is that the psychic state may contribute to a number of disease processes, possibly through an increased biological vulnerability. The possibility of organ weakness playing a determining factor in the specificity of the disorder is not precluded.

The pathways by which the psychic state contributes to or is expressed in specific disorders are not yet clearly defined. It is known that in some instances emotions have a direct and immediately activating effect on an organ system—for example, the role of anger in circulatory changes. Among the physiological changes similarly occurring in depression, diminution of salivary secretions has been noted by many observers. In relation to the burning mouth, however, the significance of this finding is difficult to evaluate. Salivation studies on comparison groups have not adequately been controlled for such factors as age, sex, diet, state of oral hygiene, and other relevant variables. Particularly relevant to the burning mouth is the fact that the complaint occurs more frequently with the aged, although not exclusively so, as was once thought to be the case. Moreover, decreased salivation is also related to aging. Whatever role decreased salivation may play in facilitating the development of the symptom, however, other factors also operate, since evidence clearly shows that the sensation of burning is not the inevitable consequence of decreased salivation. Similarly, not all complaints of burning mouth are correlated with decreased salivation.

At this point it appears that somatic symptom formation is multi-determined and may reflect many of the same mechanisms that operate with psychoneurotic symptoms. In relation to burning mouth, the symbolic meaning of the symptom seemed obvious in some instances. The mouth is commonly regarded as an instrument of attack. Expressions such as "sharp," "biting," "or "cutting" tongue, are indications of the common acceptance of the tongue and mouth as a weapon.

F. V. was a 57-year-old widow who was depressed over the death of her mother with whom she had lived and from whom she was inseparable for many years. She developed painful burning of the tongue and mouth the morning immediately after an argument with her sister about the disposition of her mother's estate. She attributed the onset of her symptoms to her violent verbal attack on her sister.

T. H. was a 53-year-old clergyman whose sermons were enjoyed because he spoke of "peace and tranquility" rather than "fire and brimstone." Shortly before the onset of his burning sensation, he had become angry with a parishioner who had made false accusations against him. One afternoon, the patient became consumed with rage and threw the parishioner from his porch. Remorseful over his loss of temper, he became dejected upon discovering the parishioner was suffering from a brain tumor. On projective tests, it was obvious that the patient's defenses involved denial of and reaction formation against strong hostile impulses as well as much guilt about them.

The notion of burning or burning sensations as punishment for guilt is basic to the belief in hell and damnation, as illustrated in the Biblical story of burning coal placed in Isaiah's mouth to cleanse him of his sins.

In some instances, the burning mouth symptom appeared to reflect identification with a family member who had had a similar complaint.

B. A. was a 69-year-old woman who complained of soreness and burning of the upper and lower lips; she also complained of indigestion, paresthesias, bodily concerns, and insomnia. Her husband had died of "cancer of the mouth" about six years earlier. She did not cry or mourn at that time because, she maintained, she had been cautioned not to upset herself since she had previously had a myocardial infarct. Shortly after, she developed mouth ulcers which did not heal for a long time. Approximately one year ago she experienced the onset of the burning sensation.

Although she did not associate her symptom with her husband's illness, its relationship seemed apparent. She now cries when she thinks of her husband and apparently out of guilt visits his grave as often as possible.

Displacement upwards in the context of hysterical conversion reactions sometimes also seemed obvious:

H. B. was a 60-year-old married woman who described her problem as "a burning sensation in the oral cavity which travels; it goes to the chin and palate at times, and lips, also the tongue." She indicated the burning began nine years ago and readily associated this with the end of her menstrual cycle. She indicated that at that time she lost her migraine headaches ("as if somebody took a wand") which she had had for 25 years and which coincided with her menstrual cycle. During the interview it became obvious that she was distorting her age. She stated she didn't believe the burning was due to "nervousness" but thought it might be neurological since her "hot flashes" still continued after menopause.

The oral cavity is an erogenous area and a body orifice, and readily becomes a zone of displacement from other parts of the body. Psychoanalytic studies and investigations of dreams indicate that bleeding from the oral cavity may be unconsciously experienced as menstruation, abortion, sexual invasion, rape, castration, or death.

A. Z. was a 47-year-old man who complained of burning of the tongue. Following the initial interview, in which he cried over his father's death, he reported that he experienced relief from symptoms. He was referred for psychotherapy because of his depression. His first dream in psychotherapy was as follows: "My wife and I were invited to see a painless execution. A hammer with a long pick-like thing on it hit a man in the head. He collapsed smiling; then he started screaming. His mouth—I mean, tongue —kept coming out of his mouth, getting longer and longer." He stated that there seemed to be many physical similarities between the victim and himself. He supposed that the execution followed a trial and conviction for murder. A few moments later he related that he did not feel guilty over the death of his father as he had taken his father for adequate medical care

46

preceding his death. Then, making a slip, he told how as a child he had wished his father would die.

Conclusion

In summary, the evidence relating object-loss to somatic symptom formation is largely correlational, and does not prove a cause and effect relationship. Nevertheless, both in quantity and quality the evidence strongly suggests that the psychic state emanating from separation and object-loss may contribute to a number of diverse somatic reactions, ranging from those which involve actual cellular changes (for example, cancer) to those which comprise such subjective sensations as pain (for example, burning mouth). While consistent with generalizations concerning the intimate relation between psyche and soma, the relationship between object-loss and symptom formation carries implications for prevention and management which have hardly been touched upon in our present approaches to physical illness. While it has sometimes appeared that the great lack is that of appropriate theoretical models to explain "how" psyche and soma influence each other, the much greater practical need is for approaches to prevention and management which take the relationship for granted.

REFERENCES

1. W. D. Rees and S. G. Lutkins, "Mortality of Bereavement," *British Medical Journal,* 4:13, 1967.
2. C. M. Parkes, "Effects of Bereavement on Physical and Mental Health—A Study of the Medical Records of Widows," *British Medical Journal,* 2:274, 1964.
3. A. H. Schmale, Jr., "Relationship of Separation and Depression to Disease," *Psychosomatic Medicine,* 20:259, 1958.
4. S. J. Kowal, "Emotions As a Cause of Cancer," *Psychoanalytic Review,* 42:217, 1955.
5. L. L. LeShan and R. E. Worthington, "Personality as a Factor in the Pathogenesis of Cancer: A Review of the Literature," *British Journal of Medical Psychology,* 29:40. 1956.

CONCEPTS CENTRAL TO LOSS AND GRIEF

6. J. Paget, *Surgical Pathology*, London: Longmans Green, 1870. Quoted in Kowal (4).
7. W. Parker, *Cancer: A Study of Three Hundred and Ninety-Seven Cases of Cancer of the Female Breast*, New York, 1885. Quoted in Kowal (4).
8. E. Cutter, "Diet on Cancer," *Albany Medical Annals*, July-August, 1887. Quoted in Kowal (4).
9. H. Snow, *Cancer and the Cancer Process*, London: Churchill, 1893. Quoted in LeShan and Worthington (5).
10. C. B. Bahnson and M. B. Bahnson, "Cancer as an Alternative to Psychosis: A Theoretical Model of Somatic and Psychologic Regression," *Psychosomatic Aspects of Neoplastic Disease.* Edited by D. M. Kissen and L. L. LeShan. Philadelphia: J. B. Lippincott Company, 1964.
11. S. Peller, *Cancer in Man*, New York: International Universities Press, 1952.
12. H. F. Dorn, "Cancer and the Marital Status," *Human Biology, 15:*73, 1943.
13. W. A. Greene, Jr., "Psychological Factors and Reticuloendothelial Disease: I. Preliminary Observations On a Group of Males with Lymphomas and Leukemias," *Psychosomatic Medicine, 16:*220, 1954.
14. W. A. Greene, Jr., L. E. Young and S. N. Swisher, "Psychological Factors and Reticuloendothelial Disease: II. Observations On a Group of Women With Lymphomas and Leukemias," *Psychosomatic Medicine, 18:*284, 1956.
15. W. A. Greene, Jr. and G. Miller, "Psychological Factors and Reticuloendothelial Disease: IV. Observations On a Group of Children and Adolescents with Leukemia," *Psychosomatic Medicine, 20:*124, 1958.
16. A. H. Schmale, Jr. and H. P. Iker, "The Affect of Hopelessness and the Development of Cancer," *Psychosomatic Medicine, 28:*714, 1966.
17. L. L. LeShan, "A Basic Psychological Orientation Apparently Associated With Malignant Disease," *Psychiatric Quarterly, 35:*314, 1961.
18. B. Schoenberg, "Psychogenic Aspects of the Burning Mouth," *New York State Dental Journal, 33:*467, 1967.
19. B. Schoenberg, et al., "Idiopathic Orolingual Pain (Burning)." Submitted for publication, 1969.

II

Loss and Grief
in Childhood

4

The Child's Reaction to His Own Terminal Illness

John E. Schowalter

Calm, calm me more! nor let me die
Before I have begun to live.
                    Matthew Arnold

The death of a child is one of the outrages of nature. The basic efforts
of childhood are toward completing development by attaining physical
and emotional mastery of the self and the environment. For the dying
child, this effort is rudely thwarted. Instead of mastery, there is failure.
Instead of growth, there is wasting. Instead of joy, there is grief.

How children face death depends on their developmental capacity
to understand its meaning and on the environmental climate provided
by their caretakers. In this discussion of children's responses to impending death, it is assumed that the child knows he is going to die
and that he knows what death means. These assumptions may or may
not be warranted. Death has been treated as a taboo subject (1) and
the twentieth-century American mystique of vigor and sex has monop-
olized most parents' energies with teaching their children about their
origin rather than about their departure (2). Thus, it is seldom that a
child with terminal illness is told he is going to die.

It is very difficult to obtain direct information on death from dying
children (3). They seldom talk of their impending death. Because of
intellectual immaturity or emotional defenses, some children do not

realize they are dying. A greater number do not talk about their death because those around them overtly or covertly forbid it. Thus, while some of our information is first hand, the greater portion was necessarily obtained through detailed observations of dying children, discussions with parents and hospital staff, and studies of other children's attitudes toward death.

The children discussed here suffered from fatal diseases of a chronic rather than acute nature. Acute deaths are usually accompanied by great pain or impaired consciousness. Individuals faced with acute death use denial as their primary emotional defense (4). Denial is also the initial response of many chronic patients, but weeks, months, or years of increased debilitation provoke, in addition, a variety of other responses. This is particularly true for patients with disorders such as lymphocytic leukemia, in which case the patients may repeatedly swing from the despair of deterioration to the false hope of remission, and back again.

The variety of children's responses to terminal illness can be partially understood as a reflection of their emotional and conceptual development at a given age. For this reason the following discussion will examine attitudes toward and conceptualizations of death in four developmental periods: the infant and toddler period includes the first three years of life; the preschool period refers to the child from ages three to six; the latency age period considers the child up to about the age of ten; and the last period deals with the preadolescent and adolescent. It is understood that these attitudes and concepts do not change abruptly at a given age but evolve gradually and with wide individual variation.

The Infant and Toddler

The younger the child the more his affective responses to dying will be influenced by those around him. The exceptions, of course, are infants under six months of age. They do not yet recognize the environment as separate from themselves and therefore suffer only the physical ravages of the terminal process. From this age on, however, the child's response to his approaching death is significantly affected, for better or for worse, by those about him.

The experience of aggression predominates in all aspects of terminal illness. This is true for both the parent and the child. The fact that not only do children have occasional murderous impulses toward their parents, but also that parents experience the same impulses toward their children, is commonplace. In a setting of terminal illness these latter impulses are now experienced with special repugnance.

The child during his first three years regularly harbors resentment toward and fear of his parents. It is at this time that he realizes he is not omnipotent and that he is completely dependent on his parents. This realization is the source of separation anxiety. It is also at this time that definite demands (the prototype being toilet training) are first made upon him. Dreams in two-and three-year olds show a predominance of themes concerning being chased and involving oral incorporation (5). When the child becomes sick, he feels anger at the parent for failing to protect him and experiences a fear that he will now be abandoned. If anger is greater than fear, the child will tend to become rebellious. If fear is dominant, he will tend to become overly compliant. Thus, for the child under the age of three, while death is not yet a familiar nor realistic concept, the fear of separation from protecting, comforting objects is present in its most terrifying intensity.

Rank believed the traumatic separation at birth of the infant from the mother was coincidental with the initiation of the child's death fear (6). Freud, on the other hand, pointed out that the newborn's insufficient psychic organization prevented any direct memory of this event, and suggested that it would seem more reasonable to conclude that it is the separation from those nurturing him which provides the prototype of death anxiety (7). Death anxiety and separation remain juxtaposed at all ages, but their fusion is greatest while the organism is youngest and most dependent.

A dying child inevitably evokes parental emotions of guilt, grief, and anger. Depending on the parents' own past and their relationship to the child, these emotions will be expressed in different proportions. Parents, the mother especially, may unremittingly and exclusively dedicate themselves to the care of the child; or they may become overwhelmed with the tragedy of their child's suffering and impending death. In the case of the second reaction, parents will often find it difficult to spend time with the devastated patient who looks and acts so differently from the active toddler they remember.

It is impossible for parents to view the death of their child as anything but unnatural, and thus parents may respond to the fatal prognosis with feelings of responsibility and guilt (8, 9). Their past aggressive impulses toward the child, conscious and unconscious, hauntingly return. Such guilt is often too painful an emotion to endure along with grief, and the parent frequently projects it onto the attending physician and hospital staff (10). Direct anger at the child for being the source of inconvenience and anguish is also often too painful for self-realization and is displaced likewise onto the staff.

It is crucial to the child's morale that parents spend as much time as possible with him. It has been shown that even the non-fatally ill child reacts strikingly to the absence of the mother during the experience of hospitalization (11). Severely ill children may show severe signs of regression, such as prolonged periods of anger or withdrawal. Bowlby describes three phases of response to separation. These are protest, followed by despair, and then detachment (12). Once the latter stage is reached, the child may begin to ignore the parents even if they do begin to spend more time with him, and a vicious cycle of mutual withdrawal often takes place.

During the first few years, the mother *is* the child's whole life. She not only emotionally cares for him but also literally keeps him alive. Eissler states that the knowledge of time is necessary for the knowledge of death (13). The toddler does not yet know death—only absence. Since this concept of time is still faulty and incomplete, any departure is viewed as an abandonment. If the mother is not frequently present in the hospital, the dying child experiences only a rotation of nurses who come, then leave, thus aggravating his terror. It may be paraphrased that toddlers may die many times before their deaths, while the older child need taste death but once.

The following case history describes the difficulties one family had in providing the necessary support for their dying child, the child's response to their behavior, and one way the hospital staff attempted to compensate.

Tim was a twenty-eight-month-old Catholic child who developed a neuroblastoma and was hospitalized seven times over a period of five months prior to his death. He was an only child and conceived prior to the marriage of his nineteen-year-old mother and twenty-one-year-old father. During the course of his illness, Tim developed bone pain, massive liver enlargement, and exophthalmos. He was treated with surgery, irradiation, and chemotherapy. The parents' grief was accentuated by their old shame concerning Tim's untimely conception and by their feelings of guilt triggered by their inability to conceal from themselves or others the irritation they felt toward the child for causing them an impossible financial burden. As a consequence of these emotional factors the parents rarely visited the child while he was in the hospital and only mechanically cared for him at home.

During the initial hospitalization for diagnostic tests, Tim responded with anger and negativism toward the staff, but by the end of the first week he became increasingly apathetic. The same empathic and energetic nurse was assigned to Tim each time he was admitted, and she often visited him during his interim outpatient appointments. Prior to each discharge, Tim's parents were reluctant to take him home, and with subsequent hospitalizations he would return to the ward detached and withdrawn. It was recognized that this was not entirely due to his physical debilitation because following two or three days on the ward, regardless of whether or not the treatment regimen was altered, his interest and vigor would substantially increase. It was also clear that when his nurse-mother-substitute was off-duty for more than one day, Tim's anger-followed-by-apathy pattern would quickly return. During his last days when Tim needed additional care, it was arranged for this mother surrogate to "special" him. His parents were notified that he was terminal but were not present at his death. Tim remained relatively alert and died peacefully, holding onto the nurse's hand.

While death is not yet a fact for the child under three, anxiety about separation is all-pervasive. Thus, continuity of the parents' presence and the character of this presence is crucial in determining the child's response to his terminal illness. It is the responsibility of those caring for the child to offer the parents the necessary aid and support to accomplish this task.

The Preschool Child

Sometime between the ages of three and five most children first comprehend the fact of death as something that happens to others (14, 15, 16). At this time a child's response to terminal illness will reflect the beginnings of an intellectualization of death as well as the attitude of the environment. Although the preschool and early oedipal child has usually had some first-hand experience with the death of a flower, an animal,

55

or a relative, the concept is still vague, associated with sleep and the absence of light or movement, and is not yet conceived as permanent. The concept of death remains relatively unstable in children of this age group, but compared to the toddler they are better able to withstand and understand short separations. Probably because they cannot yet comprehend death's permanency (17, 18), children in this age group respond more spontaneously and with less anxiety to questions about death than do other children (19, 20). Life at this age may be attributed to anything that moves or, even, anything that is useful. Death is understood as the opposite of life (21, 22) and is often described as remote, dark, and constricted (23, 24, 25).

During these preschool years, the child begins to struggle with particular conflicts growing out of his development. It is typical that he feels fearful of retaliation from the parents for his intense sexual and aggressive impulses toward them or toward siblings. These fears may be completely repressed, only to reappear as night terrors, tics, phobias, obsessions, or compulsions. When misfortunes or illness befall the preschooler, he often identifies these as just punishment for his vivid fantasies and wishful misdeeds (26). For the child with a serious or fatal illness, guilt is often almost as common as fear. Since the child at this age cannot logically comprehend the causes of disease, he may understand his regressive illness as deserved punishment for real or imagined wrong doing. As if to confirm his punishment fantasy, hospitalization takes him from his parents, and he is subjected to numerous painful tests and therapies. Instead of being expiated by these inflictions, however, he finds himself worsening. At this point many young patients seem to give up and resign themselves to whatever may come.

The child who reacts to his illness with guilt may present as the passive "good" patient who causes trouble for neither the parents nor the staff. Experienced pediatricians know, however, that the angry, rebellious patient responds better to treatment than the one who has acquiesced to his plight. Because of this, it is important that the feelings of a passive child not be ignored, but that he be given the opportunity to reveal feelings of fear and guilt. Our experience has been that once these feelings have been expressed the child's mood brightens.

A minority of patients become increasingly rebellious and antagonistic in the hospital. This latter reaction stems from the child's denial of guilt and his projection onto and subsequent anger toward his parents or staff for either causing or allowing this tragedy to happen (27). Parent and doctor alike often correctly interpret the child's aggressiveness as a rebuke against their impotency. If they follow a natural tendency to withdraw from the attacks, this only aggravates the patient's complaint of faulty protection, and his behavior worsens. If and when the child finally convinces himself that he cannot drive away his caretakers, reassurance is usually revived, and he becomes more quiet and trustful.

Mark was a five-year-old boy with a malignant brain tumor, a medulloblastoma. He was hospitalized five times over a period of eight months. With his first two hospitalizations, Mark was extremely passive and withdrawn. He did not seem outwardly frightened and he did not cry. During his third admission, the housestaff became concerned with his apathy, and a child psychiatrist was asked to see Mark and his parents. It was learned from the parents that a few months prior to the onset of Mark's symptoms his mother had discovered him masturbating, and she warned him that such actions could make him crazy or damage his penis. His paternal grandfather had been recently hospitalized for schizophrenia, and Mark understood that being crazy meant something was wrong in your head. With the beginning of headaches, dizziness, and blurred vision, Mark reasoned that his symptoms were probably due to his masturbation. When he required urethral catheterization, the belief seemed to be confirmed. Once it was suggested to Mark that he probably worried about being to blame for his condition, the child's fears and guilt gushed forth. After the doctors, as well as his parents, reassured him that he was in no way responsible, he became more outgoing and was much better able to accept the warmth and care his parents were so eager to give.

In summary, the dying child at this age no longer responds purely with separation anxiety but often feels his illness is a retribution for bad thoughts or actions. The guilt of responsibility is either borne by the child or projected onto parents and/or staff. If the child takes the guilt upon himself, he usually becomes passive and withdrawn. When guilt is projected, he becomes angry and rebellious. It is important that those responsible for the patient's care realize the universality of guilt in the severely ill child and that they help to allay it.

LOSS AND GRIEF IN CHILDHOOD

The Early School-Aged Child

This period involves the child of six to ten or eleven years of age. Developmentally, this era spans the intensification and resolution of the conflicts involving sexuality, aggression, and rivalry, as well as the subsequent latency period. The child's response to a serious illness is not dissimilar from that already described for the preschooler, but not until this age does *terminal* illness have a meaning of its own. During these years, the permanency and universality of death gradually, if incompletely, make their impact on the child. Death in old age is grasped first. The unnaturalness of childhood death is also first understood at this age. It is interesting that a group of devout Catholic children, age six and seven, thought heaven a fine place for others, but they wished that their own arrival be delayed at least until adulthood (28). One seven-year-old child with leukemia said he hated to see children die because they should have to grow up first. It has also been reported that it was at age six and one-half that a congenitally blind girl first uttered the wail of "It isn't fair!" (29) This rebuke is echoed in many forms by dying children from this age on.

The studies of Piaget, Nagy, and Safier show that children of this age group attribute death to an external agent which causes the organism to die or cease to move (30, 31, 32). As noted previously, this belief may be enhanced by oedipal conflicts, and it appears that the fear of physical injury and mutilation is greatest in dying children of this age (33). It has also been reported that tonsillectomy patients at this age most fear the operation per se, while younger children most fear the separation, and older children most fear the anesthesia (34). Safier found children between ages five and eight most reluctant to talk about death (35), while Alexander and Alderstein found these children responded more anxiously to words associated with death than did the older age groups (36). Blanchard reports that dreams about death become more frequent at about age six (37). It seems then that the fear of death per se first makes its appearance at this time, and that the child is horrified, confused, and angered by the discovery.

What are the reactions of the terminally ill child at this age? The feeling of responsibility for the illness remains strong. One study (38) reported that in response to the question, "Why do children become sick?" 90 per cent of a group of children with diabetes or heart disease

58

responded, "Because they are bad." Kessler has reported that one of the answers universally given to the question, "Give two reasons why children should obey their parents," as part of the Binet Scale at the eleven-year level, is, "So you won't get sick or hurt" (39). A belief that they are the cause of their illness leads to the same dichotomy of passive and aggressive behavior patterns found in preschool children.

Although strong death concern has been reported in a dying three-and-one-half year old (40), and Solnit and Green discuss a four-year-old who confided that he knew he was dying (41), anticipation of death is rare prior to the age of five or six. We have no direct information about what proportion of fatally ill children realize they are dying, but probably the frequency begins to rise at about age six to reach almost 100 per cent in late adolescence. We do know, however, that it is in this latency age range that some children begin to ask if they are dying. Seldom do they really want to know the truth, but they are expressing their realization that they are very sick. Most children are content with an explanation *why* they are feeling so bad and with reassurance that they will be taken care of. If a patient continually returns to his original question, he should probably be told, but what and by whom must first be discussed with the parents. No child should be told more than he asks, and hope must never be totally abolished. Interestingly enough, patients seem more frequently to ask the doctor or hospital staff about death than they do their parents. The reason for this could be that they are too anxious to ask the parents or they believe the staff is more competent to answer such a question, but often they are attempting to spare the parents extra grief. The child knows, and the parents know, but both make believe the other does not.

Once the parents have been told the child's fatal prognosis, their whole life shrinks. There is routinely a period of denial, after which the process of mourning begins. It is impossible for the parents' attitude toward the child not to change. It is also impossible for the child not to recognize this change. This recognition may not be readily apparent, but the child senses that his parents are distressed and that his relationship with them is different. Although their attention toward him may increase, the perceptive child is also aware of the subtle intensification of feelings that anticipate the process of mourning. His parents' reaction of frantic closeness and at the same time hurt withdrawal led one seriously ill eight-year-old Jewish boy to remark that his parents' attitude reminded him of the Biblical story of Abraham and Isaac. This one association accurately expressed the boy's fear of being sacrificed, his anger at the parents for letting it happen, and his hope for a last minute reprieve.

Once a child is old enough to be aware of the possibility of death, his philosophy of a hereafter also becomes relevant. It is a clinical impression that children exposed to death in a nonfrightening way tend to be more open and less fearful about death than those without exposure. A child who believes in a benevolent God and a reunion after death with loved ones may appear less fearful than a child without this hope. Religion per se, however, is no certain safeguard against death fear. On the contrary, some of the most terrified and inconsolable children are the product of juxtaposition of earthly guilt with the belief in a malevolent God.

Stephen was a seven-year-old Catholic boy with lymphocytic leukemia. After the diagnosis was made, his family took a brief pilgrimage with him to a religious shrine in eastern Canada. When he returned, and following chemotherapy, he had a "complete" remission. Although the parents had been informed to anticipate a good initial response and also cautioned that recurrences were the rule, this information was ignored, and they assured the boy that he was completely well. Although Stephen had not been told of his diagnosis, the hurried plane trip, the hallowed shrine, and his harried parents certainly emphasized to him the gravity of his condition. Then, when further exacerbations occurred, the boy became very angry, denounced his parents and his religion. The hospital staff found him very difficult to work with and asked that the child psychiatrist and social worker enter the case. The family, who at this point were angry, guilty, and close to losing their own faith, welcomed the intervention.

Although it took some time to gain rapport with the child, it soon became clear that Stephen was not as angry at religion as he was fearful of it. His parents were strictly religious, and when he became ill Stephen wondered if his past sins might not be the cause. When his parents took him to Montreal, he became terrified that God would not help him. He found the prayers, penance, and ceremony more frightening than comforting, but his symptoms did disappear and his parents did tell him he was cured. However, rather than believing that his sins were forgiven, Stephen thought that through oversight they had only been forgotten, and that his cure was a mistake which God might at any time discover. Subsequently, relapses convinced him that this was the case, and he feared God would now blame him for the "mistake" as well as his past sins. When a staff member arrived to perform any procedure, no matter how minor, Stephen worried that he might be the Devil coming to take him. He was also terrified of going to sleep.

Once it was discovered that Stephen had not rejected his religion but feared it rejected him, the child psychiatrist worked together with a priest in helping Stephen sort out fact from religious fantasy. Although they were never completely successful in attaining this goal, the boy did begin to sleep better, to give evidence of greater inner peacefulness, and to take procedures with greater equanimity. During this time, the social worker met with the parents to help them deal with their own anger and guilt.

It is important in this age group that parents and staff do not underestimate the child's possible awareness of the seriousness of his condition. While a child at this age usually cannot emotionally handle being told he is going to die, it is not unusual for him to reach this conclusion himself. Unless a child of this age repeatedly and specifically asks whether or not he will die, it is usually better not to tell him. It is easier for him to deny his own judgment than that of his doctor or parents, and he should be allowed to use this defense if he wishes. Allowing the child to discuss his fear and guilt concerning his illness continues to be crucial in allaying his anxieties.

Preadolescence and Adolescence

It is doubtful whether an individual can fully conceive the fact of his own death. Yet, at about age ten or eleven, the fact of the universality and permanence of death finally does become comprehensible (42, 43, 44, 45, 46, 47). Since the child now has an almost adult capacity to understand death, his response to terminal illness is more like that of adults (48).

The problems of adolescence have much in common and often recapitulate those of infancy (49). The adolescent must cope with vast bodily changes as well as redirect intensified sexual impulses toward appropriate objects outside the family. The task is an enormous and frightening one even under the best of circumstances. For the dying adolescent, however, it soon becomes apparent that the changes in his body will prove not to be a vital asset to his fulfillment but a fatal liability. He will experience not only a general decrease in vitality but may also suffer the consequences of x-ray or chemotherapy (for example, increased fatigue, nausea and vomiting, easy bruising, etc.). These physical ravages of terminal illness are least easily endured by this age group. At no other time in life are physical beauty and prowess such critical standards of one's personal popularity or success. While all patients should be kept informed of the physical side reactions to treatments, this is particularly important in the care of adolescents.

Anna Freud has well described the shame and frustrations inherent in illness (50). The child is faced with regression, loss of control, and the need for external help in performing even the most basic body functions. For the adolescent who until recently was beginning to realize real autonomy and independence, such deterioration is devastating. Youngsters within this age group who become ill are especially susceptible to feelings of disgrace and lack of prestige (51). This feeling of shame is unique to this older group of children. The problem of separation experienced by the younger child in terms of *physical* separation becomes for the adolescent the problem of *emotional* separation of the self from others. Erikson exhaustively describes the importance of the adolescent attaining an identity (52), while the novelist Richard Hughes brilliantly describes the surprise and wonder of his young heroine when she startingly discovers "that she is *she*" (53). This revelation is what opens up the world and all its wonders, so that the adolescent "regards himself at an initial point and as a beginner in some all-important but dimly conceived progression toward whatever may be valuable in life" (54). To then become aware that one is going to die triggers what Solnit and Green have perceptively noted is one of man's deepest fears—death before fulfillment (55). It has been shown that dying patients turn away from the future and gain solace from the past (56). The adolescent often sees little in his past to comfort him. Although adults often find it hard to believe, a substantial number of teenagers describe childhood as a necessary evil or initiation imposed on them as preparation to join the freedom and happiness of grown-up life. For these adolescents death means not only that there is nothing in their future, but that the time spent in growing up was wasted.

The fatally ill adolescent often resents the ebullience of the unafflicted around him, especially other teenagers. They represent a constant reminder of his own frailty and lack of future. This feeling was best expressed by an intelligent high school senior who only recently had learned he had a brain tumor. He was reading Hardy's *The Return of The Native* for class and one day quoted to me a sentence he said best expressed his feelings. "Men have oftener suffered from the mockery of a place too smiling for their reason than from the oppression of surroundings oversadly tinged" (57). This young man's recitation can be readily recognized as a sophisticated and intellectualized echo of the six-year-old's anguished wail of "It isn't fair!"

Helen was a fourteen-year-old girl with chronic kidney disease which required frequent peritoneal dialyses. After a prolonged but relatively well-adjusted period of hospitalization, she was moved from a single into a three-bed room. Soon thereafter she suddenly became very agitated, told the pediatric interns she knew she was going to die, and asked to talk with a psychiatrist. Discussions with the girl uncovered the cause of her acute anxiety. The fifteen-year-old girl who occupied the bed next to hers had been hospitalized following a series of behavioral difficulties. She boasted of taking marijuana and had left the Yale-New Haven Hospital without permission to spend a day in New York City. Helen overheard the doctors question the girl as to whether or not she had had intercourse while she was gone. Helen had for years fantasized such adventures for herself but had rigidly suppressed the urges to carry them out with the self-promise that she would enjoy them when older. However, her sudden proximity to such actual happenings coupled with her knowledge that now she would never experience them caused her to become overwhelmed by the limitations of her mortality. Although she came to understand the cause of her sudden anxiety, it did not substantially decrease until the other girl was discharged.

Although it is probably true that a majority of dying adolescents sense their fate, it remains a crucial question whether or not they should be told what they already suspect. With parental consent, all children over the age of nine on a leukemia ward were told their diagnosis. It was concluded that parents and children benefited from this openness (58). On the other hand, some experienced pediatricians advocate never telling a fatally ill child his true diagnosis (59, 60). There is not, of course, one answer for all children. Such an important decision must be individualized and based on the child's requests, the parents' consent, and the staff's ability to support either decision. Studies indicate that while approximately 80 per cent of dying persons

63

believed that patients should be told, 80 per cent of doctors felt it best to withhold the true diagnosis (61). Other studies have shown that interns and residents have even greater difficulty managing dying adolescents and young adults than they do older or younger patients (62, 63).

In summary, the universality and permanence of death are painfully grasped by all within the adolescent age range. Just at the time when secondary sexual characteristics, independence, self-identity, and a lust for life begin to develop, the fatally ill adolescent is faced with bodily deterioration, forced dependency, disintegration of the self, and death. The dying adolescent may be plagued with feelings of shame as well as guilt, and classical signs of depression may be seen.

If one is willing to look and listen, most terminally ill adolescents react in such a way as to indicate that they know they are dying. Whether or not their suspicions should be confirmed depends on the persistency and meaning of their questions, the wishes of the parents, and the ability of the staff to provide support to patient and parents.

Those adolescents who will talk about dying express less separation anxiety and fear of procedures than do younger children, but despair over not being fulfilled seems almost universal. Some adolescents find comfort in anticipating a religious fulfillment in heaven. Clinically, it would appear that there are fewer religious fears of death during adolescence than during the early school age or the period of latency when conscience and ideals are often so strict.

Summary

A child's response to his death is predicated on his understanding of death and on the reaction of the people around him. Based on the evolution of the child's understanding of death, four developmental periods have been discussed. All children develop at their individual pace, and for biological and psychological reasons dying children regress. The age ranges, therefore, vary for different children but do indicate a developmental sequence of responses. Remnants of reactions characteristically formed in one developmental period may be seen in response patterns during all following ages. Each of the four developmental periods is summarized below.

Under the age of three, death is not yet a fact, but separation is, and the child's reaction is exquisitely sensitive to the caliber of mothering he receives. The dying preschool child recognizes the fact of death but does not understand it. Although he may express less death anxiety than children in other age groups, and no longer responds to his illness purely with separation anxiety, he commonly believes his illness is a retribution for bad thoughts or actions. If the child accepts this guilt, he often becomes passive and withdrawn. If he denies guilt and projects it onto others, he may become angry and rebellious. This complex interaction between guilt, denial, projection, passivity, and aggressivity will continue to be seen at all ages.

During his early primary school years, the child begins to comprehend the permanency of death. The concept of *terminal* illness first makes its impact, and death anxiety is greatest during this period. The severity of the recently formed superego and its self-punishing characteristics increase the child's fear of physical procedures, and he conceptualizes death as an external force which will malevolently stop his life. Religion begins to play a more important role, positively or negatively, with this age group, and although some children realize they are dying, they may be reluctant to voice these fears to their parents but rather confess to the staff that "I'm not supposed to know" (64).

After age ten or eleven most children intellectually understand the universality and permanency of death. This is also the time of life when physical and sexual maturation, self-identity, and independence begin to develop. Most terminally ill adolescents know they are dying and may be overwhelmed by the despair and resentment of unfulfillment. Shame, guilt, anticipatory mourning for oneself, and depressive symptoms are not uncommonly seen.

Along with the child's understanding of death, the other most important influence on his attitude and response toward death comes from those around him (65). Staff as well as parents feel guilty and uncomfortable in the presence of a dying child because his condition and often his attitude rebuke their failure and impotency. The wish to withdraw is omnipresent, but human presence and communication must not be withheld (66). One has to listen to hear, and this is both taxing and painful; but parents' positive involvement with the child facilitates their and the child's response to his condition (67, 68, 69). The competence, constancy, and availability of the staff are paramount in supporting these efforts (70, 71).

65

LOSS AND GRIEF IN CHILDHOOD

REFERENCES

1. H. Feifel, "Death." *Taboo Topics,* edited by N. L. Farberow, New York: Atherton Press, 1963.
2. S. Yudkin, "Children and Death," *The Lancet, 1:*37, 1967.
3. M. Green, "Care of the Dying Child," *Pediatrics, 40* (suppl.)492, 1967.
4. I. W. Browne and T. P. Hackett, "Emotional Reactions to the Threat of Impending Death," *Irish Journal of Medical Science, 6:*177, 1967.
5. J. L. Despert, "Dreams in Children of Preschool Age," *The Psychoanalytic Study of the Child, 3/4:*141, 1949.
6. O. Rank, *The Trauma of Birth,* New York: Harcourt, Brace, 1929.
7. S. Freud, "Inhibitions, Symptoms and Anxiety" (1926), *Complete Works,* Standard Edition, *20,* London: Hogarth Press, 1959.
8. M. F. Bozeman, C. E. Orbach, and A. M. Sutherland, "Psychological Impact of Cancer and Its Treatment. III. The Adaptation of Mothers to the Threatened Loss of Their Children Through Leukemia: Part I," *Cancer, 8:*1, 1955.
9. S. B. Friedman, et al., "Behavioral Observations on Parents Anticipating the Death of a Child," *Pediatrics, 32:*610, 1963.
10. C. E. Orbach, A. M. Sutherland, and M. F. Bozeman, "Phychological Impact of Cancer and Its Treatment. III. The Adaptation of Mothers to the Threatened Loss of Their Children Through Leukemia: Part II," *Cancer, 8:*20, 1955.
11. J. Robertson, "Some Responses of Young Children to the Loss of Maternal Care," *Nursing Times, 49:*382, 1953.
12. J. Bowlby, "Grief and Mourning in Infancy and Early Childhood," *The Psychoanalytic Study of the Child, 15:*9, 1960.
13. K. R. Eissler, *The Psychiatrist and the Dying Patient,* New York: International Universities Press, 1955.
14. S. Anthony, *The Child's Discovery of Death,* New York: Harcourt, Brace, 1940.
15. A. Freud and D. Burlingham, *War and Children,* New York: International Universities Press, 1943.
16. R. A. Furman, "Death and the Young Child," *Psychoanalytic Study of the Child, 19:*321, 1964.
17. H. von Hug-Hellmuth, "The Child's Concept of Death," trans. from Das Kind und seine Vorstellung vom Tode in *Imago, 1:*286, 1912, by A. O. Kris, *Psychoanalytic Quarterly, 34:*499, 1965.
18. G. A. Safier, "A Study in Relationships Between the Life and Death Concepts in Children," *Journal of Genetic Psychology, 105:*283, 1964.

66

19. W. Gartley and M. Bernasconi, "The Concept of Death in Children," *Journal of Genetic Psychology, 110:*71, 1967.
20. G. A. Safier, "A Study in Relationships Between the Life and Death Concepts in Children," *Journal of Genetic Psychology, 105:*283, 1964.
21. F. S. Caprio, "A Study of Some Psychological Reactions During Prepubescence to the Idea of Death," *Psychiatric Quarterly, 24:*495, 1950.
22. W. Gartley and M. Bernasconi, "The Concept of Death in Children," *Journal of Genetic Psychology, 110:*71, 1967.
23. J. Piaget, *The Child's Conception of the World* (1929), New York: The Humanities Press, Inc., 1951.
24. G. A. Safier, "A Study in Relationships Between the Life and Death Concepts in Children," *Journal of Genetic Psychology, 105:*283, 1964.
25. P. Schilder and D. Wechsler, "The Attitudes of Children Toward Death," *Journal of Genetic Psychology, 45:*406, 1934.
26. *Ibid.*
27. W. S. Langford, "The Child in the Pediatric Hospital: Adaptation to Illness and Hospitalization," *American Journal of Orthopsychiatry, 31:*667, 1961.
28. W. Gartley and M. Bernasconi, "The Concept of Death in Children," *Journal of Genetic Psychology, 110:*71, 1967.
29. E. B. Omwake and A. J. Solnit, " 'It Isn't Fair'—The Treatment of a Blind Child," *The Psychoanalytic Study of the Child, 16:*352, 1961.
30. M. H. Nagy, "The Child's View of Death," *The Meaning of Death,* edited by H. Feifel, New York: McGraw-Hill Book Co., 1959.
31. J. Piaget, *The Child's Conception of the World* (1929), New York: The Humanities Press, Inc., 1951.
32. G. A. Safier, "A Study in Relationships Between the Life and Death Concepts in Children," *Journal of Genetic Psychology, 45:*406, 1934.
33. A. G. Knudson and J. M. Natterson, "Participation of Parents in the Hospital Care of Fatally Ill Children," *Pediatrics, 26:*482, 1960.
34. G. E. Blom, "The Reactions of Hospitalized Children to Illness," *Pediatrics, 22:*590, 1958.
35. G. A. Safier, "A Study in Relationships Between the Life and Death Concepts in Children," *Journal of Genetic Psychology, 45:*406, 1934.
36. I. E. Alexander and A. M. Alderstein, "Affective Responses to the Concept of Death in a Population of Children and Early Adolescents," *Journal of Genetic Psychology, 93:*167, 1958.
37. F. Blanchard, "Study of the Subject Matter and Motivation of Children's Dreams," *Journal of Abnormal and 'Social Psychology, 21:*24, 1926.
38. B. I. Beverly, "The Effect of Illness Upon Emotional Development," *Journal of Pediatrics, 8:*533, 1936.

39. J. W. Kessler, "The Hospitalized Child," Round Table, 1954, *American Journal of Orthopsychiatry, 25:*297, 1955.
40. J. R. Morrissey, "Death Anxiety in Children with a Fatal Illness," *American Journal of Psychotherapy, 18:*606, 1964.
41. A. J. Solnit and M. Green, "The Pediatric Management of the Dying Child: Part II. The Child's Reaction to the Fear of Dying," *Modern Perspectives in Child Development*, edited by A. Solnit and S. Provence. New York: International Universities Press, 1963.
42. S. Anthony, *The Child's Discovery of Death*, New York: Harcourt, Brace, 1940.
43. I. M. Greenberg, "Studies on Attitudes Toward Death in Death and Dying: Attitudes of Patient and Doctor," *Group for the Advancement of Psychiatry Reports and Symposiums, 5:*623, October, 1965.
44. M. H. Nagy, "The Child's View of Death," *The Meaning of Death*, edited by H. Feifel, New York: McGraw-Hill Book Co., 1959.
45. J. Piaget, *The Child's Conception of the World* (1929), New York: The Humanities Press, Inc., 1951.
46. G. A. Safier, "A Study in Relationships Between the Life and Death Concepts in Children," *Journal of Genetic Psychology, 105:*283, 1964.
47. A. J. Solnit and M. Green, "The Pediatric Management of the Dying Child: Part II. The Child's Reaction to the Fear of Dying," *Modern Perspectives in Child Development*, edited by A. Solnit and S. Provence. New York: International Universities Press, 1963.
48. R. D. Abrams, "The Patient with Cancer—His Changing Pattern of Communication," *New England Journal of Medicine, 274:*317, 1966.
49. E. Jones, "Some Problems of Adolescence (1922)," *Papers on Psycho-Analysis*, London: Baliere & Cox, 1950.
50. A. Freud, "The Role of Bodily Illness in the Mental Life of Children," *The Psychoanalytic Study of the Child, 7:*69, 1952.
51. G. E. Gardner, quoted in W. S. Langford, "The Child in the Pediatric Hospital: Adaptation to Illness and Hospitalization," *American Journal of Orthopsychiatry, 31:*667, 1961.
52. E. H. Erikson, "The Problem of Ego Identity," *Journal of the American Psychoanalytical Association, 4:*56, 1956.
53. R. Hughes, *A High Wind in Jamaica* (also published as *The Innocent Voyage*) (1928), New York: The New American Library of World Literature, Signet Classic Edition, 1961, p. 98.
54. R. Kastenbaum, "Time and Death in Adolescence," *The Meaning of Death*, edited by H. Feifel, New York: McGraw-Hill Book Co., 1959.
55. A. J. Solnit and M. Green, "The Pediatric Management of the Dying Child: Part II. The Child's Reaction to the Fear of Dying,"

Modern Perspectives in Child Development, edited by A. Solnit and S. Provence, New York: International Universities Press, 1963.

56. A. Verwoerdt and J. L. Elmore, "Psychological Reactions in Fatal Illness. I. The Prospect of Impending Death," *Journal of American Geriatrics Society, 15:9*, 1967.

57. T. Hardy, *The Return of the Native* (1878), New York: Charles Scribner's Sons, 1917, p. 4.

58. J. Vernick and M. Karon, "Who's Afraid of Death on a Leukemic Ward?" *American Journal of Diseases of Children, 109:393*, 1965.

59. A. E. Evans, "If a Child Must Die . . . ," *New England Journal of Medicine, 278:138*, 1968.

60. D. A. Howell, "A Child Dies," *Journal of Pediatric Surgery, 1:2*, 1966.

61. J. M. Hinton, "Facing Death," *Journal of Psychosomatic Research, 10:22*, 1966.

62. T. Rich and G. M. Kalmanson, "Attitudes of Medical Residents Toward the Dying Patient in a General Hospital," *Postgraduate Medicine, 40:*A127-130, October, 1966.

63. J. E. Schowalter, "Death and the Pediatric Houseman." Presented at The Hezekiah Beardsly Pediatric Meetings, New Haven, Conn. October 4, 1967.

64. A. J. Solnit, "The Dying Child," *Development of Medical Child Neurology, 7:693*, 1965.

65. R. Zeligs, "Children's Attitudes Towards Death," *Mental Hygiene, 51:393*, 1967.

66. J. R. Morrissey, "A Note on Interviews with Children Facing Imminent Death," *Social Casework, 44:343*, 1963.

67. S. B. Friedman, et al., "Behavior Observations on Parents Anticipating the Death of a Child," *Pediatrics, 32:610*, 1963.

68. D. A. Howell, "A Child Dies," *Journal of Pediatric Surgery, 1:2*, 1966.

69. J. B. Richmond and H. A. Waisman, "Psychologic Aspects of Management of Children with Malignant Diseases," *American Journal of Diseases of Children, 89:42*, 1955.

70. M. Green, "Care of the Dying Child," *Pediatrics, 40*(Suppl.):492, 1967.

71. J. E. Schowalter, "Death and the Pediatric Houseman." Presented at The Hezekiah Beardsly Pediatric Meetings, New Haven, Conn. October 4, 1967.

5

The Child's Reaction to Death in the Family*

Robert A. Furman

It is difficult to influence the management of a child who has lost a loved one without first understanding his attitudes toward death and others' responses to his attitudes. Beginning our discussion in this fashion may point the way for the family physician or pediatrician to avail himself of his unique opportunities for prophylactic mental health work.

Attitudes Toward Death

Many pediatricians and family physicians have learned to use the periodic medical examinations of the two-, three-, four-, and five-year-old to inquire of parents their attitudes toward sexual enlightenment of the child and to assist them in recognizing the need for and guiding them in such education. But few have utilized these occasions to inquire and assist parents in educating their small children about death.

The physician who indicates that he believes the child's early education about both life and death is important, and that these subjects, like any others, can be freely discussed, is apt to be consulted when

*What I present in these pages has been developed over years of thoughtful collaborative work with my colleagues in the Cleveland Center for Research in Child Development. Too many have contributed to list each by name but special mention must be made of my indebtedness to my wife, Mrs. Erna Furman, and Dr. Maurits Katan.

tragedy has struck. Without such a relationship, it is hard for parents in distress to turn to their physician for assistance.

It is important to acquaint the small child with the facts about death, so as to help him acquire a realistic concept of death as a prerequisite to mastering his emotional response to death.

Some years ago I was working with the mother of a kindergarten girl who was attending the Hanna Perkins School, our therapeutic nursery school and kindergarten. Quite without warning we were faced with the death of a mother of a nursery school girl. The child, with whose mother I was working, knew the bereaved child and her mother from a relationship that antedated their attendance at school.

The kindergarten girl's mother felt she had to inform her daughter of the death of the other mother and, after some initial hesitancy, did so. Her daughter asked what dead was and the mother answered that when people die they go to heaven. The mother was troubled because the daughter asked nothing further; she was also dissatisfied with her own explanation since she really was not a religious person. In discussion it became clear she wanted to explain death to her child in a realistic fashion. She was not sure how to go about it and, in fact, had avoided previous opportunities to discuss death (such as the death of insects and animals).

I shared with her what other parents had told their youngsters: that death was the end of life, or the absence of life. I also suggested that she speak of life in terms that the child, according to her age, could best understand. When someone is dead and is no longer alive, he will no longer eat or sleep or run or play or feel, or be sad or happy or angry. A wise two-year-old who had just mastered his toilet training put this explanation in terms that were age-appropriate for him by adding "and then he won't do wee-wee or BM anymore either."

The mother was concerned with what she could say about the disposition of a dead person's body. She felt she could explain the process of decay and return to earth by telling how the bodies of dead birds when left in the woods ultimately return to the earth, even as dead trees do. In response to the question of what happens to the personality of a person, she prepared herself to remind her daughter that it dies as do all other aspects of living, but added also that a part of the person lives on in our memories and love.

The mother's second discussion with her child about death was more satisfactory: her daughter asked the questions she had anticipated, obviously trying to grapple with the new concept. When the child asked

71

what heaven was all about, her mother replied that it was something that some grownups believed in and thought about, something that made them feel better about death. She went on to say they could talk about the matter again when the girl was a bit older. The girl, of course, asked her mother what she believed and the mother quite honestly said she wasn't sure. Again, the child evinced no true feelings of sadness or of compassion for her little bereaved friend. The mother consoled herself, saying that it seemed all her daughter could do at this point was to grasp these new concepts and that perhaps the lack of emotional response reflected unfamiliarity with death.

A few months later the mother of a kindergarten classmate died. This time, when she was informed by her mother of what had happened, the little girl burst into tears, and expressed great pity for her classmate. She asked who would take care of him and what she might do to help. Her mother suggested that she might just tell him how very sorry she felt. This she was able to do to the great relief of the bereaved child as well as to his classmates, who were very uncertain about how to respond to this event.

Later, the child asked her mother when she, the mother, would die and when she herself would die. Her mother explained that ordinarily mothers did not die until they have grown quite old, to be grandmothers or even great grandmothers (this little girl's great grandmother was still living) and that she, the little girl, would be a grown-up lady with a husband and children of her own long before her mother died. In time, the same would be true for her and her children.

In this instance it was necessary for the child to have some intellectual understanding of death before she could respond to it emotionally.

When can such understanding be offered to children? Certainly they must have developed meaningful speech and an ability to differentiate the living from the nonliving, the animate from the inanimate. Usually by two years of age a child can be helped to understand that the chair and table are not alive, do not feel, and that the dog, cat, or other children are alive and do feel.

If the very young child is taught about death, he will accept this education with equanimity as a part of all the information he is busy acquiring about the world around him. When the explanation first comes to him later (at four, five, or six), his fantasy life is much livelier, and contains many aggressive thoughts that are difficult to master. Any explanatory facts about death are apt to become integrated within

72

the fabric of these fantasies. They become harder to assimilate for that reason.

If parents are not trying to avoid discussing death, opportunities will readily present themselves. Dead flies, mosquitoes, birds, and animals beside the road are instances which will arouse the child's interest and curiosity without overwhelming him. If the explanation is postponed until the death of someone deeply loved by the child, either the emotional turmoil will complicate the acceptance of the reality of death or in grappling with reality, the concept of death may preclude for that occasion the appropriate emotional response.

What of religious explanations of death? It has sometimes seemed that the surest way to make a confirmed atheist of a young child may be to tell him of a God who takes from him the ones he loves; the surest way to frighten a young child about religious concepts may be to tell him of an ill-defined place where everyone goes after death.

A mother complained that her four-year-old son had great difficulty in falling asleep. In addition, he demanded that all the windows be kept locked even in the heat of summer and he was unwilling when outside to cross streets or to be out of the shade of trees. In consultation, the mother soon revealed that when his infant brother had died the boy had been told that God had reached down from heaven and while his brother slept had picked him up and taken him to heaven.

Unrealistic explanations about death—that it is merely sleep or that the person has gone away—aside from simply being untruthful, can also lead to sleep disturbances or anxiety reactions about the trips anyone might take.

Attitudes Toward a Child's Feelings of Loss

No child can live very long without suffering loss. Even the process of growing up may be seen as a loss of accustomed forms of support and attention.

A nursery schooler had just mastered tying her own shoe laces, something that had taken her weeks of diligent effort to achieve. She was duly proud of her new skill, and even untied her shoes before her grandparents to be able to demonstrate this accomplishment. But one afternoon she suddenly balked at tying her laces. Her mother was puzzled and pointed out how proud she had been of her grown-up skill. Her daughter was thoughtful, but then replied, "Yes, but I do sometimes miss your doing it for me."

Entrance into school brings with it a great loss, marking the end of the close relationship with the mother. Other losses are common to childhood. In our mobile society each year many children must give up their rooms, their homes, their friends, and their schools to move to an entirely new environment. Every time a physician takes on a family who has just moved to the neighborhood, the opportunity exists to explore how they deal with feelings of loss. The physical examination for the new entrant to nursery school, kindergarten, or summer play camp presents the same opportunity.

Allowing a child to express his sadness, worry, or anger about a loss seems so simple and sensible that it is impossible not to wonder what makes it hard for many parents to accomplish. Some parents cannot because of their own depressions, which they fear would come flooding upon them if they were to allow open expression of feelings by their children. In other instances the response of the parents may reflect losses they suffered as children.

A mother requested help for a ten-year-old daughter who exhibited delinquent behavior for the first time immediately after a sudden family move made under trying circumstances. When the obvious relationship between the two events was suggested to the mother, she dismissed it as nonsensical. Her own father had been in the regular Army and she had attended nine different public schools and had moved an unaccountable number of times before school age. But she was sure of one thing and that was that the moves had all been educational, exciting, and gratifying with never a sad or unpleasant moment. What could have been resolved by understanding on the mother's part required instead therapeutic intervention.

For the purposes of exposition we must stress another aspect of the difficulties inherent in confronting loss in childhood. Somehow the myth of innocent happiness through childhood seems destined never to be weakened. The psychiatrist who assists adolescents struggling painfully through their years before adulthood never ceases to wonder

74

how quickly people forget the pain of these years, and instead stress the bliss of being "sweet sixteen." Perhaps, it is because some sadness of childhood is so intense that people find it difficult to bring back these unpleasant memories and therefore idealize childhood as a period of constant bliss.

Children do not always directly confront their parents with their sadness. They prefer to avoid any open confrontation that might bring with it the threat of what they feel to be infantile tears. Often they will act as if nothing has occurred or, if it is impossible to avoid or deny, they will often act as if they really did not care at all. But their distress becomes evident in indirect ways that the sensitive parent will immediately detect: a change in usual cooperation, a change in moods, the appearance of minor symptoms such as physical aches or pains, sleep or eating difficulties, or more serious symptoms such as bedwetting, lying, or stealing. Some parents sense that such changes must have a cause or reason and seek it out.

Many children can verbalize feelings of sadness without crying. A nine-year-old boy was asked how this was possible for him. He explained that it was not really true that he did not cry, but rather that he usually cried when he was alone because he did not want to let anyone see him weep. He was not sure why he felt this way, but he thought it was because crying was babyish. "I know you have explained to me it's maybe babyish to cry when there is a little hurt or you just can't get your own way, and I know you say it's grownup to be able to cry when you're really sad about something and I know you're right, but I don't think all of me believes it yet."

But whether these difficulties in recognizing the child's real feelings spring from the child's way of managing his emotions or from the wishes of many adults to deny these emotions, the difficulties do exist and are most apparent when the child has suffered a severe loss.

The Child Who Has Lost A Parent: Initial Presentation

Unless a physician can be comfortable within himself about death and accept children's feelings about loss he will not be able to assist them when they suffer grievous loss. For those who cannot achieve such an equilibrium, perhaps it is best to call upon colleagues or other profes-

75

sionals such as psychiatrists, social workers, or child therapists for guidance or consultation.

Why is it important that a child master his emotional response to the loss of a loved one? First of all, not to assist a child in perceiving and understanding his responses to the most important event of his life would be to participate in denying him something of his basic birthright as a human being. In addition, psychoanalytic studies have shown that when a person is unable to complete a mourning task in childhood he either has to surrender his emotions in order that they do not suddenly overwhelm him, or else he may be haunted constantly throughout his life with a sadness for which he can never find an appropriate explanation.

How old must children be to approach this very difficult task? The evidence indicates that at about the age of four the child can be helped to begin mastering such loss, although opinion varies as to the exact age when the mourning work can begin.

How does one assist a child in coping with the loss of a parent? As indicated above, a realistic and honest approach to death and to feelings of loss is the best we can offer our children in preparation for any of life's grim pitfalls. The premature loss of a parent can come after a long illness or with brutal suddenness; in the case of a long illness it is not reasonable to expect a child to recognize his parent's impending death and to be able to cope with it. It would prevent him from enjoying the limited time he has remaining with his ill parent. It would be impossible for him not to ask the ill parent about the impending death, and if this were an especially painful confrontation it would only serve as a later source of guilt.

A father of boys six, eleven, and thirteen years of age whose wife was slowly dying of cancer dealt with this problem by telling his sons "what the doctor told mommy." In this way they could always be with their mother without fear of betraying what would have otherwise been a dreadful secret. The father encouraged visits and daily phone calls as often as their mother could enjoy them. He never allowed visiting when pain was not controlled or when she was receiving intravenous medication or any other medical procedure. When the older boys persisted with questions as her condition deteriorated, he listened patiently and replied he could understand how worried they were but that he could only tell them what the doctor told mother. He maintained this position, though painful to him, until it was clear her condition precluded any further contacts with her children, either personally or by telephone from the hospital. Then he explained to them the real prognosis and why he had evaded it with them—to protect their last days with mother and to ensure that nothing anyone did would possibly interfere with her most treasured pleasures, her moments with her family.

In the case of sudden loss—in many cases due to accident—the child may be witness to horrible scenes. It is particularly important to give him the opportunity repeatedly to talk out his feelings about an event for which he could have no preparation.

The tremendous strain on the surviving parent of either a sudden death or a gradual demise is self-evident. For this reason consultation with a professional person on a regular basis for a period of several weeks or many months can provide both support and guidance for the surviving parent. The surviving parent often can find purpose and comfort in devoting himself to the task of assisting the children in their bereavement.

While the physician cannot tell a person exactly how to inform his child that a parent has died, he can emphasize honesty in the emotional expression. It is often asked if the child should see the parent crying. It offers great support to a child in facing his own tears to see and feel his parent's ability to experience fully his own grief.

The father described above met this terrible moment by telling his sons, after informing them of their mother's death, that they would have many sad moments together in the days ahead but that there were no feelings they could not share together and that he would see to it that they stayed together as a family. One son immediately asked who would take his mother's place and the father replied that no one would or ever could, but that he would see to it that her jobs would always be done. In these words he made clear to his sons that there were no feelings to be avoided and that he would make sure that all their needs would be met. We will return later to both these points.

Often it is asked if children should attend the funeral of a loved one. In general it would seem fair to allow a child the opportunity to share this important event with the remainder of his family. It is unwise to exclude a child from participation as a member of the family, particularly at this time. On the other hand it is also unwise to force him to attend something he might not be able to manage. The most reasonable solution is to explain to him exactly what will be entailed, express the wish that he be there, but also express acceptance of the child's feelings if he prefers not to attend. The final decision can be left to the child. If a child elects to attend a funeral, it may prove helpful to insist that no lines of people be greeted and that the casket remain closed. Simple, brief, and dignified services can be tolerated advantageously by a child if he is told beforehand what will happen, can have his questions answered, and can have his choice about the degree of his participation.

How something is done, however, may be more important than what is done. For example, the Jewish custom of sitting *shivah* may in its traditional form be quite frightening and confusing to a child. In its contemporary form of a prolonged series of social evenings it may resemble a continuous and inappropriate cocktail party. But the recurrent gathering together of friends and relatives can be comforting and reassuring in the days following a loss, something a child can profitably share in at least to some extent. Some adjustment of procedure to the child's perspective may be important. What will not offend the sensibility of a child may be best for all—perhaps a fair guide in making certain that the best of old customs are retained with no loss of what is helpful and dignified.

The Child Who Has Lost A Parent: Emotional Response

If a child is told with feeling of the death of a loved one he will respond with feeling. But just as grownups at the moment of awareness may cope with shocked disbelief, so may the child. The child's almost immediate return to play may appear a heartless denial of what has happened, but would in reality be a return to the familiar to allow himself time to assimilate and accept what is horrible, new, and unfamiliar. If he can be allowed this retreat, he can accomplish by himself what grown-ups do when they slowly get over their feelings of disbelief.

An apparent indifference during the first few days or weeks

should be considered as serving an adaptive function and should be distinguished from the child's pretending the death has not occurred as a form of denial.

A six-year-old who always had a lively interest in school lost his mother. He suddenly stopped bringing home any of his school papers. He forgot them, leaving them in his desk at school. The boy was not able to explain this to his father. Overhearing one of these conversations, his older brother said, "I know why. There is no mother home to bring the papers to. It would make him too sad so he forgets them at school." The six-year-old nodded a begrudging agreement and the school papers began coming home.

The same child became reluctant to get his hair cut, always being some place else at the time he was scheduled to go to the barber with his father. Again his brother pointed out, "You know, mother always used to take him."

The six-year-old was simply avoiding those situations which would underscore his loss and stimulate his sadness and pain. That he was not denying the fact of his mother's death is borne out by his ready acceptance of his brother's explanations and the consequent changes in his behavior. The father soon found himself thinking in terms of the loss of the mother in every instance when the six-year-old's behavior differed from his usual pattern. Every time the child had to face without mother something he had previously done with her, the father spoke of the feeling of missing mother that was invariably present. This occurred particularly at the time of birthdays, holidays, shopping for clothes and groceries, and change of seasons. These occasions were most trying for the father and the need to assist his son delayed for some months the full impact of his own mourning.

The perceptive understanding of the older brother merits special explanation and leads to the most difficult feeling the bereaved child must manage, namely, anger. At the time the eleven-year-old was told of his mother's death, he became distressed. He told his father he feared it was his fault his mother had died because he had been angry with her just before her last admission to the hospital. He had wished that she would never come back. His father immediately reassured him that such wishes never could hurt anyone and that this was a problem they would all have to face. It appears that he was then able to be helpful and realistic because his aggression and guilt had come to the fore immediately after the loss and had been dealt with adequately.

A few months after his mother's death, the six-year-old boy whose avoidance patterns were discussed above experienced a period of denial —for example, he began going for walks to places that his mother had frequented in the hope of seeing her. Denial is a common defense mechanism in both children and adults. Many older bereaved people, for example, manage their lives as if a lost husband or wife were still living, such as by not disposing of their clothes, or leaving a room exactly as the lost one had last used it.

Four months after his mother had died, the patient's denial was first noted when he took, from his teacher, two tickets rather than one ticket for a PTA meeting. He did this though he was aware that the teacher knew of his recent loss. In addition, in his psychoanalytic sessions he wanted to walk to an adjacent hillock a few blocks away where his mother had sometimes parked while waiting for his session to end. In exploring this behavior it emerged that he feared his anger had made his mother angry and that this anger had caused her death. After this was discussed his denial stopped. Whenever it recurred, we found that he had again become convinced that he was in some way responsible for her death. It also recurred when he experienced anger toward her for having died and left him.

What often appears to be a child's intolerance for the reality of a loss is actually his unsuccessful struggle with guilt over his anger toward the lost loved one. The ubiquity of this response in children is understandable when we realize that all child-parent relationships are at some time marked by anger. Children also engage in magical thinking, insofar as they believe that feeling, wish, and action are equivalent. Children will feel angry at a parent who is seen as abandoning them even if the abandonment is caused by death. It is the apparently selfish aspect of these feelings that make the child feel guilty and hesitant about verbalizing his anger. Denial is utilized to avoid profound guilt as well as sorrow.

Professional assistance is often needed to help the child cope with his anger as well as with his sadness at the loss of a parent. The professional must be aware that the child will have to come to grips with guilt over his anger toward the lost loved one, and that the struggle

with these feelings will frequently be evidenced by denial of the death
of the loved or valued person.

The Child Who Has Lost A Parent: Fulfillment of Needs

Need fulfillment is a term that refers to the early and helpless period
of an infant's life when immediate satisfaction of his needs is of primary
importance to him. The person who fulfills these needs at that period is
of secondary importance. It is, however, in the fulfillment of needs that
the infant experiences the crucial relationship of his life, his relationship with his mother. Until full, independent adulthood is achieved
every person continues to have needs which his parents must fulfill,
although with time and growth the necessity for parents to fulfill needs
slowly decreases.

A starving person can think of nothing except his struggle for
food and survival. His feelings become expendable luxuries until his
future is safely assured. Similarly, until children are certain that the
needs the lost parent fulfilled for them are going to be met, they will
not be free to deal with their feelings. With the child under three or four
years of age, his need is for the same person consistently to meet his
bodily needs: to feed, dress, bathe, and protect him.

The needs of small children who have lost their mother will in most
instances have to be met by professional community resources. In this
regard four points should be emphasized: 1) Consistency is a vital key.
Every change of the need-fulfilling person constitutes a repetition of
the trauma of the original loss. The fulfilling of needs should be the
responsibility of a single person. If this is not possible and more than
one person is required, then each person who participates should remain constant in the role he fulfills. 2) Since the small child has lost
an irreplaceable part of his environment, all the other parts of his environment that can be maintained unchanged should be kept, as far as
is possible, exactly as they were. Relatives or friends who offer should
help in the child's home. The child's home, room, daily schedule, toys,
and associates should remain constant as far as is possible. 3) It is
difficult to know when a young child can fully understand what is told
him. Because of the emotional difficulty engendered in those who talk
to him about the loss of his mother, such discussion is often by-passed

81

on the pretext that "he is too young to understand." However, those responsible for the child must explain simply and repeatedly what has happened. If the small child cannot understand fully, nothing is lost; if he understands only a small part, much is gained. 4) Anna Freud* has made the important observation that the change in care from a mother to a substitute can be best effected if the mother herself can gradually transfer the care of her small child to her successor. On the one hand, this is, of course, brutally difficult for an ill mother in full consciousness to do. On the other hand, when the terminal illness gradually increases in severity, this transfer is naturally accomplished and the mother can find gratification in the fact that her child will have many of his needs met in his accustomed way. She can derive additional gratification from sharing her special caring techniques with the surrogate, knowing that her child will be well cared for.

In the case of the toddler and preschool age child a similar situation exists. The fulfillment of needs is of primary importance, and painful feelings of loss cannot be meaningfully approached until the child has been told and has verified that his needs will be met. With the school-age child fulfillment of needs is not the massive task that it is for the younger child, but otherwise what has been said holds true for him as well.

There are three needs of children that deserve special mention because they can easily be overlooked. The first concerns the small child's ability to remember a loved one in his absence. Although this ability begins even in the first year of life, the child requires assistance until much later in life, perhaps around puberty. Pictures of the lost one, particularly those taken with the child, not only are cherished mementoes but also serve to recall that person so that the feelings associated with him or her remain available for resolution. The recall of dates of important birthdays and the anniversary of the death should be respected and observed by those with the surviving child to help him keep alive the memory of the one who was lost.

Second, a child has many "firsts" ahead of him in his life that he wants to share with loved ones. Every step forward in growth or achievement will recall for him the one he misses. Thus, in a special way the management of the child who has lost a loved one is a task or responsibility that continues for years. This does not mean that the loss

*Personal communication.

should be belabored, but it does mean that this most important event in the child's life must never be denied its continuing significance.

The third special need of young children is to have both a male and a female figure to whom to respond. Older children will often select parent substitutes from among their teachers or family friends. In the case of the younger child, however, relatives and family friends must take the initiative in the substitute relationship. They should not be merely the supplier of good things and special times but should also make themselves consistently available to the child to help him deal with his day-to-day activities and problems. This does not mean that a surviving parent must hasten to remarry "for the children's sake." Such a marriage will impose unnatural burdens on grownups and children alike. It does mean that for the little girl who has lost her father, other males in her family take on a special meaning and special role. This special role is not just that of the supplier of good things and special times but entails being available on a consistent basis to allow the child to experience and work out some of the feelings she would have had with her father. It means allowing her to find out something of what grown men are.

Loss of A Parent as the Model for Other Losses

It is impossible in a single chapter to cover all the varieties and circumstances of loss to which any child might be subject. Not only will the nature of the losses differ, but so also will the relationship that antedated the loss, the personality of the child both as far as age and emotional maturity are concerned, and the exact circumstances of the loss. Some losses are premature, others a natural part of life. Because of the inherent complexity of this topic, the first two sections of this chapter deal with topics that are common to all losses through death in childhood. If the attitude to death and loss have a sound base, then the child can deal with all the natural losses through death to which every child is subject, such as the loss of grandparents, which so often constitute the first experiences of this nature.

Earlier, the example of the death of a parent was used to put into some context the many practical questions dealing with death that offer concrete examples for the application of the principles elucidated in the first two sections. In addition the major problems that are peculiar to the child who has endured a premature loss were stressed. The general applicability of the questions regarding the death of a parent can hopefully be extrapolated to other premature losses, for example the death of a sibling. Here the question of needs will occupy a much less paramount place in management except insofar as the natural depressed reaction of the parents to the loss of one child will temporarily decrease their accessibility to meet the needs of their other children. The parents' awareness of their natural mourning response to the loss and their explanation in words to their children can help the children greatly in accepting the transient deprivations. The physician who is aware of this situation and its implications can be most helpful in assisting parents to be aware of their mourning, its impact on their other children and the need to explain verbally what is happening.

The feelings that are observed with the loss of a sibling will be sadness and guilt. Both feelings will be present for the surviving child and will have to be felt, expressed, and mastered over a long period of time. I would be as suspicious of the child who experienced only sadness as I would be of the child who is only aware of his guilt or his anger toward the departed sibling.

But perhaps of equal importance to the management of these tragedies would be the question of whether we can utilize our knowledge of loss in the approach to mental health prophylaxis. Can we learn from our focus on these acute difficulties something that has a much wider applicability and significance? Can we as professionals assist parents to help their children deal with the many instances of loss that are inherent in childhood? Can we help more parents to understand the importance of their children's feelings? Can we develop a more healthy attitude toward death and impart that attitude to the parents with whom we deal? Can these attitudes exert influence on the mass media and current mores regarding violence and death?

Perhaps it will seem out of place to raise these questions in the context of a chapter on a child's reaction to death. It is our thesis that the proper management of a child who has suffered a loss through death does not depend alone on what is done at the time of crisis, but rather on what have been the attitudes to death and to his feelings for those with whom the child has lived.

BIBLIOGRAPHY

Barnes, M., "Reactions to the Death of a Mother." *Psychoanalytic Study of the Child, 19*:334, 1964.

Bergen, M., "The Effect of Severe Trauma on a Four-Year-Old Child." *Psychoanalytic Study of the Child, 13*:407, 1958.

Bowlby, J., "Grief and Mourning in Infancy and Early Childhood." *Psychoanalytic Study of the Child, 15*:9, 1960.

Chaloner, L., "How to Answer the Questions Children Ask About Death." *Parents' Magazine, 37*:48, 1962.

Deutsch, H., "Absence of Grief." *Psychoanalytic Quarterly, 6*:12, 1937.

Eissler, K. R., *The Psychiatrist and the Dying Patient.* New York: International Universities Press, 1955.

Freud, A., and D. Burlingham, *War and Children.* New York: International Universities Press, 1943.

Freud, A., "Indications for Child Analysis." *Psychoanalytic Study of the Child, 1*:127, 1945.

———, Unpublished Lectures given in New York City, 1960.

———, "Discussion of Dr. Bowlby's Paper." *Psychoanalytic Study of the Child, 15*:53, 1960.

———, "The Concept of Developmental Lines." *Psychoanalytic Study of the Child, 18*:245, 1963.

———, Personal Communication to the Cleveland Child Analytic Group, 1963.

———, Unpublished Lectures given in Cleveland, Ohio, 1964.

Freud, S., "Mourning and Melancholia" (1917). *Complete Works.* Standard Edition, Vol. XIV. London: Hogarth Press, 1957.

Furman, E., "Treatment of Under-Fives by Way of Their Parents." *Psychoanalytic Study of the Child, 12*:250, 1957.

Furman, R., "Death and the Young Child: Some Preliminary Considerations." *Psychoanalytic Study of the Child, 19*:321, 1964.

———, "Death of a Six-Year-Old's Mother During His Analysis." *Psychoanalytic Study of the Child, 19*:377, 1964.

———, "A Technical Problem: The Child Who Has Difficulty in Controlling His Behavior in Analytic Sessions." *The Child Analyst at Work.* Edited by E. R. Geleerd. New York: International Universities Press, 1967.

———, "Case report: Sally." *The Therapeutic Nursery School.* Edited by R. A. Furman and A. Katan. New York: International Universities Press, 1969.

85

LOSS AND GRIEF IN CHILDHOOD

————, "Additional Remarks on Mourning and the Young Child." *Bulletin of the Philadelphia Association of Psychoanalysis, 15,* 1968.

Katan, A., "Experience with Enuretics." *Psychoanalytic Study of the Child,* 2:241, 1946.

————, "The Nursery School as a Diagnostic Help to the Child Guidance Clinic." *Psychoanalytic Study of the Child, 14*:250, 1959.

Katan, M., Personal Communication, 1964.

————, "Fetishism, Splitting of the Ego and Denial." *International Journal of Psychoanalysis, 45*:237, 1963.

————, "The Origin of 'The Turn of the Screw'." *Psychoanalytic Study of the Child, 21*:583, 1966.

Lindemann, E., "Symptomatology and Management of Acute Grief." *American Journal of Psychiatry, 101*:141, 1944.

McDonald, M., "A Study of the Reactions of Nursery School Children to the Death of a Child's Mother." *Psychoanalytic Study of the Child, 19*:358, 1964.

Meiss, M. L., "The Oedipal Problem of a Fatherless Child." *Psychoanalytic Study of the Child, 7*:216, 1952.

Nagera, H., "Children's Reactions to the Death of Important Objects: A Developmental Approach." Unpublished paper, 1968.

Peller, L., "Further Comments on Adoption." *Bulletin of the Philadelphia Association of Psychoanalysis, 13*:1, 1963.

Rochlin, G., "Loss and Restitution." *Psychoanalytic Study of the Child, 8*:288, 1953.

————, "The Loss Complex: A Contribution to the Etiology of Depression." *Journal of the American Psychoanalytic Association, 7*:299, 1959.

Scharl, A., "Regression and Restitution in Object Loss: Clinical Observations." *Psychoanalytic Study of the Child, 16*:471, 1961.

Shambaugh, B., "A Study of Loss Reactions in a Seven-Year-Old." *Psychoanalytic Study of the Child, 16*:510, 1961.

Spiegel, L., "Affects in Relation to Self and Object: A Model for the Derivation of Desire, Longing, Pain, Anxiety, Humiliation and Shame." *Psychoanalytic Study of the Child, 21*:69, 1966.

Wolf, A., "Helping Your Child to Understand Death." New York: Child Study Association, 1958.

Wolfenstein, M., "Death of a Parent and Death of a President: Children's Reactions to Two Kinds of Loss." *Children and the Death of a President.* Edited by M. Wolfenstein and G. Kliman. New York: Doubleday, 1965.

————, "How is Mourning Possible?" *Psychoanalytic Study of the Child, 21*:93, 1966.

6

Reaction of the Family to the Fatal Illness of a Child

Jerry M. Wiener

There is no more devasting experience in the life of a family than the fatal illness and death of a child. It tears into the family's life as a functioning unit and confronts each family member with a crisis in coping with loss and grief. The shock extends from parents and siblings to involve grandparents, other family members, and friends. At the time of diagnosis, during the period of illness, when death occurs, and in bereavement there are pervasive and changing stresses for which different behavior, attitudes, and adjustments are required.

Characteristic as well is the mobilization of new ways of coping with stress. Reactions ranging from adaptive, to temporarily disruptive, to more severely maladaptive may occur in each individual and in the family as a unit. Each family member is affected in a way which reflects his previous adjustments, the realistic impact of the illness and loss, and the psychological meaning of the illness and loss. The anticipation and experience of loss are associated with intense emotional pain, and there are characteristic ways that each family will have for coping with it. The physician called upon to manage a fatal illness in a child should have a grasp of the general reactions he can expect in the family members and the child and the effect of the loss upon the family as a whole.

Ideally, he would have had an earlier relationship with the family and thereby be aware of their strengths and vulnerabilities, the way in which the family manages their difficulties, and some notion of any specific problems they might have. In many cases, however, the doctor will be a specialist—not the family's regular physician. In these instances, a special effort should be made early in the course of treatment to inquire into the child's developmental history and personality, as well as the family constellation, nature of the parents' relationship with each other and to the child, and their own personality types. An alternate approach would be to request assistance from a hospital social worker to obtain this information in the course of her liaison relationship with the family. This information will make it possible to provide comprehensive and responsive medical care. The fatal illness and death of a child confronts the physician with a challenge and opportunity to exercise all his skills and resources toward insuring optimal medical care—not only for the child, but for the family as well, assisting them by his awareness of their needs, his sympathetic understanding of their reactions, and his ability to minimize extremes of disruption. The emphasis of this discussion will be on the impact of a child's illness or death on individual family members and the family as a unit. The two are closely linked, and an understanding of each requires a grasp of some basic concepts about the family.

A central consideration is the nature of the marital relationship. The physician must determine whether the parents are facing the crisis together, each providing the other with support, comfort, and strength, or whether the stress is making worse already existing weaknesses in the substance of the marriage. While it is true that in some cases a strained marital relationship may be strengthened by a shared response to such a stress, it is more likely that this will be only a temporary moratorium.

Ackerman (1) describes the healthy marriage as characterized by a "mutuality and interdependence of the respective family role adaptations, the complimentarity of sexual behavior, the reciprocity of emotional and social companionship, the sharing of authority, and the division of labor," with the addition of "shared parental responsibility" when there are children. In a marriage approaching this description, reflecting mutual respect and affection as its major elements, there will be a sharing of and adequate adaptation to the short and long term strains presented by this stress to the family's integrity.

There are, on the other hand, many strained, alienated, fragile, or borderline marital adjustments. Here one will observe less than adequate mutual support, each parent reacting and coping in isolation, or in ways which compromise the reactions of the other. In many marriages consideration for the children has been the overt reason for the parents remaining together, but the children are covertly assigned responsibility for the parents' unhappiness or have become pawns in a parental power struggle. In such cases both children and parents will have an undue amount of mixed feelings toward each other. When a child in such a family develops a fatal illness, his parents may experience further discord in the marriage, inappropriate and nonsupportive reactions toward the child, and feelings of guilt about such reactions.

Related to and yet also somewhat independent of the character of the marital relationship is that of the parent-child relationship. Here, too, one can define in broad outline a healthy relationship as one in which the parent-child unit is characterized by respect, affection, honesty in communication, well-defined roles, empathy, flexibility, and tolerance of each other's independent needs. Disturbed parent-child relationships are expressed in a variety of ways. For example, there may be parental feelings of rejection, hostility, guilt, or envy. These may then be reflected in overprotectiveness or emotional isolation, permissiveness or harshness, marked inconsistency or inflexibility, and other varied reactions.

Reactions to the illness on the part of both the ill child and the parents depend upon these background factors as they influence the parents' perceptions of what is happening to the child, themselves, and the family. These factors affect the child's interpretation of his illness, his adaptive capacity and coping behavior. As used here, adaptive and coping behavior in the child and parents refers to the entire repertoire of defenses, characteristic reactions, social interactions, and behavior which are available to an individual in aiding him to master inner conflicts and environmental stresses. When presented with a major crisis such as the fatal illness and death of a child, parents must have resources which help to temper the pain, in order to allow for continued contact with reality, and to keep them available at a time when the child has a heightened need for support and care. This then permits them to participate effectively in the medical and psychological care of the child.

There are common reactions that most parents will experience when faced with the diagnosis and subsequent course of fatal illness in a child (2, 3, 4, 5, 6, 7). These reactions will be discussed in terms of initial responses, interim period of adjustment, terminal period, and sibling reactions.

Initial Reactions

Although the parents may suspect a serious illness, possibly hinted at during the diagnostic evaluation, there comes a point at which the physician must share with them the diagnosis and its implications. The initial reaction to the diagnosis has been described by parents in terms of being shocked, feeling numbed or faint, and being unable to remember or comprehend what was said. This sense of shock can last over a period of hours or days, may be accompanied by various somatic sensations, and may severely restrict adequate role functioning. Perhaps all parents experience this reaction to some degree. It should at least be anticipated by the physician so that he can assist the parents, realizing that much of what he has presented and explained about the diagnosis and prognosis will require patient and even frequent repetition.

Perhaps as frequent as the "shock" reaction is the response of initial disbelief and refusal to accept the diagnosis or its implications—the reaction of denial. Denial is usually directed not toward the fact of illness but to the fatal prognosis. Denial may take the form of a request for consultation with another physician, and this request should, of course, be honored without question except in the most unusual circumstances. Nevertheless, some parents may maintain denial until the terminal stage of the illness. This may be encouraged by well-meaning relatives and friends who raise doubts about the diagnosis or who know of rare cases of long-term "cure"; it may also be supported by a clinical course of remissions during which the child appears entirely healthy.

It should be emphasized that there is a great deal of difference between denial and hope. There is general agreement on the importance of presenting the facts in such a way as to allow the parents to maintain hope for as long as it can be reasonably sustained. Prolonged denial can lead to a disruptive insistence upon endless consultations and seriously interfere with the parents' capacity to be helpful to the child and to plan the program of care realistically with the physician. Hope, on the other hand, can be the ingredient which makes possible a mobilization of those resources necessary to maintain self-control and

90

respond adequately to the situation. In most cases, as the need for denial recedes, the diagnosis and its implications are accepted and more adaptive coping behavior becomes possible.

Other mechanisms for dealing with stress are attitudes of stoicism and detachment, which may appear as unusual strength or as indifference, coldness, and lack of concern or affection for the child. Such a protective reaction allows for immediately necessary decisions and plans to be made before the emotional impact begins to be felt. This reaction of stoic acceptance is more often seen in fathers than in mothers, possibly because our culture allows women more overt expressions of grief than it does men. Men are expected to maintain emotional control and be a source of strength in times of crisis. Indeed, Friedman and his co–workers report the impression that when told the diagnosis "the fathers generally took the major responsibility for such decisions at this time, and also tended to offer emotional support to their wives" (8). The parents themselves may be aware of their lack of feeling and will frequently express concern, guilt, and bewilderment at its absence.

Although observers disagree as to the intensity and significance of guilt (9, 10, 11, 12), all agree that guilt feelings are a normal part of parents' reactions. It is natural that parents would attempt to structure the illness within some comprehensible framework of cause and effect, to give the illness some meaning by searching for an etiology. Thus guilt may be felt and expressed in terms of not having recognized or taken seriously early symptoms, or not having prevented some type of exposure which they consider responsible for the illness (many parents are aware of the virus theory of the etiology of cancer). Despite intellectual awareness to the contrary, parents will conduct an agonizing search of their pre-illness behavior and come up with notions about diet, punishment, type of maternal care, and earlier illnesses as etiologically implicated. If the previous parent-child relationship has been adequate, patient reassurance by the physician should suffice to gradually resolve these feelings of self-blame. On the other hand, there may be more persistent or extreme guilt reactions, reflecting a premorbid disturbance in the parent-child relationship, which do not respond to factual reassurance or diminish with the passage of time. To alleviate his feelings of guilt, the parent may become overprotective or overindulgent, interfering with necessary diet or activity restrictions. He may be unable to set and maintain any reasonable limits on the child's behavior, thus

91

surrendering his parental role. These types of behavior may interfere with the child's medical management and with his ability to adapt both in the hospital and during periods of remission; they also foster disturbed relations with the other children in the family. These reactions, including exaggerated overt expressions of self-blame, will not be as easily influenced by education and advice. Attempts to intervene may precipitate angry, defensive reactions coupled with rationalizations. It is important for the physician and medical personnel to be alert to such behavior and reactions, understanding that they may indicate a need for psychiatric consultation.

Angry, hostile feelings are often, if not always, mobilized in the parents. Such feelings may be related to feelings of guilt, futility, and helplessness. Anger may be directed toward the physician as the one who first conveys the diagnosis and prognosis. It may be directed at the nursing staff as criticisms and complaints about the quality, efficiency, or responsiveness of nursing care, or may occur at a time of relapse when hopes are shattered and final acceptance of the prognosis sets in. Parents may feel very critical of the way in which they were told the diagnosis or prognosis—that it was presented too abruptly or coldly, and as hopeless. The parents may be angry that the physician has only limited powers, that he is not omnipotent or possessed of healing magic, or that he is not really doing his utmost, but rather is withholding something that is available. They may express resentment that their physician has withdrawn and is unavailable after the initial period of contact.

While in some cases hostility is based on a variety of illogical or ill-founded notions, it is equally true that in many instances the physician and other members of the medical team are guilty of insensitivity, of aloofness or bluntness, or of being unavailable, in defense against the emotional demands made upon them by parents who are distraught, demanding, dependent, or guilty. These responses of medical personnel are mentioned here as a reminder that the parents' anger should not automatically be considered "their problem," but that it requires honest self-appraisal, as well. If the members of the medical team expect and can accept these initial angry expressions without becoming defensive, reacting in kind or withdrawing, a more constructive collaborative partnership will be possible between the parents and staff.

92

Interim Reactions

After the initial reactions and the first period of crisis have been weathered, a second phase sets in, often coinciding with the period of active treatment. The fatal illnesses of childhood generally are not immediately terminal. In many instances one can expect a course which includes periods of relapse and remission, surgical procedures, and trials on various drugs. During this period the stresses and demands on the family are different from those at the time of diagnosis. The child requires ongoing care, in and out of the hospital. Job, home, and other children in the family must receive attention.

Many parents will actively seek information during this time. They become highly knowledgeable about the illness by way of every resource available—the lay literature, medical texts, relatives and friends, or other parents whose children are in the hospital with the same or other illnesses. To some degree the acquisition of this knowledge serves as a defense of intellectual mastery over the condition; at the same time it fosters co-operation with the child's medical care and may clarify questions and misconceptions about the illness.

It may also lead to many misconceptions and doubts, which, when expressed, must be patiently clarified. However, the search for information about the illness can at times become an all-consuming preoccupation directed toward maintaining denial that the child has a fatal illness. Parents will read incessantly, want to know details of the laboratory results, and request or demand endless consultations, or ask why certain treatments are not being used. Such behavior may well provoke the medical team to angry, defensive, or avoidance responses and generate even more problems in communication. When the parents' behavior can be recognized and understood as an attempt to cope, appropriate responses can then be made.

It is during this interim period of treatment that the parents can and should be available to help care for the child. The degree to which the parent, primarily the mother, participates in the child's care in terms of bathing, feeding, dressing, and providing companionship must be allowed wide latitude and should be decided jointly by physician, nurse, and parents. Institutional routines, procedures, and preferences should not automatically be allowed precedence. What could be more tragically unfair to parent and child in these circumstances than to limit contact to arbitrary visiting hours, or to limit the relationship by not allowing and encouraging parents to continue providing parental care to the fullest extent possible? Many parents will not insist or even ask if they may bathe or dress the child, or be with the child during certain procedures. They should be informed of these options, indeed prerogatives. Even if a parent is initially reluctant, he should be urged to participate for his own peace of mind; the mother will appreciate that she is still needed and is essential to the care of the child and, later, that she has done all she could. This also helps to preserve the child's sense of continuity and security. Children early become aware of the transfer of authority from parents to professional staff; at the same time they may angrily blame the parents for their inability to prevent pain and separation experiences (13). While this is to some degree unavoidable, sensitive hospital personnel could do much to mitigate such reactions. When parents become overprotective, excessively solicitous, or withdraw completely from the child, they will require frank and tactful counseling to help them provide optimal care for the child, themselves, and other family members.

The parents' presence in the hospital allows them opportunity to become acquainted with other parents of seriously ill children. There is the opportunity for sharing experiences, exchanging information, receiving and giving both emotional and practical support. This lessens the sense of isolation and self-recrimination. The association provides examples of how other parents react and cope with similar kinds of stresses and crises. Parents often report later that these relationships were a more important source of support than relatives or friends, who often were too detached from the situation or hindered their adjustment by raising questions about the diagnosis, citing cases from their experience which contradicted the medical management, or conveying certain stereotyped expectations of the parents' reactions to the illness.

Anticipatory Grief

Many of the fatal illnesses of childhood take a prolonged course and allow the parents time for preparatory mourning (14, 15, 16, 17, 18). Anticipatory grief appears in cases of illness of four months and longer and can be seen concomitant to a gradual relinquishing of hope as the illness progresses. This process of anticipatory grief is a further step in adaptation to the child's illness, making possible a return to more normal functioning and attention to other responsibilities during the illness, and serving to cushion the parents against the massive and disorganizing impact of their child's death.

Lindemann (19) outlines five major manifestations of normal acute grief reactions: 1) somatic distress, such as sighing, weakness, fatigue, and gastro-intestinal symptoms; 2) preoccupation with the image and memories of the deceased; 3) guilty self-blame in the search for cause; 4) irritability, impatience, and social withdrawal; and 5) inability to maintain normal patterns of conduct and functioning, with overactivity, restlessness, and lack of initiative. When the mourning occurs as a preparatory process, the symptoms are not as dramatic or condensed as in acute grief reactions. They are diluted over time and vary in intensity according to individual patterns over the course of the child's illness. Their expression should be sympathetically respected rather than discouraged or aborted by the child's physician or others of the professional staff. As this work reaches its completion, parents may then be observed to share their attention with other children in the hospital, manifesting a less intense relationship with their own child and tolerating separations with more equanimity. This new behavior may be puzzling to and criticized by members of the staff who mistake its meaning. It should be recognized and accepted as evidence that the parents are prepared to accept the child's actual death with appropriate affect, composure, and even a sense of relief that the inevitable is finally over, and that the child's suffering has ended.

When the illness has been acute, short-term, or when denial has been maintained until the end and the parents have not been able to prepare and mobilize their resources, they will experience a more acute and prolonged grief reaction in which final integration and acceptance of the loss can be delayed for as long as several months.

Siblings

The impact of these events upon other children in the family should be given attention by the managing physician or other members of the hospital staff. They can inquire as to the children's adjustment, the questions being asked by them, and the parents' responses to their questions. The staff's concerned interest will encourage the parents to attend to these issues, which may be overlooked out of more immediate concern for the ill child. Early inquiry regarding siblings may provide the physician with cues that the family needs help in coping with the stress. "The disintegration of a family group precipitated by an impending catastrophe is a sequel that the physician, more than anyone else, can attempt to prevent." (20)

The reaction of siblings will depend upon their age, maturity, ability to comprehend and integrate the meaning of the illness, the particular relationships of the siblings to the ill child, the siblings' own place and adjustment within the family, and perhaps most importantly the honesty and appropriateness with which the parents communicate with them about the ill child and the nature of the problem. Much depends on how they are included, as part of the family, in the adaptation to the crisis. Older children and adolescents can comprehend fairly completely the full implications of the illness, and the parents can be frank in sharing information and answering their questions. For younger children with less mature conceptual capacities, too much and too complete an explanation will confuse instead of clarify. For them, it may well be the separation from their sibling and their own reaction to changes in the parents which dominate their concerns. It is generally agreed that whatever is told the siblings by way of explanation and in answer to their questions should be the truth; parental judgment, individual needs, and the family's values will shape the specifics and determine the extent of the truth to be shared, but the truth it should be. Deception, however well-meaning, is ultimately self-defeating and a disservice to all concerned. Although degrees of deception are often practiced in telling the siblings about the illness, under the rationalization of sparing their feelings, the reason will more often be the parents' understandable need to protect their own feelings.

Much of this difficulty may be prevented by early discussion with the parents, initiated by the physician, about how to help the ill child's siblings during the course of the illness—while he is in the hospital, at home in remission, or at the time of relapse.

Since competitive and hostile feelings among siblings are ubiquitous, varying degrees of guilt feelings generally may be expected in the others when one of them falls ill. These feelings of guilt may be expressed, for example, by depressive symptoms, nightmares, or reactive aggressive behavior. When the ill child is at home he is often given special attention and dispensations regarding the usual rules and limits on behavior. Since the ill child often looks and acts quite well during remissions, it may be particularly difficult for the other children to understand such favoritism. They may deeply resent this and be caught in a confusing welter of angry and guilty feelings. These conflicts may be most acute and poignant in the school age child whose younger sibling is ill, since it is in their relationship that issues of rivalry, envy, and hostility are likely to be most current.

Terminal Reactions

Despite all preparation through anticipatory grief, the actual loss is a blow to the family which removes the last protection that fragments of hope and denial were able to sustain. While true emotional acceptance and the final work of mourning may take several weeks or longer, the actual fact is irrevocable and may bring with it a revival of reactions already experienced.

The more acute and dramatic reactions at the time of death tend to occur in those parents who continued to maintain denial throughout the illness and those who, because of the rapid course of illness, had little time to accommodate themselves to the prognosis. They, too, experience the aforementioned feelings of guilt, self-blame, and anger toward the physician or nurse, as well as uncontrollable grief. It is important that the parents be able to feel that they did everything possible for their child, and be convinced that no medical stone was left unturned in his treatment. Parents should also have an opportunity to satisfy themselves on these issues at a time after the death of the child. Thus, the physician should be aware that his presence and availability are crucial to the parent's security not only during all stages of the illness but also for one or more contacts after the child has died. Then the parents have a chance to review once again the care of the child, raise questions about hereditary or transmissible etiologies, and express feelings of gratitude to the physician for his attention and understand-

97

ing. If an autopsy was obtained, they will want to hear that nothing more could have been done, and that the autopsy had been of value to the physician in helping him to manage the care of other children. They may feel the need to say good-bye to the physician and others who helped care for the child, as a means of final closure as well as to express their thanks.

Questions often arise as to whether siblings should attend the funeral. Here again, answers must be individually tailored. Solnit and Green (21) maintain that children who are old enough to understand the cause of the sibling's death are usually old enough to attend the funeral if they desire to do so. They describe most children under six as too young and most over nine as able to benefit from the experience, pointing out that any child who is reluctant or frightened should not be forced to attend. In many cases a child need not be old enough to understand the cause of death to attend this last formal rite when the final separation occurs. Death is a difficult conceptualization and this is particularly true for the preadolescent child; the funeral is a concrete, realistic experience which will provide a counterbalance to the fantasies every child elaborates to fill in the cognitive and emotional limitations to his understanding of death. It is also an experience into which he can later integrate knowledge unavailable to him at the time of the funeral with more mature awareness. If the parents are able to prepare the child, and if they are themselves able to maintain sufficient composure so that a young child will not be unduly frightened by extreme manifestations of grief, the children of four years of age can and should be included in the funeral. If a child is frightened or reluctant, efforts should be made to explore these feelings and their source with a view toward making it possible for him to attend. The family that has together endured the fatal illness of one of its members also benefit from sharing the experience of the funeral.

One 12-year-old boy did not see his younger brother after this brother entered the hospital with a terminal illness. He was not allowed to attend the funeral for reasons partly related to his own reluctance. Subsequently, he elaborated the fantasy that his brother was not really dead, but had been removed for a variety of mysterious reasons and would eventually return.

Attendance at the funeral would not alone have prevented or resolved this development, but it would have added a reality experience and a buffer to the sense of conviction attached to the fantasy. It might also have facilitated the ultimate development of a grief reaction.

Suggestions for Health Care Personnel

Each member of the health care team should understand his personal responses to and philosophy regarding fatal illness, death, and his role in relationship to the bereaved family.

The physician should be prepared to speak with the parents for a sufficient length of time, telling them the diagnosis and discussing with them the treatment plan, expected course, and prognosis. This discussion should take place as soon as can be arranged after the diagnosis is established, and should of course be conducted by the child's primary physician. Some parents will already suspect the seriousness of the illness, or will have been given such an indication by the referring doctor; others will have no suspicion whatsoever. In either case the news will be upsetting. It cannot be properly handled in a brief time or without consideration for the parents' need to be alone with the physician where they will not be disturbed. *It should be remembered that the parents may not really hear, accept, or retain much of what is told them at this time, and will require patient repetition, reemphasis, and reassurance.* Unless the physician is himself the consultant, it is often wise that he take the initiative in suggesting a confirmatory consultation to reassure the parents that the diagnosis and treatment plan have received every consideration, and that all available treatment will be provided. Beyond this he should be prepared to be firm in limiting unrealistic and indiscriminate consultative alternatives, recognizing that such demands often reflect excessive denial or guilt.

Some anger must be expected toward the bearer of news which causes great pain and its expression should not antagonize or cause resentment. If excessive anger toward the physician or others of the medical team continues to be expressed it may be necessary to request that a staff psychiatrist or social worker be available to work with the family.

During the course of treatment the physician should make a point of being regularly available to the parents to answer questions, to provide more detailed information about the illness if this is requested, and to reassure them by his responsiveness and concern that everything possible is being done.

In many instances a physician may delegate much of the contact with the parents to the house staff in his wish to avoid the parents' anger or anxiety, or as a way of dealing with his own feelings of frustration, guilt, or inadequacy in not being able to effect a cure. Needless to say, there should be one physician clearly designated as in charge of the child's care; if the child is being cared for by house staff who are on rotation, continuity should be provided by assigning one physician to meet with the parents and to answer their questions.

The physician must decide what and how much will be shared with the child, and be prepared, particularly with older children and adolescents, for more direct awareness and questions from them. He should discuss these decisions with the child's parents so there will be agreement and coordination in whatever is communicated to the child. While the parents' wishes and decisions regarding what the child is to be told must ultimately prevail, most will appreciate the opportunity to consider the question beforehand and be guided by their doctor's advice.

There should be awareness of the parents' need to sustain a caretaking relationship with their child, and support and encouragement of their desire to do so. The physician's authority is augmented in these cases by the desperateness of the situation; as the parents transfer authority, the child perceives the shift and may do likewise. The physician should discuss with the parents the role they should continue to play in the child's care and should share his preferences and decisions with the nursing staff so that the effort will be coordinated.

The physician should discuss the child's condition, treatment plan, and family constellation with the hospital personnel who will have daily contact with and responsibility for care. By doing this he will obtain valuable feedback not only on the child's condition but also on the parents' adjustment.

REFERENCES

1. N. W. Ackerman, *The Psychodynamics of Family Life*, New York: Basic Books, 1958.

100

2. M. F. Bozeman, C. E. Orbach, and A. M. Sutherland, "Psychological Impact of Cancer and Its Treatment. III. The Adaptation of Mothers to the Threatened Loss of Their Children Through Leukemia: Part I & Part II," *Cancer, 8*:1. January-February, 1955.

3. S. B. Friedman, "Care of the Family of the Child with Cancer," *Pediatrics, 40*:498, 1967.

4. S. B. Friedman et al., "Behavioral Observations on Parents Anticipating the Death of a Child," *Pediatrics, 32*:610, 1963.

5. J. M. Natterson and A. G. Knudson, "Observations Concerning Fear of Death in Fatally Ill Children and Their Mothers," *Psychosomatic Medicine, 22*:456, 1960.

6. J. B. Richmond and H. A. Waisman, "Psychologic Aspects of Management of Children With Malignant Diseases," *A.M.A. American Journal of the Diseases of Children, 89*:42, 1955.

7. A. J. Solnit and M. Green, "Psychologic Considerations in the Management of Deaths on Pediatric Hospital Services—1. The Doctor and the Child's Family," *Pediatrics, 24*:106, 1959.

8. S. B. Friedman et al., "Behavioral Observations on Parents Anticipating the Death of a Child."

9. M. F. Bozeman et al., "Psychological Impact of Cancer and Its Treatment."

10. S. B. Friedman, "Care of the Family of the Child with Cancer."

11. J. M. Natterson and A. G. Knudson, "Observations Concerning Fear of Death in Fatally Ill Children and Their Mothers."

12. J. B. Richmond and H. A. Waisman, "Psychologic Aspects of Management of Children With Malignant Diseases."

13. S. B. Friedman et al., "Behavioral Observations on Parents Anticipating the Death of a Child."

14. S. B. Friedman, "Care of the Family of the Child With Cancer."

15. S. B. Friedman et al., "Behavioral Observations on Parents Anticipating the Death of a Child."

16. Erich Lindemann, "Symptomatology and Management of Acute Grief," *American Journal of Psychiatry, 101*:141, September, 1944.

17. J. M. Natterson and A. G. Knudson, "Observations Concerning Fear of Death in Fatally Ill Children and Their Parents."

18. J. B. Richmond and H. A. Waisman, "Psychologic Aspects of Management of Children With Malignant Diseases."

19. Erich Lindemann, "Symptomatology and Management of Acute Grief."

20. Personal communication from Harold Dargeon, M.D.

21. A. J. Solnit and M. Green, "Psychologic Considerations in the Management of Deaths on Pediatric Hospital Services."

101

Response of Medical Personnel to the Fatal Illness of a Child

Jerry M. Wiener

"A physician unaware of his personal feelings about death and dying by the same token permits them to interfere with his effective treatment of patients. . . . It is our duty to examine death and dying just as we should study anything else that involves man . . . , but death and dying have been taboo" (1).

The medical and nursing care of a fatally ill child is an emotionally demanding responsibility which exposes each member of the medical team to the danger of overinvolvement on the one hand, and of protective withdrawal on the other. Meeting the needs of child and parent appropriately, humanely, and yet with equanimity is a task requiring the personnel's repeated re-examination of their own values, attitudes, and convictions about life, dying, and death itself. They must be aware of the parents' typical responses to their child's terminal illness and the sources of these parental responses. They must possess insight into their own reaction to both child and family. Otherwise, their responses and actions may be inappropriate to the needs of the situation.

Early in his practice a physician was asked to see, in consultation, a child with leukemia who had developed some behavior problems. He agreed reluctantly, wondering what he could contribute to the situation. He did not want to "intrude" upon a family facing such a tragedy, and thought that a behavior problem was the least of their worries. Gradually he became aware that he was annoyed with the referring physician, and felt uneasy in "confronting" the child and his family. This awareness allowed him to be of help, since he persevered rather than withdrew, and assisted the family and child in resolving a profound emotional crisis.

Deepseated and ubiquitous feelings of unease are frequently mobilized in staff personnel engaged in caring for a fatally ill child. The intensity of these feelings, their particular meaning for each member of the team, and the way they are handled will determine the degree to which they permit or interfere with appropriate care.

Factors in the Choice of Medicine as a Career

Central to the choice of medicine as a career is certainly its function in the alleviation of pain and the prevention of death. The physician's role is invested with authority and power, with realistic expectations on the part of the patient for care, as well as magical expectations of omnipotence and infallibility. During the course of his education and training the physician acquires knowledge and skills which make it possible for him to fulfill his realistic obligations. When the physician is significantly influenced by unconscious needs for power over illness and death, his care of patients will be inappropriate, nowhere more so than when he tries to provide comprehensive care to the fatally ill child and his family.

The physician may be susceptible to needs for mastery, control, omnipotence, or dependency gratification. In allowing others to be dependent, the physician may vicariously receive gratification of his own repressed wishes to be cared for. At the same time he appears and feels himself to be strong, resourceful, and self-sufficient. The need for mastery, control, and omnipotence may be the outcome of struggles with the various fears and normal feelings of inadequacy which exist during childhood. The existence of these needs is not in itself pathological, nor is the choice of medicine as a profession inappropriate or misdirected. It is the intensity of the conflicts which is important, as well as the degree to which magical and unrealistic self-expectations influence the physician in his choice of career.

103

LOSS AND GRIEF IN CHILDHOOD

Identification may also be a factor in the choice of career. Identification, referring in this context to the process by which one models his behavior, attitudes, and values on those of another person, results in a change within the self. Related to this is the process by which we establish an "ideal-self"—that set of standards, values, attitudes, and behaviors which form an inner picture of what we feel we ought to be. Both the process of identification and the formation of an ideal-self can be important factors in the choice of medicine as a career and in the way a physician perceives his role. If during development the child establishes very high or unrealistic ideals, as a physician he may continue to expect more of himself than is realistic. This, in turn, may result in painful self-doubt, inappropriate feelings of inadequacy, or avoidance when he is called upon to make the diagnosis of fatal illness, provide subsequent care to the child, and support the family.

A further factor is the physician's attitude toward dying and death. Feifel (2) offers the hypothesis that one of the motivations in the choice of medicine as a career is the physician's need to deal with his own fears of death by means of power over illness. The fatally ill patient would, then, represent a threat to the doctor's self-assurance and stir up his own personal anxieties about death. Feifel's hypothesis is based on measures of the degree to which physicians, when compared to other groups, had above-average or excessive fears of death. His results indicate that "physicians were significantly . . . more afraid of death than both the physically sick and healthy normal groups" (3). In those physicians for whom this motivating factor predominates, the anxiety mobilized by a fatally ill patient may lead to an unwitting avoidance reaction which functions to make the physician psychologically unavailable to the patient. Several authors (1, 3, 4, 5) have commented on the lack of attention paid to the subject of death in medical school teaching. They stress the great need to deal with death as a natural subject of study, emphasizing the importance of learning by example, from respected and experienced clinicians, how to deal honestly and humanely with the dying patient. The absence, in medical school, of such teaching surely represents in part an unconscious avoidance.

These influences are, of course, important in varying degrees to all those who choose a career in health care, including nurses, social workers, hospital chaplains, medical technicians, and hospital aides.

Care of the child with a fatal illness produces entirely normal re-

104

actions which may interfere with the exercise of the art as well as the science of medicine. Rothenberg describes these reactions as stemming from a core conflict mobilized by treatment of these patients. The conflict is between forces of compassion, producing impulses to move toward the child, and forces of "repulsion," impelling treating personnel away from the child, to assure protection from the threat of death and the "impending shock of separation and loss." (4) The manner of resolution of this central conflict determines the capacity to make an appropriate emotional commitment to treatment. If recognized, those tendencies to reach solutions by means which compromise holistic medical care can be anticipated and dealt with constructively.

The care of a child with a fatal illness does not provide the usual satisfactions of medical care and may result in considerable frustration. Frustration of satisfactions leads to reactions of anger and resentment. It is generally unacceptable to feel angry at the ill child, so these feelings unconsciously become redirected. Anger may be displaced onto other members of the medical team or hospital staff, or upon the parents, when they press for information, request consultations, or make other requests. These angry feelings frequently result in guilt. Guilt also may be exacerbated by pre-existing self-doubts and feelings of inadequacy unrelated to the specific presenting problem. The combination of anger and guilt may be dealt with by becoming overprotective and overindulgent of the child, responses frequently noted in parents. Thus, the staff will not be able to help the parents, but, instead, become partners in mismanagement. Guilt may lead them to unnecessary or futile treatment which merely serves to allay their own nagging self-doubts.

Avoidance reactions also occur in response to frustration, reflecting the need to put distance between oneself and the perceived source of frustration. Here the physician may unduly delegate care of the child to the house staff, or may find ways of making rounds when the child is asleep or when the parents will not be visiting. Often the child with a fatal illness is passed by quickly by personnel, as if interest in him has already been detached and invested elsewhere. Another expression of this tendency is the practice of discussing the child's illness in his presence as if he were not there. The assumption is made that the child cannot really understand what is said. Even if true, what could be more frightening for a child than to know or suspect he is being dis-

105

cussed, and at the same time to understand only partially what is said, filling in the gaps with his own fears and misconceptions?

When interest in the child is maintained, the physician may protect himself by intellectualization, making paramount the disease rather than the child. His feelings are controlled and his personal involvement limited; he is comfortable, but the child and the parents, sensing his emotional unavailability, become more anxious. Even if the child has fears and questions about his illness, he will be discouraged from initiating discussion or open communication. The parents will also be left stranded, uneasy about revealing their own feelings. They may complain angrily to others about their doctor's coldness or insensitivity. The physician can err as much by maintaining too exclusive an involvement, as in excessive delegation of responsibility. The need to exercise exclusive management may exclude the parents from sufficient involvement, and encourage the child to turn to the doctor for decisions and authority over issues which should properly remain the parents' responsibility.

When the doctor has "above-average" fears of death, (5) he may become very anxious when confronted directly by its reality—as, for example, when he makes the diagnosis of a fatal illness. To cope with his anxiety he may interject excessive hopefulness into his discussions with the parents, making more difficult their adjustments. While the prognosis should be presented so as to assure them that everything possible is being done for their child, the physician must be realistic and provide them with the opportunity to prepare for the loss.

Depression is another response experienced by personnel while caring for a child with a fatal illness, as well as at the time of death. One can regard many of the reactions previously discussed as ways of avoiding painful depressive feelings. If the physician and other personnel allow a normal emotional investment to occur, then a degree of depressive feeling is probably inevitable during the process of anticipatory grief while the work of emotional separation occurs. The degree of depression should remain within limits of tolerance so that it does not disrupt an ongoing relationship with the patient and family during the course of the illness. Within these limits there can be communicated to the child and family the physician's emotional commitment, compassion, and capacity to share in their painful experience while still providing appropriate care. When the depressive reaction is more severe, there are additional factors which require inspection and attempts at resolution. For example, the health care worker may be reacting to a loss in his own past, overidentifying with rather than empathizing with the patient. Depression may also be the expression of unacknowledged feelings of anger and guilt.

Easson has discussed the health care personnel's reactions to death in terms of age-appropriate and age-determined factors (6). He describes the young physician and nurse as reacting with a sense of outrage at death as an enemy to be battled, as refusing to consider death an inevitability. The possibility of excessively vigorous treatment to combat death is seen as one consequence of this normal response of youth. In middle age the physician's reaction is more likely to be one of intellectual acceptance coupled with emotional detachment. The elderly physician is described as likely to have a more calm, personal acceptance of death and may, therefore, be less aware of or insensitive to the intense emotional reactions stirred up in the patient, family, and younger members of the health care team.

Nursing Personnel

Some special attention should be given to the pivotal role of the nurse in the hospital care of the child with a fatal illness. Her daily responsibilities with their maternal connotations, make the nurse a key figure in his management. The nurse must often bear the brunt of the child's distress and the parents' anxieties. Through her are mediated the doctor's orders as well as the behavior and attitudes of those under her supervision.

It has seemed that early in their experience nurses tend to greater emotional involvement with dying children under their care than is so later in their careers. Many nurses have described an increasing emotional perspective (or emotional detachment) which develops with increasing experience. The impression has been that the early, more intense involvements had been quite painful, resulting in a grief reaction when the child died. After a few such experiences, a protective development takes place in which a more "businesslike" approach counterbalances those forces which lead to greater involvement. This may result in a healthy emotional equanimity which allows sufficient invest-

107

ment for compassionate and sensitive nursing care, or it may result in a detached efficiency unresponsive to special needs or circumstances.

The prevailing climate of a pediatrics floor is determined more by the nurses than by any other medical personnel. Visiting hours, attitudes toward parents, the methods of handling children, and reactions to their behavior are generally determined by the nurses. Indeed, nurses' preferences may solidify into inflexible rules which fail to answer the patients' and families' real needs. The nurse may look upon the child's mother either as a partner or as a competitor in the care of the child. In the former case, encouragement will be offered to the mother to maintain appropriate maternal care during the hospital stay— activities such as bathing, dressing, feeding, the giving of medication, and even assisting at dressing changes, are all within the purview of usual maternal care. These activities should be viewed as the mother's right, rather than as a privilege. However, competitive feelings toward the mother can lead to a possessive attitude toward the child. This may cause less difficulty in the nursing care of routine pediatric patients, but may evoke pervasive problems in regard to the care of a child with a fatal illness. In individual and group discussions with nurses the question of such competitive feelings was raised and almost unanimously denied. They generally agreed that mothers should participate in the routine care of their hospitalized children, but felt many mothers were reluctant to do so. Further, the nurses were generally in accord that mothers should not come in before visiting hours, which began at 11:00 A.M., by which time, of course, the children were generally up, bathed, and dressed. Only one nurse was in favor of placing no limitations on visiting hours for any child. The remainder felt visiting hours should be observed even in the case of children with serious illnesses, except when the illness was terminal. As a group, the nurses interviewed were aware of the parental tendency toward overprotective and permissive behavior toward their hospitalized children. While their own reactions to this type of behavior varied, they tended to deny that these children represented special nursing problems, preferring to treat them like "all the other children." Perhaps this is one means of protection against the impulses leading to a more intense involvement. While attitudes were less harsh toward children in the terminal phase of illness, there was still an undercurrent of feeling that this change represented special concessions made to parents at the time of terminal illness.

Hospital Care Team

In effect, a *team* of health care personnel is responsible for the care of a child. Members include the attending physician, house staff, nurses, aides, and other personnel, such as social workers, teachers, occupational and recreational therapists. Surgery may be required, bringing the surgeon and anesthesiologist to the team as well. Parents may also be included as participating members. While the team ideally should function as a coordinated unit, a lack of coordination may occur so that each member functions in isolation. The personal dilemma of each member can best be resolved when mutual respect and channels of communication exist among all members, whether these be on a formal or informal basis. Each member of the team should have a clear definition of his or her own role, and an understanding of the contribution that others can make to the care of the child and his family. Management of the child with a fatal illness and the reactions of his family can open up areas of conflict and misunderstanding among members of the caring team. Unacceptable angry feelings toward the child who is not responding to treatment, and toward the parents who are anxious and hovering, may be displaced onto other members of the team as criticism and accusations. Some may project feelings of inadequacy, while others may withdraw by inappropriately delegating duties to other personnel, and yet harbor resentment over the consequent loss of authority. These responses, mentioned in previous sections, are reviewed here from the perspective of their effect on the emotional climate in which care is provided. Such responses undermine the morale and shared objectives of holistic medical care. As Green has stated, the emotional and even physical demands made upon the hospital staff by a number of children with fatal illnesses are exhausting and frustrating, making it important that all personnel share the effort of care and, thereby, soften its impact (7). The physician and head nurse usually share the responsibility of initiating and maintaining a climate in which direct expressions of feelings, questions, criticisms, doubts, and attitudes are possible. Channels of communication need to exist vertically between medical student, intern, resident, attending physician, and student nurse, staff nurse, and head nurse, as well as horizontally among physicians, nurses, social workers, and ancillary personnel. The tone is set by the attending physician in terms of his attitudes, accessibility, and sensitivity—not only to his own reactions, but also to tensions, anxieties and needs of the other members of the team. Moving toward rather than away from these issues requires greater efforts but also delivers justifying rewards. The treatment plan is coordinated, a common purpose is shared, and parents are not confronted by misunderstandings and conflicting attitudes. Staff differences and cross-purposes can be reconciled before they become disruptive. Such issues as visiting hours and the degree of parental participation in the care of the child can be jointly discussed and agreed upon. Even though total agreement may not be possible, policy can be clarified, areas of disagreement acknowledged, and alternative approaches discussed before necessary decisions are made by the physician.

Addendum: Survey of Pediatricians' Attitudes

In order to assess some of the attitudes and practices which influence pediatric care of the child with a fatal illness, a questionnaire was submitted to 160 pediatricians. The sample included residents and staff at a large midwestern clinic, those at a metropolitan general voluntary hospital, and pediatricians in private practice in suburban areas of New York City. A total of 97 questionnaires were returned—18 from pediatric residents, 36 from pediatricians in practice 10 years or less, and 43 from physicians in practice more than 10 years. This division was made to assess differences in attitudes and practices with increasing experience; such differences could also reflect differences in training and scientific advances made in medicine over a period of time.

1) Do you believe the parents should be given the diagnosis (of a fatal illness)?

	Residents	Practice under 10 years	Practice over 10 years
Always	78%	86%	77%
Usually	22%	14%	23%
Seldom-Never	—	—	—

All were in agreement that the parents should be told the diagnosis, but roughly 1 out of 5 of the respondents answered "usually."

This is surprisingly high, since there would seem to be few indications for withholding the diagnosis from the parents. This result may only reflect a reluctance on the part of some to give an unqualified answer. On the other hand, it may reflect a tendency to avoid the distress of giving parents the diagnosis of a fatal illness.

The next two questions deal with informing parents of the prognosis:

2) If parents ask about prognosis, do you feel they should be accurately informed?

	Residents	Practice under 10 years	Practice over 10 years
Always	72%	64%	79%
Usually	28%	36%	21%
Seldom-Never	—	—	—

3) If parents do *not* ask about prognosis, do you make it a point to inform them?

	Residents	Practice under 10 years	Practice over 10 years
Always	28%	41.7%	60%
Usually	72%	55.5%	37%
Seldom	—	2.8%	3%
Never	—	—	—

The responses to these two questions demonstrate an interesting trend in both attitude and practice. Consistency of practice was lowest in the group in practice under 10 years—86 per cent believed the parents should "always" be given the accurate diagnosis, but only 64 per cent believed they should be given the accurate prognosis even when they ask about it directly. Among residents there was a slight shift in the same direction. To question 3, an average of 55 per cent of all respondents answered "usually" instead of "always." This rises to 63 per cent if the first two groups—residents and those in practice under 10 years—are considered together. When parents do not specifically ask about the prognosis, there is a greater likelihood that a discussion of it will not be introduced by the physician. One explana-

111

tion could be that these physicians judge that the parents may not be prepared to accept it or that they really don't want to know. On the other hand, these judgments may represent rationalizations which allow the physician to avoid a situation which creates unease and anxiety within himself. The parents may not ask about the prognosis for a variety of reasons: dread, denial, shock, ignorance, passivity. The physician must be alert to his own feelings about discussing the prognosis with the parents, and aware when those feelings, and not the parents' needs, lead him away from such a discussion. It is possible that the response "always" may reflect a certain unwillingness to modify procedures in accordance with exceptional circumstances.

However, most would agree that the circumstances are rare in which parents would not be informed of the prognosis, since such information is vital in securing their full and understanding cooperation with the treatment plan and in setting in motion their own coping reactions.

Another set of questions deals with attitudes and practices toward discussing the nature of the illness with the child (questions 4, 5, and 6). Here, 67 per cent believed that children "always" or "usually" know or suspect that they have a serious or fatal illness, even if not told directly, and 33 per cent believed children "seldom" or "never" know or suspect it if not told directly. Nevertheless, a majority of the respondents believe most children should seldom or never be informed of the nature of their illness.

4) Do you believe most children routinely should be informed, at their level of understanding, of the nature of their illness?

	Residents	*Practice under* *10 years*	*Practice over* *10 years*
Always } Usually }	47%	38%	33%
Seldom } Never }	53%	62%	67%

A majority favors giving accurate information when it is directly requested by the child.

5) If the child *asks* directly about the nature of the illness (that is, the diagnosis or kind of illness) should generally accurate information be given?

112

Response of Medical Personnel

	Residents	Practice under 10 years	Practice over 10 years
Always / Usually	72%	60%	52%
Seldom / Never	28%	40%	48%

A majority believes that an accurate answer to inquiry about prognosis should seldom or never be given to the child, even when the child initiated the question.

6) If the child asks directly regarding prognosis (for example, "Am I going to die?" or "What is going to happen to me?") a majority believes that an accurate answer should seldom or never be given to the child.

	Residents	Practice under 10 years	Practice over 10 years
Always / Usually	45%	33%	40%
Seldom	55%	67%	60%

In summary, a *majority* of respondents believe: most children know or suspect they have a serious illness; children should not routinely be informed as to the nature of their illness; if the child asks directly about the *diagnosis* he should be fully informed; but, if he asks directly about *prognosis*, he should not be fully informed.

It would seem the inconsistency of these responses might reflect, in part, a natural reluctance to discuss issues involving serious or fatal illness with a child or adolescent. Perhaps no issue arouses more controversy than the approach to discussing with a child the nature and prognosis of his fatal illness. Reactions vary from total denial that such a discussion can or should be conducted with any child under any circumstances, to compromise or temporizing, even when the child himself initiates the discussion. Certainly there is no stock or programmed answer to the problem. Some physicians suggest asking the child such questions as "What is it that you have been thinking about?" "Is there something you have been worrying about?" or "What have you heard or been told about your illness?" (or "trouble" in the case of a young

113

child), letting the patient continue to take the lead so that the answers do not go beyond his immediate concerns. Some believe in giving immediate reassurance and others suggest diverting the child. Perhaps the most that can be said is that the approach chosen should be the one that provides the patient with trust and security in the honesty, concern, and dependability of those caring for him. This may well necessitate a realistic and frank discussion of the diagnosis and even the prognosis in some cases, providing at the same time what hope, reassurance, and support are appropriate to the age, maturity, and specific fears of the child.

The final set of questions deals with physicians' attitudes toward parental involvement in the care of the child.

7) Do you believe it desirable for a parent to be in the hospital with the child to whatever extent the parent chooses?

	Residents	Practice under 10 years	Practice over 10 years
Usually } Always }	59%	78%	91%
Seldom	41%	22%	9%

Here, an overall majority is in favor of unrestricted visiting hours. It is an impressive fact that this attitude is expressed more frequently as the physicians' experience increases.

8) Do you believe parents should be allowed and encouraged to assist in the hospital management of their child, for example, feeding, bathing, giving oral medication where feasible, etc.?

	Residents	Practice under 10 years	Practice over 10 years
Always } Usually }	83%	90%	93%
Seldom } Never }	17%	10%	7%

Here there is general agreement by a significant majority of all groups.

A question not explored here is the degree to which the physicians'

114

attitudes are shared through discussions with the nursing staff, and to what degree they actually help to shape hospital policy regarding visiting hours and parental participation. It is through such discussion that a coordinated policy can be effected which reflects the attitudes of all involved in the care of the child and his family.

SUMMARY. This chapter has discussed some of the reactions health care personnel may experience in the care of a child with a fatal illness, and some of the antecedents to those reactions. It has pointed to the importance for all personnel to be aware of their attitudes and values regarding death, dying, the patient, and his family, in order that these attitudes and values might not lead to inappropriate management and treatment. Communication between all members of the medical team has been stressed as a way of clarifying and coordinating policy and procedures so that intrastaff conflicts and reactions which affect patient care and confuse parents can be avoided. Results from a questionnaire surveying pediatricians' attitudes have been presented as one means of assessing the variety of attitudes and procedures applied in the care of a fatally ill child.

REFERENCES

1. C. D. Aring, "An Appreciation of Death and Dying," *Hospital Tribune,* June 26, 1967, p. 6.
2. H. Feifel, "Death," *Taboo Topics,* edited by N. L. Farberow, New York: Atherton Press, 1963.
3. H. Feifel et al., "Physicians Consider Death" (Proceedings, 75th Annual Convention, American Psychological Association, 1967).
4. M. B. Rothenberg, "Reactions of Those Who Treat Children With Cancer," *Pediatrics, 40*:507, 1967.
5. H. Feifel et al., "Physicians Consider Death."
6. W. M. Easson, "Care of the Young Patient Who Is Dying," *Journal of the American Medical Association, 205*(4):103, July 22, 1968.
7. J. Green, "Care of the Family of a Child with Cancer" (Panel Discussion), *Pediatrics, 40*:506, 1967.

115

III

Reaction to
and Management of
Partial Loss

8

Loss of External Organs: Limb Amputation, Mastectomy, and Disfiguration

Bernard Schoenberg and Arthur C. Carr

Although the concept of loss is generally discussed in relation to dying and death, physicians must frequently treat patients who have experienced many other kinds of significant loss, often ones related to the body, its parts, and their functioning. Such losses include, among others, those involving the external bodily organs such as occur through limb amputation, mastectomy, and bodily disfiguration.

With modern advances in medical treatment and surgical techniques, amputation of body parts has become prevalent. A total of 35,000 limb amputations are performed in the United States annually, in addition to amputation of other external organs. Cancer of the breast accounts for almost 25 per cent of all malignancies in women, the majority of which are treated by breast surgery in combination with other forms of treatment. Loss or disfiguration of external organs through other than surgical means occurs increasingly, particularly as a result of highway accidents. Such "partial loss" in relation to external organs of the body is an increasingly common experience, and may present complications for the patient, his family, and his physician, which, although similar to those which occur with fatal illness and death, may also involve less commonly expected reactions.

Understanding some of the diverse reactions which may accompany change or loss of external organs can be best conveyed by reference to the concept of body-image, an important construct which in recent years has gained wide recognition in psychology, psychiatry, and neurophysiology. Defined by Head (1) as a schema of the individual in terms of which all postural and bodily movements are integrated, the meaning of the concept was extended by Schilder (2) beyond the neurological sphere to include psychological correlates, as indicated by his statement that "The image of the human body means the picture of our own body which we form in our mind, that is to say the way in which the body appears to ourselves. . . . The body schema is the tri-dimensional image everybody has about himself." The pervasive importance of the concept was emphasized by Kolb (3), who, in a summary of body-image disturbances, related the construct to patterns of development, physiological factors, family and cultural attitudes, and prognosis for therapy.

In clinical usage the concept of body-image has been extended to include a wide variety of phenomena, not all of which have been shown to be related to each other: dependence on bodily cues for establishing the upright position; conscious attitudes about the body and its parts; symbolic and/or unconscious values placed on the body and its parts; the stability of the view of the body; the ability to perform complex motor tasks (for which the integrity of the body-image is assumed to be basic); permeability of body barriers, presumably reflected in Rorschach test content; anesthesias; hypochondriasis; preoccupation with the body, and familiarity with the body and its parts.

The wide range of normal and abnormal disturbances included in the concept raises the question of whether it is justifiable to discuss it as a single concept. Kolb (4) finds value in distinguishing the "perceptual image" (referring to the postural model of the body as described by Head) from the "conceptual image" (referring to the emotions and attitudes attached to the body and its parts). In what follows, however, we will continue to use the single concept, body-image, as a convenient abstraction referring to how one experiences, differentiates, conceives of, and perceives his body and its parts, and to the relationship of this experience to reactions accompanying loss or change in the body.

The infant is first able to distinguish self from nonself by perceiving the body through external tactile and kinesthetic sensations and internal sensations (for example, depth sensibility). The formation of the body-image is brought about and constantly modified through an accumulation of memories from every sensory modality. The constant experience of motility of a body part, whether active or passive, helps to orient that part in space for the body-image. Vital functional psychological factors also contribute to the structure of the body-image and its subsequent awareness by the ego. The socially determined qualities begin to appear with the earliest experiences of the individual in relation to the significant person in his family or home environment. Toward his body and its various parts, the child acquires social percepts, attitudes, and affects from his interaction with parents and members of the family. The attitudes of parents impart an indelible impression on the child's concept of himself, his body, and its functioning. Depending on the experience with the parents, the body and body parts may be conceived of as good or bad, pleasing or repulsive, clean or dirty, loved or disliked. Such attitudes and values about the body are an integral part of the body-image.

The body-image has an integrity and intactness which are presumed to reflect basic aspects of one's ego integration. When this integration is weak, disruption of the body-image through surgery or amputation may precipitate blatant psychotic or delusional behavior. Even in well-adjusted persons, however, the almost universal reaction to such loss is that of grief, accompanied by depression and anxiety. On occasion, such emotions may be expressed only through somatic equivalents, but they are nevertheless invariably present in some form. Recognition of the diverse reactions that accompany changes in body-image is helpful for the patient, his family, and his physician and may forestall serious psychologic complications.

The phantom limb, for example, is an almost universal reaction following amputation and reflects an aspect of the body-image which is anchored in a neurophysiologic substrate developed fairly early in life. The phantom phenomenon is observed after removal of a body part such as breast, penis, nose, nipple, and most commonly after amputation of limbs. In less extreme circumstances, the phenomenon may be noted after sudden change in body size (such as that which occurs following childbirth) or subsequent to alterations in body appearance. Generally, the greater movement of a body part the more sharply defined will be a later phantom. Most amputees will report some physical sensation associated with the lost extremity. Immediately following amputation the patient usually experiences the phantom as the entire extremity, the distal portion most vividly. The sensations may be tingling "pins and needles," or disagreeably painful sensations. The initial experience of the phantom gradually diminishes for most patients. With some patients the total disappearance of the phenomenon may take as long as several years. It is of interest that children who have amputations before the age of six or seven, or children who are born without limbs, do not experience the phantom phenomenon, reflecting the fact that the neurophysiological patterns of body-image are not firmly established before this time.

In contrast to normal resolution of phantom phenomenon are certain maladaptive developments. If the mourning process over such a loss is unresolved, complications such as a persistent phantom, denial of a phantom, or the painful phantom may occur. Psychogenic pain in the stump or phantom limb may present major problems for rehabilitation. Such a symptom formation may serve the function of keeping anxiety and grief (the usual emotions accompanying limb amputation) unconscious through the experience of a somatic substitute. No matter how distressing physical pain may be, it may be more tolerable than the emotionally painful feeling it replaces. Physical complaints also result in increased interest and attention on the part of family, of friends, and especially of the physician, a figure who may unconsciously represent to the patient the primary source of love and the gratification of infantile needs. The symptom of pain may also offer a socially acceptable retreat from everyday burdens and responsibilities. The sensation of burning pain has been revealed in some patients to be a reflection of the fantasies about what is done with the amputated extremity: "I've heard what happens to organs that are removed. I know they are put in the incinerator and burned." Kolb (5) has shown that most amputees with painful phantoms have a past history of significant emotional attachments to other amputees and have fathers who overemphasized physical strength and athletic skill.

The patient's response to loss of a body part varies with the specific significance of that part to the patient. The emotional impact of a mastectomy, for example, has a significance to a woman that transcends functional or cosmetic factors, since a breast, like the uterus, is far more likely to symbolize a woman's femininity. Her reaction to losing a breast will therefore depend to a great extent on her feminine identity, which in turn is determined by her previous relationships with parents, other family members, and more currently, her relationship with her husband.

In our own culture breasts have been idealized and have come to symbolize a woman's sexuality. There is considerable emphasis in magazines, the news media, and movies on the size and shape of breasts. In the United States, breast stimulation is an integral part of sexual behavior, although reports indicate that the female breast is of greater significance to the male than the female. In other cultures and societies there is considerably less emphasis on breast development.

The initial reaction to a mass or lump in the breast is anxiety, since it is widely known that such a mass or lump may be due to cancer. Denial and avoidance are common reactions and are frequent causes of delay in seeking treatment. Any surgical procedure to the breast is likely to arouse fear and anxiety despite reassurance that the lump is probably benign or that chances of survival are good. For many women, feelings of self-esteem, desirability, and sexuality are closely related to the breast. Therefore, the patient about to undergo mastectomy may expect to be regarded by others as defective and may consequently anticipate sexual rejection.

As with the loss of a limb, the loss of a breast will be experienced as the death of a body part and may symbolize or be psychologically comparable to the loss of a significant person. The reaction to the loss is grief persisting during a period of mourning for the lost breast and what it may symbolize. Generally speaking, women who have high emotional investment in their breasts are more likely to suffer severe postoperative depressions. If the normal process of mourning is prolonged or unusually severe, the physician should regard it as an indication of an emotional complication. Likewise, if there is no visible reaction to the loss the physician should be alert to the likelihood of future difficulties in the patient's adjustment.

Bodily disfiguration may occur through other than surgical intervention. Some deformities exist at birth or early in life through birth injuries, congenital defects, or childhood diseases. Disfiguration may be secondary to physical trauma or may be the result of chronic deforming diseases such as the arthritides, leprosy, endocrine dysfunction, poliomyelitis, and hyperobesity.

123

REACTION TO PARTIAL LOSS

The patient's ability to adapt to disfigurement depends not only on its extent but also on how he emotionally experiences it. This in turn is related to his body-image and his previously existing personality. The nature of his emotional and perceptual reaction will also vary over the course of time. In contrast to the gradual changes of the body surface characteristic of some chronic diseases (for example, rheumatoid arthritis), sudden changes resulting from surgery or trauma will evoke greater anxiety. The anxiety reaction is related to fear of rejection by significant figures because of the deformity, and because the abruptness of the alteration in body appearance has not yet permitted the formation of a new body-image.

The common feelings that accompany anxiety are shame, hostility, and guilt, followed by emotional withdrawal and physical avoidance of others. Patients with disfiguration also react with depression, since any alteration in the body-image is experienced as loss of a body part and reduction of self-esteem.

Management

If we accept the likelihood that the patient will mourn any change or loss of a body part, it would appear necessary that he be granted the opportunity to discuss his anticipated loss as well as his feelings following the change. Perhaps no better single rule of management exists than that of allowing for meaningful expression of feelings which may range from despair and hopelessness to unwarranted optimism and euphoria in the stages preceding the final adjustment to serious disruption of the body-image. Too often, physicians, relatives, and friends, because of their own personal anxiety, discourage not only expression of feeling but also legitimate curiosity and desire for relevant information. Out of his own anxiety and guilt, the physician, in particular, may defensively present himself as someone whose decisions should not be questioned.

An example of the educative, reassuring role which the physician might play is that of his response to the patient's attitude toward the amputated limb and its method of disposal. During the nineteenth century, when modern surgical practices were first introduced into China by medical missionaries, the Chinese would allow the doctors to ampu-

124

tate only after receiving the doctor's assurance that he would save the severed limb, which would then be buried along with the rest of the body after death. Among orthodox Jews, the amputated limb is buried, and when the person dies he is reunited with the severed part of his body. The Talmud states that all organs necessary to sustain life, such as the heart and kidney, should be treated in a similar way. Whatever the original basis for these beliefs, there is an intrinsic wisdom in these cultural practices which should not be overlooked, as it is relevant to our present understanding of the psychology of mourning. It is not surprising that an individual might want a prized or loved part of himself to be disposed of with respect, tenderness, and dignity, or to know the whereabouts of his body parts. This is illustrated in Carson McCullers' *The Heart Is a Lonely Hunter* (6) by Willie, who has lost both his legs.

I feel like my feets is still hurting. I got this here terrible misery down in my toes. Yet the hurt in my feets is down where my feets should be if they were on my l-l-legs. And not where my feets is now. It a hard thing to understand. My feets hurt me so bad all the time and I don't know where they is. They never given them back to me. They s-somewhere more than a hundred m-miles from here. . . . I just wish I knowed where my f-f-feets are. That the main thing worries me. The doctor never given them back to me. I sure do wish I knowed where they are.

Preoperative preparation should include a discussion both of the patient's wishes and fears regarding the disposition of the body part and of the phantom limb phenomenon.

In evaluating the effect of the loss, the special or unique significance of the organ or limb to the individual should be considered.

A 54-year-old unmarried man, intellectually gifted, had compensated for an unhappy childhood relationship with his parents in which he felt weak, ineffective, and feminine, by undue emphasis on physical strength and athletic ability. He discontinued his doctoral studies in mathematics to become a high school football coach and prided himself on his ability to surpass his students. He refused to cooperate with his physician in the control of his diabetes. Following a leg amputation for gangrene, he became profoundly depressed. Despite strenuous efforts at rehabilitation by his physicians, he committed suicide.

REACTION TO PARTIAL LOSS

Males are often concerned about the significance of loss in relationship to their masculine adequacy, particularly in relation to their jobs and their earning capacity. Women, in general, tend to be more preoccupied with the cosmetic aspects of the change, although either type of concern may be of major importance to patients of either sex.

The indirect effect of amputation or disfigurement can sometimes be anticipated from the previous medical history of a patient.

A 42-year-old woman with a life-long history of hypochondriacal symptoms and somatic complaints was discovered in a routine examination to have a lump in her breast. Prompt treatment by mastectomy and radiotherapy resulted in a 5-year cure. However, despite reassurance by numerous physicians, she has remained a chronic invalid, dependent on her mother and older sisters to manage her household.

In this case, a "real" illness allowed the patient to regress to an infantile, helpless state, a situation which might have been anticipated from the patient's history of hypochondriasis and somatic preoccupation prior to the onset of her illness.

The symbolic aspect of loss is illustrated in those situations where the body part had a special unconscious significance to the patient. When examined closely, the reaction of grief may be related not only to the loss of body function but also may be related to a revival of feelings about a previous significant and symbolic loss:

A 45-year-old mother of three children had a bilateral mastectomy for cancer. Because of a complicated convalescence and difficult rehabilitation she was referred to a psychiatrist for consultation. During the interview she readily discussed her sexual frigidity and great doubts about her femininity. She regarded her breasts as her only "physical asset" and was certain that her husband had lost interest in her. Her associations to her breasts led to her mother who was hospitalized several times during the patient's childhood for severe depression and who ultimately committed suicide when the patient was 10 years old. The patient admitted recurrent thoughts of her own suicide and it became apparent that she had become dependent on alcohol.

Her first year of psychotherapy dealt to a large extent with her unresolved grief over the loss of her mother.

126

An individual's body-image is dependent on his ability to perceive his body and its parts realistically and to adapt to them as they actually exist. The ability to assess one's body and its parts is in turn related to early life experiences, especially the relationship with parents and other family members.

A 38-year-old unmarried "career" woman had an unhappy childhood and felt rejected by her father who would have preferred a son. He openly expressed disappointment that his wife was unable to bear more children. The patient, an attractive woman, experienced great fluctuations in weight since early adolescence and spent many hours in beauty salons "being made over." She admitted that many times in looking at herself in the mirror she did not recognize herself. Following a minor automobile accident in which she injured her nose, she sought rhinoplasty. Although the surgeon considered the operation successful, the patient had numerous complaints and threatened litigation. Her major complaint was that she was now unable to recognize herself.

Our own observations indicate that patients after breast surgery are more able to express resentment over the loss of pectoralis muscles and axillary contents than over the loss of the breast. In some cases patients feel they have been deceived by the surgeon who did not warn them of the body defect. This reaction occurs most frequently when the physician has not been frank in discussing the possible results of surgery.

Preoperative preparation by the surgeon may profitably include an interview with the husband to explore his reaction to the anticipated mastectomy. If the preoperative marital relationship has been intimate and mutually supportive with a good sexual adjustment, coping with the postoperative period will present fewer problems. When the husband's self-concept is fragile and his own anxiety over mutilation is great, he is likely to react to his wife's "mutilation" with avoidance or repulsion. The patient's feelings of being defective may cause sexual withdrawal, thus provoking feelings of rejection in her husband.

A 42-year-old energetic and attractive woman reacted to radical mastectomy with depression and sexual withdrawal from her husband. She told her physician that her husband had always admired her breasts, and breast stimulation had always been a significant aspect of foreplay. She was convinced that her husband no longer had "any use" for her. The physician

127

requested an interview with her husband, who reported that although 8 months had passed, he still regarded his wife as being too fragile for sexual intercourse. The physician remarked that his wife did not appear too fragile for strenuous housework. The husband added that his wife gave him no indication of wanting sexual relations and wondered if as a consequence of her operation she had lost her sexual drive. The physician encouraged him not to take her "disinterest" personally. He explained to the husband that the patient felt defective and undesirable. Several days later they resumed sexual relations.

Through reassurance and encouraging verbalization of feelings, the physician usually can alleviate some of the interpersonal problems posed by mastectomy. At times, however, the problem requires more active intervention.

A 54-year-old post-menopausal woman sought psychiatric help three years following a radical mastectomy. She was moderately depressed with multiple minor somatic complaints. Since her hospitalization she had suffered from insomnia and nervousness. She became frightened when recently "for the first time I began to contemplate suicide." She admitted, with embarrassment, that her husband had not approached her sexually since the surgical procedure. Although sexually frigid, she had always enjoyed intercourse because of its physical intimacy and closeness. An interview with her husband revealed that his mother had died of breast cancer after several operations. Currently, he lived in fear of seeing his wife's "wound." He expressed guilt over his mother's death 20 years earlier and realized that he was still mourning for her. He readily accepted the suggestion that he be referred for psychotherapy.

Establishing a warm supportive relationship with both members of the family can be the most important step in preventing emotional complications.

A 40-year-old woman, mother of four children, delayed entering the hospital because she felt uncertain about the consulting surgeon who examined her. She sought another consultation, despite her personal physician's assurance that the surgeon was an outstanding specialist in breast surgery. She was favorably impressed with the second consultant, who appeared "interested and unhurried." He explained to her why biopsy and surgery could not be separated. He discussed with her in a straightforward man-

128

ner that she may have cancer and reassured her that if she did, he thought they could "get it out." Together with her husband they discussed her responsibilities at home and he explained hospitalization and convalescence in detail. He suggested that the husband come to the recovery room so that he would be there when she was told the results of surgery. During the postoperative period the surgeon saw her twice a day—once alone and again when her husband was present. He encouraged the patient and husband to ask questions, constantly reassuring the patient that she was a "good patient." He openly admired the results of surgery and spoke freely of his excellent results. They both reacted positively to the surgeon's pride in his work (he referred to the "beautiful scar") and his "compulsive" attitude over details of postoperative care. At the end of hospitalization he discussed with both of them the chances of spread and metastasis and was hopeful about her future. He encouraged the patient to stuff her brassiere with cotton upon leaving the hospital, and arranged for further discussion regarding a prosthesis. The husband reported that the surgeon had "set the stage" for open discussion among the three of them.

A measure of the patient's capacity to adapt is his willingness to express feelings regarding his change or loss and his willingness to participate in a program of restoration or rehabilitation. The eventual failure to reorganize the body-image leads to emotional complications and usually requires psychiatric treatment. Individuals with disfigurement frequently suffer social discrimination in a society that places such great emphasis on physical appearance. They are regarded by most people with a certain degree of fear, pity, or revulsion, the deformity being reacted to by the observer on the basis of his own anxiety and phantasies.

The impact of the loss of a body part through amputation or the "loss" of appearance through facial disfiguration depends greatly on feelings of the individual about himself. If he is secure in the feeling that he is loved for himself and not for his appearance, physical ability, or his capacity to work, he is more capable of adjusting to the loss. His earlier relationships with significant people in his environment, especially parental figures, will be the principal determinant of his self-regard or self-esteem. In turn, attitudes of family members depend on their previous background as well as their relationship to the patient. The attitudes of hospital personnel toward amputation and disfigura-

129

tion will also be significant in determining the patient's reaction. Reactions to major disruptions of the body-image may require intensive psychiatric treatment as well as the services of prosthetic experts, vocational counselors, physical rehabilitation and occupational therapists, group psychotherapists, and other professional workers. Numerous studies have illustrated that the physical improvement made in the hospital is frequently lost when the patient returns to his home if he and his family are not psychologically prepared to cope with the disability. It has been observed that the attitude of the family member caring for the patient is crucial in rehabilitation, and particularly that the individual's opportunity for relief from responsibilities may determine success or failure. If the family member is not provided opportunity for "role relief," he may become as sick as the patient and rehabilitation of the patient will be greatly disrupted.

Thus, a reaction to the loss of a part of the body and the psychology of the mourning reaction which accompanies this loss depend on many factors. Basic to this reaction is the body-image, which is an expression of the emotional adjustment of the patient prior to the loss. Reactions to changes in the body-image are intimately related to previous losses, patterns which have been established in early relationship with parents and family members. Reactions to body-image changes depend, in addition, upon the nature of the change and the lost part's conscious and unconscious significance to the patient. The strategy taken by physicians, relatives, and friends in dealing with the patient's attitudes and feelings, as well as their own attitudes and feelings regarding the loss, will be crucial to the ultimate adjustment to and acceptance of the loss or change.

REFERENCES

1. H. Head, *Studies in Neurology*, London: Oxford, 1920.
2. P. Schilder, *The Image and Appearance of the Human Body*, London: Kegan Paul, 1935.
3. L. C. Kolb, "Disturbances of the Body Image," *American Handbook of Psychiatry*, New York: Basic Books, 1959.

4. L. C. Kolb, "The Body Image in the Schizophrenic Reaction," *Schizophrenia; An Integrated Approach*, edited by A. Auerback, New York: Ronald Press, 1959.
5. L. C. Kolb, *The Painful Phantom*, Springfield: Thomas, 1954.
6. C. McCullers, *The Heart is A Lonely Hunter*, Boston: Houghton Mifflin, 1940.

9

Loss of Internal Organs

Richard S. Blacher

A surgical procedure may precipitate a profound, often long-lasting psychological reaction which is often obscured to the casual observer. The fact that these reactions are usually unexpressed suits the needs of both patient and physician. The surgeon would prefer to think that his work is not only helpful and even life-saving—which it is—but also emotionally easy for the patient—which it is not. It is only in the uncommon instance when the usual postoperative course is uneven that the physician becomes aware that operations may lead to upsetting emotional reactions. For his part, the patient struggles to appear calm and self-possessed both before and after his operation. Indeed, overwhelming anxiety before surgery is treated as an ominous sign by most surgeons, who would prefer delaying any but the most urgent operations. One is struck by the almost casual attitude of most patients on the day preceding surgery. While some patients do admit to mild anxiety, and a rare person will describe feeling "frightened to death," the average patient appears quite calm. However, in a series of patients studied by Meyer et al. (1), psychological tests administered both before and after surgery revealed marked changes in the emotional state of such patients. While clinically they seemed in good control of themselves, preoperative drawings frequently showed severe regressive and even psychotic trends. This evidence of extreme, though clinically hidden, anxiety disappeared after the operation. Postoperatively, the patient may also attempt to hide his fears.

A young man was seen the day after repair of a cardiac septal defect. He appeared paralyzed with fear but vehemently denied these feelings.

After recovery, he was able to admit how he had really felt. "But doctor, I'm *too old* to be frightened."

Most patients utilize mechanisms of denial against the underlying dread they must deal with, lest they be overwhelmed by it. Nor is this dread surprising. To the physician, illness and surgery are matters of his everyday life; to the patient, his operation is a unique experience which is not only a therapeutic procedure but a danger of his life. In studying reactions exhibited in the recovery room (2), we were struck by the frequency with which herniorrhaphy patients would ask, "What did they find?," clearly alluding to a concern with cancer. A surgeon preparing for an apparently benign procedure might not think of reassuring such patients preoperatively, but the patient can imagine any operation as a most hazardous undertaking.

In a sense, the physician's competence may make things more difficult for the patient. As medical technology advances, and more complicated procedures and technical improvements become routine, the experienced doctor may tend to forget that certain procedures are commonplace to him, but not to the patient. Misunderstandings are fairly common, but because of the patient's reluctance to complain they are not discussed with the physician. For example, patients with tracheotomies after cardiac surgery are understandably anxious, not only because of their inability to talk at the time; many of them suffer quietly with the fear that they will never again be able to speak. The explanation that the condition is transient often does not register and repeated reassurances may be necessary during the course of recovery.

Reactions to the loss of internal organs must be viewed in terms of the psychological significance of the surgical procedures. The significance of the disease treated by surgery will in large part determine the patient's reaction to surgery. Obviously, a patient hospitalized for cancer surgery will react differently than one who has a drainage for infection. These factors in turn are interwoven with the reactions related to the significance of the diseased organ to the patient. These interrelated factors are usually inseparable. However, at any time and for any patient, one or another of these factors may predominate, overshadowing and even hiding the others, which nevertheless are present. For example, the dread of a diagnosis of cancer is often present despite the nature of the surgical procedure.

133

REACTION TO PARTIAL LOSS

For some patients their first postoperative response is often, "What was found?" If only the disease process is benign or at least curable, they can tolerate the loss of almost any organ. For these patients, any opening of his body cavity may well reveal some dread illness.

Frequently, however, the patient does not even express concern over the disease process. Here the mechanism of denial comes into full play and the focus of anxiety is typically displaced to postoperative woes—often to realistic concerns such as pain in the incision, but just as frequently to seemingly trivial concerns having no direct bearing on the illness as such. Denial can be a useful adaptive device, especially when the danger is overwhelming.

A young woman with a pneumonectomy had developed a complication of excessive bleeding, a symptom which worried her surgeons and which, one might expect, would alarm her. When asked how things were going, she burst into a tirade, her main concern being that the nurse who had made her bed that morning had left a crease in the sheet. She also described other minor imperfections. Clearly this was easier to worry about than cancer. Only weeks later could she discuss the real fears her surgery and bleeding had aroused.

The disease process rather than the surgical procedure can be the predominant fear in procedures such as adrenalectomy for breast cancer; here, the adrenal glands have minimal psychological significance to the patient, but the disease is of great importance. So it is for thymectomy for myasthenia gravis, and even appendectomy for an acute abdomen. It is rare indeed to find a person who experiences much regret over loss of the thymus or appendix. Rather, the concern is with the possibility of being overcome by infection, debilitating disease, or terminal illness.

The meaning to the patient of the loss of an internal organ may be viewed under two rubrics. The first refers to the characteristic relative importance of specific body organs to human beings; it is to be expected that cardiac surgery will elicit a stronger response than cholecystectomy. The second category is one in which the specific organ has unique or special significance to the individual. Thus, for some patients, an organ ordinarily considered psychically insignificant may take on great importance because of previous experiences or fantasies associated with it by the individual. The removal of a spleen might ause great anxiety in a patient whose younger sibling died of a spleen injury and in whom guilt from the earlier experience is mobilized at the time of the current surgery.

A young woman who had had three previous operations for unrelated conditions was told that she needed a gastrectomy for pyloric stenosis subsequent to long-standing duodenal ulcer. She became panicky and confused and refused to sign the consent for surgery, a reaction which seemed strange in light of her easy tolerance of three major procedures in the past. Psychiatric consultation revealed a similar confusional episode six months before, at the time of her father's death. She had originally stated that he had died of leukemia, but his symptoms did not fit this illness, and on further questioning she revealed that he had actually died following surgery for gastric cancer. Although her symptoms were different, she worried lest she, too, had this disease—a possibility not seriously entertained by her physicians. When the situation was clarified, her anxiety subsided and she underwent surgery without incident. Clearly, the stomach, in her experience, was of utmost importance, not only because of her own chronic illness with its attendant pain, but also because of her father's fatal disease. In telling her doctors that he had had leukemia, she attempted to deny the association.

The significance of the organ may be understood not only in terms of symbolic displacement but also in terms of function of the organ. The exteriorization of the ileum with colectomy for chronic ulcerative colitis highlights the results of the loss of an organ and the loss of the usual mode of carrying out a vital function. This function of evacuation of feces is not merely a life process, but in addition has acquired profound psychological significance for humans. Not only does the act of defecation provide gratification for the child, but in the development of control of this function, one can trace the child's first attempt to give up such gratification in order to satisfy those in his environment. Psychoanalysts have pointed up the connection between anal functions and orderliness, frugality, obstinacy, and compulsive traits. Disgust is the usual emotion evoked in the handling of human feces, so it is understandable that a procedure which results in the expulsion of the fecal mass through an opening in the front of the abdomen would be anticipated with dread. Yet surprisingly, most patients make a good adjustment to cleaning and manipulating these stomata. They

135

are helped in large part by the excellent work done by "ostomy" clubs These organizations are composed of patients with various ostomies who advise each other regarding management, and provide the support only those with a similar disability can give. The awareness that others can live full and productive lives professionally, socially, and sexually despite the disfigurement, makes it possible for many patients to become rehabilitated.

An entirely different response than disgust may be elicited by the stoma. For some patients, pleasure may be derived from the manipulation and successful management of the new opening. This process may then occupy many hours each day and can become the new focus of the patient's life (3).

The loss of function that predominates in such conditions will in most cases obscure the patient's reaction to the actual loss of an organ—in this case, the colon.

A young man who had made a rapid and excellent adaptation to ileostomy underwent a total colectomy a while later. He reported that for over a year he continued to have a desire to pass gas and would have to remind himself that this was impossible. It was the loss of his anus that he experienced as his real loss.

The most awesome sense of loss is experienced by patients undergoing cardiac surgery. The heart as the central organ of life is naturally the organ most important in the psychic representation of the inside of the body (4), and any procedure involving its handling and cutting must evoke a major emotional response. We are not accustomed to viewing such procedures as resulting in loss, but careful interviewing of many patients with valve replacements and pacemaker implantations has convinced us that this is often how the patients view their situation. While emphasizing how they have been given a new lease on life or new abilities, many of these patients also struggle with the sense that something was taken from them and then replaced. A man who suffered repeated episodes of heart-block and syncope was provided with a pacemaker. Although he became asymptomatic, he not only felt different from other people, but he also felt strongly that he had lost the ability to run his own body and prayed that something could be done to remove the device. This loss of function that the pace-

136

maker highlights is most keenly experienced by those people who must feel in control of things. One such woman stated, "I'm really not a person anymore; I'm a robot run by a machine" (5).

In patients with valve replacements, there is a common though reluctantly expressed regret that the new valve is artificial. A common analogy used is that of an automobile engine valve that must be replaced. "I guess my valve had too much carbon and needed overhauling," one woman stated quite seriously. "My valve is plastic and *so far*, it's holding up," said a man who was an auto mechanic. "So far" indicated his concept of the durability of a plastic valve in an engine. "I have a metal valve now—I hope it's stainless steel," said one patient who immediately denied a concern about its rusting. There is widespread feeling that a prosthesis is not as good as the real thing.

Aside from the removal of organs damaged by trauma, it is uncommon for significant organs to be extirpated without a history of acute or, more commonly, chronic disease. Thus, one might expect that the removal of a healthy organ from a donor, as in renal transplant, would provide an opportunity to study reactions to the loss of that organ in pure culture. However, clinically we do not find such a simple isolated response. While the fact of giving the organ is in the forefront, ambivalent feelings toward the recipient and toward the medical staff who encouraged the procedure and the sacrifice predominate. One woman, for example, experienced giving her kidney to her child as a revival of childbirth—"I'm giving him a new life"—and then re-experienced a postpartum depression (6). In some patients the removal of a kidney represents the loss of a pelvic organ which might hinder reproduction.

Management

The physician dealing with patients who face the loss of organs must bear in mind the various problems which confront such a patient. An awareness that the patient must deal with his feelings about the organ, the disease, and the surgical procedure will allow the doctor to give support in the areas most pressing. For many people, the anesthesia may be more frightening than the surgery, since it is equated with dying, forced passivity, or loss of control. In addition, it frequently re-

137

vives traumatic childhood experiences of surgery. A preoperative visit from an understanding anaesthesiologist may be far more efficacious than chemical sedation (7).

The need for the patient to prepare himself for an operation is clear to anyone dealing with emotional responses to surgery. While it is difficult to determine what might constitute an adequate period of preparation for surgery, the danger usually lies in too *short* a preparation. The tendency of some surgeons to give only a day's warning lest they upset the patient may reflect their own anxieties, especially when the surgery is disfiguring or life-endangering. Giving a patient adequate warning is to give him an opportunity to worry in advance which may lead to a smoother postoperative course (8).

A patient who has suffered disabling illness for many years would be expected to react to surgery differently than the asymptomatic patient who is referred for an operation following routine examination. Oddly enough, the former patient may at times suffer more. The person who has adapted to his initial valve disease, and has even unconsciously welcomed it as an honorable means of avoiding an aggressive role in life, may react to a valve replacement with profound depression.

Ultimately the patient must face surgery alone. The most his medical advisors can do is prepare and support him as he faces his ordeal. The physician who would undertake guidance of the patient through the emotional hazards of surgery must accept his role with the realization that the burdens for both guide and guided are heavy and that the trail markings are not always clear. But such guidance may well make the difference between hope and despair, between a rapid and delayed convalescence, and even between recovery and death.

REFERENCES

1. B. C. Meyer, F. Brown, and A. Levine, "Observations on the House-Tree-Person Test Before and After Surgery," *Psychosomatic Medicine*, 17 (6) : 428, November-December 1955.
2. C. Winklestein, R. S. Blacher, and B. C. Meyer, Unpublished Data.
3. S. Margolin, "Psychophysiological Studies of Fistulous Openings into the

Gastrointestinal Tract," *Journal of the Mt. Sinai Hospital,* 20(3):194, September-October, 1953.

4. B. C. Meyer, R. S. Blacher, and F. Brown, "A Clinical Study of Psychiatric and Psychological Aspects of Mitral Surgery," *Psychosomatic Medicine, 23*(3):194, May-June 1961.

5. R. S. Blacher and S. H. Basch, "Psychological Aspects of Pacemaker Implantation," *Archives of General Psychiatry* (in press).

6. S. H. Basch, Personal Communication.

7. L. D. Egbert et al., "The Value of the Pre-operative Visit by an Anaesthetist," *J.A.M.A. 185*(7):553, August 17, 1963.

8. H. Deutsch, "Some Psychoanalytic Observations in Surgery," *Psychosomatic Medicine, 4*(1):105, January, 1942.

10

Reaction to and Management of Sensory Loss: Blindness and Deafness*

K. Z. Altshuler

The eye and the ear are distance receptors. Through them man extends his awareness and mastery beyond finger-tip reach. Through the eye he gains color, and integrates form, distance, and the perspective of self and horizon. The ear brings the word, and from it, language, which extends the reach deeply into himself, the past, and even the future.

Since both are openings as well as appendages, the eye and the ear may symbolically represent the mouth, anus, or genitals of either sex. Because of their unique importance in adaptation, threats of any kind are referable to them and can be reflected in myths of their destruction or dreams of their functional loss. Fears of retaliation are related not only to the implied sexual use of these senses but to their aggressive roles as well, that is, spying, eavesdropping, and incorporation. The real loss of sight or audition, in addition to posing legitimate difficulties in adaptation, can also be experienced as a punitive measure for some transgression, real or imagined.

Of the two senses, vision has carried with it the more dramatic associations. From ancient myths to contemporary films, the blind have been cast to evoke extremes of feeling; as supernatural seers command-

*The author gratefully acknowledges the general and research assistance of Miss Mima Cataldo.

ing awe and deference, or as the totally helpless beggar or outcast, to be regarded with pity or disgust. The deaf, too, have inspired mixed feelings, and were considered defective and uneducable until only relatively recent times. As a result, stereotypes abound, and where there are stereotypes there is misinformation. This chapter will attempt to put some of the facts into perspective, to touch on the role of hearing and of sight in development, and to discuss reactions to their loss. As a first organizing principle, one must recognize that loss of vision or hearing in the adult is an entirely different matter, with entirely separate sequelae, than loss of either of these sensory modes at birth or in early infancy. Indeed, there is evidence to suggest that while loss of vision is the most fearsome to the adult, it is congenital loss of hearing that has the most far-reaching consequences.

Loss of Vision or Hearing in the Adult

It could be argued with some validity that people often grow old without growing up, but the fact is that—physiologically at least—the adult is a mature organism. His character is either formed or malformed, and ordinarily is not likely to change in any major fashion. It is this formed character, with its equipment and impediments, that determines the ultimate outcome when loss of vision or hearing supervenes.

Blindness

The shock of sudden blindness is enormous. The immediate reaction generally is one of immobility, facial blankness, hypoesthesia, and depression. Depersonalization may occur, perhaps as an emergency defense to separate the person from his plight and to allow the realistic impact of blindness to emerge gradually. Blank (1) observed that these initial reactions last two to seven days, but the depression may normally persist from three months to a year. According to personal accounts, it is the total dependency and loss of individual freedom that preoccupy the individual at this time — as Chevigny puts it, ". . . being observed without knowing it [and] being unable even to commit suicide without help" (2).

The period of shock and subsequent depression is a normal re-

141

action; indeed, the prognosis is ominous if no signs of disturbance appear. The dynamics of loss and mourning which have been reviewed elsewhere in this text (See Chapters One and Two) are also characteristic of loss of vision. The blind person in addition must discontinue relying on his eyes and accept himself as blind. The fact that vision has a realistic as well as symbolic meaning is important since changes imposed by the loss of sight require physical as well as psychological efforts at adaptation. On the one hand the reality factors increase the difficulty and may prolong the mourning; on the other hand, mastery of any real step toward mobility, reading, or the reestablishment of friendships can increase the individual's self-esteem and hasten further adaptation.

Studies of war-blinded veterans and other adults suggest that 60 to 80 per cent traverse the path to rehabilitation and acceptance of the handicap with reasonable success. In reading personal accounts one is impressed by both the difficulties encountered and man's inveterate resiliency. When the initial shock wears off, the healthy person's persistent concerns are related to economic loss, the loss of freedom, and feelings of disfigurement.

The sense of disfigurement derives from difficulties in maintaining an appropriate range of facial expressions without another face to respond to, a tendency to assume hesitant, protective posture to ward off the inevitable bump, and a host of problems in manners and appearance. One memoir, for example, suggests the use of an aluminum fork, the weight of which makes it easy to judge a proper load of food (3). The blind man is also advised to sit touching the garment of the person with whom he speaks, so as to avoid the embarrassment of talking into empty space should his companion depart. Others emphasize difficulties in maintaining cleanliness and the need for order in arranging household objects. Keenness of memory becomes most important, as well as auditory, tactile, and olfactory senses. Success and satisfactory adaptation can be achieved when the handicap is accepted, confident mobility established, and when the individual has returned to economically productive work and renewed social relationships. There is even a potentially positive aspect of blindness in its freedom from the prejudicial aspects of vision; thus the blind man reports he can hear the guilty girl in a beautiful woman, or the sincere friend despite physical ugliness.

142

Those who do not succeed in adjusting to the handicap continue to show symptoms of anxiety, mood disturbances, aggressive asocial behavior, or excessive dependency. These symptoms may be the result of prolonged mourning and may extend into a masochistic state of angry depression, or they may appear as an exacerbation of prior character traits. The dependence can be such that the blind person never undertakes mobility training, but remains in virtual confinement for years. In contrast, one healthy survivor was both shocked and offended to learn that, once blind, he could be pensioned off and never expected to cope or contribute again. Another compromise is a minimal effort accompanied by a defensive rage at the "stupidity" and lack of understanding of the sighted, usually a reflection of self hate indicative of the subject's own attitudes toward his blindness.

Society's attitudes are continuing sources of discomfiture to the blind and may retard progress in readjustment. For example, a social agency may assume too much responsibility for a client and squelch the first tentative moves toward independence. Solicitude can also be insulting or painful: imagine a well-meaning dinner companion moving the water glass from its place to put it closer to the blind man's hand, or obviously avoiding such conversational topics as a busy street scene or an unusual visual event. Frank acceptance by the sighted that blindness is a handicap but is not totally incapacitating is the most positive approach.

A physician's efforts to be "merciful" may in some instances be more for his own emotional protection than for that of his patient. A straightforward statement of fact is advisable when blindness is irrevocable, with a clear recognition that a painful experience for the patient is unavoidable. To prolong hope where none exists can intensify anxiety, encourage denial, delay the inevitable depression, and postpone the required participation in rehabilitative measures. Slow, progressive blindness may be more difficult to adapt to than blindness of sudden onset, for the former generally occurs in late middle life, when real options for adaptation as well as psychological flexibility to a new pattern of living are reduced.

Specific preexisting unconscious conflicts referable to the eye or excessive premorbid concerns with guilt can also contribute to prolonged rehabilitation, while a healthy prior personality, success in previous education, and the ability to establish a marriage and respon-

143

sible social relationships before blindness are all associated with success in adjustment to the handicap. Psychiatric consultation and psycho therapy can be effective in many seemingly intransigent cases. Above all, time, in its classic role of healer, must be appreciated and allowed to play its salient role.

Deafness

As in most situations where we are ignorant, theoretical contributions are rife but little practical observation has been made on the consequences of severe hearing loss in the adult. An obstacle for such study arises at the first step, that is, the matter of definition. Whereas blindness, by legal dictum, can be said to be present when vision is less than 20/200, the borderline for deafness is nebulous. Losses greater than seventy or eighty decibels are generally accepted as profound, but such losses are not necessarily consistent across frequencies, and for reasons unknown some people make better use of residual hearing than others. The most common causes of deafness in the adult are otosclerosis, chronic middle-ear disease, industrial noise, and old age. With the exception of the last, all are treatable or on the wane, and psychiatrists venturesome enough to study the aged have seldom wanted to complicate their task by taking on the additional handicap of impaired hearing.

The result is that there are only a few studies on severe hearing loss in the adult, and the majority of these focus on noise-deafened soldiers. According to Knapp (4) only about 8 per cent of affected soldiers developed chronic neurotic reactions to the physiological loss. Factors contributing to the reaction are anxiety, related unconsciously to experiencing the loss of function as a mutilation; the persistence of other somatic symptoms (tinnitus and other head noises) ; difficulties related to sensory deprivation; and social insecurity based on problems in communication. The initial reactions in acute cases are anxiety and depression, though hypochondriasis and compulsive behavior are also seen. While the former reactions may be considered a normal response to loss, the latter probably stem from earlier problems in character and personality.

With time, an adequate adjustment to the loss of hearing is gen-

144

erally made, the mode depending on individual personality. In some, chronic tendencies may remain toward withdrawal, denial of deficit, overcompensatory socializing, displacement to concern with other symptoms, and exploitation of the handicap for secondary gain. Ingalls (5) noted that depressive reactions are generally short-lived with acute cases of hearing impairment, while in chronic progressive cases the sense of loss may be less, yet give rise to more severe problems. As the deficit progresses, exaggerated efforts at concentration may result in fatigue, anxiety, and irritability, and can increase the tendency toward withdrawal. While society's impatience with the hard of hearing may indeed induce paranoid feelings in some patients, the stereotype of the deafened person as paranoid is more frequently found in psychiatric folklore than among the affected themselves.

The majority of the deaf accept their handicap with some degree of stoicism and ultimately reach an acceptable psychological denouement. As with the blind, forthright assessment of the degree of impairment by the physician is advisable and hopes of recovery should be honestly and realistically discussed. The individual's natural reaction of grief, depression, and anxiety should be respected. Since hearing loss in the adult has little effect on language or mobility and since it does not always lead to major economic and interpersonal dislocations, a generally good result can be anticipated with supportive therapy and appropriate rehabilitative measures.

In individuals with a severe preexisting personality or character disorder, the preoccupation with power and intactness may be so overwhelming that any deficiency is intolerable. Individuals who have spent a life-time struggling with their passive wishes and retaliatory fears may react with massive efforts at denial when confronted with chronic, progressive impairment. The denial of what is perceived, accompanied by a heightened sense of vulnerability may, in rare cases, lead to a paranoid reaction.

Blindness and Deafness From Birth or Early Childhood

A loss of vision or hearing at birth or in infancy is much more serious than in adulthood. The human infant has been designed to mature in an average predictable environment and with certain average equip-

145

ment. Departures from the average environment (the culturally disadvantaged, the institutionalized infant) inflict heavy penalties, and failures in expected equipment also lead to skewed development and maturational detours.

The eye is involved in object recognition and location, and hence in prehension, hand-eye coordination, free and safe mobility, and the expansion of awareness that comes with exploration. Relationships with the external environment, psychosexual development, and the ego functions that depend on these abilities are retarded, impaired, or rendered out of phase in the absence of vision.

The sensory isolation imposed by deafness blocks the reception of auditory stimuli and the learning of meaningful sounds for communication. Bowlby (6) has noted that sound plays an essential role in the child's bond with his mother, and a quieting emotional response can be generated by the sound of a mother's voice as early as the first few weeks of life. Spitz (7) includes speech (along with the smiling response and stranger anxiety) as one of those primary organizers of the psyche which, by their impact on the surrounding world, initiate a new expansion of personality. Stimulating affectionate interchange between child and parent, these "organizers" are prerequisites for the development of object relationships in the human pattern. The absence of hearing and verbal language—part of the foundations of intelligence—also limits the ability to acquire and associate symbols that are required to define feelings, to develop empathy and a sense of mutuality. Thus, by interfering with codification and expression of age-specific interests, deafness has been shown to impede certain aspects of abstraction (symbolic recall, recognition of similarities, and deduction of consequences) that may be necessary for thinking, feeling for others, and exercising effective self-control.

The blind infant may lie quiet and expressionless, fists clenched in eyes; and the deaf child does not respond as expected to peek-a-boo or sound games, or to vocal expressions of coddling or disapproval. Before the limitation is recognized, these failures in expected response create confusion and bewilderment in the family and interfere with the mutual reinforcement which is the basis of loving, parent-child relationships. When the diagnosis is made, parents react with depression, guilt, hostility, and ambivalence, and they may become unnecessarily

146

and unwaveringly solicitous or cling to unrealistic, overoptimistic expectations.

Further studies of children and adults afflicted with either handicap from birth or early childhood should prove invaluable. Such studies would amplify our knowledge and test psychoanalytic and learning theories with regard to the role of perception in personality development. Investigations would define the role of sight or hearing as each has been determined by social and physical development. Aberrations would be determined not only by the handicap itself but in large measure by factors such as the reactions of parents and other important figures to the handicap, by the experience of other losses such as those consequent to separation, etc. In those situations in which the diagnosis is made early, and in which therapeutic counsel is used to normalize early relationships, the effects of the handicap itself might then be defined, i.e., the minimum deviations which must derive from a life-time of different and limited experience.

Psychological Studies

Interestingly enough, the role of either perceptual mode has not been traced satisfactorily with regard to personality development. Until recently, psychiatrists and psychoanalysts have avoided studies which elucidate the effects of these handicaps. Through the late 1950s all significant research was done primarily by psychologists and educators. In a study using the Rorschach test, Levine (8) reported that the average deaf adolescent typically showed mental and emotional impassiveness, strong egocentric affectivity and personal inflexibility, with a notable absence of anxiety, depression, or paranoid feelings. Norris, *et al.* (9) reported that intelligence can progress in an orderly fashion in the blind child and sometimes can reach normal expectations; his work dispelled the idea that "blindisms" (rhythmic movements, head punching, hypokinesis) were due to associated brain damage.

Considerations of space make it impossible to provide a thorough review of psychological research on either the blind or the deaf. The interested reader is referred to the work of Barker, *et al.* (10) for reviews of both subjects up to the mid-1950s; to that of Cowen, *et al.* (11) on blindness, and to Levine (12), Myklebust (13), or Hess (14) for

147

comparable reviews of the psychological studies on the deaf.

It is generally agreed that neither handicap necessarily limits intellectual potential, although failures of the environment to provide adequate stimuli can stunt its achievement. In the deaf, full verbal facility is seldom reached, and the average deaf child leaves school at age eighteen with about fifth-grade skills in reading and mathematics.

Personality studies suggest that blind children and deaf children earn scores indicative of "maladjustment" more frequently than the unaffected, and that they are retarded in social maturity. For example, Myklebust (15) suggests that deaf college students may have less empathy and less ability to develop normal feelings of what is expected of them and may be more impulsive than their counterparts who hear. Most impressive is the fact that a range of "normal adjustment" and "normal functioning" is present in the majority of affected adults. Furth (16, 17), in a series of experiments modeled after Piaget (18), and Oleron (19, 20), argue that all aptitudes are available and capable of developing, if only we properly assess and encourage them.

Psychiatric and Psychoanalytic Findings

Psychiatrists and psychoanalysts have more recently expressed interest in these complex problems, approaching blindness from one end of the age spectrum and deafness from the other. Interest in the blind has been for the most part child-oriented, with the data derived from observations of the normal blind child and from treatment of the deviant (21-34). Some investigators have observed a prolonged oral phase with a delay in hand dominance. Purposeful reaching in response to a sound stimulus usually does not appear till eleven months of age, in contrast to six to seven months in the sighted, and objects are most often brought to the mouth for exploration. Thus, coordinated prehension is retarded and separation of hand-function from the mouth delayed. Indeed, in the deviant child, use of the hand may remain modeled after the mouth, with a peculiar type of chewing grasp retained well into latency.

Blind children also show a delay in mobility and a lengthened period of dependence on the parent. The absence of vision leaves only sound to entice the toddler to explore through movement, and realistic dangers may limit mobility. The prolonged dependence and restriction

148

of movement may also result in greater compliant behavior and a paucity of aggression.

Moreover, the absence of vision results in only a partial sense of objects, in a difference in object meaning, and perhaps in a delay in establishing a sense of object permanency. Thus, the dropped bottle is not pursued at six months, and it is not recognized if offered glass-end first until eleven months. Later, a square is perceived as four points, a paper puncher (with its click) is the same as a camera, and sand is equated with sugar. Residuals of this partial sense of objects may be seen in such questions as "Is there a hill on the road as well as the pavement?" or "Does it hurt the beads when you cut them?" Verbalization, at first delayed, may be precociously expanded in the following years, but many words may be parroted without understanding, or their meaning only partially understood.

Certain positive factors also may be recognized. What was first interpreted as withdrawal has in some cases emerged as rapt, alert attention, of which the hands fisted in eyes may even be a part. Tendencies toward independence and self-sufficiency may also be present. When the child of two or three ignores a fallen object, he may be stubbornly asserting his pride and denying the shame of his limitation, rather than failing to achieve a permanence of object representation. Self-control and high frustration tolerance are also required to limit mobility and to constrain aggressive or sudden movements. Memory, too, must develop precociously to organize and place the surrounding world and to hold in abeyance the partial meanings of words and objects for later synthesis and understanding.

The late effects of these difficult circumstances, heightened all too frequently by the depressive-withdrawal response of parents, remain speculative. The compliant parroting and dependence may lead to qualities of superficiality, hypocrisy and preening. The enforced limitation on mobility may yield obsessional characteristics, with underlying exaggerated fears of aggression and projected aggressive phantasies. Doubting uncertainty may also develop from the partial awareness of objects, or it may lead to a willingness to withhold judgment and wait patiently until all the facts are in. Impulsiveness is unlikely.

Investigators offer a number of astute suggestions to help the blind child accomplish the adaptive tasks of the early years (35). Of primary importance is the fact that the experience of the blind child is different

149

from that of the sighted and that it takes him more time to gain a working knowledge of the world. The child's growing need to hear in order to gain reassurance and encouragement can be exploited through the use of noise toys. The use of a wheeled walker, through which the child is drawn to locomotion as he leans toward the sound of his mother's voice, can encourage mobility (36). Toys that can be taken apart and then reassembled can contribute to feelings of success and to the concept of how parts contribute to the whole. Parents should feel free to talk about blindness, for acceptance of the handicap can free the child's intelligence and encourage his curiosity and reasoning. Psychotherapy for the parents, especially the mother, is often essential to develop awareness of feelings of shame and depression. Under optimal circumstances, the child may develop tortuously toward normality, despite his different framework of experience.

In the field of early total deafness, psychiatrists have worked primarily with adult patients and then extended their interest to the school-aged deaf and their families (37-43). By learning manual language, they opened up a pathway of communication that had until recently been entirely closed to psychological investigation. Thus, they found a welter of misdiagnoses, wherein disturbed, gesticulating, and nonverbal patients had been relegated to the waste-basket classification of "psychosis with mental deficiency." With the adjunct of manual communication many such misdiagnoses proved correctible, and the whole range of classical neurotic and psychotic disorders could be discerned. Treatment could then be directed to the disorder at hand and the ongoing results evaluated. Pharmacotherapy, psychotherapy, and group methods of treatment have all proven useful. Psychoanalysis, modified to permit face-to-face communication, was reported in several cases (44, 45). In hospitalized psychiatric patients, regardless of underlying diagnosis, the typical problems were found to comprise some form of impulsive, aggressive, often bizarre behavior, and in which accurate diagnosis required time and patience.

Educators plead for early recognition of deafness and prompt institution of auditory and language training. For the child, the imitation and understanding of words that appear as foreign bodies—seen or only felt on the lips and mouth of oneself or others—is a formidable task. Usually long years of residential schooling are required, and the "spoon-feeding" necessary to teach basic information may stultify creative and independent work. Under present conditions about one-quarter develop adequate speech ability, but academic achievement is limited for the majority. Education remains mostly orally oriented, and controversy exists over the use of manual language and finger spelling. Parents may even be advised to avoid using signs with children in order to encourage motivation for speech. This advice can obviously be misused in the parents' efforts to deny the handicap. In addition, the silence of the deaf child can make him particularly susceptible to serve as the screen on which a family neurosis may be projected and played out. For the child as well as the family, agonizing self-appraisal and depression commonly recur when the child reaches puberty, and motor ability at games is no longer sufficient to carry him through the enlarged scope of social relationships.

Despite these manifold problems—failure of early communication, disruption of the child-parent relationship, possible doublebinds, and uneven segmental development as maturation outpaces the tools of expression — schizophrenia is apparently no more frequent among the deaf than among the hearing. Psychological studies of the deaf have indicated ego rigidity, limitations in abstracting capacity, and signs indicative of maladjustment. In adult deaf patients, these qualities have been described by the author (46) as

a lack of understanding of and regard for the feelings of others [and] inadequate insight into the impact of their own behavior and its consequences. . . . [There is] a generally egocentric view of the world . . . demands unfettered by excessive control machinery, [and an] adaptive approach . . . characterized by gross coercive dependence. The preferred defensive reactions to tension and anxiety are typified by a kind of primitive riddance through action . . . [reflected behaviorally by] considerable impulsivity and the absence of much thoughtful introspection.

These traits are of special interest when coupled with the findings that retarded depression, accompanied by excessive guilt, seems rare among the deaf, while agitated depression characterized by anger is not. It would thus appear that the internalization of rage, necessary for the normal development of guilt and for the control of hostile impulses, may be limited in the life-long absence of audition. The findings have led to the inference that audition and verbal language are requisite parts of relationships whereby the wish to please is fostered and a conceptual level is developed sufficient to allow for the giving up of immediate gratification. Without these tools for defining feelings and nurturing empathic concern, the establishment of a system of self-restraint and self punishment based on guilt rather than fear alone may also be impeded.

In any event, the dynamic or supportive treatment of the deaf psychiatric patient is possible and can be as fruitful as the work with the hearing. The dreams of the deaf and of the blind have proved analyzable and useful in psychotherapy, although alertness must be maintained for the different associative pathways and means of symbolic expression derived from a lifetime of different experience (47, 48, 49). Preventive efforts are of equal importance, and group and individual consultation can be of great value, especially for the adolescent deaf child and his parents. Early diagnosis and prompt encouragement of open, clear, and expanded communication by all means possible is essential. Psychotherapy for parents, including a straightforward appraisal of the handicap's implications and a therapeutic clarification of the parents' response have been advocated. The exciting possibilities of direct play-therapy of the very young deaf child remain virtually unexplored.

In sum, it is clear that psychiatric interest in the blind and in the deaf has finally emerged, but our certain knowledge of the role of either perceptual mode in psychological development and function is still primitive. Sight may be helpful in the formation of psychic images, while word symbols and sound, perhaps, are required for their storage, manipulation and hierarchical organization. Continued psychiatric exploration of these areas has much to offer both clinically and theoretically. Hopefully, the work will be extended to the blind adult and deaf infant, and to longitudinal studies of sufficient depth and number to replace intelligent speculation with simple certainty.

REFERENCES

1. H. R. Blank, "Psychoanalysis and Blindness," *Psychoanalytic Quarterly,* 26:1, 1957.

2. H. Chevigny, *My Eyes Have a Cold Nose,* New Haven: Yale University Press, 1946.
3. E. Javal, *On Becoming Blind,* translated by Carroll E. Edson, New York: Macmillan Co., 1905.
4. P. H. Knapp, "Emotional Aspects of Hearing Loss," *Psychosomatic Medicine, 10:*203, 1948.
5. C. S. Ingalls, "Some Psychiatric Observations on Patients with Hearing Defect," *Occupational Therapy and Rehabilitation, 25:*62, 1946.
6. J. Bowlby, "The Nature of the Child's Tie to His Mother," *International Journal of Psychoanalysis, 39:*350, 1958.
7. R. A. Spitz, *A Genetic Field Theory of Ego Formation,* New York: International Universities Press, 1959.
8. E. S. Levine, *The Psychology of Deafness,* New York: Columbia University Press, 1960.
9. M. Norris, P. J. Spaulding, and F. H. Brodie, *Blindness in Children,* Chicago: University of Chicago Press, 1957.
10. R. G. Baker et al., *Adjustment to Physical Handicap and Illness: A Survey of the Social Psychology of Physique and Disability,* New York, Social Science Research Council, Bull. no. 55, 1953.
11. E. L. Cowen et al., *Adjustment to Visual Disability in Adolescence,* New York: American Foundation for the Blind, 1961.
12. E. S. Levine, *Youth in a Soundless World,* New York: New York University Press, 1956.
13. H. R. Myklebust, *The Psychology of Deafness: Sensory Deprivation, Learning and Adjustment,* New York: Grune & Stratton, 1960.
14. D. W. Hess, "Personality Adjustment in Deaf Children" (Nonverbal MAPS Test). Unpublished doctoral thesis, Rochester University, 1960.
15. H. R. Myklebust, *The Psychology of Deafness.*
16. H. G. Furth, "Research With the Deaf: Implications for Language and Cognition." *Psychological Bulletin, 62*(3):145, 1964.
17. H. G. Furth, *Thinking Without Language: Psychological Implications of Deafness,* New York: Free Press, 1966.
18. J. Piaget, *The Origins of Intelligence in Children,* New York: International Universities Press, 1952.
19. P. Oleron, "A Study of the Intelligence of the Deaf," *American Annals of the Deaf, 95:*179, 1950.
20. P. Oleron, "Conceptual Thinking of the Deaf," *American Annals of the Deaf, 98:*304, 1953.
21. H. R. Blank, "Psychoanalysis and Blindness," *Psychoanalytic Quarterly, 26:*1, 1957.
22. M. T. Bonaccorsi and H. Caplan, "Psychotherapy With a Blind Child." *Journal of the Canadian Psychiatric Association, 10:*393, 1965.

23. D. Burlingham, "Developmental Considerations in the Occupation of the Blind," *Psychoanalytic Study of the Child,* 22:187, 1967.
24. D. Burlingham, "Hearing and Its Role in the Development of the Blind," *Psychoanalytic Study of the Child,* 19:95, 1964.
25. D. Burlingham, "Some Notes on the Development of the Blind," *Psychoanalytic Study of the Child,* 16:121, 1961.
26. D. Burlingham, "Some Problems of Ego Development in Blind Children," *Psychoanalytic Study of the Child,* 20:194, 1965.
27. S. Fraiberg and D. A. Freedman, "Studies in the Ego Development of the Congenitally Blind Child," *Psychoanalytic Study of the Child,* 19:113, 1964.
28. S. Fraiberg, B. L. Siegel, and R. Gibson, "The Role of Sound in the Search Behavior of a Blind Infant," *Psychoanalytic Study of the Child,* 21:327, 1966.
29. W. R. Keeler, "Autistic Patterns and Defective Communication in Blind Children with Retrolental Fibroplasia," *Psychopathology of Communication,* edited by P. H. Hoch and J. Zubin, New York: Grune and Stratton, 1958.
30. G. S. Klein, "Blindness and Isolation," *Psychoanalytic Study of the Child,* 17:82, 1962.
31. H. Nagera and A. B. Colonna, "Aspects of the Contribution of Sight to Age and Drive Development: A Comparison of Development of Some Blind and Sighted Children," *Psychoanalytic Study of the Child,* 20:267, 1965.
32. E. B. Omwake and A. J. Solnit, " 'It Isn't Fair'—The Treatment of a Blind Child," *Psychoanalytic Study of the Child,* 16:352, 1961.
33. R. H. Stewart, "The Psychotherapy of a Blind Schizophrenic Child," *Journal of the American Academy of Child Psychiatrists,* 4:123, 1965.
34. D. M. Wills, "Some Observations on Blind Nursery School Children's Understanding of Their World," *Psychoanalytic Study of the Child,* 20:344, 1965.
35. S. Fraiberg and D. A. Freedman, "Studies in the Ego Development of the Congenitally Blind Child, *Psychoanalytic Study of the Child,* 19:113, 1964.
36. S. Fraiberg, B. L. Siegel, and R. Gibson, "The Role of Sound in the Search Behavior of a Blind Infant," *Psychoanalytic Study of the Child,* 21:327, 1966.
37. K. Z. Altshuler, "Personality Traits and Depressive Symptoms in the Deaf," *Recent Advances in Biological Psychiatry,* Vol. VI, edited by J. Wortis, New York: Plenum Press, 1963.
38. K. Z. Altshuler, "Psychiatric Considerations in the School Age Deaf," *American Annals of the Deaf,* 107:553, 1962.

39. J. D. Rainer et al., *Family and Mental Health Problems in a Deaf Population*. New York: New York State Psychiatric Institute, 1963.
40. K. Z. Altshuler and J. D. Ranier, "Patterns and Course of Schizophrenia in the Deaf," *Journal of Nervous and Mental Diseases, 127*:77, 1958.
41. K. Z. Altshuler and M. D. Sarlin, "Deafness and Schizophrenia. Interrelation of Communication Stress, Maturation Lag and Schizophrenia Risk," *Expanding Goals of Genetics in Psychiatry*, edited by F. J. Kallmann, New York: Grune & Stratton, 1962.
42. J. D. Rainer and K. Z. Altshuler, *Comprehensive Mental Health Services for the Deaf*, New York State Psychiatric Institute, New York, 1966.
43. J. D. Rainer et al., *Family and Mental Health Problems in a Deaf Population*, New York State Psychiatric Institute, New York, 1963.
44. K. Z. Altshuler, "Personality Traits and Depressive Symptoms in the Deaf," *Recent Advances in Biological Psychiatry*, Vol. VI, edited by J. Wortis, New York: Plenum Press, 1963.
45. J. D. Rainer, K. Z. Altshuler, and F. J. Kallmann, "Psychotherapy for the Deaf," *Advances in Psychosomatic Medicine*, Vol. III, edited by B. Stokvis, Basel: S. Karger, 1963.
46. K. Z. Altshuler, "Personality Traits and Depressive Symptoms in the Deaf," *Recent Advances in Biological Psychiatry*, Vol. VI, edited by J. Wortis, New York: Plenum Press, 1963.
47. *Ibid.*, "Personality Traits and Depressive Symptoms in the Deaf."
48. H. R. Blank, "Dreams of the Blind," *Psychoanalytic Quarterly, 27*:158, 1958.
49. E. Deutsch, "The Dream Imagery of the Blind," *Psychoanalytic Review, 15*:288, 1928.

11

Loss of Sexual Function in the Male

Alexander P. Orfirer

The tendency to evolve stereotypes is a common approach to those areas of human relationships where information is limited and emotional involvement is great. Stereotypes serve to simplify those matters which threaten to be disturbing and complicated, and in this way they seem to offer ready answers. Stereotypes exist in many areas of human relationships, and particularly in the area of human sexuality. Stereotypes are part of our culture and, except where they are countered by special experience or special knowledge, they are shared by all members of that culture. Certain stereotypes regarding the sexual behavior of the human male are shared by the general public and professional people as well. According to one such stereotype, sexual function in the adult male is seen as an uninhibited, almost mechanical and automatic activity requiring only an appropriate stimulus and intact physical equipment. The model for this is well known in literature and particularly well depicted in the movie *Tom Jones* based on the Fielding novel. The effect of the pervasiveness of such attitudes is reflected in the depression of the male who at one time or another fails to perform according to the model. What the stereotypes fail to take into account are developmental factors and special feelings which will determine sexual expression for a particular male. Another habitual attitude concerns sexual activity for the elderly male, for whom sexual interest is assumed normally not to exist. The same is assumed for patients with chronic illnesses and disabilities. As a result of these stereotypes, our knowledge of the sexual function in the male in special situations is greatly limited and our ability to deal with variations from this supposed norm is hampered.

The adult male who for some reason does not function sexually in a particular situation will usually assume that this is the result of some defect in his physical equipment, an attitude which was until recently rather generally shared by physicians who viewed the problem in purely physiological terms. The assumption exists that for the elderly man, or for the patient with chronic illness, a biological change has occurred which makes sexual function no longer possible or appealing. When, despite this assumption, he finds himself or others find him expressing a sexual interest, the reaction is often one of denial, shame, or rejection.

In recent years, however, studies have been made, notably by Kinsey *et al.* (1) and Masters and Johnson (2), in an effort to break through the stereotypes and to learn more about the realities of sexual function in the male. In addition, insights from psychiatry and psychoanalysis have given us a perspective on sexual function not previously available. As a result, we are now able to see that sexual function is determined not only by its biological basis but also by developmental, emotional, and cultural factors. For example, the young male approaching his first sexual experience often sees it as a test of his physical equipment. However, despite his conscious concern regarding his genitals and their functioning, we can recognize that his functioning will depend as much on his emotions and attitudes as on his organic integrity. We are now aware that underlying fantasies, feelings of anxiety and guilt, his attitudes toward himself as a person, and his history of relationships with other people, will determine reactions in the sexual situation. It can be generalized that everything in the individual's emotional development and current emotional experience can to some degree affect his sexual functioning. It is also important to think of sexual functioning as more than the ability to have an erection at the proper moment. It includes the attitudes which are necessary to maintain a stable and intimate relationship with a member of the opposite sex.

Among the experiences which will have a strong impact on the male's sexual functioning will be those involving losses, such as in a significant relationship, through death or separation. Any disease or injury which threatens to have an effect on his genital equipment may also evoke

157

overwhelming feelings of loss. This may affect sexual function. Since an intact physical structure has a great symbolic importance in the development of the image of masculinity, even injuries or illnesses not involving the genitals directly may nevertheless evoke a sense of loss and deprivation of sexual function.

Sexual Development in the Male

Psychoanalytic investigation and the direct observation of children gives a background for the understanding of the sexual reactions of the adult to both emotional and physical losses in later life. We begin with the observation that the sexual development of the adult male takes place over the whole period of his lifetime. It goes hand in hand with his physical and emotional development, and his relationships with important figures in his early life. These first experiences as an infant with other human beings will have an important bearing on what he brings into the later stages of his development.

If his earliest needs receive a normal degree of gratification, this will establish a background of warmth and trust on the basis of which he can move from being completely dependent as an infant, into his second and third years when he develops a sense of his own body, an ability to master some of its functions and, given proper encouragement and protection, finds satisfaction in his own thrusts toward activity and control. All of this must leave room for reassurance that he can turn again, if need arises, to the protection of a passive and dependent position from which he can again move forward. As he moves into his fourth and fifth years of life he becomes aware of the sexual differences in the people around him and that these involve definite sexual roles. At the same time he becomes aware that he himself is involved in these differences. He is no longer just Johnny, he is also a boy, "like Daddy." This gives him a certain role and certain expectations. He finds himself identified with Daddy but at the same time recognizes that there are considerable differences between Daddy and himself. Daddy is seen as a giant and appears able to do anything. He is a rival for the attentions of his mother, toward whom he feels special and possessive feelings. In the course of this period he may find himself with considerable mixed feelings toward these important people in his life. At times he will have aggressive competitive strivings with considerable overestimations in his fantasies of what he can or would like to do. At the same or other times he may feel envious, angry, and frightened in the face of the disappointment of his wishes and strivings and in the face of what he sees as his own physical inadequacies. As he confronts new challenges in his development he may feel very keenly the loss of his more dependent past relationship with his mother and attempt to retreat to that rather than meet what he may see as the almost impossible demands to measure up to the people around him, especially Daddy. Daddy appears, at times, as a model beyond the bounds of possibility and yet a very exciting one. In the normal course of development he finds he is not really expected to do as father does. That will come later. He and his parents find pleasure in what he can do now and in the perception of the growth of his own skills and abilities. The need to compete with his father and the desire for the sole possession of his mother are given up for objectives in the future. He arrives at this point of development with a certain sense of his own identity as a boy and future man, a confidence in his own integrity and a knowledge of his body and what it can do under his control. At the same time he can accept his dependence on others and the limitations on his independence. His relationships within his family give him a pattern which will serve as a background for his future experiences with others.

During this entire development he is, because of his dependent position, prone to fantasies of physical vulnerability and abandonment. Experiences such as the absence of his mother at a crucial time, the absence of supportive responses from his environment, or the experience of a surgical procedure without adequate preparation, may give rise to doubts about his intactness and to fantasies of irreversible loss and damage. The fantasies the child develops about himself and the world around him will determine the attitudes with which he will deal with future events. Fantasies in which he perceives himself as damaged may lead him to react to later events with attitudes of submission and passivity rather than attitudes of activity or assertion. If his experience leads to an image of the world as depriving and threatening he will have difficulty in accepting help or even a close relationship whenever he feels not in control.

In the course of this development there is an intricate interweaving of his sexual feelings with his attitudes toward the integrity of his body, his mastery over his physical functions, and his ability to control. Experience of loss, whether it is of an important person or of his

159

sense of physical integrity, will affect the emotional concerns on which his sexual image is based. A major loss may cause him to pull back to an earlier, more dependent stage of his development. If this is too threatening to his own ideals of what a "big boy" should be, he may cling to rigid attitudes of independence or denial which makes coping with future experiences in a flexible and realistic way very difficult. If those in this environment respond to his temporary regressions in an understanding way and help him with his feelings, he can recover with a renewed sense of mastery.

With this developmental model in mind we can approach the experience of loss in the adult and its effect on his sexual function with an understanding which takes into account both universal tendencies and individual variations. The feeling of loss can occur as a reaction to a variety of experiences. Its importance lies in the meaning it has for the individual on the basis of his past experience. The same loss will have great significance for some and very little for others. However, even with individual variations there are experiences which universally will evoke feelings of loss. Among those most commonly encountered are the loss of significant persons and the loss of body integrity through illness or injury. In addition, and of special significance here, are those injuries which involve an interference or a threat of interference with sexual function.

External Losses and Sexual Reactions

An external loss, such as the death of a significant person, will set into motion a process which is described as grief or mourning. This process (3) consists of a painful period of sadness and preoccupation with thoughts and feelings connected with the loved one. To some extent, there will be a loss of interest in other people and other matters in the outside world. By definition, normal mourning is a temporary process during which the individual, while clinging to his attachments to the loved one, at the same time engages in a painful process of gradual withdrawal from those attachments. As this gradual withdrawal is accomplished, the capacity for new or renewed attachments is again restored. Clinically, this process may extend over a period of months. The experience is often an uneven one, with alternations of withdrawal into mourning and resumptions of tendencies toward normal ties.

160

For the physician, the observation of sadness in the family is a familiar one. Less familiar are the vicissitudes of the sexual feelings during this period. For many of his patients there will be a withdrawal in the area of the usual loving and sexual feelings, which in most cases is accepted by the spouse. In a male who cannot overtly express grief there may be a silent withdrawal.

In one such instance the wife of a usually attentive husband expressed her bewilderment at the fact that for the last few months her husband had withdrawn from her sexually. She was concerned that there was some deep disturbance in their marriage. When she was reminded of his relatively recent loss due to the death of an older sister who had raised him, she reported that while he was upset at the funeral there had been no discussion of the sister since then. The wife had assumed that he had recovered from his loss and she had not associated his withdrawal from her with the death of his sister. However, she recognized that it was his pattern to conceal his feelings and she was encouraged to talk with him about his loss. She was successful in this effort and was surprised at the amount of feeling he had suppressed. As he was enabled with his wife's support to experience the painful feelings related to his grief, they were able to resume their former relationship. In talking with his wife, he confessed one day that part of his sexual withdrawal lay in his concern that his unexpressed feelings of grief were childish in their intensity and therefore unmanly. He was fearful, therefore, that he would be unacceptable and impotent. Thus, his sexual withdrawal was the only overt expression of his grief.

Since emotional withdrawal is widely experienced in mourning, the image of sexual avoidance during this period has been elevated to the status of a stereotype. This stereotype is sustained by the feeling that it is indulgent to seek pleasure at such a time. This view of sexual activity is a very restrictive one, since one of the vital aspects of a mature sexual relationship is the capacity for closeness with a loved person and the comfort and reassurance to be derived from that at times of stress. It is often forgotten that sexual activity can have varied functions other than procreation and pleasure. Since it can be expressive of warmth, love, and tenderness it can remind a bereaved person that he is not alone, that he has someone with whom he can share his feelings, all of which can be a source of considerable consolation. However, in the aftermath of loss, the expression and experience of sexual feelings may be unexpected and misunderstood.

161

REACTION TO PARTIAL LOSS

In one instance, a physician described the experience of making a condolence call on a friend who was a patient of his, and who had lost his father about a week earlier. After the usual greetings, the wife of his friend asked to see him privately in another room. She told him of her husband's evident grief at his loss, but then with much embarrassment told the doctor that for the past two nights he had wanted to have intercourse with her. She had reacted to this with a concern that this represented some gross insensitivity on his part and had refused his overtures. He had reproached her and obviously felt very hurt by her rebuff. She felt uncertain about her reaction and wanted the doctor's impression of her husband's behavior. He assured her that he thought this did not indicate anything other than an effort to find consolation. Although she was a woman with a need to be "proper," there was sufficient warmth in her relationship with her husband to enable her to accept this reassurance.

A much greater anguish is often experienced in those instances where there has been the loss of a mate. In the inevitable loneliness there is often experienced an intense desire for physical closeness. For the male this may be felt as a need for an intimacy with a woman who will be supportive and comforting, and may be accompanied by feelings of sexual desire. These feelings may also represent an unconscious effort at a reunion with the loved one. Because of the setting in which such feelings arise there is inner turmoil involving feelings of dismay and guilt. He perceives his feelings as an infidelity and may engage in severe self-accusations. Some may throw themselves into activities in an effort to ward off any such feelings. Others may use tranquillizers or barbiturates in their attempt to ward off any sexual fantasies. The sexual feelings may be experienced in unexpected and unguarded moments. Dreams of the dead mate may have an unmistakable sexual content or feeling. The sleeper arises with an awareness of a sexual longing but is self-critical for thinking of his wife in this "selfish" way.

One man, long after the event, recalled how shortly after the death of his wife, he was talking with a woman relative of his when he broke into tears. The woman reached out in a comforting way and held his hand. He was suddenly aware and perturbed by a rush of sexual longing toward this woman. In response to this event, for several days he tried to maintain a tight control over any expression of feeling in public out of fear that a sexual longing would accompany it. He gradually recognized that he need not be concerned that he would act on them.

162

For other individuals the pain of mourning may seem too great to be tolerated, the sense of loss too keen to be endured, and such persons may attempt to use the pleasurable intensity of the sexual function in a truly defensive way. Their effort is to ward off the experience of mourning by a type of denial. Through sexual activity they attempt to reassure themselves that they have not suffered a loss. The pleasurable feelings which sexual activity can offer include the response of another person, which is a reassurance that one is not alone or abandoned. The common wisdom that frowns on a bereaved person's making a permanent attachment too soon after a loss is, in part, a recognition of the defensive nature of attachments made before normal grief work has been completed.

Most people, of course, work through their experience of mourning with the help of family, friends, and their own inner resources. The process is painful and takes time. However, it is not uncommon that the professional person may be in a position to be of help to the person who has suffered such a loss or to the family who seeks an understanding of the grief-stricken. To be most helpful he must have an understanding of the basic concept of grief and at the same time of the variety of reactions which can be expected. He will know that one should avoid judgments, that each individual has his own needs and his own background. He will recognize that his greatest service will consist of supporting the process of grief. This may best be accomplished by attention to and respect for the feelings which the individual should be helped to express in words. The opportunity to talk to an interested and sympathetic person can be a tremendous relief in itself. In such a context some of the concerns and perplexities about a variety of feelings, including the sexual, may be expressed. Often, very little may need to be explained. As the bereaved one is able to discuss his feelings he may recognize, for example, that the sexual feelings causing his guilt are an expression of longing. For others, the support may make it possible to face the work of mourning and therefore make it unnecessary to use some of the defensive maneuvers mentioned to ward off the process.

The opportunity to talk may relieve two of the feelings which sometimes are related to the awareness of sexual stirrings. One of these feelings is anxiety. Anxiety is often a reflection of the concern that the sexual desires will be acted upon. The verbal expression of this anxiety may act as a reassurance that such feelings can be recognized without being acted out.

The other relates to feelings of guilt. Guilt may be associated directly with the sexual feelings or may, in a more general way, be a part of the whole experience of mourning.

A man who had already accused himself of having neglected his wife became aware of some sexual longings. In his guilt he accused himself of being a "sex maniac" who deserved punishment. This was a transient phase of his grief reaction. As he was able to discuss some of his intense feelings he found they were associated with many ambivalent feelings toward his dead wife.

The doctor's degree of self-awareness may be an important factor in his ability to be of help. If he is made uncomfortable by discussion of sexual feelings or of grief he may not respond to the cues that are offered to him. However, if he has the ability to tolerate these feelings and to recognize that his values and experiences are not necessarily universal, he will recognize the efforts of the grieving person to express his distressed feelings. Since the guilt feelings and the sexual feelings are both associated with shame the individual may show them only in an indirect way and sometimes in a fashion which implies that he is not only preoccupied with the thoughts he is suggesting.

A recent widower, with an effort at humor, told his doctor that he guessed that some men he knew would be thinking about other women. The doctor wisely used this as an opportunity to show his interest and asked him if he sometimes found himself concerned about such thoughts. The patient immediately denied this but a few days later did take the opportunity to talk to his doctor about his sexual concerns.

Losses Through Bodily Illness or Injury and Their Impact on Sexual Function

In the course of acute illnesses or injuries there is often an impact on sexual function, which for the most part goes unnoticed since it rarely presents a problem. The patient who is in a passive dependent position, anxious and self-concerned, will have minimal sexual drive. Since such illnesses are limited in time, the patient will usually return to his

164

former state of full function. The psychological impact, in most instances, is equally reversible.

However, as developments in medical science have succeeded in maintaining life in the face of illness and trauma, more people are faced with the prospect of living with a chronic disability. The disability threatens their feelings of integrity, self-esteem, and identity. The patient's identifiations may be weakened in regard to his occupational status since he is no longer able to participate in a segment of the work of the world around him, with its built-in supportive social structure. The loss of work may mean a loss of a sense of being active and in control of the environment. His relationships to other people undergo both gross and subtle changes. All of this, together with the change in his body image, may literally cause the patient to feel that he is no longer the same person. Such changes may make necessary the building of a new image and relationship to the world around him. The loss of his former image is experienced as equivalent in feeling to the death of another person, and will evoke some of the same processes of mourning. The confrontation with his defect will almost inevitably cause problems in the sexual area. His ability to operate in the area of sexual function will depend on the degree to which he can maintain his basic image of himself and his self-esteem.

The impact of this disability may cause a regression to more primitive attitudes, reminiscent of earlier stages of development, and revive old fantasies and conflicts. These fantasies will lead to difficulties in interpreting the reality of his injury and cause him to unconsciously equate damage to his body with injury to the executive organ of his masculinity, his penis. He may interpret any disability in a global way as meaning that he is simply no longer capable of any degree of function.

Some of these attitudes were illustrated in the case of a man in his early fifties who suffered a moderately disabling left hemiplegia. He was the owner of a small business which his eldest son effectively managed with advice and suggestions from him. He had a good relationship with his wife and his family. His initial reaction to his illness was a sense of hopeless grief which was, at times, overwhelming to his family. During this period he found it difficult to participate in the rehabilitation problem at the hospital. With support from the staff and his family he was able to express

165

his concern over his dependent position and with their encouragement began to accept the suggestion that he need not be a helpless invalid. The staff was careful to establish goals in a gradual way. It was essential that planning be done with him rather than for him. As he accepted the rehabilition goal he was able to resume ambulation with the aid of a cane and to recover limited function in his left arm. In the hospital he continued at times to be mildly to moderately depressed. He had always taken a great deal of pride in his physical activities, having been an excellent golfer and tennis player. He often spoke during depressed periods of feeling that he was "less than half a man." Other times he asked, "How can I hold my head up in the world?" The full meaning of these complaints became more clear during his first weekend at home following a period of progress in the hospital. He anticipated the visit with both pleasure and anxiety. Upon his return to the hospital he was very depressed and refused to discuss the weekend. His wife asked to see his physician and she described how Saturday had been a great success. On retiring her husband had asked her to "come to bed" with him. She was surprised at his wish to have intercourse since she was concerned that "he might hurt himself." However, she consented, but he was awkward because of his difficulty in movement and lost his erection. The remainder of the weekend was a disaster, nothing went well and everyone, including the patient, was relieved by his return to the hospital. If it were not for the wife's frankness in discussing the matter the staff would have been unaware of the reason for the patient's sudden depression.

The wife discussed her own surprise at her husband's sexual interest, feeling that someone this ill would not be interested in sexual intercourse. She was advised to tell her husband that she had discussed the experience with his physician. In his discussion with the physician the patient realized that he had taken his failure as proof that his illness had rendered him impotent. His previously voiced concerns that he was "less than half a man" had at times consciously included a conviction that his genitals were as damaged as his limbs. However, he had been unable to voice his concern and unfortunately the staff had not encouraged him to discuss his feelings. After several meetings with the wife and husband they were more able to realistically accept his physical limitations and also his continued ability to function in the sexual area. Together they were able to accommodate for his disability through changes in their accustomed sexual positions. Both of them were helped to accept the need for the wife's increased activity in the sexual act. With these discussions of their general attitudes toward his illness and of their feelings about sexual matters the patient recovered his sexual potency.

166

Ford and Orfirer (4) discuss the common expectation on the part of staff, family, and patients that the sexual life of such patients comes to an end with their illness. This attitude is rarely verbalized but is reflected in an unconscious avoidance of the subject on the part of physicians and other health personnel. It is appropriate to view the reestablishment of a mature sexual relationship as a factor in the rehabilitation program.

One reason for the attitudes of pessimism may lie in the physician's emotional identification with the feelings of loss and grief which the patient is experiencing. He may share with the patient the sense of helplessness and irreversible damage which causes the patient to seek security in a state of dependency and in the avoidance of efforts which would threaten to recall the impact of the original trauma which was so overwhelming.

On another level this attitude of limited expectation of rehabilitation efforts may have its roots in an era when methods of rehabilitation were primitive and meager. During that period a major disability would condemn a patient to a life of helpless invalidism, complicated by contractures and intercurrent infections which frequently led to the patient's death. With the recent developments in rehabilitation techniques and other advances in medicine, there are far greater possibilities for an active life for the patient.

As yet, there have been only a few studies of the possibilities for an active sexual life for the disabled patient. These studies suggest that our preconceived notions and stereotyped ideas prevent us from realizing that these patients may be able to achieve an active sexual relationship. In a study of patients following cerebrovascular accident, it was found that although 29 percent of 105 patients below the age of 60 reported their libido was decreased, 60 percent said it was unchanged or increased (5). The same group reported that the frequency of coitus decreased for 43 per cent but was unchanged or increased for 22 per cent. However, the information from 35 per cent was inadequate. The report that actual sexual experience is decreased more than sexual drive suggests the importance of psychological and social factors in determining the sexual behavior of the disabled patient. Among those factors are the availability of a sexual partner and the attitude of that partner toward intercourse with a damaged person.

It is quite possible that if the patient mentioned above had not precipitated the crisis, and perhaps more important, if the wife had not been willing to share her concern with the doctor, this would have been an instance in which sexual function would not have been recovered. The effect on this man's subsequent general function would be difficult to estimate. On the other hand, many such couples do overcome such obstacles on their own, but this effort must be made at a time when they are already burdened with many adjustments. It is a time when outside support and understanding could make a significant contribution. For the man, the recognition that he can reestablish his sexual function, can experience pleasure and share this pleasure with his spouse, is of special importance at this time of diminished function in other areas (6).

Impact of Feelings of Loss on Sexual Function in Illnesses Which May Physically Involve the Genital Organs

Thus far we have dealt primarily with the effect of symbolic mutilations and losses and have discussed the effects on sexual function. In this section we must deal with the combination of symbolic loss plus actual or threatened damage to the genitals. It is interesting to note how literature treats the reaction to loss of the genital function. Occasional war stories mention soldiers whose genitals are damaged—they either commit suicide or are mercifully helped to die by fellow soldiers. The emphasis, to which the male reader responds with sympathy, is that this is the one injury which no man can tolerate. In literature war is described as a situation in which a man literally as well as figuratively puts his manhood on the line.

A description of direct injury to the genitals and a study of the reaction of the man who has endured it is rare in the medical literature. However, certain categories of injury which involve the male genitalia are described in the medical literature. These are of importance since they may evoke a sense of horror and loss similar to that suggested in fiction. Two well known categories of injury and illness which pose a threat to genital intactness are, first, the group of spinal cord injuries and, second, surgical procedures to the genital area. There have been important studies which can give the physician a perspective to counter the pessimistic fantasies of his patients and their families in these instances.

Genital Surgery

The most common form of genital operation in the adult male is a prostatectomy. This operation brings together the influence of aging as well as surgery on sexual function. The common assumption shared by patients, families, and often physicians alike, is that both surgery and aging will end the sexual life of these patients.

However, it is essential to note that in regard to aging, studies (7, 8, 9) have shown that upward of 90 per cent of married men at the age of 60 continue to lead an active sexual life. Furthermore, from the ages of 65 to 70 more than 70 per cent are still active. Though this represents a decline it is not of the degree usually pictured, since these studies indicate that the most important factor in the decline is the availability of a responsive partner. Therefore, widowers and bachelors suffer the greatest decline. For the married man limitations on his sexual activity may be related to the health or attitudes of his wife.

Since the effect of aging on sexual function is not as catastrophic as once assumed, what then is the effect on the man who experiences difficulty in urogenital function and then must face the threat of surgery to his genitals? Many of the men facing this threat are married and have been sexually active. In a comparative study of surgical approaches to prostatectomy, Finkle and Prian (10) found that 88 per cent of the married men who are potent before operation retained their potency afterward; that after perineal prostatectomy 71 per cent retained potency; after an open suprapubic operation 87 per cent retained their potency; and after a transurethral resection 95 per cent retained their potency. Again, these figures are in dramatic contrast to the usual impressions and should serve to counteract the effect of those impressions.

Spinal Cord Injuries

In contrast to the above discussion, spinal cord injuries usually involve a younger age group. The effect on the genital apparatus is not as direct

169

as in surgery but often much more profound since it involves the inner-vation of the genital organs which mediate erection, ejaculation, and orgasm. This type of injury frequently evokes a nightmarish image of paralysis, helplessness, dependency, and loss of any hope of mascu-line function. Again, this type of attitude is not confined to the patient. Although professional people are, to one extent or another, familiar with the rehabilitation efforts available to such patients, not nearly enough are familiar with the nature of the neurological disturbances of sexual function in patients with spinal cord injuries. It is, of course, essential for the physician to be aware of the specific degree of sexual functioning which can be expected in the face of a particular neuro-logical deficit. An excellent survey of this topic is available in a report by Bors and Comarr (11). Their description of the effect of various neurological lesions on sexual function is helpful in pointing out the variety of ways in which the genitalia are affected. In their post-World War II survey of the effect of spinal cord damage on sexual function, they found the following: that erections are retained in from 63.5 to 94 per cent, varying from study to study, and that intercourse was re-ported by 23 to 33 per cent. Ejaculation was rarer; reports vary from 3 to 20 per cent, and orgasm was reported by 3 to 14 per cent. One to 5 per cent were reported to have fathered children. These bare figures do not do justice to the significant variations and possibilities for sexual gratification and functions. Despite the nature of the injury, interest in the other sex and the desire for intercourse or the regret of im-potence are present in all male patients.

A significant report by Guttman (12) on the married life of para-plegics and tetraplegics emphasizes that sexual relationships for patients with spinal cord injury do not stop with the injury and the subse-quent deficits in function. In his description of 1,316 male paraplegics and tetraplegics, 605 were married and living with their partners at the time of admission to a rehabilitation center. The majority of these marriages occurred after the injury. Of 678 males who were single at the time of admission, approximately 40 per cent married after admis-sion. The percentage of divorces is approximately 7.3 per cent but when adjusted to include remarriages is only 5.1 per cent. This is a report from Great Britain and it is significant that the divorce rate is only slightly higher than the over-all British divorce rate. Guttman com-ments that, "The former widespread belief that individuals with severe

170

lesions of the spinal cord are necessarily impotent and sterile is unfounded and sexual readjustment is possible." He reports further that in some studies over 50 per cent of paraplegics and tetraplegics are not sterile. (In his group, 108 males fathered 204 children.) He concludes that "it has been proved beyond all doubt that paraplegics and even tetraplegics make very satisfactory partners in marriage, and this applies to marriage both before and after injury. Their marriages are, of course, subject to all the problems encountered in marriages of the able-bodied but their divorce rate is not significantly higher."

The study by Guttman adds an important dimension to the neurological study by Bors and Comarr. Guttman brings into perspective the ability of patients to maintain their masculine role despite the loss of active muscular ability and even genital function, which in the course of development had been identified by them as essential to masculinity, and their ability either to continue or to assume the role of husband or father. We must assume, therefore, a capacity even in those men who may have lost some aspect of genital function to restructure their image of masculinity to one that enables them to achieve development in which active attitudes and more mature concepts of independence and responsibility toward others become primary. This idea suggests that masculinity consists of more than the function of the genital itself. In line with this, Guttman notes that in England adoptive agencies have placed children in families where the father is paraplegic and sterile.

We can often recognize the role of illness and loss as precipitating the regression of the individual toward earlier attitudes of helplessness and dependency. Guttman's article suggests the possibility that loss and illness can serve as a stimulus toward a new phase of development leading to a new maturity.

The Return of Sexual Function

The return of sexual function following a loss depends on the nature of the loss and the meaning of that loss to the individual concerned. In the case of the death of a significant person, the loss for most adults is a single blow (although it may have many ramifications) from which the individual recovers through the process of grief and mourning. The

171

sense of depletion and deprivation occasions a turning in on the self which is temporary. This lack of interest in the outside world will frequently be accompanied by a giving up of sexual function. Feelings of guilt based on earlier hostilities toward the one who is lost, or regret over actual or fantasized neglect may interfere with the ability to engage in activities which bring pleasure. As the process of mourning proceeds, the individual is again able gradually to turn his attachments to others. It is essential to recognize the nature of grief as a reparative process which, though painful, is necessary for the future well-being of the individual concerned. It is a time when the individual may be preoccupied with making moral judgments of himself. The mourner will need the reassurance that his feelings are normal and that any interest in sexual activity is not condemned. If he is concerned about a lack of interest in sex this also can be explained as part of the temporary reactions to mourning. Essential to all of this is the ability of the mourner to tolerate the experience of his grief. Those around him must understand the necessity of supporting his mourning. A sympathetic attitude on the part of friends and relatives will indicate that feelings of sadness and loss are accepted. If they can recognize that reminiscences have the effect of alleviating the pain of mourning they will avoid misplaced efforts at protection by avoiding the topic of the loss.

In the case of illness or injury which leaves a lasting disability the patient must deal with a loss of a different nature. He must face not only the initial recognition of the disability, but also the everyday reminder of its persistence. His grief lies in relinquishing his previous self-image and acknowledging a new and painful reality. In the course of rebuilding his image of himself he will need reassurance and support.

The grief incurred by a physical loss is particularly difficult for many people to share. Often family and friends may hinder the process of mourning and the acceptance of the reality of loss by denials of the loss and false assurances of recovery. They may see him now only in terms of his loss and therefore in a painfully inferior position. Because of the loss he experiences himself as helpless and worthless, perhaps even as repulsive and ugly. Efforts are therefore made to deny the disability or its consequences. The paraplegic patient is often told not to think of his injury and that he will soon be walking "better than ever." His denial breaks down constantly in the face of reality and it is the task of the rehabilitation team to help him with these and other feelings.

As the patient with a permanent disability embarks on a rehabilitation program he is faced not only with the loss but also with the reality of what he has not lost and what with effort he can recover. The challenge of recovering certain functions and exploiting the many functions he has not lost will evoke many conflicts. The degree to which he can resolve these conflicts will have considerable bearing on his perception of himself as a sexually functioning person.

The conflicts stem from the fact that in human development there are contrasting needs which unconsciously exist side by side: the need to be passive and helpless, active and assertive; to be dependent and protected, and independent and in control. For the average person in normal circumstances these possible responses are subject to the demands of reality. The individual can be dependent and passive in ordinary illness, and can resume his independent and active role when the illness is over. However, where there have always existed tendencies toward dependence and passivity the sense of anxiety evoked by a continued disability may enforce these attitudes. To such an individual activity and independence always represented a danger and provoked feelings of anxiety and inadequacy. An evident injury is accepted as a relief from the struggle to maintain their independence. For this type of patient independence always had the meaning of being abandoned to cope with one's own needs or outer demands with inadequate abilities, skills, preparation, or support. His tendency, therefore, is to fall back and hold on to the support occasioned by his illness even though it does put him into a child-like dependent state.

On the other hand there are patients who find their dependency needs so unacceptable that even where the reality demands a certain concession they are unable to comply. They fear that dependency will place them in a situation in which they will be either exploited or abandoned and they therefore must maintain the appearance of independence. This leads to a denial of the disability and makes it impossible to develop the new skills and mastery to overcome the threat to independence.

Individuals with backgrounds of emotional deprivation have a tendency to retreat to a passive dependent position. A long-standing conflict about their sexual role often accompanies this tendency. They may utilize their disability as a justified resolution of their sexual conflicts. LeBan, *et al.* (13) describe a group of men with back injuries

173

who came from emotionally deprived backgrounds. Following their illness they were impotent in their sexual and general adjustment. They appeared to relinquish their masculine role, made little effort to return to work and willingly accepted the function of housekeeper while their wives worked.

The first step in the rehabilitation process is to recognize the patient's need for protection and reassurance to deal with the anxiety and depression aroused by the loss. If this is made available to the patient in a manner which conveys a basic respect for him, he can allow his feelings to surface. Tactful responses to his efforts to verbalize his feelings will give him the opportunity to see himself and his relationships with others in a more realistic way.

One patient who was able to speak of his despondency about his degree of disability disparaged himself by speaking of himself as childish because of his expression of grief. The nurse to whom he spoke told him that his grief was understandable and conveyed to him by her attitudes that her respect for him as a man was neither diminished by his disability nor by his expression of feeling. He was then for the first time able to speak of his self-disgust which he was certain others must inevitably share. The next day, in a joking way he asked the nurse if she would have a date with him that night. She recognized his anxiety about his sexual role, and in a joking way told him that in time she was sure that he would find girls who would be interested in him. He was obviously relieved by her reply and went on to discuss some of the details of his physical therapy program.

As the patient experiences some relief from his anxiety, he recognizes that whatever his losses there are rehabilitative potentials which can restore him to an active role. This role may differ from his familiar past, but he will gradually recognize that it is worthy of his respect and that of others.

With the help of staff and family, he must realize that an attitude of passivity and dependency is not an inevitable concomitant to physical limitation. He should be given every opportunity to play an active role in the efforts to recover function. This will mean that he is consulted in every step, that his opinions are sought and will be respected, that he is given power over decisions when this is possible and a sense of control whenever he can accept it. Thus, his feelings of effective control over his own fate are supported in a way which emphasizes his adult and masculine role. This provides an opportunity for expression of his fantasies which can then be corrected by reality. Through this experience he can accept a definition of independence by which all of us are bound. The mature adult, healthy or sick, realizes independence only to the degree that he recognizes his own limitations and the extent to which he must realistically be dependent on others. This means relinquishing unrealistic infantile phantasies of omnipotence. Once this is accepted without conflict the patient can be free to build his life in those directions which best serve his needs.

Conclusion

The starting point in handling problems of the effect of loss and grief on sexual function lies in the recognition that such problems do, in fact, exist. It is a fact that the stereotypes which have been described are subscribed to by doctors and other professional persons who work with patients. As a consequence, patients and their families are too often forced to work out their own solutions.

Lief (14) and Castelnuovo-Tedesco (15) have described the limitations of knowledge which doctors bring to the topic of sexual function. As they point out, there are very few medical schools which even make any effort to cover this material. This is a grave defect since it is customary in our society to consider the doctor as a source of information on these problems. The origin of this confidence is felt to lie in the doctor's knowledge of anatomy. However, since such knowledge gives only a limited view of sexual function the patient who overcomes his reluctance to discuss these matters may find in the doctor the same discomfort and shortcomings in knowledge which he finds in himself. In addition, since the doctor is accustomed to dealing with problems in which he is expert he is likely to avoid those areas in which he is not, particularly where his own and his patient's strong feelings are involved.

The physician who wishes to deal with the needs of his patients must be willing to make some appraisal of his own attitudes toward the feelings they are likely to bring to him. He must be aware of his reactions toward intense feelings in general and toward sexual feelings in particular. He must try to determine whether his own attitudes will interfere with his patient's efforts to communicate with him. A knowledge of human sexual development is important. The recognition that sexual function is related to other factors of human experience is equally important. It is not necessary, however, that he be an expert in this field to make a contribution to his patients' welfare. If he can convey to the patient in a respectful and sympathetic manner his willingness to understand the conflict the patient may take the essential step of verbalizing his feelings. This in itself can be a source of great relief of guilt, shame, and hopelessness.

As the patient describes his problem the physician can explore with him the degree to which the problem is based on misconceptions and misinformation. He will then be in a position to give correct information regarding the stereotypes discussed earlier. In an excellent article, Wahl (16) has described techniques which are useful in taking a sexual history. If the doctor feels it will be too difficult for the patient to mention, he may initiate discussion of the patient's sexual readjustment along with other matters. He can then leave it to the patient to return to this topic when he feels ready. The same approach will serve in the matter of sadness and grief. It is not an intrusion for the doctor to comment on the patient's evident sadness and to indicate his interest.

The extent to which the physician will deal with the problems of his patient's reaction both to matters of loss and grief and to matters of sexual adjustment will depend on the degree of his training and understanding. When he feels himself beyond his competence he will, of course, find it helpful to consult with a psychiatrist. Such consultation can be sought by the physician or other professional as an opportunity to expand his own knowledge. In addition there is useful material which has been written with the needs of the physician in mind (17). In time, those with experience in these areas will expand the kinds of research which will make the dependence on stereotypes unnecessary. At the same time, we should be aware that much that is useful is known.

REFERENCES

1. A. C. Kinsey, W. B. Pomeroy, and C. E. Martin, *Sexual Behavior in the Human Male*, Philadelphia: W. B. Saunders Co., 1948.

176

2. W. H. Masters and V. E. Johnson, *Human Sexual Response*, Boston: Little, Brown and Company, 1966.
3. S. Freud, "Mourning and Melancholia," *Complete Works*, Standard Edition, Vol. XIV, London: Hogarth Press, 1957.
4. A. B. Ford and A. P. Orfirer, *Sexual Behavior and the Chronically Ill Patient*, Medical Aspects of Human Sexuality, Vol. I, No. 2, 1967.
5. J. L. Kalliomaki, T. K. Markkanen, and V. A. Mustonen, "Sexual Behavior After Cerebralvascular Accident: A Study on Patients Below the Age of 60 Years," *Fertility and Sterility*, 12:156, 1961.
6. A. B. Ford and A. P. Orfirer, *Sexual Behavior and the Chronically Ill Patient*.
7. L. M. Bowers, R. R. Cross, Jr., and F. A. Lloyd, "Sexual Functions and Urologic Disease in the Elderly Male," *Journal of the American Geriatric Society*, 11:647, 1963.
8. J. T. Freeman, "Sexual Capacities in the Aging Male," *Geriatrics*, 16:37, 1961.
9. A. C. Kinsey et al., *Sexual Behavior in the Human Male*.
10. A. L. Finkle and D. V. Prian, "Sexual Potency in Elderly Men Before and After Prostatectomy," *Journal of the American Medical Association*, 196:139, 1966.
11. E. Bors and A. E. Comarr, "Neurological Disturbances of Sexual Function With Special Reference to 529 Patients With Spinal Cord Injury," *Urological Survey*, 10:191, 1960.
12. L. Guttman, "The Married Life of Paraplegics and Tetraplegics," *Paraplegia*, 2:182, 1964.
13. M. M. LeBan, R. D. Burk, and E. W. Johnson, "Sexual Impotence in Men Having Low-Back Syndrome," in *Archives of Physical Medicine and Rehabilitation*, 47:715, 1966.
14. H. I. Lief, "Orientation of Future Physicians in Psychosexual Attitudes," *Manual of Contraceptive Practice*, edited by M. S. Calderone, Baltimore: The Williams and Wilkins Co., 1964.
15. P. Castelnuovo-Tedesco, "The Doctor's Attitude and His Management of Patients with Sexual Problems," *Sexual Problems: Diagnosis and Treatment in Medical Practice*, edited by C. W. Wahl, New York: Free Press, 1967.
16. C. W. Wahl, "Psychiatric Techniques in the Taking of a Sexual History," *Sexual Problems: Diagnosis and Treatment in Medical Practice*, New York: Free Press, 1967.
17. C. W. Wahl, ed., *Sexual Problems: Diagnosis and Treatment in Medical Practice*, New York: Free Press, 1967.

12

Loss of Sexual Function in the Female

May E. Romm

Almost two hundreds years ago Pietro Metastasio, the poet, stated that, "If the internal griefs of every man could be read, written on his forehead, how many, who now excite envy, would appear to be objects of pity" (1). Each human being in the process of living is at times subject to grief. How he reacts to it, whether physiologically or pathologically, depends to a great extent on his emotional-developmental pattern and the state of his ego-capacity to handle pain.

The loss of a loved person through death is the most frequent and poignant precipitating factor in mourning and grieving with concomitant depression. In normal bereavement, sadness, low mood and some somatic reactions (such as weeping, disturbance of sleep and appetite, or lack of usual interest in the environment) may last six to ten weeks. During this period, the process, by means of which the mourner can gradually rehabilitate himself and accept the fact that death is final, involves facing the mourning overtly. Repression of the pain connected with the loss, avoidance of it by distractions, stoicism, or denial, may lead to both emotional and somatic disturbance.

Women, in their unique sensitivity, as a rule react more intensely than men to the death of a loved one, particularly to the death of a child, a mate or a lover. Generally, the self-esteem of women is not as greatly involved with material possessions, competitive strivings with peers, or status in society as is that of men. In our culture the mature female usually cherishes and derives her greatest satisfactions through emotional investments in loved ones. To a great degree, her life is usually enmeshed with her mate, her children, and her household. Being cherished, loved, and protected by her mate (especially during her vulnerable states, such as pregnancy and maternity) is more important to her than is personal success in other areas. Her competitive strivings outside the immediate family are much less than those of her mate who, as the cardinal provider of the family, has less time and energy to invest in his wife and in his children. Therefore, women often react to the loss of a member of the immediate family more intensely than do men. A woman may also be greatly affected by the death of a parent since she frequently spends more time with relatives than does her husband.

We can speculate that a mother may react to the death of a child with guilt and intense frustration as well as with grief. This may be due to the fact that she harbored the child in her body, went through the travail of pregnancy, labor and childbirth, and was more or less grounded during the offspring's infancy and childhood. After such an intense investment, she may respond with guilt and anger at her irreparable loss. The woman who has no awareness that it is normal for a mother occasionally to feel angry, helpless, and frustrated in the process of nurturing a child, may react to the death of the child with feelings of guilt, anger turned toward herself, and need for punishment. She may feel that she is in some way responsible for the child's death. In some cases there is an intense identification with the child, and the reaction may be one of melancholia, suicidal rumination, and even suicide. In such cases, even a short history may disclose intense traumatic situations in the early life of the bereaved. It is as if the death of her loved one reactivated the pain experienced early in life but subsequently repressed. The "If-only-I-did-differently" complex obsesses her and acts as an inhibiting factor in lessening her grief with the passing of time. A short case history illustrates how enveloping and rigid grief can be.

An attractive, intelligent woman of 50, married to a successful man who cared deeply for her, lost her adult daughter from cancer. She reacted with intense grief and anger. Her frustration was of such intensity that instead of facing her loss and going through a period of mourning with decreasing pain, she isolated herself, responded with grim silence, and for years refused to enter into any social contact or take part in activities which she enjoyed before the death of her daughter.

This woman was orphaned when she was nine years old by the death of her mother. Her father remarried within a year after his wife died. The patient refused to accept the new wife who tried to mother her. Early in life she developed a need to control everything, including the people around her. Her inflexibility extended toward her two children. She expected total obedience from them long before they were chronologically ready for any sort of discipline.

Within the first two years following her loss she became subject to a number of organic conditions. She was operated on for gall stones, she began to suffer from Menière's Syndrome, and fifteen months after her bereavement she had a coronary occlusion. Her grief dissipated somewhat as her body became damaged. Whether she felt that she atoned for her daughter's death by her illness is open to speculation.

The antithesis to the above case is the following.

A 45-year-old woman lost her only child from polio not long before the polio-vaccine became available. For about two months after this death she grieved intensely. She then began actively working for the prevention of the disease that killed her daughter. She raised money for research, worked with crippled children, and traveled with her husband. While on occasion she spoke lovingly and poignantly of the times that she had enjoyed her daughter during the latter's short life, she did not cast a gloom on her family and friends. She was sought after by old and young. Her interest in people and general self-tolerance prevented her from feeling angry or inordinately guilty when she met with her tragedy. She suffered in her mourning, she faced her loss, and after a period of time she rehabilitated herself to the point where she could become useful to herself and to others.

Grieving and the depression which accompanies it may occur in women in situations not connected with death. Some of the precipitating factors may be amenorrhea, infertility, abortions or miscarriages, sexual incompatibility, the birth of an infant, or even the adoption of a child.

While on occasion the onset of menstruation may produce anxiety, once it is established it is usually considered by the female to be a cardinal part of her femininity (in spite of the fact that it is frequently referred to as "the curse"). Menses assure women of their fertility. Women frequently feel that the sexual orgasmic response is dependent

180

on menstrual functioning. When the menstrual cycle ceases, as it may in certain depressions or severe emotional illnesses, or when it stops as a result of the menopause or gynecological surgery, the woman may react with a feeling of intense loss. Women frequently feel that they are no longer desirable sexually, and may repress their sexual desires and drives. Under such conditions, a state of mourning occurs which at times may lead to melancholia. It must again be pointed out that this untoward reaction is usually based on a personality and character structure which suffered many points of traumatic fixation. It seems that the emotional response to the amenorrhea, for whatever reason, brings forth repressed painful feelings in a hypersensitive individual.

A case in point is that of a 35-year-old married mother of three children, who, following a mastectomy for carcinoma of the breast, had a hysterectomy and oophorectomy as precautionary measures against a recurrence of the malignancy. Adequate hormone medication kept her symptom-free from menopausal reactions. In spite of the fact that for a number of years before her operations she used contraceptive measures and did not want any more children, she reacted to her imposed menopause and infertility with a feeling of intense loss. She presented the picture of a person in deep mourning. Her husband, who accepted her physical condition without changing his attitude toward her, continued to be a tender mate and a desirous lover. This did not neutralize her sadness, and her depression deepened. She disclosed during her first interview that since her mastectomy she refused to undress in the presence of her husband and slept in a brassiere although he assured her that she was as wanted and loved by him as she was before her operations. Her fantasies and dreams dealt with menstrual flow and contraceptive devices. The latter were depicted in her dreams explicitly or symbolically as diaphragms (which she used before her hysterectomy).

In psychotherapy, her condition improved when she understood her intense rivalry with her older sister, whom she considered the favorite child of her parents. Her sister had four children. Now that the patient was no longer fertile she resented her inability to have another child so as to equal her sister. It became apparent to her how controlling she was of members of her family since her early childhood and how much her rivalry, anger, envy, and unrealistic inferiority interfered with her pleasure. She began to realize that life could still offer her many desirable opportunities if she were willing to take advantage of them. She decided to complete the college training which she interrupted when she married. She later became a nursery school teacher, an occupation which she enjoyed thoroughly. This woman responded adequately to the realization that she did have a severe illness, a malignancy, but that skillful surgery had given her the chance for recovery. Also, she realized that she had been fulfilled in her marriage and maternity and that she could, through her own efforts, be useful to herself, to her family and to society.

Every woman has some reaction to the menopause. Many consider it a benefit in that the discomfort of menstruation is eliminated and contraceptive measures can be discarded. These women react to the physiological endocrine changes with relative equanimity and with a continuation of their usual activities. Most of them are occasionally subject to hot flushes, increased perspiration, and occasional bouts of tachycardia. They may react with slight irritability to situations which were taken calmly in the premenopausal state. However, the transition into the menopausal and postmenopausal state is accepted by them as a routine change in the process of living. Generally, these women are not too disturbed about aging.

Other women consider their "change of life" a crisis or even a tragedy. They think and feel that it is an indication that the pleasures of life, including attractive appearance, health, and sexual enjoyment are no longer available to them. Hostility, anger, envy, and general mistrust take over and they regress to an early state of helplessness. They evaluate themselves as old, unattractive, and rejected by nature, by fate, and by those whose love is essential to them. They have a tendency to become unrealistically suspicious of their mates, whom they frequently accuse of infidelity, and they seek and demand attention through the development of psychosomatic symptoms. Their anxieties are likely to create severe tension which may interfere with the physiology of the body. It is possible that under such conditions latent organic weaknesses become intensified to the point of becoming actual organic pathologies.

Even when menopause is precipitous, as after surgery of the procreative organs, mature women meet it without undue stress. Other women who are weighed down by emotional sequelae of infantile dependence have a tendency to regress to unresolved fixation points in their early lives. The result is some form of pathology, either psychic, somatic, or a combination of the two. The grief connected with what is considered to be the loss of youth, sexuality, or the possibility of accomplishment can range from mild depression to severe melancholia. Invariably their history discloses that these patients have led inadequate premenopausal lives. Evaluation of their personalities frequently shows that they were inordinately dependent, that they suffered from the inability to enjoy a satisfactory interpersonal relationship, and that they were dissatisfied with their lot, their sexuality, and the important people in their lives. Their tendency is to project onto others their failure to utilize their potential and to blame fate, parents, mates, children, or friends for what they consider their pitiful state. They feel misused by the world and, rather than facing their inabilities to invest emotion and effort in the pursuit of realistic enjoyment in order to acquire more out of life, they settle for secondary gains from illness. They hope in this way to gratify their insatiable need for dependence on others. Since they believe that they have been cheated by life, menopause represents to them another loss for which they grieve interminably.

The physician who is aware of the personality of his patient may be able to anticipate some of the untoward reactions to menopause. In certain cases he may succeed in forestalling or at least modifying these reactions. Merely explaining to the woman the meaning and the process of menopause can at times save her a great deal of emotional tension. It is surprising how many intelligent persons have erroneous and even bizarre concepts about the functions of their bodies. It is therefore both a wise and a therapeutic step for the physician to enlighten the woman about the changes in the body during menopause. The patient should be permitted to express her own ideas of what she anticipates or anticipated. In addition to the decrease of anxiety, the patient may also benefit in other ways. For example, she may feel that her doctor is vitally interested in her and will stand by her and help her if and when she needs him. When the patient's pathological reaction is severe, the physician should refer her to a psychiatrist. The latter may treat her on an ambulatory basis or, if indicated, may have to hospitalize her.

In considering the advisability of an indicated abortion, the physician should evaluate the personality of the patient. There are, on occasion, guilt and inferiority feelings and erroneous inculcated concepts which, after the interruption of the pregnancy, can produce a depression in the woman. The depression may be either mild and tem-

183

porary, or of psychotic magnitude with a poor prognosis. In order for the physician to be aware of the possible untoward effects following such surgical interference, he should spend sufficient time evaluating the woman's background and psychological status. A spontaneous miscarriage is usually not as psychologically traumatic as an abortion since the patient considers the former an "act of God" rather than something for which she herself is responsible.

An inordinately attractive woman of 50, who already had had five years of psychotherapy for depression, still continued to lament that she had ruined her life because she had two abortions before her marriage. Part of her problem was that she had been unable to become pregnant when she married at the age of 35. (Whether her inability to conceive was due to the aftermath of her interrupted pregnancies was never determined.) Her history disclosed that she was a middle child with two male siblings. Her mother was a very neurotic person, who relegated the responsibility for her sons to the patient when the latter was eight years of age. Her father, an alcoholic, paid no attention to the patient. Her constant weeping and laments revolved about her feelings that she was a sinner who was undeserving of the miracle of motherhood and that her future would bring her nothing but pain and disaster. She suffered from innumerable psychosomatic symptoms and exaggerated the importance of a slight osteoarthritis. It became obvious that what she feared most was that she would lose her attractiveness. She frequently referred to how beautiful and slender her hands were in the past, and that numerous male admirers would kiss her hands in admiration of her beauty. While therapy decreased her psychosomatic symptoms, her narcissism remained intact.

Now, close to 70, she is still having therapy and still spends most of the session weeping and lamenting her sorry state. We can speculate that if her physician had discussed with her the possible sequelae of induced abortion and had advised psychotherapy earlier in her life, she may have been a more productive person to herself and others.

It seems paradoxical that a woman who may have planned her pregnancy and overtly looked forward to being a mother may develop a severe depression or even a psychotic state after delivering a healthy infant. A number of theories have been proposed to throw light on the cause of such an unexpected emotional reaction. Frequently the pregnancy is normal and pleasant. The length and severity of the labor does not seem to influence the likelihood of a depression. There are several possibilities which may produce such a reaction. The history of such a woman invariably reveals her to be a dependent, infantile person for whom adjustments to life with its vicissitudes were always threatening. The change of her body to a nonpregnant state, after the feeling of fullness and well-being of pregnancy, may be a shaking experience for her. What are probably more threatening to her are the demands which an infant makes on a mother. Being herself a dependent individual, she may have fastened her ego on her parents or parent surrogates and then transferred her dependence to her husband. With the birth of a child she is called upon to accept the dependence of the helpless infant. Her fragile ego, incapable of handling the responsibility of nurturing her newborn child, collapses under the strain. What a mature woman accepts as a privilege and as a joy represent to her a disaster. She mourns the loss of her dependent state. The baby, toward whom she is ambivalent, creates anger and guilt within her. This may account for her fear, which may be turned into action, that she will injure or murder the child. When such rage is repressed by her, it may be internalized with the possibility that she may attempt suicide. A short case history may exemplify some of the dynamics of a postpartum depression.

A young married woman became intensely depressed following the birth of her son, a second child. She already had a 2½-year-old daughter. Several days after the delivery she developed an intense resentment toward her newborn infant. She feared to remain alone with him and expressed ideas that she might injure him. Her depression deepened and within a week after giving birth she refused all food, became noncommunicative and sat immobile, staring into space and drooling. She gave the impression of being in a schizophrenic state. Since she refused to talk it seemed indicated to inform her of some speculative reasons for her state and her behavior. It appeared that unless there was some radical improvement within a short period of time she would have to be hospitalized. Her husband refused to consider this possibility. Taking a calculated risk, the physician soliloquized that she may have reacted with anger and frustration to the birth of the infant because she was unhappy with her marital state, and that she may have considered that having two children instead of one would interfere with the possibility of an escape from her marriage. Although she seemed not to listen to what was said, there was a sudden change in her expression, and she slowly and with considerable effort verbalized that she did not want the child. After a long silence she whispered that he reminded her of her husband. Within several days she began to improve.

185

She started eating and began to take an interest in herself and in her surroundings. However, for a number of months she did not trust herself to be alone with the infant for fear of hurting him. She disclosed later that she was inordinately attached to her father who, she felt, preferred her brother to her and rejected her. The birth of a male infant reactivated in her many painful experiences that she had with males in her formative years. In addition to her unhappy relationship with her husband, this solidified her hostility toward the male child whom she considered an obstacle to the release from her unhappy marriage. Fearing that her hostility might destroy the infant, she attempted to escape into a sort of immobilized pseudo-catatonic state. It may be that one reason for her quick recovery was that the confrontation struck a propitious note in her before she regressed further in her attempt to escape from painful reality. This in turn, depended on her acceptance of the idea that she did not lose freedom of action in her marriage, a freedom whose loss she so extremely mourned.

A feeling of loss and grieving may occur after the adoption of a child. The loss of the dependency state which has to give way to the responsibility of taking care of a child may bring out in a woman who has an infantile character the same reaction as a postpartum depression. She is incapable of investing adequately in the interpersonal relationship which is required in the process of mothering.

In his appraisal of grief, Eric Lindemann equates it with an illness (2). Anyone who has been in the presence of a mourning person can fully appreciate that he is symptomatically ill. His pain and suffering impair not only his bodily functioning (such as motility, sleep, and appetite) but also his ability to relate to people and to work.

Normal mourning is distinguished from pathological mourning not only in terms of the intensity of the grief, but in terms of length of time that the mourner withdraws himself from the demands of his environment. During the acute mourning period, it is essential for the individual to tap his painful feelings, to face and to experience his loss emotionally as well as intellectually, and to realize that every relationship has some ambivalence in it. Just as each metal, no matter how pure, has some alloy in it, so love—no matter how tender—has in it a certain amount of ambivalence and resentment. Pain, irrespective of source or cause, produces anger. The reaction of "How could the death of my loved one happen to me!" may be a defensive maneuver against the anger which could read "How could you be so cruel as to die and leave me?" This in turn reactivates guilt connected with the idea of "Had I done enough? If only I did more or something different, my loved one would have survived." These feelings are related to the universal feelings of omnipotence of early childhood. The mourner feels as if he had the power to prevent the tragedy but failed to utilize it. Such an unrealistic reaction, if it is more than a fleeting thought, can prolong or solidify through concomitant guilt feelings the grief and mourning.

One of the most painful components of mourning and grief is the bereaved's feeling of helplessness. This helplessness and the finality of the loss combine to reactivate in certain hypersensitive individuals the early helplessness that every person experiences in childhood. Consolation or attempts to distract the person during the acute phase of mourning are definitely contraindicated, since they may even serve to increase the pain and make the grief more poignant. According to William F. Murphy (3), "In the long run the neurotic person must learn how to mourn, forgive, forget, renounce, and try again." One of the most difficult things for the inordinately dependent person to do is to give up the wishful thinking connected with his feelings of invulnerability, immortality, and magical maneuvers. Since one's own ego is averse to accepting the concept of nonexistence after death, the mourner, through identification, is threatened by the finality of his loss. Physiological mourning through the process of grieving adjusts one to the realistic concept that man is vulnerable and mortal. One must agree with C. W. Wahl, who claims that "any defense which enables us to *persistently* escape the perception of any fundamental internal or external reality is psychologically costly" (4). The energy utilized in hiding from one's self what is essentially the truth leaves one depleted, hampered, and enslaved. When an individual after a severe loss fails to experience normal grief and mourning, the absence of such reactions may be later replaced by severe emotional or somatic illness.

Not every person in mourning requires psychotherapy. The person grieving over the death of a loved object or objects can be greatly benefited by his family physician, a person of the cloth, a relative, or a close friend who, by his very presence, can help him during and after the working through of grief. A great many of the depressive states connected with mourning are self-limited. When grieving is repressed or inordinately prolonged it may become the more severe illness of melancholia, and thereby become a danger to health or life. In the latter case, a psychiatrist is necessary in order to get to the deeper layers and roots of the emotional problems.

REFERENCES

1. *The New Dictionary of Thoughts*, reprinted by Doubleday and Company, Inc., New York. 1969, p. 139.
2. E. Lindemann, "Symptomatology and Management of Acute Grief," *American Journal of Psychiatry, 101*:141, September 1944.
3. W. F. Murphy, *The Tactics of Psychotherapy*, New York: International Universities Press, 1965.
4. C. W. Wahl, "The Fear of Death," in *The Meaning of Death*, edited by H. Feifel, New York: McGraw-Hill Paperback, 1965.

13

Reaction to Chronic Illness

Richard S. Blacher

I feel so sad when I think of how I am, I could cry. I think of all the things I could do before. Then I look around me and see all the healthy people my age, and get jealous, and begin to hate them. But then I get to feeling guilty because they've never done any harm to me, and I'm overwhelmed by a blue feeling.

This poignant recital of her emotions by a young adult victim of myasthenia gravis describes a sequence much more common in patients with chronic disease than most physicians realize. What this young woman relates is a progression from grief to depression, from an initial sadness over her illness and the loss of her usual functioning, to an unacceptable rage and jealousy, with her angry feelings turning upon herself.

Every victim of a chronic disease must make a series of adaptations to the disease and to treatment, but above all, to the loss of function and sense of well-being the illness brings. Loss of health is dealt with in the same manner as other experiences of loss—namely, by grief and mourning. But so prominent are other aspects of chronic illness, both for the patient and for the doctor, that the elements of loss and grief often go unrecognized.

For example, an outwardly calm and unperturbed woman with a long history of heart disease and a recent myocardial infarct constantly spoke to the nurses of her reminiscences with the emotional tone of a wake. Here though, the "deceased" was the patient herself as a robust person and her mourning was for the loss of her health. To consider this a reason for sorrow does not require an extension of our concept of grief. One mourns not only the loss of a person, but other things as well—health, parts of the body, employment, valued objects, social status, and ideals. And in all instances of loss, classic indicators of mourning are apparent. These were described by Freud (1) as profoundly painful dejection, loss of interest in the outside world, loss of the capacity to love, and inhibition of activity. These symptoms are also characteristic of depressive states and it is common for ill patients to be depressed. While they may indeed be depressed, they are not *necessarily* so. In depression, one finds a lowering of self-esteem, with guilt and self-accusatory feelings. In the case of the patient with myasthenia gravis who described her sadness, it was when her envy came to the fore that she felt guilty, and only then did her mourning turn to depression.

Reactions to any illness are determined by a multitude of factors involving the nature and severity of the illness, the personality of the patient, and the interplay between personality and illness. For example, heart disease may be unconsciously welcomed by the passive, dependent individual who finds the disability a solution to his conflicts about asserting himself. For the hyperactive individual the necessary limitations and restrictions may be intolerable.

A 55-year-old corporation executive suffered a myocardial infarction. He could never delegate responsibility, would work long hours, and was known to perform heavy manual tasks if he felt that a workman was slow or inefficient. After his coronary occlusion, his doctor urged him to reduce his working hours and avoid spasmodic outbursts of heavy manual labor. He followed instructions for a short while, but gradually his hours lengthened, and he began to lift heavy objects once again. He casually mentioned to friends that perhaps the doctor had misdiagnosed his "case of indigestion." For this man, who could not allow himself a vacation, the prospect of enforced idleness was intolerable.

Denial is perhaps the commonest mechanism utilized in adjustment to chronic illness. Patients frequently remark that they can't accept the fact that they are ill. For example, a young woman who was known by her friends to be intolerant of illness was unusually cheerful when she developed diabetes. She quipped, "They can't understand why I don't just fold up. What *they* don't know is that *I* don't know yet that I'm sick."

Observers on coronary intensive care units in a hospital are struck by how indifferent these critically ill patients may seem. They are, after all, people whose immediate environment indicates the danger they are in. Nevertheless, overt anxiety is rarely observed. It is apparent that this calm facade covers up a great deal of internal turmoil.

It is of interest that the usual initial response to a loss is one of disbelief. Indeed, there is often an unconscious denial of the loss that is consciously accepted. As used here, the term *denial* refers to the unconscious mechanism whereby something real and perceived is repressed from conscious awareness. The patient who consults his physician with an obviously advanced lesion, and states that he noticed this large tumor on the previous day, has denied its presence. While denial may be a useful adaptive mechanism in the face of a threat to one's well being, it may prevent one from seeking treatment or following a prescribed therapeutic regimen.

The more serious the condition, the more one might expect denial to operate. Patients with cancer and heart disease show denial to a remarkable degree. In a group of patients with valvular disease selected for open-heart surgery, a careful explanation of the procedure was given by the surgeon, who often illustrated his remarks with drawings. When these patients were later asked to describe the locus of their illness, however, they spoke of the valves as part of the blood vessels outside the heart. The ability to tolerate something wrong *within* the heart, with the implication that the heart would then have to be opened to repair the valve, was more than these patients could bear.

There is a broad spectrum from fantasy to reality along which any patient may view his disease. Certain conditions, such as cancer, are viewed with anxiety by most patients. In chronic illness which is not immediately life-threatening, the range of reaction depends to a great extent on the personal meaning of the disease to the individual. Such meaning, if recognized by the patient, is not easily expressed because of the emotional significance of the situation.

For example, a patient with diabetes with no previous contact with the disease and no preconceived notions about it may be stimulated to learn all he can about the condition. The patient whose con-

191

cept of the illness is determined by a parent's mild case of diabetes with casual control by diet may experience only minimal anxiety. To a patient who has witnessed progressive deterioration in a family member involving neuropathies, blindness, and amputations, the diagnosis may elicit a reaction of severe anxiety and depression. Such a patient may not report this family history to the physician and the emotional reaction may, therefore, be a source of confusion to those in attendance. Often the patient regards historical data as irrelevant in denial of their highly-charged implications. The reluctance to share these innermost thoughts is overcome only after a relationship of support and comfort is established.

A woman who became severely depressed upon recovering from an episode of congestive heart failure felt her family history was not related to her condition. Only after several sessions did she reveal that a younger sister had died during a similar attack a number of years earlier. She felt that she should have sought better medical care for the sister and had always felt guilty. Her own subsequent recovery revived and intensified these guilt feelings and only this exploration of the "unimportant" data relieved the depression.

This reluctance to discuss highly-charged material increases the distance between physician and patient and renders it difficult to understand the inner life of the patient. Often a persistent, gentle exploration by a physician who is prepared to deal with the repressed material will open what may be a Pandora's box of emotional content.

Chronic illness may be schematically divided into several categories in which the problems confronting the patients are somewhat different.

1. Life-endangering illnesses which may be cured but which are potentially recurrent—such as cancer or coronary artery disease following a single myocardial infarction.

2. Illnesses for which there may be no cure but for which there may be reasonable control, such as diabetes, some heart conditions, certain muscular diseases and neurological conditions.

3. Illnesses marked by exacerbations and remissions such as chronic ulcerative colitis, asthma, myasthenia gravis, and multiple sclerosis.

4. Illnesses marked by a progressive downhill course, such as some forms of chronic leukemia and lymphosarcoma.

Responses to diagnosis, treatment, and the illness itself differ markedly from group to group.

Minor aches and pains, usually ignored by the healthy person, can become an ominous threat to the chronically ill person. A mild chest pain has a different meaning to a person with a previous myocardial infarction than to someone without such a history. To the patient with a chronic intestinal disease, food poisoning may lead to the same emotional reaction of despair as an attack of ulcerative colitis. A vital function which the normal person barely notices is always at the surface of awareness of the chronically ill. Thus the cardiac patient is more attuned to sensations in his chest and the asthmatic to his respiratory process. The awareness of a symptom may lead not only to anxiety but also may stimulate the defense of denial.

A young man came into his psychiatrist's office with the statement, "I must be very nervous today; I have a severe pressing pain in the middle of my chest." Immediate referral to his internist revealed no evidence of organic disease, and his original statement was borne out. However, exploration revealed that this symptom, which he had never experienced before, indicated to him the onset of a heart attack. The overwhelming anxiety was warded off by an unconscious denial and he was not consciously aware of the fear of cardiac illness.

Denial is not limited to the patient. His physician may also utilize this mechanism to deal with the painful implications of the illness.

A physician's mother was admitted to the hospital with a textbook history of advanced carcinoma of the stomach. Careful histories were taken by the intern and two residents whose conclusion was unanimous that the patient was suffering from a gastric ulcer. One resident suggested carcinoma, but only as a remote possibility.

A similar response was seen when an adolescent girl with congenital heart disease suddenly developed a massive cerebrovascular accident. The nurses, who had known this patient a long time and were quite fond of her, first called the psychiatrist excitedly explaining that she had developed some sort of hysterical state. These experienced nurses had seen many such attacks in other patients, but could not bear the thought that this affable youngster was in a perilous condition.

The patient with chronic illness may be very attuned to the nuances of bodily change. Joseph (2) has reported a series of patients with ulcerative colitis who had dreams of bleeding. Upon arising, they proceeded to have bleeding episodes. His assumption that these patients were unconsciously aware of the disease process seems reasonable.

A key factor in determining response and adaptation to those conditions for which there is good control but no cure is the age of onset. The patient who develops a chronic illness in early adulthood or later life obviously has different obstacles to overcome than the child whose entire development has been influenced by chronic disease and who has *developed* within the framework of medical treatment. The limitations of activity imposed on the congenital cardiac patient may create havoc in a young child's development. The child is torn between obedience to his parents and physician and his desire to enjoy the pleasures of play and physical activity. Unless his symptoms are severe, he cannot understand what may seem to him to be unreasonable restrictions on his pleasure, nor does he tolerate easily the constant comparisons he makes with other children who can run and jump. Anna Freud has described how children, through adolescence, act as if it were their right to endanger their health while leaving it to their mothers to protect and restore them (3). Constant nagging restrictions, alternating frequently with overindulgence, often complicate such a child's develment. Certainly the connection between an abstraction such as "heart disease," and practical problems such as mastery of motor skills and enjoyment of physical activity, may be difficult for the child to make.

The problem of the juvenile diabetic has always plagued the pediatrician. Here, the loss of such a fundamental pleasure as eating sweets that companions enjoy is experienced by the youngster as a severe deprivation. Perhaps the parents and medical attendants may only too well appreciate this loss and deny its impact in order to carry out a medical regimen for the child's welfare. A full realization of how hard it is for the child might impair an effective enforcement. Frequent hospitalization of chronically ill children leads to a sense of having been deserted by the parents, adding an additional burden to their development. That children manifest signs of grief as well as depression is

194

apparent in many chronically ill children, and the effect of such experiences on later development is seen by every psychiatrist.

A 35-year-old man became agitated after a mild heart attack. Only extensive exploration revealed that the anxiety was not so much in response to heart disease, but to the experience of *hospitalization*. Repeated and prolonged hospitalizations for a chronic bone disease marked his earliest years and resulted in a life of immobility and complete dependence on his family. When he was finally able to make his mark in a learned profession, his main difficulties centered around his persistent need for activity and his independent attitude. Hospitalization for his myocardial infarction revived the painful early experiences and increased his need for independence and activity. In addition, this man showed to a marked degree the almost universal childhood reaction to illness—namely, a sense of responsibility for it, as if the illness was a punishment for some previous wrongdoing.

Patients who have been taught to regard self-pity as an immoral indulgence quickly develop a sense of guilt when confronted with the difficulties imposed on them by chronic illness.

A young woman with a Tetralogy of Fallot, which had severely restricted her activity since early childhood, was taught by her mother that it was not good to feel sorry for herself. While perhaps originally intended as an encouragement, it clearly assumed a strong moral tone and the patient would show characteristic acceptance whenever she was hospitalized. She could not talk or even think of her narrowed existence without a sense of guilt. Not to feel a sense of sadness was impossible; yet to be sad was wrong.

The role of the parents in such situations is a most difficult one—torn between a desire to infantilize the sick child, on one hand, and to encourage him to go beyond his limits on the other, they often resolve the issue in a guilt-laden manner by a confusing mixture of both. Unless they themselves can be helped by the physician to come to grips with their feelings in a realistic way, their own confusion may serve only to complicate the child's adaptation.

Occurrence of such illnesses in adult life revives early modes of response to stress and it is not unusual for the patient to resort to infantile regressive behavior. Any chronic illness provides a stage on which all emotional problems can be expressed.

195

REACTION TO PARTIAL LOSS

In those illnesses marked by remissions and exacerbations, the dreaded expectation of a recurrence is ever present. Denial of the illness predominates during remissions, while the reaction to exacerbation is determined by the patient's usual mode of coping with stress.

A young man with frequent bouts of chronic ulcerative colitis would withdraw into a shell whenever he had an episode of diarrhea. His history revealed a fear of sexual encounters with women, as well as a deep sense of guilt in surpassing an incompetent older brother. Thus, it was not surprising to find him utilizing his illness to withdraw from both social and professional experiences. In contrast, an active and independent single man in his mid-twenties was loathe to give up his social and professional life whenever he had an exacerbation of his colitis. He found his life limited only by available toilet facilities and he would plan his activities around the proximity to a men's room to which he might have to make a frenzied dash.

Patients with chronic fatal illnesses must make a double adaptation: 1) to illness and impending death, and 2) to living as productive a life as possible in the time left to them. It is striking how uncomfortable the hospital staff feel in the face of terminal illness. When the patient most requires intimacy and support, he is avoided by doctors and nurses, and even by his family. The doctor's feelings of anxiety result from his own feelings about death and from the frustration of his desire to help the patient (4).

Anticipatory mourning is quite common and explains the frequent lack of a strong grief reaction in the survivors when death follows a prolonged illness. On the other hand, when this anticipatory mourning involves withdrawal from the dying patient and thus the realistic self-accusation of "we could have done more for him," the grief reaction may in fact be prolonged (5).

That these reactions may be present in situations where death is anticipated sometime in the more distant future is not surprising. In both cases, the mourning may occur too early for the patient. The process of mourning entails the gradual giving up of the dead person by the living, and when this occurs too soon, it may result in feelings of emotional isolation for the patient. The patient, too, may mourn the loss of his loved ones because of his dying.

The family appears to struggle between the polarities of treating

196

the patient as if nothing were changed and moving away from him—as if to disengage themselves and thus not have part of them die with him. The guilt this latter path may engender can result in overindulgence of his slightest whim. As with children so treated, solicitude may make the patient more anxious. A more realistic and open situation is to be preferred wherein the patient and his family can share the experience rather than be alienated by it.

Management of the Chronically Ill

The treatment of patients with chronic illness makes greater emotional demands on the physician than the treatment of those who are acutely ill. In the case of the latter, the usual successful outcome is rewarding to the doctor's self-esteem and the gratitude of the patient and his family may be an added bonus. In contrast, chronic illness requires a long-standing "contract" between patient and physician, with inevitable frustration on both sides. Cursory physical treatments without consideration of the emotional impact of the illness may protect the physician from his personal anxieties concerning illness and death, but hardly constitute optimal care. It is important to distinguish between what the patient needs and what he wants. He *wants* complete relief from discomfort and even restoration of health. He wants reassurance that these are forthcoming. What he *needs* is support in accepting the illness and the medical treatments necessary for its control. He needs a feeling of being understood and that come what may, he will be taken care of and not be abandoned by his physician.

Only an awareness and appreciation of the patient's inner turmoil on the part of the physician can create the necessary setting for sound medical treatment. The physician must recall that everything that he says or does carries enormous weight with his patient. The casual flippancy may well strike terror in the patient's heart. A competent and sensitive internist was asked by a coronary patient whether it was safe to resume sexual relations. The doctor assured him that it would certainly do no harm, but then laughingly quipped, "What a way to go!" The apprehensive patient could not accept this as a joke and was plagued by a fear of sudden death for months afterward.

In a delightful paper, the novelist Ben Ames Williams (6) describes

197

the doctor-patient relationship from the patient's point of view and reminds us of the omnipresent fear with which the patient faces illness and medical treatment. He closes with:

It is the hard lot of the doctor to know that in the end he is always defeated; his victories at best are temporary. Death he can never finally conquer. But death's ally is fear, and this ally the doctor can defeat. Let him help the patient to conquer fear, and he will win many a skirmish; and if he can never hope to win the last grim battle, he can at least do much to rob that ultimate defeat, for his patient and for the patient's family, of the terror that is its most grievous pain.

REFERENCES

1. S. Freud, "Mourning and Melancholia" (1917), *Complete Works,* Standard Edition, Vol. XIV, London: Hogarth Press, 1957.
2. E. D. Joseph, Unpublished data.
3. A. Freud, *Normality and Pathology in Childhood,* New York: International Universities Press, 1965.
4. R. S. Blacher and C. Winkelstein, "The Initial Contact with the Cancer Patient—Some Psychiatric Considerations," *Journal of the Mount Sinai Hospital* (New York, New York), 35(4):423, July-August, 1968.
5. G. Rochlin, *Griefs and Discontents,* Boston: Little, Brown and Co., 1965.
6. B. A. Williams, "The Greeks Had a Word for It," *New England Journal of Medicine, 233*(15):427, October 11, 1945.

14

Reaction to Loss in the Aged

Alexander R. Broden

Physicians, psychiatrists, and other health workers in allied fields studying the aged population are particularly aware of the reality of loss, grief, and consequent depression. In this country over 18-million people are over 65 years of age. In ten years, this number will be substantially increased. As medical science develops new methods of prolonging life, certain problems for the aging individual become proportionately greater. The biological processes of aging are associated with a decline in efficiency and functioning that eventually result in death. Although some people think of aging as both growth and decline, scientists prefer to see aging as a deteriorative change over the life span. This decline consists of a series of accumulated and compounded losses. Thus, loss may be not only psychological and physical, but also social and economic, and any one area of loss can effect any other area. For example, a debilitating illness in an aging individual may precipitate a loss in social standing in the community, result in economic changes, and alter his status within his family.

The individual who suffers one or more functional losses may react with loss of self-esteem, grief, or depression. The same will be found for the individual experiencing loss of status, job, or loved one. He will express his reactions to his family, physician, or religious advisor in various ways. The physician may be confronted with inordinate somatic complaints; the nurse or social worker in an institution for the aged may bear the brunt of complaints about food or room arrangements; the family may be plagued with overwhelming expressions of helplessness; the religious advisor may be the recipient of confessions of guilt. Thus, not only do losses affect the individual himself, but they also present specific difficulties for the family and at times the community itself.

In recent years, the aging individual and his problems have become an increasing source of interest to the health professions. The psychiatrist has made new efforts to understand the effects of chronic disease and loss of loved ones upon the intrapsychic economy of the individual and the impact of these effects upon medical personnel. Community mental health clinics have turned their attention to elderly individuals in recent years; homes for the aged have increasingly included psychiatric service in their programs; and the rapidly expanding field of community psychiatry has begun to educate the public about the problems facing the elderly and those in contact with them.

Loss of Body Functions

Radical shifts take place as the individual approaches old age—shifts that involve both *somatic* and *psychological* functions. These include the following: a) altered sensory perception; b) altered motor capacity; c) altered functions of internal organs; d) altered sexual capacity; and e) altered control of physical and mental functions.

Loss of vision is brought on by cataract formation, by presbyopia, and specific diseases such as retinal detachment, by diabetic retinitis, and by arteriosclerotic disease of the eye. The most common of these—presbyopia—produces impaired vision at low levels of illumination which often results in disorientation during the night not evident during the course of the day.

Loss of hearing can serve to shut off the individual from his environment, creating feelings of isolation, rejection, and distrust of those around him. Initial hearing loss may be limited to reduction in perception of background noises. The patient is unaware he is missing them, but feels merely that the world is less alive. Sensory stimulation is essential to alert and adequate psychological activity. Prolonged sensory deprivation as experienced in impairment of sensory perceptions leads to psychological isolation. Society often promotes the physiologic process of aging by not supplying the elderly with the necessary environmental stimulation.

200

In most aged individuals there is a 50 percent loss of taste and smell so that foods become less palatable. Staff members of institutions are often confronted with complaints about food that are partly an attempt to rationalize this loss. Muscle mass and strength become diminished as one ages and there is also a decreased tolerance to exercise. Arthritis, the number one disease impairing older Americans, can severely limit movement of the extremities and is a common source of discomfort and pain to the aging individual. Circulatory and neurological diseases of the extremities contribute further to loss of limb function. Hypertension, coronary artery disease, and cerebrovascular disease contribute largely to decrease in motor functioning, as do various respiratory and digestive system diseases. Defective teeth and gums make chewing food a source of distress. Fear and ignorance about these limitations often cripples an individual to a greater extent than do the actual physical losses.

As we age, the functions of the internal organs are subject to deterioration and chronic disease. Between the ages of 45 and 64, chronic conditions are present in 61.3 per cent of the population, and serve to limit activity in 18.3 per cent. After age 65, the incidence of chronic disorders increases to 78.7 per cent and disability to 45.1 per cent (1). Disease processes lead to the need for dietary restrictions; there is also a decreased tolerance to exercise. In chronic neoplastic diseases, the patient not only suffers from severe limitation in function, but may experience severe pain as well. Mutilating operations, which must often be performed as a lifesaving measure, place an additional burden upon the patient's ability to adapt to an altered body image. Chronic disease brings about a marked increase in dependency upon other persons, and with dependency may come hostility. When increased dependency needs are not met, resentment may remain unexpressed for fear that such expression would bring further neglect. The aged individual who has always feared helplessness and passivity is particularly vulnerable when debilitated by chronic illness. Fear of death and of the dying process is, of course, more marked in progressive illnesses. The individual realizes that thoughts of death can no longer be put aside as something that happens to others. In many, insomnia, a common complaint, is related to a fear of dying.

The waning sexual function in females and decreased potency in males represent an enormous blow to the individual's self-esteem. In post-menopausal women, there may be an exaggerated longing to be loved, or there may be a turning away from painful reality. Although decline in sexual function may be primarily organic, it may also be affected by fears that sexual activity will result in severe illness. A man who has had a myocardial infarction may become "impotent" to avoid facing the possibility that during intercourse he would suffer another coronary thrombosis. Changes in secondary sexual endowments and subsequent loss of attractiveness to the opposite sex are, in themselves, blows to self-esteem. Although the climacteric and potency decline means loss and disillusionment to some, they are usually accepted with reasonable complacency.

The group of disorders known as the organic brain syndrome include both the acute and chronic brain syndrome. The former is characterized by the sudden development of disorientation, confusion, lethargy, hallucinations, bizarre behavior, and personality changes. The acute symptoms, usually reversible, frequently accompany severe febrile states, hospitalization following a fracture or operation, or merely an abrupt change in environment. The chronic brain syndrome includes severe loss of memory, misidentification, disorientation, chronic confusion, loss of initiative, delusional preoccupation, and defects in thought and judgment. Loss of instinctual control is evidenced by asocial sexual activities such as exhibitionism, sexual fondling of children, and eventually soiling and overt masturbation. The chronic brain syndrome which is often associated with cerebral arteriosclerosis (commonly referred to as senile brain disease) is present to some degree in most individuals of advanced age.

In cerebral arteriosclerosis, the structural alteration of cerebral tissue results in a deterioration of ego-function and consequently in a decreased ability to deal with sexual and aggressive drives. Many old people exhibit childish sexual behavior and uncharacteristic aggressiveness. For example, a 70-year-old man began to make sexual overtures toward nurses and social workers after he suffered a cerebral thrombosis, although he had been quite inhibited and restrained earlier in life.

Investigations have not as yet revealed a clear corroboration between the degrees of chronic brain syndrome and actual organic cellular changes. There are individuals with early senile manifestations who do not have diagnosed arteriosclerosis or evidence of cerebral circulatory or metabolic changes. Both senility and arteriosclerosis are

202

fairly common occurrences in old age, but may not bear any essential pathogenic relationship to each other. Some observers explain symptoms commonly associated with senility (such as forgetting and disorganization) as adaptive defense mechanisms against death fears, aggressive impulses, and loss. Others feel that the senile process itself is a regression to infantile states since senile behavior is, in many instances, analogous to behavioral patterns of infants at various stages of development (2).

Socioeconomic and Psychosocial Losses

In addition to organic decline, the aging individual also experiences a decline in influence over his environment. His children leave home and marry, his advice is no longer respected, and he becomes less useful to his offspring. He loses friends and relatives through death, and he experiences difficulty in establishing new associations. Since his productive capacities have been lost he may be rebuffed or ignored. At the same time that his influence on his environment declines, he becomes more dependent on that environment, especially on family members. These psychosocial factors may influence the outcome of changes of health and personality. Retirement, for example, though devastating to a physically healthy individual, may come as a welcome relief from pressure to one who is physically ill. Loss of mastery over one's own bodily functions may be tolerated only as long as protective, supportive persons remain with the individual.

A 75-year-old resident of a home for the aged, suffering from severe osteoarthritis, rarely complained about his illness while his wife was alive. Upon her death, he rapidly developed severe limitation of movement, becoming quite helpless, and bitterly complained to doctors and nurses that he was in great pain. Examination and laboratory tests revealed no significant change in the severity of his illness. His complaints, which expressed helplessness and represented a desperate plea for emotional support, highlighted the somatic reaction to the fact that his wife's emotional support had been lost. They also represented an attempt to justify his continued residence in the home which was, until her death, rationalized as something he did for his wife.

REACTION TO PARTIAL LOSS

Loss of a dependent partner can have just as profound an effect as loss of a partner upon whom the individual had been dependent. This loss is analogous to the experience of no longer being needed by one's children. As long as one is needed, he can experience mastery over his environment. Once this is lost, however, a severe challenge to the individual's self-esteem must be overcome.

Socioeconomic factors have resulted in a decrease in size of families and geographic dispersal of family members. This separation, in addition to other factors, usually makes family members unavailable for the care of aged persons. Although they may receive continued respect from their children, the parents are, in many cases, no longer looked to for advice and assistance. When the elderly must share a small apartment or home with their married children, resulting in overcrowding and lack of privacy, they usually feel unwanted. Few families are any longer capable of supporting the burden of an aged relative, and the extended family as a functional unit is a thing of the past.

It is difficult for the aged individual to find new friends. Individuals in his own age group may shy away from him because they see in him their own aging and approaching death. As one individual put it: "All my old friends seem to be so old and shriveled. Can it be that I am this way too? I don't believe it." Younger people may withdraw from the aged individual as a defense against anxiety over aging and death. In addition, as organic processes progress, the elderly become less articulate and interesting to others.

A sexual life is possible for most aged individuals, even if only in fantasy. Many married men in their 70s continue a reasonably active sexual life. Limitations are more often imposed by the environment than by actual physical decline. In interviewing elderly people, the physician tends to avoid detailed questioning about sexuality. Cultural attitudes limit dating for the aged person and he may feel humiliated if his children or friends become aware of his sexual interests. Aging people in this country feel more apologetic than proud of their age and many try to keep up with the younger ones, often in an inappropriate manner.

Very often the elderly must face being placed in a nursing home or old age home by their children. The initial reaction to such a move is often a feeling of having been rejected by the family. In others, an old age home can represent a temporary solution to environmental pressures they are unable to tolerate, and feelings of relief may be the predominant reaction. One woman described her entrance to an old age home as an admission to a final resting place.

Reactions to Loss

The following are examples of some common reactions to loss:

1) An aged hemiplegic stumbles out of his wheelchair in an attempt to walk without adequate support or refuses to admit to being unable to undress himself and goes to bed with his clothes on.

2) An old woman with rapidly progressive wide-angle glaucoma blames the doctor's eye drops for causing her visual difficulties.

3) An elderly man who has undergone prostatic surgery and suffers periodic urinary incontinence complains of hoarseness for which no organic cause is found. He displaces his concern and shame over the urinary incontinence, which represents a loss of masculine independence and control, to the hoarseness which interferes with his vocal production, because he can more easily accept loss of function associated with his voice than with his genitalia.

4) A resident of an old age home complains bitterly about the quality of her meals. Although there may be some justification for this, the complaints represent an effort to blame the environment rather than recognize diminished sensory perception.

5) A woman who has lost her roommate seems either indifferent or only very mildly concerned with her death, as a way of denying anxiety about her own anticipated death.

6) A husband seems indifferent to the loss of his wife, but expresses his feelings of helplessness and despair by increased senility or withdrawal.

7) A recent admission to a geriatric institution becomes helpless, clinging, and demanding. Another resident insists that she is different, of a higher social class and moral standard than the other residents. She treats the staff, nurses, and aides with contempt, and engenders a good deal of hostility in return. Another resident criticizes doctors for their inefficiency and describes other residents as being "senile, stupid, or crazy."

REACTION TO PARTIAL LOSS

Reactions to the perception of physical, social, and mental losses range from healthy or adaptive responses to comparatively unhealthy or maladaptive reactions. At one end of the scale is the individual who accepts and compensates for his loss. At the other end clinical syndromes such as depression and hypochondriasis are substitute expressions for the painful experience of loss.

Reactions to loss are determined, in most cases, by the individual's experiences in early life, his present personality and character structure, and the capacity he has developed to deal with losses. People who have high self-esteem, self-confidence, and an active approach toward facing life's challenges are less likely to develop feelings of helplessness and anxiety when confronted with losses associated with old age.

Reactions to aging have been categorized (3) into five reactive modes: 1) Compensation—a reaction which repairs, modifies, avoids, or substitutes for a decrease in function. 2) Acceptance—understanding the change as unavoidable, inevitable, and beyond changing. 3) Limitation—experience of the change as an interference with some explicitly stated needs or necessary daily functions. 4) Complaint—a response of discomfort, pain, annoyance, or embarrassment. 5) Qualification—importance of the loss is minimized by indicating that the change was insignificant. This last type of response is a form of denial which will be discussed later in more detail. Another form of denial is an attitude which leads the individual to engage in physical activities obviously excessive and probably dangerous to life and limb. It is, of course, much easier for a passive, dependent individual to tolerate imposed physical losses in old age than it is for an individual who was extremely active and found it necessary to master his environment through activity.

Since medical personnel and psychiatrists are often called upon to manage the maladaptive or pathological responses to loss in the aged, discussion will be confined to this group of reactions.

Denial

Denial is a defense against the pain of loss and is expressed by a refusal to acknowledge its existence. One woman who suffered a radical mastectomy attempted to minimize her loss by referring to her breasts

206

as "they never did me any good anyway, so I certainly don't need them now." Denial may also be expressed by acting in such a way as to recapture the lost function. This can lead to structural damage: for example, the individual with severe arthritis may attempt to walk without support; a nearly blind person may refuse assistance.

A poignant example of denial was a physician who continued to perform major surgery, although he suffered a tremor of both hands. The individual who has suffered the loss of a loved one may deny his loss by persisting in a fantasy of living with the lost object:

A widower quit his job after his wife's death and angrily refused to support himself in any way. He continued to act as if he were being protected and taken care of by a nonexistent wife, until one day he was robbed by hoodlums. He then developed a morbid fear of being attacked and robbed with the realization that there was no one to take care of him and that he was quite vulnerable.

In senile states, denial may take extreme forms. The individual may be convinced, for example, that his mother or father is waiting to take him home from the institution. As noted earlier, senile states may represent a turning away from the present reality of multiple loss and an overemphasis on the remote past when achievements, prestige, and expectations of a future predominated. Moss (4) feels that dulling of recent memory helps the patient to turn away from the painful present by denying its existence.

It is suggested by Weisman and Hackett (5) that denial is not simply a negation of objective reality, but is something people do to contend with a potential danger, such as death. In order to deal with this eventuality, the aging person may deny its possibility or even more subtly isolate its significance. Thus, conversations about death and infirmity can take place with comparative alacrity. However, if this attempt to separate fact from feeling becomes too pervasive, an inaccessibility is conveyed to others that may further interfere with the older person's maintaining close relationships.

There are individuals who develop an awareness and readiness to face dying. One factor mitigating fear of death in the aged is that incapacity and waning power is familiar to them. For some, the loss of independence and dignity may be more threatening than the concept of death. Death can even mean relief from pressures accompanying loss.

207

REACTION TO PARTIAL LOSS

Paranoid States

In the elderly who have suffered physical losses feelings of self-contempt may become overwhelming. In many such cases such self-contempt cannot be tolerated. As a result it is changed to contempt for others via a mental mechanism known as projection. A patient suffering from vision loss may accuse her doctor of causing it through his incompetence. Accusations of theft may reflect a patient's attempt to minimize his incapacity to arrange his belongings. Grandiose behavior may represent a pathological attempt to master imposed helplessness and passivity. People with such attitudes often become either troublesome or aloof to the point of withdrawal from the environment.

Hypochondriasis

In the process of disengagement, the decreased interest in the outside world is paralleled by an increased interest in one's own body functioning. Many old people seem to be self-centered and reveal little interest in developing friendships. Somatic complaints which have no organic basis and which do not respond to medication often point to an attempt to control people who are significant to the patient.

Shortly after admission to a home for the aged, one patient literally controlled her new environment from her chair. Since she claimed to be too ill to move, she arranged to have people bring her food or sent other residents and staff members on errands, while she maintained a "throne" in her own room. This woman had always been the dominant member of her household and was able to control her relatives by much more direct means in the past. The perception of loss of strength, compounded by the loss of her husband, led her to develop a "useful" illness.

As gradual body losses or depletions strike a blow to an individual's feeling of invulnerability, he is required to face the fact that he can no longer master various activities. His observations of ailing friends and relatives lead him to identify with them. The outcome may be a severe anxiety reaction or a hypochondriacal state. Preoccupation with a body organ may in some instances be a direct substitute for preoccupation with a lost loved one. On the other hand, one who has lost

208

a loved one may hold on to the illusion that the lost person still lives by identifying with him and his illness and may even begin to resemble the lost person. His hair may turn gray like the hair of the one he mourns; he may develop cardiac symptoms if the person died of heart disease; he may assume gestures and peculiarities of speech of the lost loved one. Hypochondriasis is often intimately connected with and may be symptomatic of depression, the most common pathological reaction to loss.

Depression

Depression is often not recognized in elderly people because weakness, apathy, irritability, and delirium are often considered manifestations of a chronic brain syndrome.

When an only daughter who had been a frequent visitor to the patient went abroad on vacation, the patient became disoriented, with garbled speech, accompanied by an alteration in consciousness which resembled apathy. When the daughter returned from vacation, these symptoms proved to be reversible manifestations of depression.

Another individual developed a confusional state with memory loss when hospitalized for physical illness. Separation from familiar surroundings precipitated a depressive state which was reversible.

In some depressions there is a loss of normal organized activity represented by extreme restlessness, aimless moving about or searching for something to do. Activity which formerly seemed to be centered around the lost object cannot be continued in an automatic way in the absence of the object. There is also a lack of capacity to initiate or organize one's activity patterns.

A seemingly trivial loss may be the occasion for the expression of depression over a significant loss. Deutsch (6) describes a woman who suffered a marked depression when the death of a pet dog rekindled memories of an earlier abandonment by a sister who had been dependent on her. Such depressions have as their source anger and hatred of the abandoning loved one (such as a dead spouse or, as occurs with great frequency in today's social structure, a rejecting child) and consequent guilt for experiencing these feelings. The child who sends his elderly

209

parent to a home for the aged may become the object not of direct hatred, but of overconcern.

One patient who disclaimed any anger at her son who arranged for admission to the home because she was "in the way" became depressed. She blamed herself for traits that any observer could easily ascribe to her son, while expressing a constant concern over her son's health.

Suicide

Suicide rates increase with age in both sexes and there is a peak suicide rate for men in the age group 60 to 69. Although women approach their peak suicide rate at about age 55, the number of elderly female suicides has increased. Suicides of both sexes, in the later years, have increased proportionately over the past three decades. Physical illness in the aged individual fosters dependency needs and concern over who will take care of him. Death is often sought as a solution. In paranoid states, suicide serves as an attempt to escape from tormenting delusions. The loneliness stemming from a lack of companionship and from a feeling of uselessness in both family and community life, and economic loss as a consequence of the decline in earnings, may also foster thoughts of suicide. Painful losses, such as loss of function through illness or the infirmity of advancing age, or severe guilt reactions following the loss of a love-object may be resolved by suicide. In the latter case, suicide can also serve the function of rejoining dead loved ones in some better world. Some people will threaten their loved ones who have abandoned them with statements about wanting to kill themselves and attempt suicide as a manipulative or coercive gesture. The most common internal conflicts in the suicidal individual are those associated with murderous impulses toward a loved person. These impulses arise out of an actual or imagined rejection, abandonment, or withdrawal of love by a person of significance to the patient. In severe depressions, the object of the patient's loss is in effect "swallowed up." Thus, many suicide attempts can be understood as an attempt to murder the hated but swallowed-up loved person.

Questioning both the patient and his family about the subject of suicide may aid in the recognition of a potential suicide. Many physicians avoid the subject of suicide in the belief that it may precipitate a suicide. Rather, patients are often relieved to be able to talk about their suicidal preoccupation with a supportive and willing listener.

Management in the Community

It is important to understand that the aging individual cannot be treated in isolation, since he is often dependent upon his family. His behavior has profound repercussions upon his children and their marital partners. It is often the children and their spouses who must be helped to understand the behavior of their aging parents and in-laws. Counseling or psychotherapy in many instances can provide a basis for reducing or ameliorating aberrant behavior of the aging individual. The physician, social worker, and psychiatrist may collaborate to change the environment and influence the attitudes of family members.

The number of social agencies specializing in services for the aged has increased rapidly in this country in the past decade. Community agencies provide counseling to older persons and their families with an emphasis on dealing with stresses of retirement planning, changes in living arrangements, health care, financial management, and social relationships with relatives and friends. Services of some agencies include housekeeping assistance and home visiting by volunteers. More recently some agencies have developed a public affairs program which seeks to improve community conditions for the aged and to promote study programs which aim at influencing legislation pertinent to the aged. Religious organizations and churches have expressed increased interest in the aged by providing family services and activities in neighborhood settlement houses. Recreation and vacation facilities have become more prominent. Day centers with recreational, educational, and social activities for aging men and women have included club programs, discussions, lectures, music and dance, fine arts, crafts, outings, and community service projects.

REACTION TO PARTIAL LOSS

Management in the Hospital and Home for the Aged

Teamwork on the part of the entire staff is necessary for the understanding and management of the elderly patient. Providing continuity for the patient by assigning one physician or nurse to administer his care may reduce the need for medical attention and give the patient a sense of security. The more independence a patient is given the longer he preserves personal habits. A patient's excessive concern about himself can be reinforced by unnecessary nursing care. "Spoon-feeding" attitudes of nurses toward a senile patient may lead to more rapid deterioration. Staff members should try to recognize and work with the intact personality remaining in the individual and intervene promptly to counteract tendencies toward withdrawal and isolation.

Some authorities feel that reminiscence is early evidence of chronic brain syndrome; others feel that it has a positive adaptive value and should be encouraged since it enables patients to reestablish the fact of past accomplishments, thereby raising self-esteem. In order to avoid disorientation, confusion, and depression, adequate preparation should be made if there is a need to change a patient's accommodations. Sympathetic understanding of offensive, irritable, and selfish qualities in the elderly individual should be maintained.

For many individuals, placement in an institution represents a major loss—whether the loss of familiar surroundings and of authority over one's own household, or abandonment by family members. Such losses may be mitigated not only by supportive attitudes on the part of the staff, but also by making possible personalized and individualized living arrangements. Depression is often precipitated when an individual has to give up not only his residence but his own articles of clothing and furniture for which he has developed a life-long attachment. They may represent lost love-objects, social achievements, or an extension of the person's body. Rooms in institutions should be made as attractive, cheerful, and individual as possible, and institutional clothing should be avoided. The residents should be encouraged to use personal articles, furniture, pictures, and other mementos of their pre-institutional life. There should be a place for storing food brought by friends or relatives, and even some personal kitchen utensils (an old tea-pot, a familiar mug). Beds should look like apartment furniture

212

rather than hospital beds. Unnecessary use of bed siderails may foster feelings of helplessness and loss of independence.

Periods of work, play, and recreation should be included in a program of activities for aging patients. Group participation, training and industrial workshops aimed at improving the physical, psychological, and socioeconomic status of the patient should stress individual needs and be geared to enhancing self-esteem. Tasks too difficult to master can foster feelings of worthlessness in a depressed person. On the other hand, very simple stereotyped activities can present an affront to the individual's intelligence.

Many professions may contribute to the program. For example, in cases of aphasia a speech therapist can offer invaluable opportunity for self-expression. Individual and group psychotherapists should be available, and a social worker can be helpful in dealing with social security problems, job placement, rehabilitation services, and referral to special clinics or hospitals.

When food, shelter, medical care, and recreational facilities are provided, the individual may be relieved of anxiety but lack the gratification that is ordinarily derived from successful mastery of the physical and the social environment. Goldfarb (7) has described how illusory mastery over the powerful physician may be a source of pleasure for patients in whom healthy affectionate attitudes are poorly developed, and whose sense of worthlessness is so great that the only bond between people is one of power.

The physician should understand the patient's behavior not as a personal assault but as an attempt to dominate the powerful authority both of the physician and of the illness, and to overcome a sense of lowered self-esteem. If the physician understands the potentially threatening aspect of his authority, he will see that at times he should permit the patient to believe he can dominate him. Staff members can be made aware of their own reactions to the normal frustrations of working with the chronically ill since they may develop attitudes of excessive pity or compassion or they may carry out hostile acts disguised as kindly measures.

Patients will occasionally be suspected of intending suicide. In these instances appropriate measures and approaches are suggested. While a 24-hour watch of suicidal patients is usually indicated, some

213

individuals feel that such precautions at times can become too repressive. When suicidal precautions are taken, they must not indicate a lack of faith or respect for the patient's sense of self-esteem and integrity. Interest and sincerity on the part of the physician can serve to mediate suicidal feelings. It is important that the physician not belittle hypochondriacal complaints since they may often represent the only verbalization of the patient's depression and suicide intent. Depression is, of course, not the only precipitant of suicide. Many would-be suicides show agitation, psychotic symptoms, or symptoms ordinarily associated with organic brain syndromes. However, depression is the best single indication of potential suicide.

The Physician-Psychotherapist

In many communities the general physician or medical specialist is often called upon to treat emotional disorders in the aged in lieu of any available psychiatric facilities. A few general principles may serve as helpful suggestions in such instances.

It must be borne in mind that the physician often represents to the patient a substitute parent who can help him regulate his everyday functions. He prescribes medications for pain relief, sleep, and bowel regulation. Quite often patients respond to medications according to their relationship to the physician. Also, suggestibility may govern the patient's response to medication. Vitamins, for example, have a symbolic "building-up" quality and can often be administered most effectively to elderly patients. Analgesic drugs administered to relieve prolonged states of pain at the same time may relieve depression and feelings of helplessness. The physician can often provide magical relief from suffering and misery by simply offering reassurance or suggestions.

Just as the physician as a powerful parental substitute is endowed with authority and magical omnipotence, so his medication is endowed with similar qualities. Because of the nature of physical illness in old age, however, the individual's magical expectations are easily shattered. In such instances, he may become openly demanding and complaining when the medication is ineffective; the doctor's advice is regarded as worthless. The physician, in response, may develop an

214

attitude of therapeutic nihilism, for his own sense of mastery is threatened. His failure may revive memories of earlier real or imagined failures of care on his part or on the part of those responsible for him.

In addition to the failure of mastery over the environment, there is an increasing limitation of whatever capacities remain. It is the physician's task to try to relieve the anxiety surrounding these limitations. He should avoid explaining to the patient that he has no organic ailment when the patient presents with hypochondriacal complaints. Such explanations may deprive the patient of psychological defenses that he needs to preserve his self-esteem.

A blind woman who had lost part of a finger trying to open a door subsequently feared renewing her social activities. She remained in bed most of the time complaining of severe arthritis. Therapeutic intervention revealed a mild depression based on the fact that the referring physician considered her complaints psychological and told her so. He had, in effect, stripped her of a necessary defense. The fact that she was afraid was too intolerable for her to admit.

The patient must be helped to ventilate his angry feelings, his feelings of hopelessness and worthlessness. In some cases loss of self-esteem may be reversed if the physician expresses the patient's anger and rage for him, thus enabling him to avoid the guilt which would result from such self-expression.

The doctor's helplessness in dealing with physical and mental losses in the elderly and the patient's angry response to him may evoke strong feelings of hostility, even to the extent of an unconscious wish to kill a chronically ill or demanding patient. These patients are frequently avoided or dealt with by oversolicitous attitudes which represent a defense against such unacceptable wishes.

Psychopharmacotherapy is an important aspect of geriatric management, especially in depressive states. In reviewing the various studies on drug therapy, one finds a paucity of discussion of the physician-patient relationship and its influence upon the effectiveness of drug-therapy. The practitioner who finds it necessary to administer one or more drugs should be aware that his attitude toward this specific drug and toward the patient in question will greatly influence the effectiveness of the patient's response. Many elderly patients are loathe to take medications. Some will ascribe their symptoms

215

to the fact that they are taking the drug, while other patients will try to control the physician by insisting that whatever drug he gives is of no use. Because of his guilt or because of his own wish to help the patient, the physician may be tempted to keep changing the medication. This can have negative results since it becomes a reversal of the usual relationship of patient to physician. If the physician can convey to the patient a sense of conviction about the medication he uses, along with a keen interest in helping and understanding the patient, the drug therapy will frequently be more effective. The physician should avoid drugs and dosages that unduly relax and confuse the elderly patient.

In his dependence upon the physician, the elderly patient may react to him very much as a child would toward a parent upon whom he delegates a magical omnipotence. At times the patient is determined to belittle the physician's efforts. If this is permitted, the sense of guilt may be merely furthered. The physician-parent image may be destroyed, with increased guilt and depression the consequence.

REFERENCES

1. E. W. Busse, "Research on Aging: Some Methods and Findings," in *Geriatric Psychiatry: Grief, Loss, and Emotional Disorders in the Aging Process*, eds. Martin A. Berezin and Stanley H. Cath, New York: International Universities Press, 1967.
2. R. E. Moss, "Aging: A Survey of the Psychiatric Literature 1950-1960," in *Geriatric Psychiatry: Grief, Loss, and Emotional Disorders in the Aging Process*, eds. Martin A. Berezin and Stanley H. Cath, New York: International Universities Press, 1965.
3. S. Perlin and R. N. Butler, "Psychiatric Aspect of Adaptation to the Aging Experience," in *Human Aging, A Biological and Behavioral Study*, eds. J. E. Birren et al., Washington, D. C.: U. S. Public Health Service Publication #986, 1963.
4. R. E. Moss, "Aging: A Survey of the Psychiatric Literature."
5. A. D. Weisman and T. P. Hackett, "Denial as a Social Act," in *Psychodynamic Studies on Aging: Creativity, Reminiscing and Dying*, eds. S. Levin and R. J. Kahana, New York: International Universities Press, 1967.

6. H. Deutsch, *Neurosis and Character Types,* New York: International Universities Press, 1965.
7. A. T. Goldfarb, "Psychotherapy of Aged Persons, *Psychoanalytic Review,* *42*:2, 1955.

IV

The Dying Patient

15

The Patient's Reaction
to Fatal Illness

Bernard Schoenberg and Robert A. Senescu

Recent advances in medicine have resulted in increasing numbers of patients being treated for chronic illness over longer periods of time. For patients with cancer, for example, earlier detection, more strenuous surgical treatment, new chemotherapeutic agents, and better combinations of treatment have increased the chances of survival and the period of illness preceding death. Unlike deaths in some other cultures where patients are moved back home with their families to die, more than one-half the deaths in the United States occur in the hospital.

In the health professions in general, minimal attention is paid during training to the psychosocial care of the dying patient. Hospital personnel receive meager support in caring for dying patients and minimal opportunity to deal with their emotional reactions to death. Care of the dying patient usually induces so much anxiety in health personnel that in many hospitals emphasis is placed on the routine technical aspects of physical care rather than on the development of close interpersonal relationships with patients.

Cancer presents a realistic as well as a symbolic threat to the welfare and survival of a human being. The threat is magnified by the fear with which cancer is viewed by laymen and the health professions. Other diseases which may carry an equally serious threat to the biological welfare of the individual and which may be less amenable to treatment are frequently approached with less apprehension. The word *cancer* evokes thoughts of an eroding, devouring, and mutilating illness. This reaction may exert its damaging effect long before the patient seeks medical assistance and may contribute to an unfortunate delay in seeking treatment.

At present, one in three cancer patients is cured of his disease—that is, he remains free of disease for at least five years. It has been estimated that if everyone saw a physician when the first symptom appears, the cure rate could be increased to 50 per cent. Studies of patient-responsible delay in seeking treatment indicate that total ignorance of the significance of a sign or symptom is extremely rare, and most patients have knowledge of the treatability of cancer, especially in its early stages. In one study (1), psychological determinants and their incidence in a group of delay patients were shown to include fear of punishment (26.7 per cent), fear of death in surgical treatment (15.3 per cent), reaction formation or overcompensation to dependency needs (13.7 per cent), shame or the wish to avoid exposure (13.0 per cent), and suicidal wishes or resignation to a fatal outcome (9.2 per cent). In another study (2), the fear of cancer was shown to be usually expressed as fear of losing a job, of leaving the family, of dependency, of fear of surgery, or as an indication of weakness. Some patients sought assistance only when forced to by the severity of their symptoms. Recent research has demonstrated that patients who are more anxious over their health usually seek early assistance. Contrary to expectations, a study of a group of women with breast cancer who delayed seeking treatment indicated that they were not passive but rather showed indications of strength and independence. This group had a well-defined sense of body boundaries and less anxiety over the discovery of physical symptoms. The investigators concluded that the person who is autonomous, self-delineated, and independent is resistant to assume the role of patient and "submit" to the physician (3, 4).

Individual differences in response to the threat of illness, helplessness, disability, pain, and separation are based on differences in personality patterns which in turn are derived to a large extent from past personal experiences. The patient's responses to life-threatening illness may be considered maladaptive if the reactions are stronger than the danger warrants, if they persist when the threat no longer exists, or if the appropriate responses to danger are lacking. At what point the emotional response is to be labeled a psychiatric problem depends on how the physician views his function and his ability to manage the emotional complications. The major behaviorial criteria of a significant emotional complication in a patient with cancer or chronic disease are when the emotional reaction 1) prevents him from seeking or cooperating with indicated treatment; 2) significantly increases the pain and distress of the illness; 3) interferes with effective functioning in the vocational, social, and familial spheres; 4) results in a disorganization of his personality with the appearance of psychiatric symptoms. In the latter instance, an essential feature is the tendency of the patient to misinterpret his environment in terms of his feelings, particularly those of fear, anger, and guilt. These feelings occur to some degree, often automatically and unconsciously, as a reaction to a threatened loss of function or the prospect of pain and mutilation. The physician's reactions to these feelings will determine to a considerable degree the course of his future relationship with the patient.

Pain and Fear

Pain and fear are closely related—pain is a reaction to damage while fear is the anticipation of pain and damage. The patient who experiences pain may be regarded as fearful in the sense that he expects more pain or can not anticipate the alleviation of pain. Emotional or feeling states such as fear and depression are also painful and contribute to the experience of pain, regardless of the degree of physical damage. Fear of an imaginary danger is difficult to manage but when the fear is related to a realistic danger, encouraging the patient to express it and offering reassurance may be helpful.

A 50-year-old grocer was admitted to the hospital for removal of cancer of the large intestine. During the workup he openly expressed his fear of pain and death, and told of his hope of coming through the operation alive. He admitted great confidence in the hospital and the surgeon who was to perform the operation. Physical examination revealed moderate anxiety, with sweaty palms, a slightly increased pulse rate, and elevated blood pressure. After several conversations with the surgeon regarding the procedure and anticipated postoperative course, his anxiety decreased and he stated he was "no longer afraid." His postoperative course was uncomplicated.

223

THE DYING PATIENT

For a patient with a life-threatening disease, fear can be both realistic and/or exaggerated. A patient's magnified fear of dying may be the result of displacement from other sources of anxiety, such as fear of separation, abandonment, loneliness, mutilation, loss of control, loss of identity, and infantile behavior. One may say that the fearful patient imagines dangers which then elicit more fears. Many patients regard fear as an indication of weakness, inferiority, or immaturity and therefore are reluctant to express it. The conscious awareness of fear may be hidden and express itself only in physiologic disturbances, fearful dreams, or emotional withdrawal. Terms such as tension, restlessness, "butterflies," and nervousness, are common indications of the underlying fear and anxiety.

A 46-year-old bank clerk was admitted to the hospital with a diagnosis of cancer of the large intestine. During the initial examination he was agitated and interrupted many times to ask what was going to happen, stating that he was sure he would die during the operation. Ordinarily not suspicious, he expressed the thought that the surgeon might "cut him to bits." Several times during the examination he insisted on sitting upright and walking around the room complaining that he felt tense and nervous. His pulse rate and respiration were elevated and he reported that he felt a "lump in his throat" and a headache. During the first night in the hospital he awoke several times short of breath and feeling "panicky." He told the nurse he feared he was going to die and additional sedation failed to give him relief. In an interview the following day with the psychiatrist he talked of an older brother who died of a ruptured appendix when the patient was 10 years old. One week prior to his brother's death the patient hit his brother in the abdomen causing him to double up with pain. For many months afterwards he was "haunted" by the episode and felt that he was responsible for his brother's death. On many occasions previous to his current illness he awoke with great anxiety and abdominal pain.

Dependency

In chronic disease or in any illness requiring repeated and prolonged hospitalization, the patient is inevitably placed in a dependent position which causes him to feel childlike and helpless. Many patients react to this state with resentment since it reawakens feelings of weakness and

224

smallness, and arouses feelings of inferiority and shame. How the individual manages these feelings is related to how his dependency needs were met in the earlier relationships of childhood. If he felt secure and loved in early life he will find it easier to depend on and to trust the physician and nurse. For the patient who fears dependency, surgical procedures are particularly threatening since anesthesia and surgery require a total submission on his part. Out of fear and shame of being in a dependent position a patient may adopt a façade of independence and present serious problems in management. He will fight off any indication that he cannot care for himself: he makes his own rules, resists the nurses' assistance, and second-guesses his physicians. If his illness is too overwhelming, he may give up the fight and become depressed. At that time he may become clinging and exaggerate relatively minor physical complaints. He may be unaware of how losing his self-sufficiency influences his behavior and he may suffer severe loss of self-esteem before there are clinical indications of his distress.

Mrs. I., a 55-year-old married woman, was seen by the psychiatrist following an unsuccessful suicide attempt. She had suffered from hypertension and peripheral vascular disease which progressively forced her into a position of complete dependency on her husband and family. She was blind and unable to walk and realized that she had "a short time to live" but presented a façade of courage and "good spirits." She claimed that her suicide attempt was accidental and that she had taken an overdose of barbiturates during a period of nocturnal confusion. In psychotherapy she became aware of her shame, humiliation, and guilt over her helpless, dependent state and was able to admit her profound feelings of despair. She realized that the "accidental overdose" was an unconsciously motivated attempt to escape from an "impossible situation." She had always prided herself on her self-sufficiency and resourcefulness and found it humiliating to be dependent on family members who she felt were condescending and oversolicitous.

A fundamental characteristic of the dependent patient is his tendency to parentify the physician and nurse. The behavior of the patient toward the parentified figure is much like a child toward the all-powerful parent. In order to "remain in the parent's good graces," the patient is likely to be compliant and ingratiating, since loss of the

225

parental figures' approval is a threat to his security. He views the physician and nurse as potentially punitive and is reluctant to voice complaints or to make demands. If he disagrees or resists treatment, he is inclined to feel guilty even if his reaction is appropriate. The consequence is usually guilt and depression which may be expressed in his relationship with other health personnel or with the family.

Mrs. B., a 53-year-old housewife, was readmitted to the hospital with a tentative diagnosis of subacute bacterial endocarditis. During her two previous admissions to the ward with acute rheumatic fever she was considered an ideal patient—cooperative, cheerful, and undemanding. The medical staff were in disagreement over her diagnosis—the attending staff assumed it was acute rheumatic fever and the house staff asserted that it was subacute bacterial endocarditis. At the beginning of her fourth hospital week she suddenly burst into tears and said she wished she were dead. Psychiatric consultation revealed that during her previous hospitalizations she was terrified but was reassured by the physician regarding her diagnosis and treatment. During her current hospitalization she became increasingly aware of the uncertainty and insecurity of her physician. As she became more apprehensive over her lack of progress, she felt angry and defiant and found to her surprise that she was being "unreasonable" and demanding with the ward personnel. She felt the nurses were avoiding her because she was being a "bad girl." The psychiatrist assured her that it was permissible to discuss her doubts about her doctor and her anger with the nurses. She gradually realized that there were possibilities open to her other than complete submission or open defiance and that her physician was not omnipotent.

Anger

Like fear, anger can be an anticipatory response to the threat of pain, damage, or loss of function. In the hospital, the expression of anger is discouraged even more strongly than fear. The fearful, compliant, ingratiating patient is likely to be rewarded, while the angry, demanding, complaining patient often elicits punitive or retaliatory behavior by hospital personnel. In the dependent patient anger often stimulates feelings of guilt and fear of retaliation. It is frightening for a patient in a dependent position to express anger toward a physician or nurse upon whom he feels totally dependent for survival. To control or hide

226

anger, he may withdraw from all self-assertive behavior and become emotionally inaccessible. He may experience a feeling of great relief when his anger is acknowledged and he discovers that he will not be punished. The patient who is allowed to discuss his angry feelings is far less likely to regard the environment as hostile and to develop feelings of guilt and depression.

A 35-year-old unmarried woman was seen by the psychiatrist with members of the radiotherapy unit as part of a study project. She had received intensive treatment and her prognosis was considered poor due to abdominal metastatic disease from a primary cervical carcinoma. She was irritatingly demanding to know when she was going to die. The patient entered the conference room in a challenging, pugnacious manner and immediately asked the psychiatrist if he were the expert who would answer her question. He replied that he did not know the answer and that it was a painful subject for her to be preoccupied with. When the patient asked if he were trying to tell her that she was feeling more miserable than she should be, the psychiatrist agreed and she proceeded to tell the group how much she blamed herself for her difficulties. She feared that the physicians were angry with her for not seeking help sooner. The group reassured her that her anger was not an uncommon response to her illness and that no one blamed her. When interviewed three months later she was pleasant and cooperative and reported that she was seeing her friends again and was keeping herself busy although her physical condition remained rather poor (5).

Loss of Self-esteem

Although most patients feel somewhat damaged by their illness, there is greater likelihood of these feelings in chronic disease and cancer. Damage to the individual's self-esteem is initially a result of the patient's reaction to his primary disease and is closely related to a variety of emotional reactions. In general, the factors that contribute most to the reduction of self-esteem are: a) illness and the loss of capacity to function; b) loss of the feeling of self-sufficiency and independence; c) fear; d) guilt; e) inability to gain gratification; and f) the individual interpretation of the attitudes and feelings of significant figures (family, physician, and nurse) toward him.

Bibring (6) describes the common aspirations of individuals:

227

a) to be worthy (loved and appreciated); b) to be good (not aggressive or hateful; and c) to be strong (not dependent and helpless). The failure to fulfill these aspirations can lead to a serious reduction of self-esteem with depression as the consequence. Generally, health personnel tend to underestimate their influence on the patient's feelings about himself. Even subtle manifestations of the physician's feelings and attitudes, such as condescension, disapproval, irritation, frustration, or fear, may have a profound effect on the patient's feeling of well-being. One experienced surgeon reports that he has learned to express his appreciation or admiration to patients following surgery by saying, "You've done a good job," "You are a good patient," or "You should be proud of yourself," before he even discusses the operative findings.

Guilt

An integral part of guilt is the fear of punishment based on the child's belief that the all-powerful parent sees, hears, and knows all. The physician, who is the most likely person to be cast in the benign parental role by the helpless patient, is also most likely to be cast in the punitive role. The guilty individual may feel bad, dirty, and unworthy, and may anticipate punishment, the consequence of which is anxiety and the reduction of his self-esteem. The patient may feel guilt over hostile thoughts and feelings as well as overtly angry behavior. An ill patient may view his disease as a punishment visited upon him for past sins or indiscretions—"If I hadn't been bad, this wouldn't have happened to me" or "What have I done to deserve this?" More often than not the patient cannot say what he has done that is so bad, while the indiscretion is rarely of the magnitude to explain the guilt.

A 55-year-old man, separated from his family for 15 years, was admitted to a large municipal hospital with the diagnosis of chronic alcoholism and hepatic cirrhosis. Diagnostic procedures substantiated the impression that he had hepatic carcinoma with widespread metastases and would probably die in a short time. He was emotionally withdrawn, made no demands on hospital personnel, and showed minimal curiosity over his diagnosis or prognosis. He appeared despondent, fatalistic, and the ward nurse felt he was reconciled to dying. He was generally avoided by the medical staff until one evening the intern initiated a conversation with him. He readily

228

told the physician that fifteen years ago he had been dismissed from a responsible position as sales manager because of drunkenness, and that he was unable to tolerate the shame and humiliation he felt in his relationship with his wife and her family: "For the sake of my wife and children I disappeared and have been on skid row ever since." He knew he was dying and felt that it was just punishment for his "rotten behavior." He regarded his cancer as a result of alcoholism and regretted that he had "strayed from the church." The intern asked him to discuss his situation with the hospital chaplain, who assured him that anyone could develop cancer, "even the Pope." Following a conference with the social worker the intern contacted the patient's family, who readily forgave him and visited him daily. His depression gradually lifted and he remained in good spirits until he died two months later. Shortly before dying he told the nurse he could not recall ever being so happy, and that he now regarded his cancer simply as bad luck.

Angry feelings toward the physician and nurse, whether justified or not, are a common source of guilt. The greater the feelings of gratitude, the more likely the patient is to hide his anger and feel guilty. Patients, especially those receiving palliative treatment such as radiotherapy, are given minimal opportunity to express their feelings of anger and tend to feel ungrateful when they do.

Feelings of envy, jealousy, and dependency also contribute to feelings of guilt. In a study of 60 patients with cancer (7), feelings of guilt were noted in 93 per cent of the patients. These feelings contributed significantly to delay in seeking treatment, stimulated feelings of inferiority and dependency, and inhibited communication. Relief of guilt feelings was frequently accomplished by giving the patient and his family the opportunity to discuss them.

Loss of Pleasure

It is understandable that the patient with chronic illness or cancer will be preoccupied with his disease. However, this can result in a serious reduction in gaining pleasure from other sources and life activities. Pleasure may be viewed as having a "buffer effect," neutralizing the inevitable pains and frustrations which accompany loss of health and function. A common clinical problem is how to persuade a patient who recognizes that his life span is limited to engage in pleasurable activity.

229

THE DYING PATIENT

Although modern hospitals have emphasized making physical facilities more attractive, they tend to ignore the patient's personal sources of pleasure. In most hospitals the opportunity for pleasurable activity is usually limited, highly routinized, and quite peripheral to the therapeutic program.

A 57-year-old woman, hospitalized for bronchogenic carcinoma with metastases, was overtly depressed and considered suicidal. When interviewed by the psychiatrist she described her previous behavior and her numerous activities which served to make her feel worthwhile and adequate. She had maintained a meticulous home, cooked for her married daughters, engaged in a number of charitable activities, babysat, and knitted and crocheted. In consultation with occupational therapy she was encouraged to knit a sweater for her daughter's birthday. Although her strength was failing, she worked at the sweater, at times assisted by the nurses. She expressed the hope that she would complete the sweater before "it was too late." The psychiatrist spoke with her during brief daily visits and devoted his efforts to raising her self-esteem and directing her toward more pleasurable activities. The ward personnel noted that knitting had become a major project for her and a source of great satisfaction.

Dying

To some extent the term dying is inappropriate, since the patient may have a fatal illness and yet enjoy good physical health. The process of dying is temporal and at different stages of illness the patient's needs and the requirements of care differ. In our own approach to the problem we have found it useful to separate the initial stages of illness into detection (the first symptom), diagnosis (including biopsy), intervention (such as surgical treatment, chemotherapy, radiotherapy, or palliative treatment), remission, progression, and the terminal stage. Glaser and Strauss (8) describe critical junctures which may occur in the terminal stage: 1) patient is dying; 2) patient, family, and staff prepare for death; 3) the point is reached where there is nothing more to do; 4) the final descent; 5) the last hours; 6) the death watch; and 7) death itself.

How an individual faces death is inevitably related to his manner of coping with life. Shneidman (9) describes five patients dying of cancer as examples of the 1) "postponer" (wishes not to die and exerts his will to live) ; 2) "acceptor" (resigned to his cessation) ; 3) "disdainer" (disdainful of what is occurring and does not believe death will take him) ; 4) "welcomer" (welcomes the end) ; 5) "fearer" (fights the notion of cessation). The defensive process of denial is common, to a greater or lesser degree, in all patients with a fatal disease. The mechanism is one of avoidance that is integrated into the adaptive system of the individual and serves the temporary function of negating intolerable or painful stimuli and rendering it unconscious. The process consumes energy and avoids reality but at the moment makes life more tolerable. The emotional defenses of a patient should be respected unless there is clear evidence that the advantages of breaking down a patient's defenses outweigh the advantages of maintaining them. Confronting the patient with evidence that he is dying may precipitate a reaction which can cause further depression, emotional disorganization, or further withdrawal from reality. Sudden disclosure of evidence may stimulate even more denial and make the patient less accessible to the physician and other hospital personnel. Denial may lead to unwise decisions or behavior. An example is a patient with widespread metastases who decided to expand his business operations. Another example is a patient who had several myocardial infarcts and suffered from cardiac failure and angina but who was determined to continue strenuous recreational activities. These patients may identify with the physician and speak of other patients as being in "bad shape." A self-defeating means of strengthening the denial is to isolate oneself from the source of truth—the physician. This can result in failure to keep follow-up visits or continue essential medications. A patient may project his fear of death onto others and may devote time to reassuring his family or to telling the nurse that other patients are fearful and are in need of reassurance. Avoidance of drawing up a will or making financial provisions for the family are other typical manifestations of denial. Other patients may show compulsive reactions and engage in ritualistic behavior, intellectualizations, and ruminations.

Recent surveys indicate that most patients want to be informed of potentially fatal illness while only a minority of physicians are willing to provide this information. Other studies have indicated that when given the opportunity to speak freely; 75 per cent of terminal patients in a general hospital discussed dying with hospital personnel. Terminal patients are frequently avoided by hospital personnel, thereby increasing their sense of loneliness and isolation. Physicians and nurses may avoid conversation or otherwise distract a patient when he begins to discuss death. When the patient feels that hospital personnel are uncomfortable in allowing him to discuss the taboo topic, he will gradually erect his own communication barrier. It is the conspiracy of silence that is most destructive since it tends to separate the dying from the living and offers the patient no opportunity to verbalize his feelings and thoughts, or allow his positive feelings for others to emerge.

A 56-year-old carpenter was described by nursing students as cheerful, affable, cooperative—in many ways, an ideal patient. The students and ward personnel assumed he was unaware of his condition. An abdominal exploration had revealed a cancer of the pancreas with widespread metastases and he was "quickly closed up." The resident surgeon told him that his gall bladder had been removed and he would be as good as new. Interviewed in a patient care conference, the patient expressed his gratitude to the nurses and the doctors and assured the students he would "be back on his feet in no time." When the psychiatrist asked him if he had felt "blue or weepy recently," he burst into tears and asked if "they had gotten it all out." A follow-up interview indicated that he had been aware that he had a malignancy but felt there was no one willing to discuss it with him.

Feelings of grief and depression gradually emerge as the patient recognizes the potential loss of loved ones. To protect himself from the painful feelings of separation and loss, the patient tends to withdraw from important relationships. Unable to cope with their painful feelings of loss, friends and family members tend to withdraw. This process of gradual mutual withdrawal or disengagement results in painful feelings of isolation and loneliness, diminishing the patient's capacity for living during the last days.

Some of these feelings are poignantly described in Tolstoy's *The Death of Iván Ilých*. (10).

Iván Ilých saw that he was dying, and he was in continual despair. Why deceive myself? Isn't it obvious to everyone but me that I'm dying, and it's only a question of weeks, days. . . . And none of them knows or wishes to know it, and they have no pity for me. . . . The deception, the lie, which for some reason they all accepted, that he was not dying but was simply ill, and that he only need keep quiet and undergo a treatment and then something very good would result. This deception tortured him—their not wishing to admit what they all knew and what he knew, but wanting to lie to him concerning his terrible condition, and wishing and forcing him to participate in that lie. . . . He wept on account of his helplessness, his terrible loneliness . . . during that loneliness in which he found himself as he lay facing the back of the sofa, a loneliness in the midst of a populous town and surrounded by numerous acquaintances and relations but that yet could not have been more complete anywhere—either at the bottom of the sea or under the earth—during that terrible loneliness Iván Ilých had lived only in the memories of the past. . . . It was true, as the doctor said, that (his) physical sufferings were terrible, but worst were his mental sufferings which were his chief torture.

A recent study of advanced cancer patients showed that although the group did not manifest more emotional disturbance than a group with another debilitating disease, 25 per cent of the cancer patients manifested marked depression. Interviews and clinical observations suggested that significant factors in the depression were feelings of hopelessness, the lack of a future orientation, and the feeling that control had passed from the patient's hands.

Depression may disguise itself in a wide variety of symptoms, including insomnia, lethargy, anorexia, fatigue, or constipation. Somatic complaints unrelated to the illness may predominate and mask the other symptoms of depression leading to a situation in which the physician and nurse are unaware of the underlying feelings of loss and low self-esteem. At times the significance of the complaints associated with depression can be overlooked since the symptoms can be attributed to underlying disease. Following a biopsy or surgical procedure severe depression may become manifest by a process of somatic self-scrutiny, soon followed by bizarre or complex symptoms.

Personnel in a general hospital are usually not alert to the possibility of suicide. Nurses' notes frequently describe progressive changes indicative of a deepening depression but do not label it as such. This may, in part, be related to the fact that so many hospitalized patients are moderately depressed. When a patient shows bizarre behavior, paranoid ideation, or severe depression, he should be observed carefully and referred for psychiatric consultation. Reference to suicide, the wish "to get it over with," or sudden alleviation of a severe depression warrants further investigation.

THE DYING PATIENT

All patients with chronic or terminal disease, especially those in which delirium or confusion play a part, and those with previous histories of chronic alcoholism or severe psychopathology, should be observed carefully as potential suicides. The period preceding discharge from the hospital after "everything possible has been done" is when careful observation is necessary since the unrealistic hopes and fantasies of cure have been deflated. The suicide attempt may be related to a wish to punish a member of the family or the physician. In others, it may represent the need to relieve the individual's intolerable guilt feelings or to regain control over a process which is no longer in his hands. For some, the experience of pain, isolation, loneliness, or the loss of a valued function or body part may be unbearable. For example, one patient dying of cancer with no previous history of depression left a suicide note stating that he could not endure the waiting and that he wanted to get it over with. Personal ideologies of death and the afterworld may make immediate death for some patients more tolerable than gradual deterioration. In contrast to the above patients, one chronically depressed patient welcomed serious illness as a substitute for committing suicide. It has been suggested that in 18 per cent of suicides the principal cause was physical illness, frequently cancer.

Surgery

With recent advances in chemotherapy, radiation therapy, and surgical techniques, cancer surgery has become more prevalent and surgical procedures more extensive. Following a tentative diagnosis of cancer, a patient is often told that he requires an operation to remove a "growth" or tumor. Although terrified and overwhelmed by thoughts of mutilation, injury, and death, the patient may avoid asking the basic reason for surgery. When the patient is left with fantasies of his illness, his tendency to see it as punishment, mutilation, or shame is markedly increased. Since cancer is a dreaded disease, the implication is that extensive or mutilating surgery is necessary to cure it. The patient may also view surgery as a magical intervention which will "clean him out" and cure him of cancer. Surgery usually requires a

234

period of postoperative convalescence and implies loss of work ability, financial hardship, anxiety over mutilation, cosmetic disfigurement, and alteration in body-image.

The first indications of emotional problems are in the preoperative stage but frequently are not recognized until after surgery. In his studies of surgical patients, Janis (11) noted that those who anticipate the stress with a *moderate* degree of fear were able to withstand surgery better than those who were completely without worry, or unduly apprehensive. The latter group felt highly vulnerable to body damage and developed pre- and postoperative emotional complications. This group of patients was found to have a long-standing history of anxiety and psychoneurosis. The group that displayed the least amount of fear and minimized the operation reacted postoperatively with anger and apprehension and would have been able to cope much better if given more adequate preparation. The group that was moderately fearful engaged the staff in reassuring conversation and sought advance information regarding the postoperative period. The results emphasize the positive value of moderate anticipatory fear in creating a psychological rehearsal of the impending danger and allowing the individual to develop coping mechanisms and effective defenses. Patients who are provided with information to facilitate the work of worrying and are provided with some reassurrance require less sedation, complain less, and recover more quickly. If the patient is forewarned of the anticipated effect of surgery, the preoperative period can be utilized to adjust to the prospect of functional loss or body alterations. It also gives him the opportunity to view the surgeon as a life-saving force rather than as a destructive one.

Important factors to be considered in anticipating a patient's response to surgery are: 1) how much the healthy function of the organ contributed to the individual's self-esteem and pleasure; 2) how much guilt is present in connection with the specific part of the body; 3) the degree of preoperative anxiety.

For example, if a woman's self-esteem is based to a large extent on bearing and raising children, surgery to any part of the reproductive system will have a profound effect. If, for any real or imaginary reason, the individual feels guilty about the particular organ, the disease and surgical treatment are far more likely to be viewed as punishment.

235

THE DYING PATIENT

A woman with a strict Catholic upbringing was coerced by her husband to limit the size of their family through birth control. She submitted and developed cancer of the cervix after several years of using a diaphragm. She clearly viewed her disease as punishment for her transgressions.

For some individuals, self-esteem is based to a great extent on the appearance they present to the world. In such instances, mastectomy or any operation leading to body disfigurement may result in severe depression.

Biopsy, which is regarded by most physicians as a simple diagnostic procedure, is frequently regarded differently by the patient and may elicit as much anxiety as extensive surgery. This is especially true when the patient has no opportunity to learn the results of biopsy before surgery, as in the case of mastectomy.

A 25-year-old unmarried woman sought surgical consultation when she discovered a lump in her breast. The surgeon assumed the lump to be a benign cyst but because of the high incidence of cancer in the patient's family, he suggested a biopsy. He scheduled the patient for hospital admission 5 weeks later when he was to return from vacation. During that period the patient developed severe tension and insomnia and her mother developed severe anxiety. When he returned, the surgeon realized that he had underestimated the patient's anxiety and had failed to give the patient and her family sufficient reassurance.

In summary, the dying patient's reaction to his disease, treatment, and impending death must be understood in terms of numerous and sometimes conflicting factors. The patient with a life history of previous relationships and numerous experiences related to loss, illness, and medical care must be approached as an individual. An evaluation of his current situation involves an understanding of the significant aspects of his life in the familial, social, occupational, and religious areas, as well as in the external sources of love, comfort, and support which are derived from relationships with others. What is the patient's concept of self and body-image, his ability to recognize and cope with reality, his reaction to dependency, pain, and uncertainty? What are his sources of pleasure, his state of conscience, and his philosophical approach to life and death? Other crucial factors are the nature of the specific illness; the organ or body system affected, and its symbolic

236

as well as realistic significance to the patient; the type of treatment required (surgery, pharmacotherapy, radiotherapy, etc.); and the degree of functional loss and disfigurement which accompanies the illness. Hospital personnel must also be aware of the reaction to his illness on the part of themselves and his family and friends, and of the extent to which they withdraw from him emotionally and physically, since this may impose further isolation and loneliness and add to his grief and despair.

REFERENCES

1. J. L. Titchener et al., "Problems of Delay in Seeking Surgical Care," *Journal of the American Medical Association, 160*:1187, 1956.
2. J. Aitken-Swan and R. Paterson, "The Cancer Patient: Delay in Treatment," *British Medical Journal*, March 12, 1955, p. 623.
3. S. Fisher, "Motivation for Patient Delay," *Archives of General Psychiatry, 16*:676, 1967.
4. C. A. Hammerschlag et al., "Breast Symptoms and Patient Delay: Psychological Variables Involved," *Cancer, 17*:1480, 1964.
5. R. Senescu, "The Development of Emotional Complications in the Patient With Cancer," *Journal of Chronic Diseases, 16*:813, 1963.
6. E. Bibring, "The Mechanisms of Depression," *Affective Disorders*, edited by P. Greenacre, New York: International Universities Press, 1953.
7. R. Abrams and J. E. Finesinger, "Guilt Reactions in Patients With Cancer," *Cancer, 6*:474, 1953.
8. B. Glaser and A. Strauss, *Time for Dying*, Chicago: Aldine Publishing Company, 1968.
9. E. S. Shneidman, "Orientations Toward Death," *The Study of Lives*, edited by R. W. White, New York: Atherton Press, 1963, p. 201.
10. L. Tolstoy, *The Death of Iván Ilých*, in *Short Novels*, translated by L. A. Maude, Vol. II, New York: Modern Library, 1966.
11. I. L. Janis, *Psychological Stress*, New York, J. Wiley and Sons, 1958.

16

Management of the Dying Patient

Bernard Schoenberg

Health personnel place great emphasis on preservation of life and generally view a patient's death as a personal failure. For the physician, avoiding issues associated with death is related to prized institutional values of success and to maintaining self-esteem. In general, physicians have a greater fear of death than others and are very likely to utilize their profession to control their personal concern over death. Appropriate management of a dying patient, more than any other medical problem, endows meaning to the cliché of comprehensive medicine and significance to the art of medicine. The primary goal of the physician who assumes the responsibility of rendering this care is that of establishing a relationship with the dying patient based on trust and confidence, in which the patient feels safe to express his fears, feelings, and thoughts. The physician should be honest, consistent, supportive, and sympathetic yet, at the same time, maintain the qualities of equanimity and imperturbability.

In Osler's terms, the physician must have "coolness and presence of mind . . . clearness of judgment in moments of grave peril. . . . The physician who has the misfortune to be without it (imperturbability), who betrays indecision and worry and who shows that he is flustered and flurried . . . loses rapidly the confidence of his patients" (1). The goals of this patient-physician relationship are that the patient 1) maintain the maximal social, familial, and vocational functioning of which he is capable; 2) be enabled to cooperate with measures directed toward his welfare and survival; 3) derive the maximal pleasure and gratification of which he is capable; 4) does not cause more pain and distress to himself and others than is inherent in his painful situation; and 5) maintain a positive self-image and attain a dignified death (2).

The physician's response to the patient may vary between two extremes: On the one hand there is a tendency to emphasize the life-threatening aspects of the illness and regard all else as of minimal importance. This approach is easier to follow during the most active phase of diagnosis, surgery, and palliative treatment than during the terminal stage. With this approach the patient is placed in the position of organizing his life around his disease, rather than viewing his illness as an interruption of his life. On the other hand, some physicians regard even minor emotional complications as problems for the psychiatrist, social worker, or hospital chaplain rather than issues to be dealt with by the physician. Lack of a clear definition of what constitutes emotional illness increases the likelihood that the physician will assume that emotional problems related to dying are not in his domain. Physicians skilled in the art of medicine realize that to treat the "whole patient" effectively implies an involvement in the emotional, social, economic, and religious aspects of his patient's existence. To delay this involvement until the development of gross emotional complications increases the difficulty of effective treatment of the disease.

The patient who unrealistically fears he has cancer is not unusual. Fear of certain conditions such as dying is common in anxiety reactions, and fear of certain diseases such as cancer is common in hypochondriacal reactions. Calm but authoritative reassurance by the physician is usually adequate. Words should be chosen carefully. (For example, biopsy results or clinical studies should be described as *normal* rather than *negative*.) Exploration of the underlying fear can be helpful in most instances. For those patients who are persistent in their belief in spite of reassurance, a consultation with a psychiatrist may be necessary, since the fear may represent a delusional idea or an impending psychosis.

Clinical investigators have recently been preoccupied with the question of whether to tell the patient with terminal illness the truth about his disease. What or when to tell the patient requires a thorough awareness of the patient and his family, their level of understanding, and the state of their feelings. Most patients, on a conscious or unconscious level, already know the truth. The patient's awareness of dying comes from external as well as internal cues. In this regard, the nurse's communications to the patient are especially significant since she is engaged in meeting the patient's daily physical needs.

A "conspiracy of silence" is, in nearly all cases, most destructive, since it erects a barrier between the patient and others in his environment which compounds his feelings of estrangement. To isolate the dying patient from others also removes the opportunity for him to express his thoughts and to allow his feelings for others to emerge. The decision of whether or not to verbalize his prognosis is determined by the healthy individual, the physician, who is unable to identify totally with the dying patient and his needs. In Freud's words, "Our own death is indeed unimaginable and whenever we make the attempt to manage it we can conceive that we really survive as spectators" (3). When the physician is able to tell the truth about the illness, the patient is given the opportunity to settle financial affairs, resolve religious problems, express feelings to family members, and resolve differences with friends. He can be given a sense of confidence and a feeling of control if he is allowed to make decisions regarding family and business matters. He will feel included in future plans and therefore will be in control of the situation to some extent. For example, one patient expressed the thought that he would do things he *really* wanted to do for the first time in his life.

In discussing the patient's illness with him it is sometimes better to present the facts gradually, emphasizing those aspects of the situation over which he and the physician have control. As one surgeon stated it,

We who are constantly dealing with the physical aspects of cancer should realize that the words "incurable" and "hopeless" are not synonymous. To tell a patient that his condition is hopeless is both cruel and technically incorrect. Incurability is a state of body, whereas hopelessness is a state of mind, a giving up—a situation which must be avoided at all cost. A patient can tolerate knowing he is incurable; he cannot tolerate hopelessness. . . . Since most malignant diseases develop slowly, the patient should be given to understand that his cancer did not begin yesterday; rather he has been living with it for months or years and, still more important, he will not be dead tomorrow. . . . At this stage, the surgeon's approach must be directed toward *hope for control* of the cancer rather than *hope for cure* (4).

When the patient and physician have discussed the situation realistically, the patient can be actively engaged in the struggle against death. Because of physical impairment the patient may abandon some activities but can be effectively engaged in new, less strenuous ones. In this situation the physician can be most helpful in assisting the patient in the problems of living as well as the various aspects of dying.

Most patients seem to fear the process of dying more than death itself. The process of dying implies pain, deterioration, helplessness, dependency, humiliation, loss of loved ones, and loss of control. Assurances by the physician that he will control pain and suffering can serve to support the patient in accepting the truth with dignity and with a will to enjoy what time is left for him.

Those patients for whom denial is predominant will not accept the truth no matter how directly they are told. Every patient should be offered the opportunity to choose between acceptance and denial. During various phases of his illness the patient's receptivity should determine what the physician tells him of his condition. Communicating the truth should, in some situations, be done in stages and not viewed as an *all* or *none* process. *When* to tell the patient is also important—too often the patient is placed in limbo while he awaits his verdict.

Experienced clinicians suggest that in all cases *some* hope be maintained by emphasizing recent developments in medical research. The patient can be told the nature of his illness and the general prognosis (which is, in fact, as much as the physician really knows). Saunders has stated that "once the possibility of talking frankly with a patient about death has been admitted it does not mean that this will necessarily take place, but the whole atmosphere is changed. We are then free to wait quietly for clues from each patient, seeing them as individuals from whom we can expect intelligence, courage and decisions" (5). An essential element in the approach to any patient is that the approach not be ritualized or routinized, but *individualized.*

This approach requires that the physician and hospital be flexible enough to modify established routine in order to provide comfort for the patient. There are major differences in the manner in which various ethnic groups confront death, and hospital routines should, if possible, be adapted to the particular patient's needs. Providing insight for the family can be helpful. The spouse of a dying patient became much

241

more effective when she realized through her conversations with the social worker that although she could not prevent her husband's death, her presence made living much more pleasant for him. Visiting hours can be made less rigid and rules can be altered to allow children to visit a dying parent.

Too often patients are transferred from familiar surroundings, thus undermining feelings of security.

After five weeks, a patient was to be transferred from the medical service to a surgical ward for a minor surgical procedure. The nurse recognized that the patient expressed more apprehension over the transfer than the surgical procedure and she convinced the physician that the transfer was really unnecessary. Following surgery the medical ward nurses willingly accepted the minor tasks of postoperative care and dressing the wound.

For the physician, the care of the dying patient presents numerous problems. The usual gratifications of success are absent. In his identification with the patient his own childhood feelings of separation, abandonment, and injury are recalled, as well as the consequent feelings of grief and depression. Feelings of helplessness and ineffectuality commonly result in anger toward the patient, soon followed by guilt and emotional withdrawal. In order to overcome feelings of helplessness the physician may engage in premature activity or needless surgical procedures. The physician should experience the whole process of care, even waiting, as challenging and active. Minor problems such as pain, constipation, odors, menu, sleep, and activities can be seen as major challenges which the patient and physician can collaboratively surmount, thus overcoming feelings of passivity and helplessness on the part of both. Management problems are inevitable since the dying patient frequently has an altered sense of time and views waiting, especially for medications or visitors, in an unrealistic way. Although the physician cannot provide cure or relief, he is always in a position to offer comfort and support.

Physicians respond differently to being placed in the parental position by the patient. Some physicians are fearful of the patient's need for him to be omnipotent, while others exploit the relationship, forcing the patient into a childlike position. The most successful interactions with patients are those in which the physician accepts the parental role and utilizes it in a supportive manner for the patient's benefit.

242

In chronic illness, and with cancer in particular, how the dependency problem and the parental role are managed are crucial factors in the patient's outlook.

A 65-year-old woman was dying of cancer. The primary source of cancer was unknown but her major discomfort was related to metastases to the lung with frequent accumulations of fluid requiring repeated thoracentesis. She became aware of her internist's discouragement and emotional withdrawal, and for the first time became overtly depressed. The surgeon who had performed the exploratory abdominal operation vigorously assured her that "I am determined to keep you comfortable even if I have to tap you every day." She became more cheerful and told her family, "I believe that man can do anything." The surgeon's attitude was also a source of encouragement to the internist.

The painful feelings of guilt, depression, and helplessness engendered in the physician are usually alleviated by emotional withdrawal and avoidance. Due to the modern trend in medical care toward the strict division of labor in caring for the patient, many traditional functions of the physician and nurse have been transferred to others, resulting in a dilution of the traditional one-to-one relationship. This situation allows the physician to withdraw by delegating numerous responsibilities to others. The end result of this process is the disruption of the "continuity of care" which is of primary importance in establishing a feeling of security in the patient. The emotional withdrawal of hospital personnel is frequently related to protecting themselves against feelings of loss and the consequent feelings of grief. Often the result is that the patient is prematurely dealt with as if he were already dead.

Surgery

The management of the surgical patient starts with the first visit to the surgeon's office. Two relationships are established simultaneously: the first, a reality relationship, the second, a symbolic one. The surgeon is in a unique position since he is the one who intervenes actively and presents the opportunity for cure. The symbolic relationship has started before the patient has entered the office and is based on the image of

243

a surgeon as one who has therapeutic and even magical powers.

The immediate goal in seeing the patient for the first time is not only to learn of his illness in order to establish a diagnosis and institute a course of treatment, but also to establish rapport and confidence. How the first meeting is conducted will usually determine the future pattern of the relationship between the patient and surgeon.

An apprehensive 40-year-old woman who had delayed seeking consultation for a lump in her breast was finally referred to a prominent surgeon by her family physician. When she was ushered into his office by the nurse, he was in his shirt sleeves, eating lunch and leafing through a stack of papers on a cluttered desk. He took several minutes before looking up and greeting her. Despite reassurances by her family physician that the surgeon was an expert in his. field and a warm sympathetic person, she requested referral to another specialist.

In conducting the initial interview and examination, an unhurried, uninterrupted period of privacy, no matter how brief, is preferable to a longer period interrupted by the nurse, phone calls, or people walking in and out of the room. It is essential to ascertain the significance of the illness for the patient and the accompanying underlying fears. Primary sources of fear in this setting reside in early experiences with surgical procedures, and with previous relationships with physicians. If the surgeon is interested and listens attentively without interrupting, jumping to conclusions, or offering premature advice, the first step has been taken to reduce the patient's apprehension. The patient's train of associations will sometimes indicate if he has bizarre concepts regarding the nature of his illness. Information about a patient's emotional life can be gained indirectly if the patient feels sufficiently secure in the relationship to talk freely and spontaneously. For example, if the patient is unduly apprehensive and is withdrawing, it can be helpful to state, "You seem frightened and I suspect you are avoiding certain questions that are on your mind. What is it you are afraid of?" This type of statement communicates to the patient that you are aware of his fear, that you are not afraid to discuss death, that you are accessible to him to discuss whatever is on his mind, and that you regard his fear as normal.

Conversation directed to the patient should be purposeful and directed to the goal of gaining further information. As the patient begins to feel more comfortable, he will gradually expose more of his inner mental life. At times, and if the patient approves, the presence of a spouse, parent, or other family member may be helpful in discussing the diagnosis and proposed treatment. In general, terms such as cancer are preferable to mass, tumor, growth, or lesion. In most instances the favorable aspects of the surgical approach should be emphasized as the patient is made aware that something detrimental to him will be removed. A brief explanation of the procedure will also assist in keeping his fantasies under control and correct the misinformation he may have already received. A candid discussion of the postoperative period, length of hospitalization, degree of disability and period of convalescence at home can give the patient a future perspective and at the same time deflect unrealistic expectations and thus disappointment concerning resumption of usual activity.

Three operational models have been suggested for the doctor-patient relationship: 1) *activity-passivity;* 2) *guidance-cooperation;* and 3) *mutual participation* (6). The first model (for example, when the physician is active and the patient passive) usually is applicable to the operative period and may be compared to the relationship between the parent and the helpless infant or child. If the parent can be trusted, then the child is likely to be cooperative. In the postoperative period the second model can be useful. Although the patient may be in distress, he is aware of the situation, his judgment is not impaired, and he can be guided by the surgeon into a cooperative relationship. The relationship is still essentially that of a parent to a child. In the third model, which has special application to convalescence and rehabilitation, a major aspect of the treatment is carried out by the patient in consultation with the surgeon. The professional knowledge of the physician is communicated to the patient, who then utilizes the information to improve his situation. The prototype of this model is the mature adult relationship.

With different patients, and at different times with the same patient, one or another type of relationship may exist. If a patient requires immediate surgery, the relationship initially may be based on the first model, but it may quickly change to the second model, and then to the third. Because of his own needs, however, the surgeon may persist in maintaining the relationship on a parent-child level rather than allowing it to progress to one of mutual cooperation. After the acute problem subsides in the patient, the decisions must be shared with him if we expect him to collaborate in achieving the goals of treatment.

Some patients fear anesthesia more than surgery since it variously implies giving up control to a stranger, a state of helplessness, and/or sleep (the unconscious equivalent of death). The patient's apprehension can be decreased if he becomes acquainted with the anesthetist preceding surgery and can discuss the process in nontechnical terms. Reassuring words prior to administering anesthesia can also be a supportive measure. Visits to the recovery room by the surgeon, anesthetist, and the personal physician can be beneficial, especially when a trusting relationship has already been established.

The postoperative period presents some special problems in management. If surgery has resulted in the loss of an important function, organ, or body part the anticipated reaction is depression. The process of mourning will depend on the extent of the real loss, the symbolic aspect of the loss, and the preoperative personality of the patient. The most important preventive measure is for the surgeon to establish a trusting relationship with the patient and initiate early and frequent postoperative contact. One aspect of depression is the sense of futility in dealing with life following discharge from the hospital. During hospitalization the patient and his family should be engaged in planning and dealing with problems of rehabilitation.

The incision or wound, especially when it indicates mutilation or radical surgery, is a good meeting ground for the patient and surgeon. The surgeon can communicate nonverbally, in his examination of the site, that he is neither repulsed nor frightened by what he observes. This attitude can also be communicated to other personnel and the family as well, since if they find a mastectomy scar, colostomy, or amputation stump repugnant it is more difficult for the patient to accept. Some surgeons emphasize the good technical results of the procedure and/or the types of prostheses that are available. Others make sure that convalescent care of the wound is discussed and illustrated in the presence of a spouse before the patient leaves the hospital so that their feelings, too, may be uncovered and discussed.

When the patient preoperatively anticipates extensive mutilation or destruction, he frequently assumes this has occurred despite postoperative confrontation with the realistic effects of surgery. Sutherland (7) describes the reaction of marked weakness and acute depression observed in some of these patients. These reactions are reinforced by mistaken concepts of the role of the missing part or organ in the general physiology of the individual. Some concepts were related to folklore, anatomical confusion, infantile fantasies, and feelings of increased vulnerability and weakness. Postoperative depressions may result in prolonged convalescence, invalidism, and serious impairment of vocational and social activities. For such patients, extensive psychological preparation for surgery and early postoperative treatment of depression are indicated. The attitudes of the family members and hospital personnel are important in the management of postoperative depression. If the patient is convinced that he is still lovable or acceptable to others despite his loss of function or disfigurement, he is more likely to cope effectively with the results of surgery. In the immediate postoperative period, special attention to pain relief, prescribing adequate sedation to assure sleep, and providing opportunities for verbalization of feelings are important. If surgery has been mutilative or has validated a diagnosis of a fatal illness, the physician's tendency is to withdraw from the patient. The hospital atmosphere surrounding a patient who has been mutilated or amputated is filled with guilt and blame. At times the feelings of guilt are managed by projecting blame onto the patient for his delay in seeking medical assistance. If the surgeon can provide some reassurance and indicate that he understands the patient's feelings, he can reduce the feelings of isolation and depression.

Precautions against suicide, especially when depression is accompanied by postoperative confusion, should always be taken. Unobtrusive routine observations and general precautions as an integral part of ward routine may reduce suicides in the common categories of hanging or of jumping from a window. The most effective means of managing a suicidal patient is transfer to a closed psychiatric ward of a general hospital when available, or transfer of the patient to a psychiatric hospital.

Surgical management may be further complicated by a postoperative organic brain syndrome. Frequently the condition is of short duration if related to a febrile reaction or dehydration, but other causes may be metastases to the brain, toxic reaction caused by infection, electrolyte imbalance, or cerebral anoxia in elderly patients. The surgeon should be alert to the possibility of an abstinence syndrome in addicts or chronic alcoholics. Usually the organic brain syndrome is a com-

bination of organic and functional factors, and is difficult to differentiate from a functional psychosis. The syndrome is usually ushered in by delirium with disorientation, confusion, increased psychomotor activity, and varying levels of consciousness, which may be accompanied by hallucinations, delusions, and bizarre behavior. In general, the psychiatrist should be considered an adjunct to treatment and should consult with the surgeon and staff on the management of the patient. Reassurance, especially by familiar personnel in familiar surroundings, and explanations of his condition are sometimes sufficient treatment. The patient should be verbally oriented to time and place, and visited regularly by the physician and family. All procedures should be described and explained before, during, and when necessary reiterated after the procedure has been completed. Night lights are particularly important since darkness can be disorienting. The "laying on of hands" by physicians and nurses usually provides a sense of security.
When possible, the same hospital personnel should be utilized and the patient should constantly be in the presence of others.

Psychiatric Consultation and Therapy

The emotional complications that accompany diagnosis, treatment, and management of the patient with a fatal illness frequently require assistance from the psychiatrist. The psychiatric consultation should be viewed primarily as an attempt to assist the staff in more effective management of the patient. If the physician can focus on the specific management problem, the psychiatrist can advise him on measures that can be taken. Frequently the emotional complications are vague and ill-defined, but evidence is available in the nurses' notes, changes in attitude of the physician or family, or reactions of other ward personnel to the patient.

Problems frequently requiring psychiatric intervention are related to both the emotional reactions of hospital personnel and to the patient's emotional reactions and behavior. Too often the angry or demanding patient provokes a similar response in the physician or nurse, and the patient's underlying fear or damaged self-concept is not recognized. The patient's numerous complaints are not experienced as an unconscious plea for reassurance or sympathy but as ingratitude or insatiability. Complaints over waiting for meals or medication are not regarded as related to an altered sense of time but as hostility toward the staff. Overconcern with bowel movements or sleep are experienced as fussiness rather than regression to childhood levels of functioning. The emotional and physical withdrawal of staff, angry retaliation, or unsympathetic attitudes add further to the patient's anger, guilt, negative self-concept, and sense of isolation, often leading to further emotional complications.

One function of the psychiatrist is to intervene and to disrupt these "reverberating circuits" which are destructive to the patient and self-defeating for the hospital staff. Establishing communication between the patient and ward personnel can be the most vital factor in disrupting the vicious circle so characteristic of emotionally disturbed behavior. When the physician and nurse feel guilty about hostile feelings toward the patient, it is more difficult for them to know when to "draw boundaries" or "define limits" which can be reassuring for the regressed patient. The consultation itself should serve a therapeutic function in addition to providing a neutral, objective evaluation of the patient's emotional state.

Psychotherapy

Psychotherapy of the dying patient presents unique problems for both the psychiatrist and the patient. A salient problem for the patient is his realistic feelings of loneliness and isolation related to the mutual disengagement or withdrawal from others in his environment. Family, friends, or his personal physician may have already begun to protect themselves against the painful feelings of guilt, failure, helplessness, anger, or grief by withdrawing from the relationship through varying degrees of emotional inaccessibility or physical avoidance. The primary need of the patient is to alleviate his loneliness and isolation by sharing his feelings with another person who can maintain neutrality and offer support and comfort. The psychiatrist's primary goal is to assist the patient by enabling him to live at his highest level of functioning in all spheres of behavior, so that he may maintain gratifying relationships, continue activities, and approach death with a positive self-image. Too often the need for a psychiatrist is experienced by the patient as further evidence of failure, and therefore should be approached by the referring physician in a positive manner and with some promise that psychotherapy can help alleviate the emotional distress that the patient is experiencing.

The psychiatric treatment of the dying patient requires modifications in the usual techniques of treatment in that the immediate goal is usually of a reparative or adaptive nature rather than a reconstructive one. For the therapist, the usual problems are multiplied and exaggerated since as a physician he already knows that his patient will die, and feelings of helplessness, failure, and grief on the therapist's part are inevitable. In addition, even partial identification with the patient may lead to feelings of anxiety and childhood fears of separation, abandonment, and death. The pitfall is that the therapist may prematurely disengage himself from the patient, as others in the environment have done, thus adding further to the patient's feelings of isolation. Psychotherapy, once initiated, usually must be continued as long as the patient requires, despite the physical deterioration which limits the patient to his home or the hospital. A primary requirement for the therapist is his *availability*, which the patient should be allowed to test and verify for himself.

Therapy should focus on the patient's ability to live deeply and meaningfully in spite of distressing circumstances. Emphasis should be placed on renewing emotional participation in life. In uncovering underlying thoughts and feelings an effort should be made not to cause more pain and distress than is alleviated. The therapist should present himself as a real person as well as a transference figure in order to decrease feelings of isolation, and should deal when necessary with the "here and now" aspects of the patient's life. At times, the patient's needs may have to be met directly through intervention with the patient's family or with other physicians, and by becoming involved in structuring his environment. The therapist should be willing to ask direct questions and to answer the patient's questions in return. The positive aspects of the transference relationship, especially those feelings about the therapist as a magical, omnipotent figure, may be supported, especially during the terminal phase.

The immediate reasons for psychiatric referral—usually the emotional complications of physical illness—should be explored as early as possible. These problems are usually related to unrecognized or unexpressed feelings of fear, the patient's state of self-esteem, and feelings such as shame and guilt related to dependency and anger. Explanations (although intellectual) of the patient's exaggerated responses and their effect on his functioning can sometimes bring relief. It may be necessary to explore the patient's fantasies related to his disease and confront him with the less frightening reality, or to encourage him to engage his physician in nontechnical explanations of the disease process. When the patient focuses his attention on death, he is sometimes seeking reassurance from the therapist that he will not abandon the patient. Simple comments, such as "I'll be there to help you" or "*We'll* deal with tomorrow when it comes," can serve the immediate purpose.

It is important that the patient's anger toward family, friends, and his physician be verbalized, but the therapist should exercise caution in not adding to the excessive burden of guilt that the patient carries. The additional sources of guilt are related to feelings of envy or jealousy toward those who will continue living, and often are the result of childhood fantasies that occur during periods of regression. The patient's guilt can be reduced if the therapist reassures him that his reactions are normal or that the therapist understands why he feels that way. Silence on the therapist's part in these situations may be interpreted as disapproval.

A prime goal for the therapist should be to bring the patient into closer relationships with people rather than increasing his sense of isolation resulting from feelings of anger and guilt. Depression and grief are a prominent aspect of psychotherapy with the dying patient since he anticipates the loss of all his human relationships. Mourning for those loved ones whom he will lose is a common reaction and generally need not be interfered with. The feelings of closeness toward the therapist, to some extent, are a protection against these painful feelings. Reassurance, patience, and tolerance can be comforting to the depressed patient. Expressions of sympathy appear to promote more depression, while understanding and clarification of the patient's emotional reactions provide reassurance.

L. R. was a 27-year-old single man first seen by the psychiatrist in a routine interview of cancer patients at a radiotherapy unit of a large general hospital. The diagnosis of cancer of the nasopharynx was made at another hospital 2 years previously and treatment (cobalt therapy) was instituted.

Following treatment he was assured that he had been cured and sought help when he noted the recurrence of symptoms. During the course of radiotherapy he asked if he might speak to the psychiatrist who had interviewed him on his admission to the radiotherapy clinic.

During his first interview he told the psychiatrist that he was aware that his illness was incurable. He had tried to discuss his condition with the radiotherapist, who had become "vague, embarrassed, and irrelevant." Following this attempt he had become profoundly depressed and was contemplating suicide. The psychiatrist suggested psychotherapy and the patient readily agreed.

Mr. R. was the son of a prominent attorney who had "disowned" him when he discovered that his son had been involved in a homosexual relationship as a college student. He felt he had always been a disappointment to his father, who was athletic, ambitious, and aggressive. His father was prone to violent outbursts of rage and had on numerous occasions tried to "make a man" out of his son by beating him severely. In contrast, his brother had been a source of gratification to his father. He was interested in athletics and was a hunting and fishing enthusiast. His brother, three years younger, was married and a practicing engineer in another city. He regarded his mother as his ally. She was sensitive, musical, and had literary interests similar to his own. He expressed sympathy for his mother, who was trapped in a relationship with a "despot" who would attack her verbally or physically at the slightest provocation. The only positive relationship with a male figure in his childhood was with his grandfather, who was a physician. In his hometown his grandfather was admired by everyone and considered to be a warm, patient, benevolent person who had dedicated his life to his medical practice. From an early age he realized that his father spoke contemptuously of his grandfather because of the latter's failure to become wealthy. He described feelings of isolation and loneliness and felt he had provoked rejection by his physician by inquiring about his diagnosis and prognosis. He laughed when the therapist suggested that his physician seemed less able to cope with his disease than he could.

Early in therapy the patient became aware of the shame and guilt he felt regarding his disease. He experienced his illness as verification of his father's accusation that he was weak and feminine and as punishment for his sexual indiscretions. His greatest fear was that his illness would render him helpless and dependent and that he would be forced back into a dependent relationship with his father. The therapist reminded him that he

252

was now an adult and if his decision was to remain at the hospital for treatment, the therapist would do his utmost to assist him in doing so. Feelings of rage toward his father were expressed throughout the initial phase of treatment until the therapist suggested one day that his father should be pitied as well as hated since he had never experienced a close relationship with anyone. He was encouraged to resume his relationships and engage in activities which were pleasurable. The theater and ballet had always been a source of gratification for him, and he began to spend his evenings with his friends.

He decided to invite his mother for a visit but wanted to do it before he became "too weak to give her a good time." He wrote to his mother and suggested she contact the therapist. In a phone conversation with her the therapist suggested that she not visit with the goal of "taking care" of her son but rather to allow her son to give her "a good time." She visited for ten days and the patient showed renewed vigor and enthusiasm. He realized the guilt he felt over having "abandoned her and leaving her at the mercy" of his father. He experienced great feelings of relief when before leaving she told him it was the best time she ever had. During an interview with the psychiatrist she supported the patient's view that a visit home would be disastrous since she was certain that her husband would exploit the patient's weakened condition.

When the patient suffered a physical set-back, he confronted the psychiatrist with the fact that he was dying and asked if the therapist were afraid. The psychiatrist admitted that he had never treated a dying patient in psychotherapy but added that he thought he could manage it. The patient answered quietly, "I suppose it will be a new experience for *both* of us."

As his weakness progressed, he was fearful that he would lose his position as personal secretary to the director of a scientific foundation. He had spoken to his employer, a brilliant, shy individual, who mumbled some reassuring words of sticking by him through this "dreadful mess." At the patient's suggestion the psychiatrist discussed the problem with his employer, who regarded his services as invaluable and stated that Mr. R. working part-time would be more useful to him than three full-time employees.

After cessation of radiotherapy he felt some relief from nausea and malaise but continued to decline physically. At that time he reported a pleasant dream of childhood in which his grandfather resembled the therapist. He laughed at the idea of the therapist as a small town general practitioner but was pleased with the dream. He had pleasant childhood

253

reminiscences and wept on several occasions in discussing his mother and brother. He prepared a will in which he left his personal belongings to his brother and a small sum of money to his brother's children for "pleasurable purposes." During this period he arrived for his biweekly sessions with two containers of coffee, the therapist always accepting his coffee with a simple "Thank you." He regretted that he would never take the trip to Europe that he had planned and the psychiatrist noted that *at present* he was too tired for such a journey. Both the therapist and patient, aware of the denial, attributed the weakness and fatigue to the effects of radiother- apy. When cancer extended to his right eye causing partial blindness, time was spent on his visual difficulties and on acquiring first eyeglasses and then an eye patch so that he could continue working. He experienced his effectiveness at work as the greatest source of self-esteem.

Near the end he expressed regret that he would have to leave the therapist and asked if the therapist were afraid of dying. He rarely com- plained of pain, which had become severe, stating that the anguish he felt before starting therapy had been much greater. He continued taking chlor- promazine in addition to analgesics because the psychotherapist had pre- scribed it during his course of radiotherapy for control of his nausea and vomiting. He no longer needed it but regarded it as a personal exchange between the two of them. During his last visits he could barely talk because of local extension of his lesion and spoke only in a whisper. Surgery had been raised as a possibility by his other physicians, who regarded it as a "useless" procedure. The patient regarded it as hastening death and the therapist supported him in his decision to forego surgery.

One day he noticed that the secretary, on seeing him enter the office, became tearful, and he commented that she was such a nice person, "She reminds me of my mother." On his last visit he sought reassurance that the psychiatrist would be informed when he was readmitted to the hospital. In his presence the psychiatrist wrote a note in the hospital chart stating that he was to be called immediately if the patient were admitted to the hospital. He asked if the therapist would walk with him to the elevator. He became tearful and smiled, "I won't say goodbye, I'll just say thank you." He died the following day.

Psychopharmacotherapy

Management of the dying patient is difficult since accompanying the illness may be symptoms of anxiety or depression. Adequate sleep is

of paramount importance and a wide variety of sedatives and hyp-
notics are available for insomnia or other sleep problems. Barbiturates
are most useful, but hangover, drowsiness, and confusion may be observed as side effects. For daytime sedative control of anxiety there is
a wide range of available drugs. For patients with confusion or organic
brain disease chloral hydrate and paraldehyde are most useful.

With states of panic, agitation, increased psychomotor activity,
and acute psychotic or manic reactions, phenothiazines are valuable
adjuncts to treatment, although side effects and idiosyncratic reactions
are not uncommon.

Two effective groups of antidepressants are the monoamine oxidase
inhibitors and the iminodibenzyl derivatives. The iminodibenzyls, such
as imipriamine and amitriptyline, have fewer serious side reactions
and are used with great frequency. The amphetamine derivatives have
also been widely used in the treatment of mild depressive conditions (8).

The medication itself may be less important than the manner in
which it is given. Having to ask repeatedly for medication is demean-
ing for patients and undermines the patient-physician relationship.
Whenever possible, patients should not be kept waiting for drugs and
a program of continuous control should be established. At the same
time, the common practice of "snowing" the dying patient with excessive medication can be demoralizing since it disrupts his relationships
with others and isolates him further from his environment.

Euthanasia

For the physician the problem of defining death posed difficulties long
before elaborate mechanical procedures were devised to prolong life.
Advances in medicine have recently made the exact timing of a patient's death a medical decision more often than physicians are willing
to admit. A disturbing question is what to do about the individual who
is in irreversible coma while his heart and respiratory system continue
to function with external assistance. Life may be sustained on this
level for years with respirators, cardiac stimulators, artificial kidneys,
and so on, draining the emotional and financial resources of family
members, straining the overtaxed facilities and scarce personnel of hospitals, and creating emotional problems for those responsible for the

patient's care. Is it the physician's duty to preserve a patient's life simply because advances in sciences make it possible to accomplish? In this section we shall be concerned with euthanasia as it applies to the dying patient. Euthanasia is defined here as the act of inducing painless death or death as relief from pain.

A university faculty committee, perhaps in response to the upsurge of controversy in the lay press and periodicals, recently proposed that death be redefined as irreversible coma. Adoption of this proposal would authorize physicians in such cases to discontinue artificial means to prolong life. An editorial in *The New York Times* (9) stated,

"No doubt many physicians have quietly done exactly that in past cases, but always at the risk of being accused of murder. The redefinition now suggested would end that problem, while providing careful safeguards against a halt in aid for those with any significant possibility of emergence from temporary coma. Most important, perhaps, this proposed definition reminds us that what we really mean by life is not metabolism alone."

Although legal definitions of death may be stated and standards of measurement (EEG, EKG, etc.) may be utilized, the tradition in medicine has always stressed the moral sensitivity and humane judgment of the physician.

In recent years there has been increasing effort toward legalizing voluntary euthanasia, a situation where the patient has consented to the termination of his life. Fletcher (10), in a discussion of the legal aspects of the problem, views the term *prolongation of life* as "a suggestion of artificially lengthening a life that would otherwise end." In contrast, euthanasia suggests a "beneficent termination of life that might otherwise continue." To those who would advocate voluntary euthanasia, they refer to situations where the *good* of ending a man's suffering outweighs the *wrong* of intentionally terminating a life.

In the United States, euthanasia—even at the request of the patient and his family—is legally murder. Although a physician may be criminally and civilly liable for failure to act to prolong life or for intentionally taking a life, there is no instance in the Anglo-American courts in which a physician has been convicted of murder or manslaughter for having killed a patient to end his suffering. Most physicians seem to distinguish between "causing" death and "permitting"

256

death. One may "cause" death by giving an overdose of a drug to a comatose patient and "permit" death by withholding strenuous therapy. An example of the latter would be discontinuing parenteral therapy or antibiotics in a comatose patient, thus hastening death. The physician may view both situations as medical intervention, the former active, the latter passive.

The problems of euthanasia were different in less developed cultures, especially among the nomadic tribes which had to keep on the move in order to survive. . . . There came a time when the aged person who could no longer play an active role was an impediment to his people. In many tribes it was accepted by all that this was the occasion for the old person to be left to die; it was not accounted cruel or ungrateful but the necessary end of a formerly useful life. Even the Hopi Indians, with their respect for the elderly, excluded those who became helpless. When this stage had been reached, the old and frail were mortally neglected. . . . This hastening of death for the old has been a worldwide custom, practiced by about half of such nomadic tribes whether they be North American Indians or Eskimo, Lapps, or Bushmen, Ainu or Australian aborigines. It has been less common among settled peoples, fishers or farmers. As cultures grow more stable and complex, with fully established laws and religion, accelerating death for the aged became rarer and is finally condemned (11).

The numerous current arguments in favor of and in opposition to euthanasia have been recently summarized by Rosner (12).

There does not appear to be significant controversy over prolongation of life when the patient is free from pain and able to gain gratification in continuing life. It is when life is maintained temporarily by maintaining vital functions through mechanical means in a patient who can not return to reasonable health that serious disagreement ensues. The physician must judge each case individually on the basis of his own conscience and his conception of the physician's role and function. Many physicians regard prolongation of life as secondary to relief of pain and suffering and allowing the individual to maintain his dignity. Some physicians state freely that they would "allow" more patients to die rather than suffer unduly if it were not for the pressures of the hospital, family, and society. It is not unusual for the physician to delegate responsibility for "termination" to the nurse by requesting that *she* discontinue intravenous fluids or oxygen or give an apparent overdose of a medication. The physician may present a difficult problem for the family by saying, "There is no hope; if you give me your permission, I'll let him die peacefully." This may well be the family members' wish, but to become an agent in terminating the life of a loved one could stimulate intolerable guilt feelings. Hofling (13) has suggested that these decisions be made only after free and honest interdisciplinary discussion, and should reflect the combined wisdom of a professional group rather than one individual. He cites instances of how these decisions precipitated or exacerbated psychiatric illness in hospital staff members.

Our own view of the medical issue of euthanasia (in contrast to the legal issue) is that in allowing the patient a fitting and dignified death, the humane physician engages in the practice of a form of euthanasia whether or not it is explicitly labeled as such.

One physician who claimed he didn't "believe" in euthanasia admitted that he recently allowed a terminal patient to remain at home rather than enter the hospital "because he would be much happier in familiar surroundings with his family." When the physician was questioned further, it was apparent that the patient's life was shortened by his decision.

Another physician advised against a mutilating palliative procedure in a dying woman to enable her to maintain her "psychological dignity" and stated that the procedure "wasn't worth the month or two it would add to her life."

Within limits, the guiding principles should be the patient's values and wishes and the family's feelings and awareness of what is happening. This requires that the physician know his patient and remain flexible, adapting to each patient's needs for support and assistance in achieving an appropriate death.

In conclusion, the management of the dying patient presents numerous problems for the patient, his family, and the many health personnel involved in the patient's illness. The formidable task of integrating the efforts of those concerned with reducing the patient's feelings of grief, isolation, and loneliness should be a shared responsibility. The complex decisions concerning when or what to tell the patient, mutilating or disfiguring surgical intervention, programs for rehabilitation, outpatient treatment, and euthanasia require the knowledge and experience of specialists from a number of different disciplines. One suggested approach is the utilization of a specialist in terminal care—perhaps a psychologist, psychiatric nurse, or social worker— who could assume responsibility for integrating the diverse efforts to provide "continuity of care." When the patient returned home, the specialist could assume responsibility for enlisting the efforts of community agencies and outpatient hospital facilities to provide physical care and emotional support for the patient and his family (14).

Many university and teaching hospitals hold "death conferences" when a patient dies in order to determine if any additional efforts could have been expended in order to prolong the life of the individual patient. An appropriate parallel would be a "life conference" preceding death to determine what steps should be taken to assist the patient, family, and hospital personnel in managing the painful feelings of grief, guilt, depression, anxiety, and anger.

Teaching the psychosocial care of the dying patient has been largely avoided in the health professions. This neglect is reflected in the common failure to provide optimal emotional support for the terminal patient and his family and in the difficulty health personnel have in coping with their own emotional response to a patient's death. Greater educational efforts are required in all the health professions in order to prepare the future practitioner to help the dying patient to maintain his dignity and self esteem, gain pleasure and gratification in his daily life, and approach death with as much truth as he and his family can tolerate.

REFERENCES

1. Sir William Osler, *Aequanimitas*, Philadelphia: P. Blakiston's Sons and Co., 1905.
2. R. Senescu, "The Development of Emotional Complications in the Patient with Cancer," *Journal of Chronic Diseases*, 16:813, 1963.
3. S. Freud, "Thoughts For the Times on War and Death" (1915), *Collected Papers*, Standard Edition, Vol. XIV, London: Hogarth Press, 1955.
4. J. S. Stehlin and K. H. Beach, "Psychological Aspects of Cancer,"

Journal of the American Medical Association, 197(2):140, July 11, 1966.

5. C. M. Saunders, "The Management of Patients in the Terminal Stage," *Cancer,* edited by R. W. Raven, London: Butterworth, 1959.
6. T. Szasz and M. Hollender, "A Contribution to the Philosophy of Medicine, The Basic Models of the Doctor-Patient Relationship," *A. M. A. Archives of Internal Medicine, 97*:585, 1956.
7. A. M. Sutherland, "Psychological Observations in Cancer Patients," *International Psychiatry Clinics, 4*(2):7, 1967.
8. C. K. Aldrich, *An Introduction to Dynamic Psychiatry,* New York: McGraw-Hill, 1966.
9. *The New York Times,* editorial, August 8, 1968, p. 32.
10. G. P. Fletcher, "Legal Aspects of the Decision Not to Prolong Life," *Journal of the American Medical Association, 203*(1):119, January 1, 1968.
11. J. Hinton, *Dying,* Baltimore: Penguin, 1967.
12. F. Rosner, "Jewish Attitude Toward Euthanasia," *New York State Journal of Medicine, 67*:2499, September 15, 1967.
13. C. K. Hofling, "Life-Death Decisions May Undermine M.D.'s Mental Health," *Frontiers of Hospital Psychiatry, 5*(5):3, March, 1968.
14. B. Schoenberg, "The Nurse's Education for Death," *Death and Bereavement,* edited by A. Kutscher, New York: C. C. Thomas and Co., 1969.

17

Pain and Addiction in Terminal Illness

Thomas A. Gonda

Most illnesses and accidents that eventuate in death involve destruction of tissue and concomitant irritation of the nerves that supply such tissue. Pain will be a common and urgent factor in nearly all terminal situations, regardless of whether the basic insult is an invading growth, degenerative process, loss of blood supply, or direct injury.

The proper management of pain in the dying patient is often a demanding and poignant task. Since clinical and experimental data regarding pain are often conflicting, a great variety of approaches to its management have been developed over the years. In medicine it is customary to conceive of pain as either "physical" or "mental." Other ways of expressing this conceptual dichotomy include "organic pain" versus "functional pain" or "real pain" versus "imaginary pain." While there is some historical basis for this distinction from the clinical point of view, such simplification greatly restricts understanding of pain in its more subtle dimensions.

We distinguish between pain at a personal level and pain at an interpersonal level, recognizing that these levels are interrelated. At a personal level pain is: 1) a feeling (a subjective and highly individual experience apparent to the patient); 2) a type of alerting signal; 3) closely related to a body part; and 4) quantifiable by the individual. Once the feeling is communicated to someone, it becomes pain at the interpersonal level, which must be considered within the context of an interaction of persons. Fundamentally, this involves the expression of pain; that is, pain behavior as contrasted with pain feeling. The essence of pain behavior is communication from one person to another. The most common message is a plea for assistance. In other words, pain behavior usually says, "I've got a signal that tells me something is wrong—now I'm telling you—help me!"

Understanding the appropriate meaning of pain behavior becomes a problem at the interpersonal or "public" level of expression. It must be borne in mind, particularly when dealing with a dying patient, that pain behavior may *not* always involve the direct expression of either pain or the seeking of assistance. Behavior associated with feelings other than pain may, at the interpersonal level, be in the form of a plea for assistance. Since it is at the interpersonal level that the physician and his patients must relate, it seems likely that many errors stemming from the communication characteristic of pain can be minimized by taking into explicit account the physician's role as perceived by the patient. In essence, then, how the dying person perceives those caring for him to an important extent determines the quality and quantity of pain complaint.

Determinants of Pain

Although the conceptual framework outlined above emphasizes a distinction between "privately felt" pain and "publicly expressed" pain, it may be assumed that a complex interweaving of neurophysiological, psychophysiological, and sociopsychological substrates underlies both.

At the neurophysiologic level, the experience and expression of pain entails a minimally intact anatomic and physiologic apparatus. To sense pain requires an afferent nervous system sufficiently intact to carry certain impulses to the central nervous system; to perceive pain requires a central nervous system functioning at least to the thalamic level, and to express pain requires motorial equipment sufficient to communicate to another. Unlike other sensory receptors that respond only to specific and limited energies, the receptors (free nerve endings) ordinarily associated with the pain experience can respond to any number of forms of energy. Thus, in everyday life, pain may result from bumping into solid objects (mechanical energy), lit cigarettes (thermal energy), faulty sockets (electrical energy), and squirting grapefruit juice into one's eyes (chemical energy).

Information at the psychophysiological level is generally based upon introspective experiences that have been objectified through clinical observations. The following inferential constructs regarding pain have been derived from this kind of data. A stimulus, whether originating from within or without the psychic apparatus, alerts the ego. The mechanisms of the ego, functioning at both the conscious and unconscious levels, scan the stimulus to ascertain whether it is of potential danger. Affects (painful or pleasurable) are engendered and to a degree are perceived. Activity is then initiated which allows the engendered affects to be discharged. For example, a stimulus arising from the skin of the hand or from the wall of the small bowel alerts the ego. The ego, in turn, begins the complicated discriminatory activity involved in perception. The eventual motor activity may be either appropriately adaptive or maladaptive. Of importance to this construct, particularly as it concerns pain, is that the various parts of the human anatomy are dealt with as objects of the ego. In other words, the ego relates with body parts through mechanisms that are similar, if not the same, as those utilized in any other object relationship. The manner in which the ego deals with an object depends upon the meaning of the stimulus received from the object and the amount of anxiety evoked by the stimulus. Both the anxiety and previously learned meanings operate to focus attention selectively on stimuli and to facilitate certain responses once stimuli are perceived. In this construct, the character of the terminal illness bears directly upon the expression of pain. Factors affecting the role of the illness as a determinant of pain behavior include whether the illness is unexpected or expected, the degree of acuteness (sudden versus prolonged illness), and the degree of incapacity as well as the degree of disfiguration.

At the sociopsychological level such social structural concepts as "role," "social class," "social mobility," and "social alienation" must be considered in accounting for the complex behavior represented by a complaint of pain. The concept of role can be regarded as the bridge between the individual's personality structure and the structure of his society. Role connotes a set of actions performed by an individual which conforms to a greater or lesser degree to expectations of others. Thus, the actual complaint of pain is determined not only by the physical stimuli present and the individual's past experiences, but also by the degree of encouragement from other individuals in the situation.

The effect of role expectation in the expression of pain is best understood within a broad social context. The importance of the social context in determining requests for analgesics has been demonstrated in a study of a group of war-injured compared to a control group with injuries of similar extent incurred in a peacetime situation. The battle-injured not only had fewer complaints of pain but also fewer requests for analgesics. The reasons for this are many and probably indicate, in addition to other social contextual factors, that respite from battle (at least for a while) is more anxiety-relieving than the injuries were anxiety-provoking.

It is well known that an experience responded to as painful in one culture is not considered painful in another. The greatly varying responses to religious practices involving significant physical trauma are an example. In addition, pain complaint is frequently related to ethnicity. Thus, it is not surprising that Jewish immigrants, those of Italian descent, and persons of British origin who have been in New England several generations show significant differences in pain behavior.

The dying patient will ordinarily experience pain at the personal level except when death is very sudden. The factors that determine the nature of pain expression of the terminal patient are essentially those determinates of pain outlined above. The following remarks primarily concern pain that is associated with fatal subacute or chronic conditions rather than pain which may accompany acute illness or accident resulting in sudden death.

Pain behavior in terminal conditions is strongly colored by the individual's feelings concerning his impending death. Feelings of anxiety, for example, often lead to exaggerated pain complaint, and may actually intensify pain feeling as well. On the other hand, the expression of pain may disguise or camouflage feelings of depression occasioned by the real or threatened loss of functions associated with the fatal illness.

In our culture, we tend to avoid discussing with the dying person the sources of his anxiety and depression; in fact, we frequently avoid direct recognition of the anxiety and depression itself. Instead, atten-

264

tion is focused on the patient's complaints of pain. The expression of pain, therefore, is very often a substitute for the expression of feelings of helplessness, dependency, and hopelessness, and fear of separation and abandonment.

The patient is necessarily dependent to some degree upon the physician from whom he seeks help for his illness. It is not surprising that the patient's early attempts to deal with the problem of impending death (whether or not he has been explicitly told that his condition is terminal) usually involve a request for his physician to "do something" to alleviate his "pain." This tendency is abetted by the physician who, in order to avoid the subject of death in his communications with the patient, focuses exclusively on his complaint of pain. Even the physician who realizes that the patient's complaint of pain may be a camouflage for depression or anxiety would, because of his own unresolved feelings about death, often choose to treat the pain complaint solely as he would treat what is commonly called "somatic pain." Such treatment is often condoned by the patient and his family.

Analgesics (usually narcotics) employed in the treatment regimen may be helpful in alleviating some of the patient's distress. Initially, the drug enables the patient to reconstitute himself sufficiently to work through his feelings of depression and anxiety. As death approaches and physical pain or pain as an expression of debility, dependency, and helplessness increases, the physician usually responds by increasing the dosages of medication, and before long the patient shows both psychological and physiological dependence upon the drugs. He is addicted. It is recognized that this manner of dealing with the patient's terminal illness might be quite reasonable, and in relatively well integrated persons drug addiction during terminal illness is of little untoward consequence. It is a trivial side effect of a management that allows the patient to carry on reasonably well and to die in relative comfort. However, narcotic addiction that complicates an already existing psychiatric disorder may make a dying patient even more difficult to manage. This is particularly true when the patient's integrative and adaptive patterns are already being severely challenged by the stresses of hospitalization, surgery, organ loss, and pain that typically accompany impending death.

265

THE DYING PATIENT

Alternative Methods to Manage Pain Behavior

Although iatrogenic addiction may ultimately be the only satisfactory solution in the management of the dying person's pain, it is usually in the best interests of the patient and his family to search very carefully for other methods. As noted previously, patients are expected, and in a sense forced, to assume certain roles. For example, the physician who is upset by talk of dying would rather hear of pain, and will tend to elicit more talk of pain and less of death. Obviously, he cannot then deal effectively with the patient's feelings about dying. The physician's first step toward an alternative management of pain is a recognition and understanding of his personal feelings toward death and the dying process. Only then will he be able to separate his patient's needs from his own and thus deal appropriately and effectively with the dying patient's complaints as well as with the problems of the family.

The physician must spend sufficient time with the patient to establish the kind of relationship that is necessary to deal effectively with his problems. This relationship entails, first and foremost, that he be supportive of the patient. He must be able to listen to what the patient is saying and accurately interpret its meaning. It is especially desirable for the dying patient to feel that the doctor has a special personal interest in him. Continuity of care by at least one physician is essential.

A substantial proportion of dying patients have great difficulty distinguishing between pain feeling and tension. With these patients the physician must try to create an atmosphere in which he and his patient can exchange information realistically. Not only must the physician pay empathic attention to the patient's assessment of his own situation, but also the physician should be able to anticipate assessment of patients too frightened or too depressed to express themselves. Reassurance that active steps are to be taken to assist the patient and the development of a supportive involvement frequently provide dramatic relief of anxiety and emotional tension. Since anxiety and tension tend to heighten pain feeling, whereas relaxation tends to aid in its alleviation, these measures aimed at relieving emotional tension are in order whenever there is a complaint of pain. Anxiety is also often amenable to the sedative type tranquilizers that are nonphysiologically addicting, such as chlordiazepoxide HCl (Librium) or diazepam (Valium). Here, too, there is often a corresponding diminution of pain complaint as the emotional tensions are relieved. Though anxiety is also responsive to narcotics, their use in that role invites addiction and fosters further regression. When narcotics are administered to treat anxiety, the pleasure accompanying the taking of drugs eventually supercedes the relief of anxiety as a goal. In effect, the use of narcotics may become a substitutive gratification for an intolerable life situation.

It is not an uncommon clinical finding that patients who communicate openly with their physician require considerably fewer analgesics. A total of only 15 to 20 minutes a day, divided into three or four visits, is usually sufficient to accomplish this result. Very likely the reduction of feelings of loneliness, isolation, and accompanying tension is an important factor in the diminution of drug demand. In spite of all this, under some circumstances as previously described, narcotics clearly do have a potentially valuable role in management of pain.

Hypnotic suggestions, reinforced daily, are often quite effective in diminution of pain complaint, reduction of anxiety, and improvement of mood, appetite, and sleep.

Much of what has been said about the management of anxiety in relation to pain applies equally to the management of depression. There are, however, certain unique problems that arise associated with depression that demand special consideration. As patients begin to face a host of unpleasant realities related to terminal illness, some degree of depression is inevitable. Very often, however, there is no direct expression of the feeling of depression. The psychic manifestations of despair and sadness are hidden completely or at most appear transiently so that only the physical complaints are presented to the observer. These "masked" or "covert" depressions or "depressive equivalents" constitute a significant and often misunderstood problem in the management of the dying. The depressive equivalents are at times difficult to separate from the unwelcome painful interludes occasioned by multiple surgical procedures. Lesions, surgical or other, are particularly damaging to self-esteem, and it is this loss that is often the source of depression. The physical complaints most commonly presented are fatigue and weakness, and only a little less frequent are complaints of muscular aches, headaches, and other pains. Such complaints of pain are best treated as depression rather than as anxiety. The establishment of a successful patient-physician relationship in the presence of covert depression depends to a large extent upon the appropriateness of the physician's condolences. It is most important for the patient to feel that the ministering physician understands what he has experienced and recognizes his despair. Responses to the patient's questions should be as simple and as encouraging as is consistent with honesty. The physician must serve as a guide for the patient's family and friends as well as for others ministering to the patient—neither aggravating the patient's feelings of isolation, loneliness, and rejection nor promoting the patient's tendency toward regressive behavior. As the substitute pain complaint subsides and denial shifts to recognition of the painful reality, the depression tends to increase. A firm insistence at this stage that the patient participate in his treatment and be consulted in family decisions often lifts the depression substantially. The greater the involvement in such tasks—in regular work insofar as possible, as well as in diversions (for example, active recreation, hobbies, passive entertainment, occupational therapy)—the less likely is pain complaint to be a prominent symptom.

Although the course of management as described above may be sufficient for the patient to carry on comfortably, at times further intervention is needed. Depression, like anxiety, is often amenable to the physiologically nonaddicting tranquilizers such as imipramine HCl (Tofranil) and amitryptyline HCl (Elavil). "Depressive equivalents" and overt depression are also responsive to narcotics. Though lifting the pall of depression, the transitory euphorogenic action of narcotics also leads to addiction and frequently results in regression.

Hypnosis is much less likely to be effective in reducing the amount of pain complaint associated with depression than it is with anxiety. The use of other methods of managing pain complaint in terminal illness, such as surgery (prefrontal lobotomy), electroconvulsive therapy, and psychedelic drugs, is beyond the scope of this section, although there are some advocates for each of these treatments.

In summary, then, while the complaint of pain is an important signal that something is wrong, it can also mask or substitute for other uncomfortable feelings such as depression and anxiety. The management of pain in terminal illnesses through the systematic use of narcotic drugs may at times be preferable to other modes of dealing with the patient's pain complaints, even though addiction may result. However, an understanding of the emotional significance to the patient of his illness usually indicates alternative approaches to the management of pain which are ultimately in the better interests of the patient and his family.

Pain Behavior of the Bereaved

In conclusion, a few remarks concerning pain complaints in those closest to the dying—medical personnel as well as close relatives and friends—seem in order.

The clinical picture of acute grief in the bereaved frequently begins long before the death of the patient, at times even before the threatened loss becomes unmistakable. There is clearly a wide range of grief reactions and a wide range of symptoms. Included in the latter is a broad spectrum of somatic symptoms, one of which is complaint of pain. Not infrequently this is expressed as a feeling of tightness in the throat and chest pain accompanied by a choking sensation. At times the bereaved has pain complaint very reminiscent of that of the dying, especially when there has been a close identification. Management of these pain complaints centers on the dissolution of 1) anxiety concerning imagined or real responsibility for the dying person, and 2) anxiety about the meaning of the symptoms of pain in the survivor. Thus, the physician must inform the survivor of the known facts about the terminal illness and must be able to reassure the survivor that all reasonable steps are being or have been taken to assist the dying. Regarding the second factor, a thorough physical examination is often indicated, followed by assisting the survivor in making an emotional reinvestment. More difficult to treat are the pain complaints that make their appearance after a symptom-free interval as long as many months or even a few years after the loss. In these rare instances pain is at times projected to the bodily region in which the deceased complained of experiencing pain. The typical history often shows not only an unusually interdependent relationship during life, but also failures to complete the work of grief and mourning. Pain must be faced and expressed or it remains a wound indefinitely.

18

The Family's Reaction to Terminal Illness

Henry J. Heimlich and Austin H. Kutscher

Perhaps it is pertinent to begin with an incident which represented the first meaningful encounter with death by one of the authors (H.J.H.):

Following my first year of medical college, I spent the summer as a camp counselor. At the end of the summer, as we were returning to the city by train, the train jumped the track. The engine and first car fell into a lake alongside of the road bed, and the engineer was killed. When it was apparent that all the passengers were unharmed, I jumped to the tracks and ran to the front of the train. The fireman was trapped beneath the understructure of the first car, struggling in about four feet of water. He had jumped clear of the train at the time of the accident, landed in the lake just off the shore, and been caught there when a car crashed into the water. I was able to raise his shoulders to keep his head above the water until other help came. We then made a sling with a blanket to support his back, tied it to the train, and thus secured him while waiting for further assistance.

The man's first cries to me were, "Help me! Don't let me die!" As my support beneath his head gave him a little more security, he pleaded with me, "I am not going to die, am I?" When he had been reassured by the fact that we would not let his head drop back into the water, he felt partially comforted, but almost at once he realized the additional perils of his situation: "I won't have to lose my leg—will I?" And later, when medical personnel had arrived and the doctor informed him that his leg would have to be amputated in order to remove him from under the train, his response was, "Please, give me something so that I will have no pain."

Thus, the fireman's fears of death were replaced by fears of mutilation and loss of his leg; and these fears were replaced by the fear of pain—once he had been reassured that his life was no longer in danger and had accepted the fact that the price for living would be the loss of his leg. During this period, I now realize, my feelings and reactions were close reflections of those expressed by him.

Among the many recognizable features of the reactions of a family confronted by the impending death of one of its members is the similarity of their reactions to those of the dying patient himself. When a patient faces death, his family's reactions will, in essence, mirror his during each stage of the downhill progression. To the extent that the physician familiarizes himself with the patient's and his family's reactions to the dying process is the extent to which he will be able to deal with the dying patient and manage the family in the best tradition of medical science and medical art.

Distinctive groups of reactions are observed following the appearance of as yet undiagnosed but conceivably lethal lesions or symptoms. These are readily evident in the case of the woman with a mass in the breast. She knows immediately that there is the possibility of malignancy. Her attitude toward the surgeon will differ according to what is found. Should the lesion be benign, she *and* her family will praise the surgeon for his skill in removing it; whether or not a scar has been left, they will feel that he has performed the surgery with great skill. Even when the surgeon might have been able to aspirate a small cyst but elects the larger operation, for one reason or another, more gratitude is expressed than when the surgeon decides that the lesion need not be removed at all. In the latter case, both patient and family may continue to demonstrate concern and doubt about the nature of the mass.

On the other hand, the surgeon who removes the breast because of a malignancy, and who may thereby have cured the patient, frequently finds both patient and family extremely bitter. Subconsciously, they feel that he has mutilated the patient when it might not have been necessary.

Attitudes toward illness and death also are subject to change according to the threat involved. For example, the agonies of a patient suffering from a gangrenous leg will evoke from the family requests for medication to relieve the severity of the pain. When all attempts are

271

inadequate, they question, "You won't have to remove his leg, will you?" If it is apparent that the amputation must be performed, they express their deep concern over the possibility of death during the operation and in the postoperative period. Should the patient recover fully, the concern with death disappears and the patient's disability becomes a major focus and problem for the family and for himself. Should death follow the operation, for whatever reason, the family, forgetting the pain that had preceded it and the extreme need for the surgery, berates itself saying, "Should we have permitted this operation?"

Certain symbolic associations also persist and color family reactions.

During World War II, I was stationed (H.J.H.) for many months in the interior of China and Inner Mongolia. One Chinese family chose me, rather than the local midwife, to deliver their child. However, after I had fixed up a small box with padding and a blanket and placed the newborn child in it, the father insisted that the baby be removed from the box since, in his mind, a baby in a box is a dead baby. Unwittingly, I had caused the beginning of the baby's life to be shrouded in the father's eyes by a symbol of life's final experience, death.

When an incurable cancer has been found during surgery, the surgeon must, soon thereafter, face the family to pronounce the unfavorable prognosis. As they await him, their primary concern is with the possibility of the patient's death on the operating table (despite the fact that this happens infrequently). Second, they are concerned with "what will be found," and this almost always infers the possibility of cancer. The patient himself, inevitably, has also previously expressed these two concerns.

It is perhaps best to announce first to the waiting family the immediate condition of the patient. "He is doing extremely well"; or "He is in the recovery room and has tolerated the operation very well." This brings visible relief. But they must then await the next words: "It was cancer"; or, "It was not cancer"; or, "It was cancer, but it was possible to remove all the visible cancer"; or, "I am sorry, but it was not possible to remove all of the cancer."

If the situation is hopeless, the family will want to know what to tell the patient, the details of his future treatment, and the expected course of the illness. Some ray of hope within the realm of truth, even if only for the patient's comfort, should be held out. The possibility of treatment that might lengthen his life span or palliate the symptoms of the disease must be outlined.

When the patient's physical deterioration becomes obvious, the family often poses such questions as, "Did the surgery cause the cancer to spread more rapidly?" As the family faces a totally hopeless situation, it becomes necessary for each member to purge himself of guilt, not only in regard to his individual relationship with the patient at this time but also in regard to their relationship over an entire lifetime. Often these feelings of guilt may be alleviated by directing their anger toward the medical personnel for "failures" in caring for the patient and, in the most extreme instances, for "having put the cancer there." Commonly, the patient who fears death and constantly questions his physician regarding his own progression toward death will be surrounded by a highly emotional family. In those cases where the patient exhibits emotional stability and accepts the fact of his own illness and death with grace, the family's responses will usually be of a similar nature.

The burdens of the family increase when the dying patient leaves the hospital to return home. There is so much care to be given at the home and so much "covering up" in the patient's presence that there is little time for any expression of grief. The slow progression of the disease, the increase of pain, the patient's general debility, his inability to eat, and, finally, his loss of consciousness bring the family to the point of being grateful for the patient's death and the termination of his suffering.

Other determinants in the family's reaction to death include the manner of death, the suddenness with which it occurs, the length of the illness prior to the death, the amount of suffering experienced by the patient, and the stability of the patient and his family.

At the time of a sudden death, such as that occurring in an automobile accident or on the battlefield, when the family is notified of the death by a stranger, the family's immediate reaction will be one of profound shock and disbelief. The grief state will depend very much on the character of the relationship that existed between the deceased and the survivor. If the deceased had been away for weeks, months,

273

or years at a time, the realization of his total absence from the family circle in the future will not have the same impact as it would if the deceased had been a husband, child, or parent who returned to the house every day and whose presence was missed almost immediately.

If a patient dies at a time when his condition seems to be improving, as after a coronary occlusion or following presumably successful surgery, the family's feelings of anxiety or encouragement are replaced by the same despair that follows a sudden death from accidental causes. This is one of the cruelest situations for a family to endure since their profound sorrow follows a period when physical and mental strain had been supported by the presence of hope.

The loss of a husband or wife is perhaps the most traumatic experience with the most profound mourning sequence. It is well to note that when a spouse has died following a long illness, the surviving mate has had time to consider what action to take following the demise. To some extent this may eliminate the confusion that occurs after a death but may, at the same time, represent a disadvantage in that the bereaved has fewer details to be preoccupied with and, therefore, may have more time to ruminate.

When the patient has succumbed to a protracted illness, nature has, in a way, softened the impact of the death. The family has already paid dearly in emotional, physical, mental, and financial stress for many months, including a long period when all hope has been dissipated. No matter what initial efforts have been made following the diagnosis and establishment of the prognosis, a time must come when the progression of the disease and the extent of the patient's disability and debilitation convince the family that all they can do now is wait for death. The unabated pain, the appearance of jaundice, the presence of colostomies and fistulas, of stomach tubes and intravenous equipment, the dramatic weight loss, weakness, and ultimate coma all prepare the family for the death and soften its impact upon them. Consciously or subconsciously, they desire to see the patient relieved of his suffering.

Another important factor determining reactions of the family to a death is the age of the deceased. The younger the patient the greater the effect of his death is on the family. Although sorrow is felt at the death of an elderly person, the family can be comforted by the thought that the departed "had lived a long and full life."

MANAGEMENT OF THE FAMILY (A Survey of Physician Opinion)

In order to provide physicians with specific suggestions regarding approaches to the management of the bereaved family, the editors present here the results of a survey of physician opinion concerning the management of grief and mourning in the bereaved (see also Chapter XIX, which presents the opinion of the bereaved). The multiple choice survey was answered by 133 professional consultants (medical, psychiatric, religious), of whom 86 were physicians.*

The need to undertake the survey was based on an observed unwillingness of numerous trained professionals to address themselves to the manifold practical problems of the bereaved. The survey dealt with 1) signs and symptoms of bereavement; 2) guilt and bereavement; 3) what the bereaved should be told by the physician; 4) what the bereaved should be encouraged to do; and 5) advice concerning remarriage. Cited below are the responses of the physician group.

The survey was undertaken with the hope that certain guidelines could be established by those most experienced in the treatment of the bereaved and in order to draw attention to the difficulties and decisions facing the bereaved as they attempt to recover from the effects of the patient's death.

Signs and Symptoms of Bereavement

Seventy-nine per cent of the physicians predict the appearance of common signs of grief and depression in the bereaved-to-be such as anorexia, loss of weight, sleeplessness, feelings of despair, and feelings of helplessness prior to the death of the patient.

Approximately 90 per cent of the physicians anticipate that dreams of the deceased will occur at least sometimes, and 67 per cent believe that such dreams will occur always or frequently. Illusions of the de-

---

*The survey was distributed to 150 members of the Academy of General Practice, 100 Board-certified general surgeons, 50 Board-certified practitioners of internal medicine, 175 Board-certified psychiatrists, and 116 psychoanalysts.

275

ceased are expected to occur at least sometimes by 74 per cent of the physicians, and only 4 per cent believe these illusions never occur.

Over three-fourths of the physicians expect angry thoughts and feelings toward the deceased to occur at least sometimes; guilt feelings are predicted to occur always or frequently by 56 per cent; feelings of infidelity are predicted to occur at least sometimes by 84 per cent.

That the bereaved will at least sometimes have subjective symptoms similar to the deceased is the opinion of 62 per cent of the physicians. Symptoms related to sexual function in the bereaved, such as diminished sexual desire, impotence, and greater inclination toward masturbation, are anticipated often by physicians. For example, 77 per cent anticipate impotence at least sometimes; diminished sexual desire is expected by 88 per cent to occur at least sometimes; 63 per cent predict an inclination to masturbation at least sometimes.

Guilt and Bereavement

Guilt is always or frequently less likely when there had been free expression of feelings between the bereaved and the patient according to 77 per cent of the physicians. Approximately 60 per cent expect that the bereaved will experience guilt at least sometimes when he begins to function on his or her own, accepts the inevitability of the death, and begins to take up old or new interests once more. When more specific questions are asked concerning putting away pictures of the deceased, having renewed interest in members of the opposite sex, and deciding to remarry, over 70 per cent of physicians expect there will be guilt feelings at least sometimes. They anticipate comparatively early experiences of pleasure in the bereavement state—52 per cent expect it within a few weeks after the deceased passed away.

What the Bereaved Should Be Told by the Physician

Sixty-one per cent of the physicians believe that it is always or frequently important to advise the bereaved-to-be how often death is faced by the dying with serenity, and 93 per cent feel that such advice is at least sometimes important. One-third of physicians feel that the bereaved-to-be should always be made aware of the patient's right to die, and only 2 per cent believe this should never be the case. Two-thirds of physicians believe that the practitioner should always or frequently advise the bereaved in detail that everything possible was done for the patient.

Physicians tend to feel that the bereaved should be encouraged to think that he will experience less fear of future tragedies following the current loss. Approximately three-fourths tend to feel that emphasis should be placed at least sometimes on the bereaved's being fortunate to have a child by the departed spouse, if that is the case.

What the Bereaved Should Be Encouraged to Do

On the subject of seeking care and advice, 71 per cent of physicians feel that regular visits by the bereaved to the physician during the first year should be encouraged at least sometimes; there is strong agreement that the bereaved should not be hospitalized for an elective procedure soon after or during the course of bereavement. Most physicians—73 per cent—suggest that the bereaved seek advice soon after the funeral; 57 per cent suggest that such advice should, at the least, be considerable. Physicians suggest turning to the physician (25 per cent) and the clergyman (25 per cent). When the bereaved is religiously inclined, 88 per cent suggest that at least sometimes the bereaved should be urged to attend religious services on the days which have special significance with regard to the deceased. More than 80 per cent agree that psychiatric advice would be of benefit at least sometimes, and 62 per cent feel that this would also be true of vocational guidance at this time.

Over 91 per cent of physicians feel that expression rather than repression of feelings and tears should be encouraged at least sometimes. Almost half feel that repression of distressing memories should rarely or never be encouraged. They favor encouraging the bereaved to speak about the recent bereavement. Eighty-nine per cent agree that the bereaved should be encouraged to talk to old friends at least sometimes; 91 per cent encourage talking with someone who has had a similar experience at least sometimes; nearly all physicians encourage the bereaved to talk to someone about feelings related specifically to the deceased.

Over half of the physicians favor keeping the deceased's wedding ring permanently. As to various other personal belongings of the deceased, there seems to be general agreement: keep some, give some to family or friends, give some to a charity. Physicians suggest that promises made by the bereaved to the deceased during life should be followed if practical and reasonable, but hardly any indicated that such promises should be followed if not practical. More than two-thirds suggest that the bereaved should always or frequently be encouraged to relinquish excessive attachments to the deceased.

Physicians feel predominantly that at least sometimes the person in grief should obtain a pet, seek a companion (if elderly), travel, change jobs if he had long wanted to do so, move to a new living location, or seek vocational guidance. They are also predominantly in favor both of continuing old hobbies and beginning new ones at this time. About half would encourage the bereaved to resume work within a week, and three-quarters within two weeks. Some physicians (18 per cent) would encourage a return to work only when the bereaved feels up to it. Nearly 71 per cent indicate that at least sometimes this might be a time to encourage the bereaved to change jobs, if this had been long desired. More than 90 per cent see working as frequently or always good for the bereaved. Many physicians (37 per cent) suggest that the bereaved always or frequently make major decisions as early as possible.

Advice Concerning Remarriage

An impressive majority of physicians (85 per cent) indicated that the bereaved should be encouraged to remarry if age permits; 52 per cent regard remarriage as the major problem of the young bereaved spouse. That those who have loved deeply and satisfyingly tend to remarry more quickly is the opinion of 70 per cent of physicians. However, 64 per cent feel that it is not desirable to encourage the bereaved to make the decision whether or not to remarry before a particular person is considered, and 83 per cent also feel that it is not desirable to inform relatives and in-laws of a decision to remarry before a particular person is considered.

Physicians should develop greater sensitivity as to what the bereaved expect, seek, and find acceptable to themselves in this most critical period. The lay public, which includes the bereaved and those who are involved with him, also should be educated as to what bereavement entails. More open recognition of the difficulties and decisions which present themselves, including the necessity of dealing with feelings which are difficult to tolerate at the time because they appear inconsistent with the feelings of loss, might help all individuals in their attempts to integrate death, separation, and loss when these occur. It is hoped that the results of this survey will contribute data in this direction.

19

Practical Aspects of Bereavement

Austin H. Kutscher

Certain conclusions are evident to one who explores in retrospect the management and resolution of "practical problems" confronting the bereaved: 1) there is a need for thorough investigation of the subject of recovery from bereavement; 2) ways must be found to communicate to the bereaved available information and advice that may be helpful; 3) bereavement should be treated as an illness which may result in serious, even fatal, physical ailments or complications; 4) an essential factor in recovery is the bereaved's acceptance and at times understanding of his grief; 5) the bereaved's efforts at recovery must be channeled into constructive efforts which will sustain him through the depths of his grief; and finally, 6) those who would minister to and care for the bereaved must be familiar with the numerous practical problems which add an enormous burden to his grief.

The discussion which follows gives emphasis to the practical problems confronting the bereaved. That the bereaved needs help in meeting the practical problems of bereavement is not simply a theoretical concept but a stern reality. Such key issues as what the bereaved can and should do, what others (doctors, family, ministers, and friends) should do in his behalf, and for how long a period of time such help should be provided must be dealt with.

The term "practicalities" refers to those concrete immediacies of day-to-day living which must be acted upon by the bereaved himself or by someone acting in his behalf. The knowledge and skills of different disciplines must be utilized in order to assist the bereaved family to regain the pleasures and gratifications of daily living. Although philosophic, psychologic, and religious determinants affect the course of action, it is important to remember that the action taken represents the need to *do* in order to relieve urgent and formidable pressures and burdens. Not only is there a tremendous gap between the bereaved's need to meet everyday problems and the quality of information and advice offered by concerned individuals, but unfortunately there is, as a rule, less than adequate recognition by the "helping professions" of the importance of dealing with such practicalities. Even when the need for advice may be recognized, there is lack of knowledge as to how such words of advice are to be delivered, how advice can be effectively utilized, and how the bereaved can find and avail himself of the specialists to advise him. By way of illustration, one individual's experience is cited below:

After the long-anticipated death of his wife from cancer, the bereaved called upon a psychiatrist, a lifelong acquaintance, for advice and suggestions as to how to proceed through the days that lay ahead. None of the questions he had in mind were unusual for someone in this situation. The questions dealt with the first moves to be taken and steps which might hasten recovery. They were concerned with such practicalities as: What should one do for the first days following the funeral? What should be done for and with the children? Should one stay about the house, or visit others, or leave home for several days? Should one accept condolence calls or simply avoid all contact with commiserators? Even cursory examination of each aspect of the life to be continued had already uncovered a multitude of such questions that required answers.

The psychiatrist replied, "What made you call *me? Why* did you call me?" As it developed, this response to what might well have been an SOS was an indication of the paucity of well-defined information available to the bereaved from any source.

Yet the psychiatrist did listen, and finally suggested that the bereaved and his sons visit with him at his suburban home that next weekend. The Sunday visit, the culmination of the first weekend of bereavement, was concluded with the accomplishment of at least the start of several important phases of the work of mourning. Words, verbalization of feelings, and advice all contributed to charting an initial course of action. Nothing actually looked brighter but beginnings had, in fact, been made, certain excesses had been abandoned, and initial perspectives had been achieved. The process of acceptance had been initiated and the past had made the first uncertain steps of retreat into memory.

The failure of anyone to provide the bereaved with comfort, information, or understanding increases feelings of isolation and despair and leads to inappropriate or detrimental responses. Such failures can create a sequence of inopportune or harmful events, just as the heeding of effective advice can create a beneficial sequence.

Dealing with practical tasks readily stirs feelings of guilt, loneliness, regret, abandonment, and despair in the bereaved. These feelings in turn, confront the bereaved with additional problems.

In grief, thoughts of what has taken place persistently reappear and reverberate. Feelings of guilt and loneliness stir up doubts and insecurities. What had one done wrong? Should the patient have been told the truth or should denial and false encouragement have been continued until the end? Should an autopsy have been permitted? If it had been performed, had it served any real purpose? Despite the suffering occasioned by ruminating on these and other matters, the practicalities of daily living must be faced. Advice is required on such basic matters as to how to take care of the children, where to live, and how to continue one's daily life. The more positive areas having to do with regaining the pleasures of living and the question of remarriage begin to emerge much later for consideration and are frequently dealt with more effectively as the result of discussions with informed friends, physicians, clergy, and family members.

It is one matter to consider how to bring comfort to the bereaved; it is another matter to consider just how well the individual can or will function in the emotional and physical turmoil of the bereavement state. Some feel that the tendency for the bereaved to drift in an unstructured and directionless manner must be dealt with forcefully. When and to what extent should the bereaved be encouraged to resume responsibilities, and how much time should the bereaved be encouraged to spend with dependent members of the family (children)? For how long should friends and relatives continue to give assistance? There are many factors, determined by individual circumstance, which materially influence such long-term goals as returning to full working capacity, resuming normal social and familial structures, and re-entry into that most satisfying social unit of all, marriage. The bereaved can be guided toward sources of advice concerned with financial arrangements, homemaker services, companionship activities, return to social living, and the myriad of other elements of daily life. Failure to do something specific and practical can have far-reaching ramifications.

The approach must be two-fold: 1) it must take into account the subjective experience of the bereaved (understood from both individual and collective accounts) ; and 2) the evaluation by the counselor of the beginning and later needs of the bereaved. Infallible guidelines cannot be formulated and applied to all bereaved, since each individual enters the bereavement state with complicating practical factors, including differences in religious, ethnic, social, and economic background as well as, where children are involved, their number, age, and sex. Timing may also be critical for those needing help. It should also be borne in mind that, for many bereaved, the problems of loss and grief do not begin at the time of death but during the period of anticipatory grief. There are also profound practical differences between the widow and widower state. By anticipating the bereaved's anxieties, fears, and fantasies, and recognizing the problems of daily practical decision-making, obligations, and household necessities, the physician can develop a far better perspective and approach to his helping role.

Bereavement as an Illness

Although it is recognized that the illness and death of a patient may precipitate emotional or physical disturbances in persons who have loved and cared for him, there is little acceptance of the concept that bereavement states *per se* may be considered an illness. The bereaved may be regarded as a patient with a definite complex of symptoms, often subclinical, which may become exacerbated, severe, and even fatal. Despite this, the bereaved's illness, in general, is left untreated. His state is usually diagnosed from the medical and psychological points of view as a normal response to the circumstances of his situation—until overt signs and symptoms reach pathologic proportions.

The bereaved, as a patient, requires treatment, especially in the early stages, to prevent a more serious progression. Unfortunately, our culture tends to ignore the fact that the problems of loss and grief do not begin at the moment of the loved one's death and that there is anticipatory grief which follows notification of the patient's unfavorable prognosis. Anticipatory grief also ushers in a multitude of prac-

283

tical problems, difficulties which cannot be deferred or ignored and which also affect events subsequent to the death of the patient.

In other areas of medicine, when an illness is regarded as being potentially serious, strenuous efforts are made to achieve early intervention and preventive treatment. In the management of bereavement, it is primarily the responsibility of the physician (perhaps the bereaved's own or that of the dying patient) to assume the initiative for the well-being of the "new" or secondary patient. Although the bereaved individual may appear to be progressing "normally," there is little reason for complacency in the physician's responses to the psychological and practical aspects of the bereaved patient's management. There always remain innumerable personal supportive measures which may positively influence the course of convalescence and the long-term physical and emotional prognosis.

Medical educators, too, must recognize that bereavement can be studied as an illness replete with multiple etiologies, diagnostic criteria, and practical features, as well as with a prognosis.

Still another problem exists which has its roots in the failure of communication among professionals. The primary physician is far too willing to ignore the entire matter or to deal with emotional complications by immediate referral to a psychiatrist rather than to see the complications in the context of an illness—bereavement. Until recently there has been a generalized apathy among professionals regarding the treatment and management of the bereaved. Compounding this state of affairs has been failure of communication between the primary physician and the specialist, as well as between the physician and paramedical personnel. The insensitive and perfunctory platitude, "Time will heal all," has often been substituted for empathic intervention. Perhaps the members of the health professions are shielding themselves from their own fears and insecurities since, in the words of La Rochefoucauld, "One cannot look directly at either the sun or death."

What is often lacking is the intense depth of feeling for the bereaved which can be summoned by few persons, regardless of training, who have not themselves passed through an intimate emotional experience associated with death. A quotation from a letter written by an eminent professional colleague speaks for itself:

One of the reasons I am so tardy in responding has been the death of my mother. Yes, grief and I have come to know one another in a very first-hand way. Mother had been making a good recovery from serious surgery—and then, a clot developed and that was it. All of the small inconsiderations—the phone call not made, the word said and the word not said, the thoughtfulness I might have shown and didn't, all of it came to me—too late. I have often heard the bereaved speak of guilt for which it is too late to atone in the way one might wish to; now I, too, have experienced it.

The practitioner, when he has gained understanding of the problems of the bereaved, can give the bereaved deeper insight concerning his problems and provide assistance in meeting the day-to-day problems. Those involved in the mourning process include the entire family, friends, as well as the physician who has just lost the battle with death. To be of real assistance, it is important that the physician make himself available to discuss the practical aspects of bereavement with the family. This availability may, in turn, be an important step toward resolving feelings of loss by the physician, so that he *can* provide comfort, reassurance, and medical care.

Few teaching or training programs exist which prepare the physician to manage the vicissitudes of grief in medical practice. Recognition of the stages of bereavement, including anticipatory grief, is important not only for the physician but also for the nurse, social worker, and chaplain. As part of his assigned duties, the staff physician should be permitted the opportunity to visit and counsel the bereaved-to-be as he awaits the termination of his vigil. How the physician should be paid for the time he spends in the management of anticipatory grief or the grief of bereavement requires mention since it, too, is very clearly a practical problem.

There is no justification for the abandonment of the bereaved immediately following the death of a loved one in a hospital. Everyone, including interns, nurses, nurses' aides, becomes submerged in routine hospital activities, apparently quite oblivious to the needs of the bereaved, at a time when innumerable problems present themselves. Abandonment should be recognized for what it is: for the professional and paramedical personnel it is a retreat from their own unresolved conflicts concerning death.

Important practical patterns to be followed by the bereaved have been established by etiquette and religion. It is ironic that certain aspects of assisting the bereaved should be well appreciated by an authority on the subject of etiquette, Emily Post, and so poorly appreciated by those who have numerous opportunities to utilize the information:

At no time are we so indifferent to the social world and all its code as when we stand baffled and alone at the brink of unfathomable darkness into which our loved one has gone. The last resource to which we would look for comfort at such a time is the seeming artificiality of etiquette. Yet it is in the hours of deepest sorrow that etiquette performs its most real service. All set rules of social procedure have for their object the smoothing of personal contacts, and in nothing is smoothness so necessary as in observing the solemn rites accorded to our dead.

The effect which the condolence call may have on the bereaved is not fully appreciated. The religious aspects of the funeral have been dealt with at great length in many writings and yet the positive practical value of these proceedings has only in recent years been duly appreciated by the health professions.

Recovery from bereavement is achieved, in part, through the management of practical day-to-day problems. In this process, we must accept the assumption that the bereaved requires "room to move around in," with as many alternatives as possible offered at the level of practical problem-solving. It is critically important to listen during this period to requests for help in regard to seemingly minor difficulties and decisions. They may represent a plea for help at a far more complex level—including a call for psychiatric assistance. If unresolved, severe emotional or physical problems may develop.

The ultimate goal is the reconstitution of the individual into someone who, having dealt successfully with grief and its attendant practical problems, has much to live for and much to contribute to his family and society. With proper support, he can emerge sustained by the knowledge that he has been able to survive his darkest hours and is able now to reengage himself in constructive living.

Four concepts which illustrate some of the practical problems confronting the bereaved are described in the following case history: 1) the numerous intellectual and psychological burdens which become practical problems as they create the milieu for emotional and physical illness; 2) the procedural details, such as funeral rites, legal routines (for example, dealing with lawyers, reading the will, opening of the vault, filing for social security, etc.) which are required by law and custom, and which may also impose unreasonable and cumulative physical burdens; 3) the additional physical strain of coping with the minutiae of daily living (for example, marketing, cooking, housekeeping, and of continuing to perform a job); and finally, 4) the compounded problems inherent in a failure to find positive solutions for many of the issues confronting the bereaved.

A 43-year-old university professor, after his wife's death from cancer, continued to face many of the uncertainties that had complicated his life during the months of her protracted and painful illness. Although he was able to function as the head of a household of three young sons, aged 17, 15, and 11, and to satisfy the minimum demands of his professional obligations, he suffered from weight loss, lassitude, fatigue, irritability, anorexia, restlessness, insomnia, physical and emotional exhaustion, and depression. Many practical problems had begun at the time of the original diagnosis and unfavorable prognosis of his wife's illness.

Initially, and again subsequently when she required hospitalization, he had encountered an emotional conflict within himself over whether or not to tell his wife the truth about her illness. His first instinct was to spare her. On the other hand, he realized that the truth might be unavoidable since she, having more medical knowledge than the average lay person, might recognize the significance of her symptoms and physical deterioration. Also to be considered was the fact that a sharing of their mutual thoughts and concerns at this time might afford both greater emotional strength. Yet at what point should he tell her, where, and in whose presence? Should he wait until her questions showed that the truth would be better than her doubts and uncertainties as she realized that she was dying? Should their physician or clergyman assume the responsibility for the decision?

Without seeking advice, he decided to withhold the truth. Their relationship had been such that words did not seem to be necessary; yet he did want to tell her of his present grief and previous happiness with her, and to share with her future plans for their children. Because he could not find the words and because he was convinced that such a course was not destructive, he did not tell her. Consequently, he was never certain of how much she did or did not know about her condition.

He was also confronted with the question of whether or not to tell the children the facts concerning their mother's illness, and if so, how—alone or together; whether to reveal the true prognosis to them or to maintain a wide margin of hope until the truth could no longer be concealed; whether to permit them to continue their visits as her condition deteriorated.

287

Could support and advice be obtained from his friends, relatives and associates, who included psychiatrists, physicians, clergy, writers? Could they provide answers to his immediate day-to-day problems? Could someone give the children the emotional support and physical presence that he realized he was withdrawing as he spent more time at his wife's bedside in the hospital?

Although those to whom he did turn for advice had few answers, they were able at times to provide temporary relief from the extraordinary and ever-present strains of the situation. He had no desire to keep up his usual social contacts but realized that the children were able to benefit from association with family and friends who tried to fill the gaps in their lives. Just finding a way to decline invitations and to respond to inquiries about himself and the family was a source of great distress.

However, he knew that more help, help of a different sort and on a permanent basis, had to be provided for the children. Some semblance of a stable home life had to be established for them. Hence, the home would have to be maintained, and a housekeeper would have to be hired. Should he advertise in the newspapers, or be in touch with community service agencies, such as Homemaker Service or Cancer Care?

Toward the end, controversial problems had to be considered concerning the administration of drugs for pain control or as psychopharmacologic agents. As body functions failed, the continuation of intravenous infusions became increasingly traumatic, and venous cut-down appeared barbarous.

When death did come in the unhospitable environment of the hospital, it was only early evening—but not a professional colleague was in sight. The heartrending task of informing the children remained for still later that night, following a visit to the undertaker. Other family members, friends, and associates then had to be notified. In each instance there were questions of how, when, and where. Strong feelings surrounding the problem of autopsy permission were avoided because the husband had reached a decision on this issue earlier. The obituary, too, had been an earlier subject for thought; he wrote it alone and readily, but no less painfully.

While most questions concerning the funeral were explicitly answered by established religious rituals, certain procedures were open to the personal preferences of the bereaved. How should a casket be chosen? In what clothes should the deceased be buried? Should keepsakes be buried? Should the casket be kept open or closed? How should the cemetery plot be chosen? Or the gravestone? Where should the family and friends go after the funeral? To what degree should the children participate in all the arrangements and rites?

Soon after her death, the bereaved husband expressed to his wife's physicians his appreciation for the care and support they had given. He knew that every available means had been used to sustain his wife's health while this was still possible. He also knew that no pain or suffering had gone unrelieved because of his own unconcern. He soon began to realize that he had neglected himself during his wife's illness; and many problems concerning his own physical and emotional well-being were becoming apparent.

Were his symptoms psychogenic or of purely physical origin? Were they what everyone called "normal?" Should he seek physical attention or psychiatric assistance, or both? Should he consider his state as "normal grief"? How would he recognize an abnormal grief pattern? What were the stages and timetable of grief and mourning? How had anticipatory grief modified his overall grief experience? How could he best counteract his despair and loneliness? Would frequent visits to his wife's grave be harmful? Should he and his family spend the mourning period away from home, with others, or alone?

Longer-range plans had to be made. Should he accept a new job offer and move to another city? What would be the advantages and disadvantages of such a move for the children? If they remained in their present house, many trivial but nevertheless emotionally stressful decisions had to be made. Should he rearrange the furniture, change the furnishings, remove disturbing mementos? Who should be given his wife's clothes, her jewelry? Should he place photos of her about the house? Should he discard keepsakes that were now painful to look at or store them until a later time when the family might better be able to live with them and perhaps enjoy them again? What kind of remembering would be of a healthy sort—deliberate recall or a simple openness to whatever memories revived from day to day? What days of commemoration should be observed—birthdays, anniversaries, nostalgic occasions? Should he participate in religious ceremonies and rites on those days?

How much should the children be included in decision-making? Would it be best for them to continue their normal patterns or should they establish new ones in order to avoid certain memories? How could the routine of their daily living be continued with no mother to see them off to school in the morning or to greet them as they returned home with tales of their daily successes and disappointments?

Legal and financial matters had to be attended to: immediate financial distress; funeral costs; service as executor of the will; the opening of the bank vault and taking inventory of its contents with a tax examiner; the problems of the joint bank account and reorganization of bank accounts; rewriting of his own will to provide guardians and care for his children in

289

the event of his own death; etc. These adjustments imposed heavy burdens on him both physically and emotionally; they also deprived him of time and energy that he preferred to spend with and for his children.

Re-engagement in any activity had to be assessed. Relationships with friends, old and recent, had to be re-evaluated. Should a widower continue to socialize with the friends he had shared as a married man? Responsibilities toward in-laws remained, but what would happen in this regard if he were to remarry at some later date?

A hopelessly desolate, seemingly unending period followed, bereft of any reason to go on, except for the children. Then the agonizing beginnings aimed at regaining the pleasures of living developed. Finally, the implications of remarriage presented problems of still greater complexity. The first difficulties involved profound feelings of guilt over having thought of meeting and loving another woman. Would this mean that the memory of his love for his wife need be diminished? If so, should he try to stand independently and allow a series of paid housekeepers to help raise his children? Should he try to assuage his loneliness in a manner that did not involve remarriage?

His own self-knowledge made him realize that his faithfulness to his wife could be only in terms of remaining worthy of her; of fulfilling his responsibility to their children; and by sharing with another wife the faith and trust in love he had experienced with her. But how was he to make such a new beginning? Should he tell his children and relatives of his intentions? Would he meet someone through friends, associates, or social organizations? How would his children react? He thought their response would be favorable, but he couldn't be absolutely sure.

Would a new marriage restore the pleasures of life for himself and his children? Could two families (presuming that he married a widow with children) learn to live together and share with each other their memories, their material possessions, and even their parents? Could two households be reorganized so that everyone's treasured keepsakes could be retained and shared to recreate a home filled with love and happiness for all?

How could new relationships be fostered in his current frame of mind, with the physical debilitation born of his grief? All the energy he could summon was being utilized in his job and in maintaining his home. He could not anticipate ever being able to make the effort to initiate new social relationships. Indeed, emotionally and physically he felt too ill to have any desires beyond those of remaining alive to care for his children.

Tranquilizers offered a modicum of relief. He was eventually able to seek out and derive spiritual comfort in diverse ways. He urgently sought a philosophy of life on which to base a pattern of living. As his physical symptoms subsided, his emotional responses became more stable, and he was able slowly to reintroduce into his life the pleasurable activities. Months later he remarried; and since then his normal health has been restored; a new mode of living, a mixture of old and new, has been achieved. The patient has attributed a major part of his recovery to his own recognition of grief as an illness.

Conclusion

The problems described in this case history are but a small fraction of those ordinarily encountered. Although some are unique to this given case, the majority replicate those faced by nearly every bereaved person. In retrospect, each aspect of daily living assumes forbidding proportions and ramifications. The conclusions become self-evident: bereavement is an illness and as such, even under the circumstances of so-called normal grief, should be considered in the context of any necessary preventive or therapeutic measures.

Research is needed to fill the void as to how, when, by whom, and through what means these measures should be provided. In virtually all health problem areas, particularly those wherein crises are encountered, research programs are organized to collect information and data to permit the purposeful design and administration of medication or care in order to effect healing. So too, in confronting bereavement as an illness, specific programs must be established for research into and treatment of this crisis.

It is hard to rechannel a life back into creative activity. Dr. George Crile, Jr., eminent surgeon of the Cleveland Clinic, has expressed the essence of the problem in his book, *More Than Booty*, written as a memorial to his wife (who had succumbed to cancer):

We are gathered together in memory of Jane Crile. If you seek her memorial, look about you—in the hearts of her family, in the faces of her children, in her writings and in her home. Life has been given and life has been taken away. Life and death are one, even as the river and the sea are one. Death is only a horizon and a horizon is but the limit of our sight.

His further message that pleasures can be restored, that a life can be renewed, is very difficult to transmit to the bereaved. Yet all who advise them should be aware that the bereaved's agony in accepting this counsel is but a small price to pay for taking the first step.

It is now more than a year since Jane died. For the first few weeks there was numbness and obsession with sorrow. Some of it may have been because of insecurity. Through the years I had become so dependent on Jane that it did not seem I could find a way to live without her. But gradually I found I was competent to do or arrange for many of the things Jane had always done for me. Interest in my work returned. I began again to find pleasure in people.

As is often the case with those who have been deeply in love and the husband or wife dies, I married again. A new life began, filled with new interests and with a continuation of the old.

I still live in the same house. Many of the same birds, the wood ducks and the swan, are still in our backyard. Many of the relics that Jane and I collected in our travels are about our house. But there are no ghosts. Memories that for a time were inexpressibly sad have once again become a source of deep pleasure and satisfaction.

Since we know nothing of death except that it comes to all, it is not reasonable to be sad for the person who has died. The sorrow that once I felt for myself, in my loss, now has been transformed to a rich memory of a woman I loved and the ways we traveled through the world together.

MANAGEMENT OF THE FAMILY Opinions of the Bereaved)

In order to provide physicians with suggestions regarding preferred approaches to the management of the bereaved family, as offered by the *bereaved,* the editors present here the results of the aforementioned survey (see Chapter 18) of attitudes of the bereaved toward problems inherent in the dying process, grief, and mourning.

The survey, to which 125 bereaved responded, also dealt with: 1) signs and symptoms of bereavement; 2) guilt and bereavement; 3) what the bereaved should be told by the physician; 4) what the bereaved should be encouraged to do; and 5) advice concerning remarriage. Cited below are the responses of the bereaved.

Signs and Symptoms of Bereavement

Regarding the appearance of grief prior to the death of the patient, 48 per cent of the bereaved predict the appearance of symptoms such as loss of appetite and/or weight, sleeplessness, feelings of despair, and feelings of helplessness in the bereaved-to-be always or frequently.

Approximately 90 per cent of the bereaved anticipate that dreams of the deceased will occur at least sometimes; 39 per cent reported that such dreams will occur always or frequently. Illusions of the deceased occur at least sometimes, according to 51 per cent of the bereaved, although 22 per cent believe these illusions never occur.

Over half of the bereaved believe that angry thoughts and feelings toward the deceased never occur; guilt feelings are predicted to occur always or frequently by only 19 per cent; feelings of infidelity are predicted to occur rarely or never by 67 per cent.

That the bereaved will at least sometimes have subjective symptoms similar to the deceased is the opinion of only one-third of the group of widows and widowers.

Symptoms in the bereaved such as diminished sexual desire, impotence, and greater inclination toward masturbation are reported relatively rarely by the bereaved respondents. For example, only 32 per cent anticipate impotence at least sometimes; diminished sexual desire is reported by 58 per cent to occur at least sometimes—but 38 per cent assume that it rarely or never occurs; one-third predict an inclination to masturbation will never occur.

Guilt and Bereavement

Guilt is always or frequently less likely when there has been free expression of feelings between the dying person and the "bereaved-to-be," according to 69 per cent of the bereaved. Approximately 60 per cent expect that the bereaved will rarely or never experience guilt under the circumstances of beginning to function on his or her own, accepting the inevitability of the death, and then beginning to take up old or new interests once more. When more specific questions are asked concerning putting away pictures of the deceased, having renewed interest in members of the opposite sex, and deciding to re-

293

marry, over half of the bereaved group expects there will rarely or never be such guilt feelings. They do not, however, anticipate early experiences of pleasure in the bereavement state—only 19 per cent expect it within a few weeks after the deceased passed away.

What the Bereaved Should Be Told by the Physician

It is always or frequently important to advise the bereaved how often death is faced with serenity by the dying, 41 per cent of the bereaved respondents believe, and 78 per cent feel that such advice is at least sometimes important. One-third of the group feels that bereaved individuals should always be made aware of the patient's right to die, although 12 per cent believe this should never be the case. More than 58 per cent of the bereaved believe that the practitioner should always advise the bereaved in detail that everything was done.

More than half of the bereaved group feel that physicians should encourage the bereaved to think that he will experience less fear of future tragedies following the current loss. Approximately three-fourths tend to feel that emphasis should be placed at least sometimes on the bereaved's being fortunate to have a child by the departed spouse, if that is the case.

What the Bereaved Should Be Encouraged to Do

On the subject of seeking care and advice, 72 per cent of the bereaved feel that regular visits to the physician during the first year should be encouraged at least sometimes; there is strong agreement that the bereaved should not be hospitalized for an elective procedure soon after or during the course of bereavement. More than two-thirds suggest that the bereaved seek advice at least soon after the funeral; however, only 29 per cent suggest that such advice should, at the least, be considerable, and more than half prefer that it be minimal. The group of bereaved suggests turning to the clergyman (27 per cent), the lawyer (25 per cent), and the physician (21 per cent). When the bereaved is religiously inclined, 79 per cent of the widows and widowers suggest that at least sometimes he should be urged to attend religious services on the day(s) which have special significance with regard to the deceased. More than 74 per cent agree that psychiatric advice would be of benefit at least sometimes, and 65 per cent feel that this would also be true of vocational guidance at this time.

Over 88 per cent of the bereaved feel that expression rather than repression of feelings, and crying, should be encouraged at least sometimes. Almost half feel that repression of distressing memories should rarely or never be encouraged. They favor encouraging the bereaved to speak about the recent bereavement: 87 per cent agree that the bereaved should be encouraged to talk to old friends at least sometimes; 92 per cent encourage talking with someone who has had a similar experience at least sometimes; nearly all encourage the bereaved to talk to someone about feelings related specifically to the deceased.

Over half of the widows and widowers favor keeping the deceased's wedding ring permanently. As to various other personal belongings of the deceased, there seems to be general agreement: keep some, give some to family or friends, give some to a charity. Promises made by the bereaved to the deceased during life should be followed if practical and reasonable, but hardly any bereaved indicated that such promises should be followed if not practical. The bereaved should always or frequently be encouraged to relinquish excessive attachments to the deceased, according to 72 per cent of the bereaved respondents.

It was commonly felt that at least sometimes the person in grief should obtain a pet, seek a companion (if elderly), travel, go shopping, change jobs if he had long wanted to do so, move to a new living location, or seek vocational guidance. They are also predominantly in favor both of continuing old hobbies and beginning new ones at this time. About half would encourage the bereaved to resume work within a week, and three-quarters within two weeks. Some 14 per cent would encourage a return to work only when the bereaved feels up to it. More than 78 per cent indicate that at least sometimes this might be a time to encourage the bereaved to change jobs, if this had been his long-time desire. More than 90 per cent see working as frequently or always being good for the bereaved—of those, nearly two-thirds emphasized "always." Many (37 per cent) suggest that the bereaved always or frequently make major decisions as early as possible.

Advice Concerning Remarriage

An impressive majority of the widows and widowers—92 per cent—
indicated that the bereaved should always be encouraged to remarry
if age permits; 78 per cent regard remarriage as the major problem of
the young bereaved spouse. That those who have loved deeply and
satisfyingly tend to remarry more quickly is the opinion of 59 per cent
of the bereaved. However, 63 per cent feel that it is not desirable to
encourage the bereaved to make the decision whether or not to remarry
before a particular person is considered, and 80 per cent also feel
that it is not desirable to inform relatives and in-laws of a decision to
remarry before a particular person is considered.

Differences Between Advice Received from the Bereaved and from Physicians

There appears to be general agreement between the group of widows
and widowers and the physicians, who were also surveyed, concerning
attitudes toward death and mourning, although some differences can
be noted.

It is relevant to consider what factors may have influenced those
differences which appear most consistently (namely, opinion regarding the appearance of signs and symptoms of bereavement), since both
groups represent, in a sense, "experts" who have had either personal
or professional knowledge of the bereaved state. It may be that physicians' impressions are in part a result of the fact that their experience is limited to bereaved persons who have chosen to turn to a
physician for help or whose reactions are so intense as to require
medical assistance.

On the other hand, the differences may testify to the lack of
understanding and the need for education on the part of both groups
concerning what occurs during bereavement. Physicians might develop
greater sensitivity as to what the bereaved expect, seek, and find acceptable to themselves in this most critical period. The lay public,
which includes the bereaved and those who are involved with him,
also should be educated as to what bereavement entails. More open
recognition of the difficulties and decisions which present themselves,

including the necessity of dealing with feelings which are difficult to tolerate at the time because they appear inconsistent with the loss, might help all individuals in their attempts to integrate death, separation, and loss when these occur. It is hoped that the results of this survey will contribute data in this direction.

20

*Awareness of Dying**

Anselm L. Strauss and Barney G. Glaser

Americans are characteristically unwilling to talk openly about the process of dying and death and are prone to avoid telling a dying person his prognosis. This is, in part, a moral attitude: life is preferable to whatever may follow it, and one should not look forward to death unless in great pain.

This moral attitude appears to be shared by the professional people who work with or near the patients who die in our hospitals. Although trained to give specialized medical or nursing care to terminal patients, much of their behavior toward the dying resembles the layman's. The training that physicians and nurses receive equips them principally for the technical aspects of patient care; their teachers deal only briefly or not at all with the management of the emotional response of patients to illness and death.

Similarly, students at schools of nursing are taught how to give nursing care to terminal patients, as well as how to give "post-mortem care," but only recently have the psychological aspects of nursing care been included in the nurses' training. Few teachers talk about such matters, and they generally confine themselves to a lecture or two near the end of the course, sometimes calling in a psychiatrist to give a kind of "expert testimony" (1).

Beyond the medical education experience, management of the dying patient in the hospital setting is quite naturally only in strictly technical medical and nursing terms. Staff members are not required

*For a more extensive discussion of this general topic, see Barney Glaser and Anselm Strauss, *Awareness of Dying*, Chicago: Aldine Publishing Company, 1965.

to report to each other or to their superiors what they have talked about with dying patients; they are "accountable" only for the technical aspects of their work with the dying (2).

Medical and nursing personnel commonly recognize that working with dying patients is upsetting and sometimes traumatic. Consequently, some physicians purposely specialize in branches of medicine that will minimize their chances of encountering dying patients; many nurses frankly admit a preference for those wards or fields of nursing in which death is infrequently encountered. Those who bear the brunt of caring for terminal patients understandably develop both standardized and idiosyncratic modes of coping with the inherent threats. The most standard mode is a tendency to avoid contact with those patients who, as yet unaware of impending death, are inclined to question staff members about their increasing debilitation. Also avoided are those patients who have not "accepted" their approaching deaths, and those whose deaths are accompanied by great pain. Staff members' efforts to cope with death often have undesirable effects on both the social and psychological aspects of patient care and their own comfort. Personnel in contact with terminal patients are always somewhat disturbed by their own ineptness in handling the dying.

The social and psychological problems involved in dying are perhaps most acute when the dying person knows that he is dying. For this reason, among others, American physicians are quite reluctant to disclose impending death to their patients, and nurses are expected not to disclose it without the consent of the responsible physicians. At the same time, personnel generally agree that a patient will usually discover the truth without being told explicitly. Some physicians maneuver conversations with patients so that disclosure is made indirectly. In any event, the demeanor and actions of a patient who knows or suspects that he is dying differ from those of a patient who is not aware of dying. The problem of "awareness" is crucial to what happens both to the dying patient and to the people who give him medical and nursing care.

From one point of view the problem of awareness is a technical one: Should the patient be told he is dying, and what exactly is to be said if he knows, does not know, or only suspects? But the problem is also a moral one. Is it really proper to deny a dying person the opportunity to make his peace with his conscience and with his God, to settle his affairs and provide for the future of his family, and to determine his style of dying, much as he determined his style of living? Does anyone, the physician included, have the right to withhold such information? And on whose shoulders should this responsibility of disclosure fall—the physician, the family, or the patient?

Both the human and the technical aspects of the awareness problem are becoming increasingly momentous. One reason for this is that most Americans no longer die at home. Fifty-three per cent of all deaths in the United States in 1967 occurred in hospitals, and many more in nursing homes (3). These people, then, pass through the dying process surrounded for the most part by strangers. Dying away from home is compounded by a noticeable and important medical trend—because medical technology has vastly improved, fewer people are dying from acute diseases and more from chronic diseases. Moreover, the usual duration of most chronic diseases has increased.

The public has become increasingly sophisticated regarding the implications of physical signs and symptoms and will not be put off by evasive or over-simplified answers to their questions. Inevitably, they will understand the truth. Therefore, it is predictable that the problem of awareness will become more and more central to what happens as people pass from life to death in American hospitals.

Awareness Contexts

There are specific "awareness contexts" revolving around the confrontation of patient and hospital personnel: for example, a patient may not recognize his impending death even though everyone else does, or he may also suspect what everyone else knows for certain. On the other hand, both patient and others may know that death is imminent yet pretend this is not so. Or they may all act on such awareness relatively openly. We shall refer to these situations as the following types of awareness: *closed awareness, suspected awareness, mutual pretense awareness,* and *open awareness.* The impact of each type of awareness context upon the interplay between patients and personnel is profound, for people guide their talk and actions according to who knows what and with what certainty. As talk, action, and the accompanying cues unfold, certain awareness contexts tend to evolve into other contexts.

300

Closed Awareness and Suspected Awareness

There are at least five important structural conditions which contribute to the existence and maintenance of the closed awareness context:

First, most patients have had little or no experience in recognizing the signs of impending death.

A second structural condition is that American physicians ordinarily do not tell patients outright that death is probable or inevitable. As a number of studies have shown, physicians proffer medical justifications for not disclosing the fatal prognosis to their patients (4). For instance, one investigator (5) found that many physicians maintain that when one announces terminality to a patient, he is likely to "go to pieces"; one must therefore carefully judge whether or not to tell after sizing up the individual patient. In actual fact, this investigator notes, the "clinical experience" is not genuinely grounded experience but a species of personal mythology. The judgment was found to be based on one or two unfortunate incidents or even incidents recounted by colleagues.

Many physicians believe that patients really do not wish to know whether they are dying; if they did, then they would find out anyhow, so there is no sense telling them directly. Presumably some patients do not wish to know their fates, but there is no really good evidence that all wish to remain in blissful ignorance. There is, in fact, good evidence that they do wish to know.*

A third structural condition is that families tend to guard the secret, thereby confirming what the physician has announced. An interesting contrast is the practice in Asian countries, where the extended kin gather around the hospital death bed two or more days before death is expected, openly indicating to the patient that they are there to keep him company during his passage to death.

A fourth structural condition is that of the organization of hospitals and the commitments of personnel who work within them by which medical information is concealed from patients. Records are kept out of reach. Staff is skilled at withholding information. Medical talk about patients generally occurs in far-removed places, and if it

---

*Eighty-two per cent of Feifel's sample of sixty patients wanted to be informed about their condition (4).

occurs nearby it is couched in medical jargon. Staff members are trained to discuss with patients only the surface aspects of their illnesses, and, as we shall see, they are accustomed to acting collusively around patients so as not to disclose medical secrets.

A fifth structural condition, perhaps somewhat less apparent, is that ordinarily the patient has no allies who reveal or help him discover the fact of his impending death. Not only his family but other patients (if they know) withhold that information.

In her book, *Experiment Perilous,* Renée Fox has described a small research hospital whose patients recognized their own inevitable terminality (6). Death was an open and everyday occurrence. Patients could talk familiarly to each other as well as to the staff members about their respective fatal conditions. Various consequences flowed from this *open* situation: patients could give each other support, and the staff could support the patients. Patients could even raise the flagging spirits of the staff! From their deathbeds, patients could thank the physicians for their unstinting efforts and wish them luck in solving their research problems in time to save other patients. They could close their lives with rituals such as letter writing and praying. They could review their lives and plan realistically for their families' futures. These consequences are, of course, not available to patients in the closed awareness situation. Instead, other consequences emerge. Since the unaware patient believes he will recover, he acts on that supposition. Thus he may convert his sick room into a temporary work-place, writing his unfinished book, telephoning his business partners, and in other ways carrying on his work somewhat "as usual." He carries on his family life and friendships with only the interruption necessitated by temporary illness. He plans as if life stretched before him. On the other hand, he may work less feverishly on his unfinished book than if he knew time was short and so fail to finish it. He may set plans into operation that in reality are useless and the plans will have to be undone after his death. The unaware patient may unwittingly shorten his life because he does not realize that special care is necessary to extend it, he may not understand the necessity for certain treatments and refuse them.

It is in some ways easier for the family to face a patient who does not know of his terminality, especially if he is the kind of person who is likely to die "gracelessly." And if an unaware person is suddenly

302

stricken and dies, sometimes his family is grateful that "he died without knowing." On the other hand, when the kin must participate in a lengthy nondisclosure drama, they shoulder a tremendous burden. They suffer because they cannot express their grief openly to the dying person; this is especially true of husbands and wives who have always shared fully with each other.

A dying man's wife had been informed of the prognosis by the doctor and had shared this information with friends, whose daughter told the patient's young son. The son developed a strong distrust for the doctor, and felt disinherited by his father since they had not (nor could they have) discussed the responsibilities that would fall to him in the future.

The closed context instituted by the physician permits him to avoid the potentially distressing scene that may follow an announcement to his patient, but such a closed context only subjects nurses to strain, for it is they who must spend the most time with the unaware patient, guarding constantly against disclosure. Nurses may sometimes actually be relieved when the patient talks openly about his demise and they no longer have to guard against disclosure. On the other hand, under certain conditions nurses prefer the closed context. Some do not care to talk about death with a patient, especially a patient who does not accept it with fortitude. An unaware person is sometimes easier to handle because he has not "given up." The closed awareness situation prevents staff members from enjoying certain advantages that accompany a patient's resigned—or joyous—meeting with death.

Important consequences of closed awareness also hold for the staff as a whole. Unaware patients who die quickly represent simply routine work for the staff. In contrast, the patient who moves explosively and resentfully from an unaware to a highly suspicious or fully aware state is quite disruptive.

The most crucial institutional consequence has already been mentioned: because American physicians generally choose not to tell patients of their terminal status, this burden falls squarely and persistently upon the nursing personnel. This considerable burden is built into the organization of the hospital services that deal with terminal patients. Another social structure condition intrinsic to the functioning of American hospitals also increases the nurse's burden, namely, the nurse's commitment to work relatively closely with and around patients. This structural condition can be better appreciated when seen in contrast to conditions in Asian hospitals, where the family clusters thickly and persistently around the dying patient, thus permitting the nursing personnel to remain at a relatively greater emotional distance from, and spend relatively little time with, the patient. In addition, the enormously high patient-to-personnel ratio increases the probability of great distance and little contact.

Mutual Pretense Awareness and Open Awareness

The mutual pretense awareness context is perhaps less visible, even to its participants, than the closed, open, and suspicion contexts. A prime structural condition of this context is that unless the patient initiates conversation about his impending death, no staff member is required to talk about it with him. The patient may wish to initiate such conversation, but surely neither hospital rules nor common convention urges it upon him. Consequently, unless either the aware patient or a staff member breaks the silence by words or gestures, a mutual pretense rather than an open awareness context will exist.

The patient, of course, is more likely than the staff members to refer openly to his death, thereby inviting them, explicitly or implicitly, to respond in kind. If they seem unwilling, he may decide they do not wish to confront openly the fact of his death, and then he may, out of tact or genuine empathy for their embarrassment or distress, keep his silence.

Staff members, in turn, may give him opportunities to speak of his death without a direct or obvious reference. But if he does not care to act or talk as if he were dying, then they will support his pretense. In doing so, they have, in effect, accepted a complementary assignment of status—they will act with pretense toward his pretense.

Staff members may rationalize pretense by maintaining that if the patient wishes to pretend, it may well be best for his health. A second rationale is that perhaps they can give him better medical and nursing care if they do not have to face him so openly. A third rationale is that this sort of action is most tactful.

During the pretense episodes both sides naturally assume certain implicit rules of behavior. One rule is that dangerous topics should generally be avoided—the most obvious being the patient's death; another, the events that will happen afterward.

Talk about dangerous topics is permissible as long as neither party breaks down. The patient and the nurses may discuss daily events—such as treatments—as if they had implications for a real future, when the patient will have recovered from his illness. Some of the patient's brave, or foolhardy activities (as when he bathes himself or insists on tottering to the toilet by himself) may signify a brave show of pretense. The staff, in turn, permits his activity.

It is customary, then, that patient and staff focus determinedly on appropriately safe topics—daily routines of eating and sleeping; complaints and their management; minor personal confidences; events on the ward, and news events. Talk about the fatal illness is safe enough if confined to the symptoms themselves.

When something happens or is said that threatens to expose the fiction that both parties are attempting to sustain, then each must pretend that nothing has gone awry. Thus, a nurse may take special pains to announce herself before entering a patient's room so as not to surprise him at his crying. If she finds him crying, she may ignore it or convert it into an innocuous event with a skillful comment or gesture. A patient who cannot control a sudden expression of great pain will verbally discount its significance, while the nurse in turn goes along with his pretense. Clearly then, each party to the ritual pretense shares responsibility for maintaining it.

A mutual pretense context that is not sustained can only change to an open awareness context. The change may be sudden, temporary, or permanent. Or the change may be gradual: nurses, and relatives, too, are familiar with patients who admit to terminality more openly on some days than they do on other days, when pretense is dominant, until finally pretense vanishes altogether. Sometimes the physician skillfully paces his interaction with a patient, leading the patient finally to refer openly to his terminality and to leave behind the earlier phase of pretense.

Pretense generally collapses when certain conditions make its maintenance increasingly difficult, for example, when the patient cannot keep from expressing his increasing pain, or his suffering grows to the point that he must be kept under heavy sedation.

The pretense context can provide the patient with a measure of dignity and considerable privacy, although it may deny him the close relationship with his family that is created when he allows them to participate in his open acceptance of death. For the family—especially more distant kin—the pretense context can minimize embarrassment and other interactional strains; but for closer kin, openness may have many advantages. Oscillation between contexts of open awareness and mutual pretense is in itself a source of stress.

But whether staff or patient initiates the ritual of pretense, maintaining it creates a characteristic mood of cautious serenity throughout the ward. Even one such patient can set such an atmosphere. Denial in the patients of a cancer hospital (buttressed by staff silence), all of whom know the nature of the hospital, can be so strong that few patients talk openly about anyone's condition.

A persistent context of pretense profoundly affects the more permanent aspects of hospital organization as well. When closed awareness generally prevails, the personnel must guard against disclosure, but they need not organize themselves as a team to handle continued pretense and its sometimes stressful breakdown. Also, a chief organizational consequence of the mutual pretense context is that it eliminates any possibility that staff members might "work with" patients psychologically on a professional basis. It is also entirely possible that a ward mood of tension can be set when a number of elderly dying patients continually communicate to each other their willingness to die, but the staff members persistently insist on the pretense that the patients are going to recover. On the other hand, the prevailing ward mood accompanying mutual pretense tends to be more serene—or at least less obviously tense—than when suspected awareness is dominant.

The context of open awareness does not eliminate complexity, and, in fact, certain ambiguities associated with two properties of the open awareness context are inevitable. Even when he recognizes and acknowledges the fact of terminality, the patient's awareness is frequently qualified by his ignorance or suspicion about other aspects of his dying. Thus, a patient who knows that he is dying may be convinced that death is still some months away. Staff members may then conceal their own knowledge of the time that death is expected to occur, even though they may refer openly to the fact that it is expected. Similarly, they may keep secret their expectation that the patient is going to deteriorate badly, so long as he is unaware of this contingency.

Of course, certain patients (such as physicians) may, as a matter of course, be aware of these subsidiary aspects of impending death. Patients who have the same disease are often kept together, so that each may observe a kind of rehearsal of his own fate by watching others who are closer to death.

The second ambiguous element of the open awareness context is the divergence in expectations about "appropriate" ways of dying which reflects in part the common tendency for staff and patients to come from different class and ethnic backgrounds. It also reflects deeply inculcated professional and institutional norms which differ from those of patients.

Once a patient has indicated his awareness of dying, he becomes responsible for his acts as a *dying* person. He knows now that he is not merely sick but dying. He must face that fact. Sociologically, facing an impending death means that the patient will be judged, and will judge himself, according to certain standards of proper conduct concerning his behavior during his final days and hours. At the same time, hospital personnel will be judged and will judge themselves in their responses to dying patients.

At first glance, the medical personnel's obligation to a dying patient seems obvious enough. If possible, they must save him; if not, then they must give proper medical and nursing care until he dies. But ethical and social, in addition to medical, judgments enter into questions such as when to try to save a patient and when to cease trying, whether to prolong life when death is certain or the patient is already comatose, and so on. These judgments, as well as less dramatic ones such as administering "better" care, depend in many instances, not on objective, but subjective criteria such as the "deserving" character of the patient.

Patients defined as less deserving risk the additional judgment that they are acting with purpose. If they know that they are dying, their improper behavior cannot be interpreted as a consequence of ignorance. Patients known to be aware of death have two kinds of obligation: first, they should not act to bring about their own death; second, there are certain positive obligations one has as a dying patient. There are no clear rules of behavior provided for the dying nor are there clear expectations on the part of the staff regarding his behavior.

Nevertheless, staff members do judge the conduct of dying patients

307

by certain implicit standards. These standards are related to the work that hospital personnel do, as well as to some rather general American notions about courageous and decent behavior. A partial list of implicit canons includes the following: the patient should maintain relative composure and cheerfulness; at the very least, he should face death with dignity; he should not cut himself off from the world, turning his back upon the living, but should continue to be a good family member, and be "nice" to other patients; if he can, he should participate in the ward social life; he should cooperate with the staff members who care for him, and if possible he should avoid distressing or embarrassing them. A patient who does most of these things will be respected.

What the staff defines as unacceptable behavior in aware dying patients is readily illustrated. For instance, physicians usually honor requests for confirmatory consultations with other physicians but object to "shopping around" for impossible cures. Some patients do not face dying with fortitude but become noisy or hysterical. Other patients make excessive demands. Some patients wail, cry out in terror, complain, accuse the staff of doing nothing, or refuse to cooperate in their medical or nursing care. Perhaps the most unnerving are the patients who become apathetic or hostile and reproachful.

In general, then, the staff appreciates patients who exit with courage and grace, not merely because they create fewer scenes and cause less emotional stress, but because they evoke genuine admiration and sympathy, as well as feelings of professional usefulness. It is difficult to admire a patient who behaves improperly even though one can sympathize with his terrible situation. People cannot help judging him, even if by diverse and not altogether explicit standards. Occasionally a patient provides such a model of courage and fortitude that the staff remembers him with admiration long after his death. The reactions of staff members include not only respect for a great human being but also gratitude for being allowed to participate in the near-perfect drama of his dying.

A few points about the consequences of open awareness are worth emphasizing here. Awareness of impending death gives the patient an opportunity to close his life in the manner he chooses. He may finish important work, establish reconciliations, make satisfying farewells, give gifts to his friends, and leave detailed plans for his family and estate.

But open awareness has disadvantages for the patient, too. Other people may not approve of the patient's way of managing his death, and may attempt to change or subvert his management. A patient may not be able to close his life usefully and with dignity because he cannot face the dying process and death. An aware patient, therefore, may be unable to face death with equanimity, dying with more anguish and less dignity than he might if he were unaware of his terminality. For some patients there is the added stress of deciding whether to accept imminent death or to perhaps prolong life through surgery.

A patient who meets death with equanimity at the same time also makes this possible for his family. They will be able to share his satisfaction and they will treasure their experience for the remainder of their lives.

REFERENCES

1. J. C. Quint and A. L. Strauss, "Nursing Students, Assignments, and Dying Patients," *Nursing Outlook*, 12:24, January 1964.
2. A. L. Strauss, B. G. Glaser, and J. C. Quint, "The Nonaccountability of Terminal Care," *Hospitals*, 38:73, January 16, 1964.
3. R. Fulton, "Death and Self," *Journal of Religion and Health*, 3:364, July 1964.
4. H. Feifel, "Death," in *Taboo Topics*, edited by N. L. Farberow, New York: Atherton Press, 1963.
5. D. Oken, "What to Tell Cancer Patients: A Study of Medical Attitudes," *Journal of the American Medical Association*, 175:1120, April 1, 1961.
6. Renée Fox, *Experiment Perilous*, New York: Free Press of Glencoe, 1959.

V

Humanistic and Biologic Concepts Regarding Loss and Grief

21

Thanatology: A Historical Sketch*

Morris H. Saffron

In the plaintive line *Timor mortis conturbat me* the English poet John Lydgate gave uninhibited and moving expression to the dread of death which in every age and land has continued to plague mankind. From that remote day when the primeval ancestor of Abel lay cold, pallid, and inanimate on the ground, the fear of dying, the fear of death, and and even the fear of the dead have persisted like so many incubi to constrict the hearts and depress the spirits of all but the bravest and wisest of men. While it is true that death is the inseparable companion of Everyman, and that man is apparently the only creature truly aware of his fate, yet the human mind refuses to accept the prospect of self-extinction, and the ego struggles against this, the greatest of all evils. Man has striven incessantly to understand the true nature of death, and has at all times attempted to alleviate by one rationalization or another his fears of death and of the unknown.

Certainly, belief in a renewal of life beyond the grave must be almost as old as man himself. Mortuary practices indicating some cult of the dead are coeval with the earliest known civilizations of the Old Stone Age. Many anthropologists have held that primitive man did not fear death in the same sense that we do today. In spite of frequent exposure to the bodies of the dead in warfare he had no clear apprehension of natural death, his mental culture apparently being insufficient to enable him to interpret his experiences accurately. Individual death, whether in the young and healthy or in the old and decrepit, was attrib-

*Two general references to supplement this chapter are Jacques Choron's *Death and Western Thought* (New York: Crowell-Collier, 1963) and *Modern Man and Mortality* (New York: Macmillan, 1964).

uted to the malign influence of a distressed spirit or a jealous god. Since the savage was unable to think of himself as ceasing to exist, and since imperishability of the personality was for him an undoubted truth, death became not so much a unique catastrophic event as a simple transition from one existence to another. The future life could thus be faced with fortitude; indeed, because the spirit takes the form of the individual in life, many persons in primitive society voluntarily sought death before the period of ultimate decline (1).

Aside from fear, death also aroused in primitive man respect and veneration. The corpse itself was tabu, and those who came into contact with it remained infectious until purified by prescribed ritual. Since the dead man continued to hear and feel until decently buried, the traditional "rites de passage" were conducted with scrupulous care in order to facilitate the dead man's transit to the spectral realm, thus avoiding his anger. Uncivilized man lived in great terror of the evils that could be inflicted by vengeful spirits of the young who died unfulfilled or by those whose neglected bodies were left unburied. Grief was shown by lamentations, and by elaborate ritual compositions addressed to the departed, bewailing his loss and imploring his benign assistance to those left behind. Ease of communication with benevolent spirits dwelling in shrines or convenient burial plots frequently led to daily contact with the dead, who could thus be consulted for guidance and advice. This cult of the dead was widespread and persistent in most early cultures, and late survivals may be observed in the ancestor worship of the Etruscans, Romans, and Chinese.

Even if we are to accept the theory that the inevitability and finality of death did not make itself felt until shortly before the period of recorded history, and that primitive man with his assurance of personal immortality did not live in morbid fear of dying and death, certainly the earliest writings that have survived present us with an entirely different picture. The Babylonians feared death with a vengeance. Personal immortality was reserved for gods and heroes, and the king annually sacrificed a young male as a substitute to avert from himself the danger of death. Holocausts at Ur bear witness to the large band of warriors and servants forced to accompany the ruler on his dreaded last journey (2). Later Babylonian mythology pictures the angel of death and his cohort scouring the land, inflicting disease and death in order to recruit new subjects for their master in Sheol. The Gilgamesh epic pictures this lasting abode of the dead as a dreary, dark, and disagreeable place, inhabited by a multitude of disembodied, frustrated spirits who live a shadowy, senseless existence, and for whom there seems to be no hope of salvation. Little wonder that man mourns: "The day of death is unknown, for it is the day that lets no one go."

But the Egyptians, perhaps more than any people in antiquity, seemed literally panic-stricken at the thought of the hated enemy, death. For the pleasure-loving Egyptian the mere idea of losing his identity and being absorbed by nature was utterly appalling, and his fears were frank and unrepressed. The perils of irretrievable annihilation could be averted only by the strictest attention to an elaborate series of rituals. Long before his own demise the prudent man began to prepare a secure dwelling place for his mortal remains. Mortuary ritual in Egypt can be traced back to Calcolithic and even Neolithic times. Their tombs or mastabas were furnished with all the appurtenances and comforts commensurate with the future occupant's earthly status. Instead of trusting to unreliable relatives the wealthier Egyptian made contracts with *ka* priests to supply the necessary incantations as well as food. We know that the greed of the tomb robber soon overpowered any fear of the dead and his curses, since every royal tomb (with the exception of Tutankhamen's) was thoroughly pillaged in ancient times.

For the earliest Egyptians personal immortality was a divine blessing reserved exclusively for the pharaoh, and it was only through this cosmic figure that his subjects could find any hope of salvation. Yet the *Book of the Dead*, which dates from the first dynasty and prescribes formulas by which the living lend assistance to the departed, already expresses a positive conviction of the soul's immortality, and insists on relating the destiny of the individual to his conduct in life. The rising cult of Osiris (*c.* 2250 B.C.) brought increased hope of resurrection and a new life to the ordinary mortal, and his fears of death abated somewhat as the underworld lost its aspect of gloom. While some now held that the soul could rejoin its *ka* in a celestial paradise, the traditional, dualistic, and more dismal view continued to retain many adherents. By 1200 B.C. the decline in primitive filial piety and the shocking desecration of many tombs led thinking men to a more skeptical attitude toward a future life. As their beliefs became more enlightened the Egyptians

315

seem to have lost their obsessive fears of dying, and with death understood as not only inevitable but also absolute, the prospect of eternal life faded.

Hebrew doctrine concerning immortality and the afterlife has gone through a lengthy and tortuous development, ranging from complete denial of personal survival to a celestial paradise. The ancient Hebrews' primitive concepts of death seem not to have varied greatly from those held by the early Semitic inhabitants of Palestine. The Phoenicians were deeply concerned with the incessant struggle between the forces of life and death, and the constant sacrifice of human lives to Moloch was part of an effort to avert a more universal catastrophe. Later cultures considered sacrifice of the first-born, symbolic castration (circumcision), and offerings of domestic animals as adequate substitutes in averting death and disaster.

However, the masses of Israelites clung tenaciously to a primitive conception of personal survival which included communication with departed spirits. It may well have been the desire to destroy this rival cult of ancestor worship which induced the priests of the postexilic period to introduce the gloomy doctrine of the Babylonian Sheol. "The dead shall not worship the Lord, nor those who go down to Sheol." A man who recovered from a seemingly fatal illness was described in the Old Testament and Koran as having been delivered from Sheol (3).

With the rise of the Pharisees as the dominant sect in Judaism, the doctrine of personal immortality, including bodily resurrection, came to the fore. The influence of Chaldean-Persian eschatology is now obvious, but the Pharisees insisted that their beliefs were plainly derived from Scripture, quoting David, Isaiah, and Job. Such liberal views were bitterly contested by the Sadducees, supporters of the priestly caste which resented the freedom from fear granted by this democratizing doctrine. For the Sadducees death is an eternal sleep, and there is no conscious existence of the soul after death. Ecclesiastes (c. 3 B.C.) is particularly pessimistic, teaching that the experience of life should induce the wise man to prefer death; indeed such is the vanity of human existence that it is probably better not to have been born at all. The somewhat more urbane Ben Sira advises us not to mourn excessively for the dead; although it is true that there is no delight in Sheol, its inhabitants have at least found rest and relief from life's distress.

Later rabbinic literature also equates death with a profound slumber from which all shall arise at the final resurrection, although a few of the holy ones may enter the blessed life at once. Even the saintly Johannan ben Zakkai (A.D. 70) wept before his death, not knowing whether he would reach Gan Eden or Gehinnom. With the rise of the Apocalyptic literature even Sheol loses some of its terrors, becoming a sort of purgatory for souls awaiting the Last Judgment. The Talmud adds that the soul mourns for seven days, knowing all that is being said until the body is finally interred. For the first twelve months the soul revisits the body and the evil soul finds no rest until final judgment. Abba Arika (3rd century) insists that even Gehenna is not a place of evil. Much later the great Saadia Gaon (10th century) asserted on rational grounds his belief in life after death, resurrection, Messianic redemption, reward and punishment.

On the other hand, Maimonides (12th century), the best representative of philosophic Judaism, was to denounce the vulgar beliefs which had grown up before his time. Resurrection of the body, torture of sinners, and sensuous pleasures of the blessed are condemned as mere allegories intended for the masses unable to serve God from love alone, and to assuage the fears of the dying and the grief of the bereaved. Like his master Aristotle, Maimonides will admit only that in the cosmic plan devised by God human existence must be meaningful in some way. His conditional immortality can be gained only by righteousness, and is not an automatic sequel to physical death for all human beings.

Like Maimonides, Judah Halevi and Ibn Daud derive their beliefs in immortality ultimately from Aristotle, but the majority of Jewish medieval philosophers, including the physician Isaac Israeli, the poet Ibn Gabirol, Saadia, and Crescas, are to all extents and purposes Neoplatonists.

Two other religions of the Near East must now be mentioned. For the Persian Zoroaster disease and death are evil. When life is extinct a demon enters the corpse and fastens on those who touch it. The corpse must be burned and the demon expelled by rites. Although there is suffering in hell and individual judgment after death, there is no eternal damnation. No soul is eternally punished and in the end Ormazd will achieve the conquest of Ahriman.

Mohammed taught that "death awaits us all, let no man seek to turn it aside from me." He adopted from the Hebrew scriptures and

317

Apocrypha much that the Koran teaches on death, resurrection, and the final judgment. Elements of Christian and Magian beliefs are also to be noted. Azrael summons the righteous and infidels alike, but the former, and especially those who die in battle for the faith, are led to enjoy the greatest felicities of paradise, whereas nonbelievers must suffer the tortures of hell until the final judgment.

The great philosopher-physician Avicenna, in spite of the strong influence of Aristotle, insisted on the immortality of the soul, and wrote a treatise on "Liberation from Fear of Death." The ascetic Al-Ghazali insisted that "the first sign of love of God is not to be afraid of death, and always to be waiting for it." It remained for Averroes, the great commentator on Aristotle, to combat Avicenna by insisting firmly on the destruction of the soul with the body. Only as a reflection of the universal Active Intellect or Divine Reason does a trace of man's personality persist. Through such men as Siger of Brabant and John of Jandun the doctrine of Averroism was to have weighty repercussions in medieval Christian philosophy.

In any discussion of the Greek attitude toward death we must first differentiate between the "thanatophobia" of the average man and the "thinking about death" of the philosopher. It is the written record of the latter which has survived, and there is no reason to believe that the Greek peasant of the countryside had any more advanced thoughts on death and the future life than his counterpart in Asia and Africa.

Indeed, the most ancient Greek conception of death was not unlike that of the contemporary Hebrews: the end of corporeal life eliminated all real sense of perception and emotion. Aesop speaks for the common man when he admits that "every human being is fearful of death even if life has been miserable," and an old Greek proverb teaches that "it is better to be the humblest peasant than King of Hades." A somewhat loftier concept comes from the Greek Anthology:

"I mourn not those who lose their vital breath
But those who, living, live in fear of death."

Euripides takes to task those who face death too abjectly: "I hate those men who prolong their lives by food and drink and charms of magic art. They ought when they no longer serve the land to quit this life and clear the way for youth." Indeed, chronic invalids, especially

318

the blind, who ended their lives voluntarily, were never condemned by pagan philosophers. Instead, Hegesias, the "Advocate of Death," influenced many of his disciples to take their own lives. The Greeks also set a pattern, followed by the Romans and subsequent cultures, in adopting all sorts of circumlocutions to avoid the dreaded name of "Thanatos" or death (4).

It has often been stated that for the Greek philosophers there was nothing funebrial about death. They do seem to have agreed that divine reason, fettered by ungodly matter, could only be released by death, that the end of life should be met in a dignified manner, and that immoderate mourning was to be condemned (5).

On the other hand, the early poets, including Homer, Sappho, and Anacreon, refused to accept the lugubrious finality of Hades. In Homer the chthonian, death-dealing figures of Moira and the Erinyes are not all-powerful, and man struggles to free himself from the superstitious fear of fate. Homer's heroes are unabashed in their explicit fear and hatred of death, nor could they find genuine comfort in a Hesiodic underworld of disembodied, alienated spirits. Homer paints a depressing picture of the "psyche flying from the body to Hades, bewailing its fate, leaving behind youth and strength," and of Achilles trying in vain to grasp the shade of Patroclus. The common people derived little comfort from the Milesian cosmologists who concerned themselves with ultimate causes and the transitory nature of things, and who could offer at best only a nebulous, impersonal immortality in the return of the soul to a primal, elemental state. The antagonists Heraclitus and Parmenides agreed only that the possibility of complete annihilation was unacceptable to the rational mind. But it was Pythagoras with his "Orphic" doctrine of the transmigration of the soul, and the release through death of the potentially divine "daemon" from the crudity of the body, who was the first to offer the solace of personal immortality. Although the teachings of Pythagoras were confined largely to his sect and had little influence on the masses, they were later to exert a profound influence through Empedocles, Socrates, and Plato.

In the sharpest contrast are the atomists Democritus and Leucippus. Their world of minute particles in whirling motion has no room for immortal souls. Death and dissolution is the fate of all animate beings and even the gods are transitory atoms subject to universal laws. This doctrine, later to receive its greatest impetus through Epicurus,

319

Lucretius, and the Roman Stoics. has persisted in one form or another to this day.

It was Socrates (or Plato) who made the bravest attempt to alleviate man's fear of death. Socrates taught that death was not something one could plan for at the very last moment, and that only the man who had lived a full and rewarding life could confront this last terror with composure. To his disciples, bewildered at his refusal to escape the final penalty, he confided "Know ye not that I have been preparing for death all my life? And since there is a God no evil can happen to a good man, neither in life or after death." Socrates hailed death as the beginning of true life. Like the brave soldier and good citizen who obeys law and order, the philosopher should be prepared to face death with composure and equanimity.

Yet at almost the same time that Socrates was displaying such fortitude, the great Pericles, having been given up by his doctors, could not conceal his fear of death, and resorted to such degrading practices as magic and incantations.

For Plato the true homeland of the soul was in the realm of eternal ideas, hence immortality must be a valid doctrine. It is certain that no writings aside from the Bible have done more to reconcile men with the thought of death than the Platonic dialogues on immortality. Aristotle, like Pericles, made no attempt to conceal his fear of death, terming it "the most terrible of all things," yet late in life he rejected his master's teaching on personal immortality, conceding only that the cosmic plan is a triumph of logic in which human existence must play an essential part. Man should live as though he were immortal in order to accomplish great things in the realm of action or of thought.

Epicurus went even further than Aristotle in denying hopes of immortality:

Since the soul does not survive to suffer the pain of the dying man death matters little to the living or the dead; for while we are living death is not present and when we are dead we are not there to fear him. Finally, if my arguments are mistaken and the soul is immortal then certainly death is not to be feared.

This specious argument, meant to minimize death by ignoring him, has had a long and eventful history. Popularized by Lucretius in the

De rerum natura, it has influenced many minds from Marcus Aurelius to this day. Jacques Choron, the leading historian of thanatology, shows the contempt with which the Platonists greeted this comfortless solution. It is interesting to note that both Epicurus and Lucretius are said to have suffered recurrent attacks of ill-health, and that for the chronically ill the prospect of death holds fewer terrors than for the healthy and vigorous; indeed, it may often be regarded as a comforter, bringing final release from pain and suffering. Lucretius saw no point in protracting life, asking: "What is there that is so very bitter if sleep and peace be the conclusion of the matter, to make one fade away in never-ending grief?" Superstition was rampant even among educated Romans, and such men as Cicero and Celsus did not hesitate to resort to magic and divination. Fear of death was aggravated by tales of premature burial, and Celsus relates how a man was discovered to be still alive while being transported to his burial place.

At the period when the world of antiquity was gradually beginning to decline, the Gnostics, Neoplatonists, and early Christians were waging a fierce war for the minds of men. All of these widely divergent sects, as well as the Essenes, offered to solve men's fears of death by offering some form of immortality. For the Gnostics the material world was entirely evil, ruled over by a Demiurge equated with the vengeful God of the Old Testament. Only those who became spiritually enlightened could find in death a blessed release and eventual mingling with the divine fire of the supreme Deity. The Neoplatonist Plotinus faced his own death with serenity, secure in the belief that death is simply the "last effort to return that which is divine in me to that which is Divine in the universe." Although the Essenes never became a major factor they were already preaching the coming of the Messiah and a universal resurrection during the lifetime of Jesus. Jesus himself had been deeply anguished at the approach of his earthly span, and the Agony in the Garden typifies man's helplessness in face of his inevitable mortality. Christ hated death; for the Christian, death was the enemy He came to conquer as well as the means by which He conquered it. The Pauline gospel broke firmly with the older Hebraic tradition of a dismal Sheol, and proclaimed not only the immortality of the individual soul, but also the eventual "expressing of the corpses," a doctrine that was to attain the greatest success and final victory. Paul knew that in a world beset with difficulties and frustrations real happiness is impossible

321

unless man can first conquer his fear of death. The true convert became no longer an object of flesh alone, but a temple of the divine "pneuma," and the man who received the last rites died secure in the belief that the unpleasant event was simply a preparation for another more blessed existence. The immediate acceptance of these "glad tidings" and the vast martyrology of the early centuries speak clearly for the attraction and effectiveness of this belief. So close was the Christian teaching on the soul's immortality to that of Socrates that by the end of the second century A.D. Athenagoras could invoke the authority of Plato in explaining Christian doctrine to Marcus Aurelius.

Zeno of Citium, the founder of Stoicism, considered the material world as real, animated by a universal soul; death implies reabsorption of the individual soul into this divine principle from which it first emanated. Although he thus precluded personal immortality from his philosophy, the aged Zeno did not hesitate to end life by his own hand. Later Roman Stoicism, tinctured by Epicureanism, moved even further away from any recognition of a conscious afterlife. Seneca, Epictetus, and Marcus Aurelius exhibit an elusive and complicated view of postmortem existence. Cicero clung half-heartedly to a belief in immortality, writing his *Consolatio* in an attempt to assuage his grief at the death of his young daughter, Tullia (6). Yet, in the later *Tusculan Disputations* he argued that death ought not to be feared whether the soul is immortal or not, adding that pain can be endured and grief overcome by the virtuous man. Indeed, it is only at death that the soul becomes truly knowing and wise. Certainly Cicero greeted his executioners with these noble words: "aequo animo paratoque moriar." Seneca echoes Socrates in considering life a long preparation for death. To avoid its terrors we must contemplate it bravely, reconcile ourselves to a temporary part in the drama of nature, and retire gracefully when our role is completed. Seneca denies explicitly the immortality of the soul, derides the wretched who through fear of death are driven to prayer; and he ended his own life like a true Stoic. Lucan and Petronius, who met a fate identical to Seneca's at the hands of Nero, are said to have faced death with indifference, quoting lightly from their own writings.

The pantheism of Pliny the Elder also has no place for the soul's immortality, and the Emperor Hadrian composed jesting verses addressed to his "immortal" soul. For Plautus an early death at a time when one is still in command of one's health, senses, and judgment is a divine blessing. The famous *Meditations* of the emperor Marcus Aurelius are greatly concerned with death and the vanity of the human condition, and may have served to relieve his own natural fears. Alexander of Aphrodisias followed Aristotle in arguing against immortality of the entire soul, and identified the Active Intellect with God.

In these early Christian centuries fear of death seems to have reached new heights; the philosophers had destroyed hopes of personal immortality, and the pagan gods, no longer venerated, were being ridiculed by a more enlightened but decadent public. Indeed, the barbarian warriors' contempt for death on the battlefield contrasts vividly with the poor morale of the Gallo-Romans (7).

The Dark Ages and later Middle Ages, with their constant succession of invasions, wars, epidemics, and famines, provided little to resolve men's terror of death, and indeed at certain periods these fears may be said to have risen to unprecedented heights. For St. Augustine, who added to the general uneasiness with his difficult doctrine of predestination, death was an anticlimax, since man has been dying from the very day of birth. From the Bishop of Hippo, who at one point of his life "hated and feared death as the most ferocious enemy," to the Venerable Bede, who exhorted Edwin to convert on the grounds that the new doctrine offered some certainty to replace the ignorance of what follows death; and from St. Bernard, who admits that life begins with sadness and ends with fear, to St. Thomas Aquinas, who notes that man fears death not only at the final moment, but also whenever he thinks of it, there is no cessation to this morbid refrain. Medieval man was constantly reminded of the frailty of human existence, the sudden stroke of Death, the tortures to be endured by those who transgress God's commandments. The skeleton now became the popular gruesome symbol of "momento mori" and the poets of the *Vado Mori* as well as artists used the theme of death and the Last Judgment in innumerable exempla, such as *Dies Irae* or *De Contemptu Mundi*. When the average span of life was well under forty, men, though ever fearful of death, were impatient to seize the pleasures and joys of earthly existence. The diversion of the Fourth Crusade to attack the Christian city of Constantinople, in spite of papal threats of excommunication and damnation provides an example of the true temper of the times.

With the final collapse of feudal order the Four Horsemen of the Apocalypse rode roughshod through Europe. Painters adorned the churches with scenes of the Last Judgment, the Triumph of Death, and Tortures of Hell, all meant to emphasize for the illiterate the vanity of worldly things. The man who had led a lusty life and died unexpectedly and unshriven was in a woeful state, and the deathbed itself became the scene of a virtual struggle between the priest and the powers of evil. The popularity of the numerous versions of the *Ars Moriendi* bears witness to the unabated preoccupation with fears of death and damnation. Yet, as the period drew to a close Death lost some of his hostile aspect, and became, for some, the benign messenger of God, the friend and benefactor of man.

With the Renaissance and the renewal of interest in the philosophy of antiquity there arose a much more skeptical approach to the insoluble problem of immortality. The tenets of the Christian church were now subjected to a grueling analysis. Such scholars as Abelard and John of Salisbury had already thrown doubts on the suprasensory world of Plato and St. Augustine. Petrarch, although nominally a believer, placed his hopes for future felicity not in a Christian heaven but in the pagan heaven described by Cicero in his "Dream of Scipio." Ficino, a leading figure in the Platonic Academy of the Medici, read Plato to Cosimo the Elder on the latter's deathbed, and Pulci would have Cosimo received in heaven by no less a person than Cicero himself. Ficino was careful to present the revival of Plato and Neoplatonism as entirely consistent with Christian doctrine, but tried desperately to escape from his own death as predicted by his horoscope through a recourse to astral magic. The cabalist Pico della Mirandola stressed the need to find the only secure refuge from death through an active life of self-fulfillment and fruitful accomplishment. It remained for Pomponazzi, less cautious than others, to maintain the thesis that belief in immortality is solely a matter of faith and not a postulate of moral conduct; indeed he argued that only an honest recognition of human mortality can provide a satisfactory basis for a fruitful existence. His contemporary, Agostino Nifo, went still further in declaring that there are no immortal things besides the intelligences of the spheres and the single intellect of man. Thus, while the terror of death was slow to diminish for the masses of men, an increasing number of defiant individuals found consolation through recourse to reflection and philosophy. Machiavelli and Leonardo da Vinci may be considered typical: the former found that through communication with the great minds of the past death no longer appalled him; the latter, "just as a good day well spent brings a happy sleep, so does a life well spent bring a happy death." Leonardo added that the happy man does not concentrate on thoughts of death or dwell morbidly on the subject. The influence of anti-Christian philosophising had now reached such proportions as to pose serious threats to organized religion, and in 1513 Pope Leo X felt compelled to order the Lateran Council to prepare a document reasserting the position of the Church on the immortality and individuality of the soul. For while the philosophers were destroying the firm beliefs in salvation and resurrection for the intelligentsia the masses were also reacting with increasing indifference to the dismal emblems of death and hell which had covered the church interiors for centuries. The grimacing skeletons of the many versions of the "Danse Macabre" and "Todtentanz" now served more to arouse levity than religious fervor. The artists managed to give a satirical or ludicrous twist to the most gruesome figures (8), and the poets joined in writing burlesque pieces about death. When a canon of Ambrun in 1658 wrote a particularly facetious set of rhymes depicting the despair of Death at the prolix excuses which detained him from carrying on his work, he was already heir to a lengthy tradition.

The deistic and anticlerical trends already so noticeable by the late fifteenth century continued unabated through the sixteenth and seventeenth. More stable governments, the availability of printed books with the corresponding decline in illiteracy, an increased knowledge of the nature of the physical world, and man's lengthening life span all combined to encourage the introspective individual to take a new look at such fundamental matters as death and immortality. Montaigne spent a long and sheltered life trying to conquer his deep-seated fears of death, but seems never to have arrived at a firm decision as to its final mysteries. He displayed a morbid interest in reading accounts of the deathbed scenes of famous men, "wishing to see by their words and actions what sort of countenance they put upon it." Montaigne reverts to the distinction, made earlier by Cicero and Seneca, between the terrifying act of dying and death itself, the latter being nothing more than a deep sleep. Even though he reluctantly gave up his belief in survival of the personality, he consoled himself with the thought that "nothing can be a grievance that occurs but once. If you had not death you would eventually curse Nature for having deprived you of it."

Montaigne thus expressed a sentiment to be echoed later on by

325

Francis Bacon, Jean-Jacques Rousseau, and many others. Bacon said: "I do not believe that any man fears to be dead, but only the stroke of death . . . death is a friend of ours, and he that is not ready to entertain him is not at home . . . . It is as natural to die as to be born, and to a little infant, perhaps the one is as painful as the other." His brave contemporary Giordano Bruno defied death, facing the flames secure in the belief that total annihilation was not possible in a universe in which God is all-Being, and an individual death simply one episode in a continuous process of "cosmic metabolism." For La Fontaine immortality rests in the works of man. "Death never takes the wise man by surprise; he is always ready to go."

Like Montaigne, Rene Descartes and Blaise Pascal were subject to severe bouts of thanatophobia. Descartes tried desperately but with little success to reconcile natural reason, the cornerstone of his mechanistic philosophy, with a metaphysical belief in the mind's immortality; and his follower de Malebranche, a true believer, spent a long lifetime defending his master's vague position. Pascal criticizes Montaigne for his wholly pagan desire to die weakly and gently, and comforts himself by recalling that even Jesus was reluctant to suffer death. Pascal anticipated the existentialists in his profound awareness of man's isolation and his terror of the nothingness after death. "Death which threatens us every minute must in a few years, infallibly reduce us to the horrible necessity of eternal annihilation and misery. There is nothing more real, more terrible than this." Pascal was a skeptic in youth, but only a deeply moving religious experience a few years before his early death, and an increasing dread of the "infinite in which man is engulfed," brought him, when sick and solitary, to desert science and philosophy and seek consolation in the bosom of the church. Perhaps it is more than a coincidence that Angelique Arnaud, abbess of Port-Royal, whom Pascal had defended so valiantly, was herself also a confirmed thanatophobe. Spinoza on the other hand refused to adhere to what he considered the outworn credo of the synagogue. "A free man thinks of nothing less than of death, and his wisdom is a meditation on life, not on death." Death completes a pattern, and the man who has conquered his fears of death through a rich and productive life can ultimately absorb and accept the concept that his self will some day cease to be. Finally, since God is the substance of all things, death is not a catastrophe, and the intellect by its love of the God of Nature finds consolation, renewal, and inner peace.

During the eighteenth century the doctrine of personal immortality was attacked with increasing fervor, and men of the Enlightenment were urged to face death with philosophic equanimity. Until this period the subject of the soul's immortality had been largely the province of theologians and philosophers, but from this time on an increasing number of physicians and scientists as well as poets had no hesitation in making their opinions felt. Such men as the Englishmen Hobbes and Toland led the way in the revival of materialism and the concept of man as a sort of mechanism. Yet Hobbes, plagued by a deep-seated fear of death, wavered between a denial of the soul's immortality and a hope for resurrection of the faithful. The complete denial of spiritual substance formed the basis of the ideas expressed in *Man a Machine*, an important book by the physician de la Mettrie. He denounced Descarte's equivocal position on immortality, and came to the conclusion that, "The soul is but an empty word of which no one has any idea." De la Mettrie advocated "until the last breath be sensual Epicurean, but a firm Stoic at the approach of death." His writings were greatly admired by Frederick the Great, Voltaire, and Baron d'Holbach, and exerted a direct influence on the leaders of the French Revolution.

In Hume skepticism about the immortal soul reached heights not attained since antiquity. Having survived an early brush with death and its attending fears, Hume determined never again to permit such terrors to disturb him. Instead he professed to a dread at the mere thought of immortality, arguing that only by recognizing the eventual extinction of the individual can we obtain complete relief from fear of death. Apparently he found this solution effective for himself, for he seemed to look forward to death, and numerous witnesses have attested to the serenity with which he met his end.

Hume's contemporary, Samuel Johnson, is often cited with Montaigne and Pascal as a supreme example of thanatophobia. Although he was undoubtedly familiar with Milton's admonition that "it is the imaginative anticipation of death rather than death itself that may be the grisly terror," he admitted that "the whole of life is but keeping away the thought of it." In spite of his firm Christian beliefs, Johnson became extremely agitated at the mere discussion of death, and on one occasion rebuked Boswell severely for pursuing the subject. He also admitted that for him an infinity of torment would be preferable to the thought of annihilation. Yet, once he was informed that there was no hope of recovery he refused opiates and all other medication and waited with resignation for his very peaceful death.

For those men of the eighteenth century who could not accept the materialist position unequivocally, some form of metaphysical doctrine, such as idealism, seemed the only answer. Leibniz combined a mechanistic philosophy with a firm belief in teleology. He argued that God will preserve not only our substance but also our person, with the monad continuing a new stage of growth after death. For Leibniz the rational soul is an image of the Deity, and the mere fact of the existence of the world implied that there was some significance to the individual self.

Others who, like Kant and Hegel, tried to defend the older position also resorted to such metaphysical expressions as "Divine Providence" and "World Spirit." Kant found a tenuous argument for immortality in the presupposition that the moral law commands us to become perfect, an accomplishment not possible in any finite existence, so that the hereafter is needed to complete the highest good. Kant's devoted follower, Fichte, although denying the existence of the individual soul, considered death a blessing since it leads us back to absolute spirit.

Hegel explains death as the "dying of God", for God loses his own sense of abstractness and alienation through incarnation and death. The act of dying thus becomes the highest manifestation of the union, through love, of God and man. Feuerbach, a student of Hegelian thought, expressed profound doubts as to personal immortality, adopting a position closer to that of Spinoza. Rousseau with customary bluntness asserted that "he who pretends to face death without fear is a liar." On the other hand, the physician Cabanis, in spite of his intensive research in physiology and psychology, seems to have clung to a belief in a spiritual and immortal soul.

Thoughts about death at the turn of the nineteenth century were dominated by a group of romantic poets and novelists who preached individuality and autonomy, rejecting all ideas of participation. They ranged all over Europe and included such famous names as Goethe, von Kleist, Novalis, and Schelling in Germany, Keats, Shelley, and Byron in England, Chenier and later Baudelaire in France, and Lermontov in Russia. Like the sixteenth-century John Donne (9), these creative spirits professed an actual yearning or overpowering wish for death as a release from the triteness and emptiness of existence and as an introduction to a new life in a blissful world of exaltation. Whether or not this "love of death" was simply a pose is difficult to judge, but many of these romanticists did die young, often under tragic circumstances. André Chenier wrote verses while awaiting the guillotine. But those who, like Schelling and Goethe, survived this phase of existence expressed a keen desire for life; Goethe indeed developed a pronounced case of thanatophobia, avoiding funerals and other reminders of death, and evincing at his deathbed "the most horrible fear of death."

As we have already noted, fear of death persists in every age, but serious study of the phenomena of death from the biological and medical standpoint may be said to have begun early in the eighteenth century with Lancisi's monograph on sudden death. From then on, such subjects as the prediction of death, the moment of death, and premature or apparent death have attracted the attention of a number of masters, including Albrecht von Haller, Marie François Bichat, and many others. Haller, like William Harvey, took a keen interest in the physiology of his own dying, and continued to count his pulse until it could no longer be felt. Brouardel in his classic *Moment of Death* (1894) revived interest in a subject which has gained tremendously in importance since his day. Strangely enough, medical historians have, until very recent times, paid little attention to thanatology as a specific entity, nor does the entry "death" appear in the indices of the most widely-read general histories of medicine (10).

Philosophers, within and without the walls of academe, social scientists, and novelists now renewed their absorption with the problems of death, and its inevitable companions fear and grief. For Schopenhauer the entire human condition is a tragedy of pain and suffering which must be met without compromise, and death is simply the last and greatest of all evils. Only through constant awareness of the imminence of death can man eventually attain an attitude of complete indifference not unlike that reached during moments of esthetic contemplation. Schopenhauer can find no rational process in nature, and the individual's death is utterly meaningless.

Less pessimistic than Schopenhauer, Nietzsche also urged men to defy death. In the evolutionary scheme of Darwin which Nietzsche adopted, death is the proper terminus of life, from which not even his Superman is exempted. The individual lives alone with his fate in his own hands. He must have courage to shape himself, counting on no supernatural help or salvation in the next world. Although plagued by years of illness and suffering, Nietzsche eventually could not reconcile himself to the idea of complete annihilation of the self, and proposed instead a process of eternal repetition or recurrence for the soul.

The influence of Nietzsche on the poet Rilke has often been noted. For Rilke death is no foe, but a complement of life, and both make an indivisible whole: "O Lord, give every creature his own death, the dying which proceeds from the same life wherein he had love, sense, affection, all."

In no previous school of philosophy has the subject of death occupied so central a position as in Existentialism and without it the problem of mortality might not have developed at all. First expounded by the theologian Soren Kierkegaard, this philosophy concerns itself with man in his concrete individuality. Since man is the only creature who knows he must die, the dreadful prospect of his individual annihilation, or nonbeing, serves to lift him from the tedium of his daily chores to a true existence. Man must face the prospect of this "imminent reality" in order to conquer his own fears and anxieties, and teach others how to avoid preoccupation with this morbid subject. Kierkegaard seems to have been more concerned with his own ability to meet death than with death itself.

For his follower Martin Heidegger "being-unto-death" differs from biological death as a phenomenon which pervades every aspect of man's existence. Although man tries vainly to escape from the thought of his own death through objectivizing and externalizing death as a universal phenomenon, and through the banalities of daily cares, it is only through contemplation of his own death that man develops a sense of his own individuality. Once aware of his own transitory and ephemeral being he realizes that each man must die alone, or as Kafka puts it, "death is a portal each man opens for himself." By thus bringing death into consciousness man disarms death, liberates himself, and becomes capable of an authentic existence.

Jasper's attitude toward death is ambivalent. For him there is no single, correct attitude toward death, nor is there any contradiction in man's clinging to life while actually longing for death. Indeed, for him the romantic death of lovers (*liebestod*) indicates that the noblest life longs for death. Man learns how to die only when he is floundering, for only by accepting absolute failure does he experience the "Encompassing of God" and make his escape into the "infinite calm." Yet before his own death Jaspers concluded that the self-conscious cannot be excluded from eternal life, and that awareness of the "eternal" already implies active participation.

Sartre ignores and despises the stranger which is death, and disputes Heidegger's position that death gives new meaning to life. Instead, death reveals our freedom and need to resort to integrity in accepting full responsibility for our choices and actions. For Sartre man is a failure, and any attempt to console him for his mortality is an infringement on his freedom. While insisting on the absurdity and meaninglessness of life, Sartre admits that death need not lead to despair but should encourage man to make constructive use of the freedom which is his greatest asset. Finally, death liberates man from the burden of existence.

Marcel, although thoroughly existentialist, adopts a position closer to Kierkegaard and Jaspers than to Heidegger and Sartre. Man, the wayfarer, is constantly passing from one situation to another. True freedom is a mystery, constituting the inner core of the self, and is found only by turning the self inward to an awareness of its capacity for good and evil. Faith and commitment to man and to God are supreme examples of man's freedom, and only through associating himself with a transcendent being does man escape from temporality and death.

Tillich stresses the courage to be or the affirmation of being in face of the threat of anxiety, which is the existential awareness of nonbeing. Individual anxiety concerning fate and death is transcended through a collective identity: the group being eternal, the part of oneself belonging to the group must also be eternal. The neurotic lacks the courage to live, and insulates himself from all threats of existence through absolutized authority.

Bergson and Jung both concede the possibility of some form of survival. Bergson argues that the brain actually translates into movement only a fraction of what takes place in the unconscious, while Jung considers that the psyche, with no knowledge of consciousness,

331

may continue after death. Scheler attributes the decline in belief in immortality to the fact that man no longer meets death face-to-face. His views approach Bergson's position on possible immortality. Man has an intuitive certainty of death, but this is constantly being repressed. While Berdyaev accepts a form of immortality which occurs in reunion with God in the creative moment, he credits Kierkegaard and Heidegger with recognizing the significance of death in relation to man's ethical position. For Ducasse, also, life after death cannot be proved or disproved, but he insists on the possibility of the survival of man's individuality (aptitudes, instincts, and proclivities) as opposed to his personality (habits, skills, and memories).

For Teilhard de Chardin the mass man in the world of Marx and Freud, socially isolated and facing the extinction of his ego at death, finds no consolation for his fears in the philosophy of a "world process" or "eternal values." Having been assured by the State of a secure and carefree old age, he feels cheated by death. Modern man has forgotten how to die with dignity because he does not know how to live.

Contemporary studies in the psychology of death and dying are still dominated by the powerful figure of Freud. He considered the "unconscious" to be ignorant of death and firmly convinced of its own immortality. Schilder agreed that while it is easy to think of another's death our own death seems remote. For Freud fear of death appears only as a reaction to external danger or as a reaction to a neurotic manifestation such as melancholia; the death fear is not a "primal anxiety" and only late in life does it become the "ultimate danger." His formulation of the dialectical nature of "Eros" and "Thanatos" as opposing instincts (the latter a malign disruptive power driving men toward death) has met with increasing opposition in recent years. Freud's assertion that the fear of death is infrequent in young children has also been disputed. Those older people in whom a longing for death has been noted have usually been exposed to repeated attacks of severe illness. Cicero had already observed that "in grief and misery death is a reprieve from the sorrows of life, not a punishment." But older people who are hale and hearty do not necessarily greet death with longing or dignity. Whitman is ecstatic about death, calling it lovely, soothing, delicate, cool, and enfolding. His famous line, "Nothing can be more beautiful than death," has often been quoted, although few persons realize that for over thirty years the poet had been suffering

from recurrent attacks of cerebral ischemia. Freud himself admitted
to a great fear of death. When recovering from a fainting spell he insisted, as had William Hunter, that dying was a pleasant experience.
Nevertheless, Freud, suffering in his last years from a painful malignancy, could not conceal as a confirmed nonbeliever his terror at the approach of death. On the other hand, three famous English physicians, Sir
Benjamin Brodie, Sir J. F. Goodhart, and Sir William Osler, studied
hundreds of actual deathbed scenes. They agreed that actual terror at the
point of death was extremely rare, and that for the vast majority death
arrived as "a sleep and a forgetting."

In America thanatology has had until very recent times few rational
students. The deist Ethan Allen, though not denying immortality of the
soul, rejected prophecy and revelation. Poe's characters, though fearful
of death, are morbidly curious about the beyond, and consider death
a release from the temporal and corporeal. Emerson could find no
rational reason for accepting immortality aside from the universal
belief in the doctrine. Josiah Royce and William James both reacted
to the current materialism by accepting immortality. The aging James
came to feel that death was a wanton and unintelligible negation of
goodness. On the other hand, Corliss Lamont picks up the strain of
Epicurus and considers that "it is positively indecent to claim that men
will act decently only if they are guaranteed the 'pourboire,' as Schopenhauer called it, of post-mortem existence."

Contemporary man now has a greater opportunity than ever to
contemplate the gradual arrival of death. The economic improvement
of the masses has intensified not only the joy of existence but also the
determination to come to grips with the last unconquered enemy. His
fear of death is now tinctured with fierce hatred. He naturally associates death with disease, and having witnessed the conquest of infectious disease and such miracles as organ transplants and the hyperbaric
chamber he is inclined even now to attribute death to negligence or
accident. Yet, if Carrel's theory is correct death can never be entirely
eliminated, no matter how long life is extended. The seeds of self-
destruction are implanted at birth and grow steadily throughout existence, with the higher organisms experiencing the greatest rate of
growth.

Medicine has until the past few decades paid little attention to
the psychology of the act of dying and to the alleviation of its fears.

Yet, the step from gerontology to thanatology is obvious and vital. The general physician—formerly the great comforter—is now more than ever overwhelmed with the problem of the "living dead" and is reluctant to tell his patient he is soon to die, since he himself has no secure philosophy of dying and death and finds it as difficult as any man to accept the "death of myself." After successive bouts of illness and depression even the strong, well-integrated personality will eventually resign itself to the possibility of his own death, and once this adjustment has occurred, he seems willing, almost anxious, to acquiesce to the inevitable.

Until recently the dying patient has had little assistance from the psychiatrist or social scientist, the latter being concerned more with the grief of the survivors. Indeed, older people are often shunned as reminders of death, even by interns and nurses. Once segregated to nursing homes or senior citizens' homes, they are no longer missed by the family. Suppression of grief and mourning is growing in America. Whereas in village society the expression of grief is specified by tradition, the current aversion to death and its symbols has caused even the traditional wakes and funeral pageantry to be curtailed, and disposal of the dead has become more than ever a private matter.

The insignificance of individual death in our large urban societies means that there is little of the consolation formerly shared by the grieved one with the group. The modern attitude is irrational—although increasingly skeptical as to immortality, man refuses to accept the existentialist philosophy which attempts to defeat death by denying its significance. He refuses to accept extinction of the ego by association with some racial or social group. Unamuno quotes an old Spanish peasant to this effect: "If there is no immortality what use is God." His own position, as stated in *The Tragic Sense of Life*, is that "immortality is essential to the self, and death as a finality is insufferable."

As our great thanatophobes (Montaigne, Johnson, Tolstoy) demonstrate clearly, a too intense love of life, its surroundings and possessions, is a poor preparation for death. All these men tried to teach themselves the necessity of reconciliation with the inevitable, yet were unable to find the tranquility with which to accept the "death of myself" (11).

Indeed, while one ought not to dwell constantly on death, it is probably a mistake to banish it altogether. Perhaps the poets have in general adopted the most sensible attitude toward death. Torn between

334

desire and fear of death they recognize its inevitability and compare it to a deep mysterious sleep. For them death is mighty yet impotent, at times it may even be ennobling. For Rabelais (as for Heine), death is simply the last act of a drama, and as he leaves the stage he shouts derisively. "Tire le rideau, la farce est jouée."

DEATH IN ORIENTAL RELIGION AND PHILOSOPHY

In general the East inclines to an impersonal concept of immortality, with the human soul being reabsorbed into the All-Soul, the human mind into the Eternal Mind, and the ego-consciousness into the void.

India of the sixth century B.C. witnessed the crumbling of the ancient Aryan-Brahmanic sacrificial cults and the rise of new religious movements. All of these taught some form of salvation and release from the pain and sorrows of the world through absolute denial or negation. In the Upanishads distress at the impermanence of life is overcome to a degree by the doctrine of recurrent death. The helpless, unpurified soul is destined to a series of rebirths until absorbed into the Universal Spirit. The radical asceticism of Jainism was too severe for mass consumption and only Buddhism, "the middle way," has continued as a potent force in the East. The Buddha refused to commit himself on such subjects as eternity of the world and immortality of the soul, and condemned all inquiry into the nature of "reality." Instead, he explained only the origin of sorrow, devoting himself to the destruction of such maladies of earthly existence as decay and death, grief, lamentation and sorrow, dejection and despair. Deliverance is obtained only when "all imaginings, or agitation, or false notions concerning an ego or anything pertaining to an ego, have perished, faded away, ceased, been given up and relinquished." Only with the cessation of all conscious experience and perception can man attain the ultimate reality of Nirvana.

This classical Buddhism, which first offered salvation only for ascetic monks, was made more palatable for the masses through absorption of traditional Indian myths, rituals, and deities, and through faith in a personal savior-god. The Bhagavad-Gita insists that "for that which is born death is certain and for the dead birth is certain." Yet, compassion which dominates this form of Buddhism becomes possible only through the denial of every reality, including the self. Only by detach-

335

ing self from Being itself and from all subject-object thinking can one reach Nirvana and the true Reality.

Confucius admits that even the sages do not know the answer to death. For the Chinese, ancestor-worship offered a vicarious alternative to personal immortality. Mencius admitted, "I hate death, but I hate some things worse than death, so I do not always flee danger."

Taoism teaches a form of quietism and dispassion. Lao-Tzu argued against an undue prolongation of life or cheating death of its due. Instead, he preached the elevation of mortal life by a transference to a higher plane of existence.

In early Japan, death was attributed to the power of evil spirits. The aristocrat was taught to be fearless in the face of death, and for the Samurai death in battle was ennobling. Continued existence after a humiliating experience was considered intolerable, with ritual suicide (hara-kiri) as the only solution.

Hinduism accepts death as the dark tones of a cosmic symphony. Everything that comes into being vanishes forever after a brief existence, absorbed by the annihilating principle, Kali, the black one, or Time. Since the theocratic and destructive principles are one and the same they unite in the divine cosmic energy that makes itself evident in the historical and biographical development of the universe.

Zen Buddhism has recently acquired many converts in the West. The moment of enlightenment or "Satori" comes suddenly and intuitively. By understanding one's own nature one understands the nature of all, acquires a sense of the Beyond, achieves Buddhahood, and thus escapes the cycle of birth and death. When the sense of individuality is replaced by this idea of oneness with Nature there is no longer any fear of plunging into the abyss.

NOTES

1. Malinowski, Radin, and other observers deny the absence of death fears among primitive people. For example, the Hopi Indians fear death and attribute little authority to spirits of the departed. The many universal myths of reincarnation and transmigration seem to indicate that fear of death of the individual was not unknown, and that

primitive man's attitude to death was not unlike that of his more civilized brother.

2. Fear of death must have inspired the desire for companionship in the grave. Herod ordered the immolation of five thousand of his subjects at his death in order to insure the mourning proper for a king. The Hindu practice of suttee which continued until modern times had many precedents. The perpetual round of sacrifices on Mayan, Toltec, and Mahua altars provided sustenance to keep the gods alive and well, thus averting fears of death and disaster for mankind.

3. References to death in the Old Testament outnumber those to life two to one. The Psalmist is especially vivid in this passage: "The terrors of death are fallen upon me; fearfulness and trembling are come upon me. The terrors of death are fallen upon me".

4. Thanatos himself is a creature of folk-lore, rather than mythology. Hesiod and Homer make him the son of Night, twin-brother of Sleep, inexorable, iron-hearted, hateful to men and loathed by the gods. Indeed, he is not worshipped as a god, nor are statues erected to him, since he refuses to accept gifts. Euripides in the "Alcestis" describes him as a dark-robed, winged figure, armed with a sharp instrument with which he cuts off a lock of his victim's hair as a sign of impending death. Yet as the god of natural death, Thanatos is sometimes compared favorably with Ker (Car) the spirit of violent death on the battlefield. The Romans made Mors, their deity of death, a female and called her a friend of the unhappy to whom she granted the tranquility of eternal sleep. The word "thanatology", first defined by Dr. Roswell Park as the "study of the nature and causes of death," now has expanded significance for social scientists and psychologists.

5. The Greeks considered it a blessing to die while in full possession of one's faculties and strength, instead of awaiting the fears and infirmities of doddering old age. Excesses of grief were decried by the Greeks, yet Solon found it necessary to legislate against offensive acts of mourning, including self-mutilation. Until recent times peasant societies of Europe and Russia continued with similar excessive, frequently artificial manifestations of grief.

6. Other well-known examples of the literature of consolation on death include: Plutarch's "Consolation to Appolonius," Schiller's "Elegy on the Death of a Youth," Tennyson's "In Memoriam," and Osler's *Science and Immortality*.

7. Fear of death for the warrior hero has been lessened in all ages by the prospect of unusual rewards. The Greek Elysium, the Mohammedan Paradise, the Scandinavian Valhalla have much in common with the Happy Hunting Ground of our native Indians. Thomas Bartholin, the Danish medical historiographer, wrote an essay in which he praised the disdain for death shown by the ancient Scandinavians.

8. The versions of the "Dance of Death" by Holbein and Rowlandson are the best known of many such productions. Although artists of all ages have been fascinated by death as a subject, the grief-laden Spaniards, from El Greco and Valdés Leal to Velasquez and Goya, have excelled in such portrayals.

9. The poet John Donne is often cited as one of the most expressive of all thanatophiles, and his youthful enthusiasm for Eros seems to have been replaced by an equally powerful longing for Thanatos. Two of his contemporaries, Robert Burton and Sir Thomas Browne, wrote extensively on the subjects of death and dying, although in a more restrained manner.

10. Several physicians have left careful records of their own signs and symptoms before death. One may cite John Hunter, Hermann Nothnagel, and, above all, Hans Zinnser, whose autobiography, *As I Remember Him,* is a classic restatement of resignation at the approach of the inevitable, and contains the moving sonnet "Now is Death Merciful."

11. Tolstoy exemplifies in his writings and his own life the obsession with thoughts of death which runs through Russian literature and history. No nation, with the possible exception of Spain, has been more preoccupied with death and the hereafter. In his *The Death of Ivan Ilých,* Tolstoy gave an authentic statement of pain and death overtaking the proud possessor of material things, no longer master of his fate. Tolstoy himself could never prepare himself for the loss of his garden, his books, and his children. Denied even the consolations of his religion, he died unreconciled.

22

Notes on Grief in Literature

Morris Freedman

"Our present business/Is General Woe." King Lear

Literary study is still much concerned with historical and biographical matters in spite of an emphasis in recent years on highly organized attempts to determine the meaning of a text and to establish ways of evaluating it. Literary evidence still is not used extensively to support research in other disciplines, although a few probes have been made to use literary sources of one sort or another to support sociological hypotheses or findings. Efforts to study literature for evidence on suicide, on how poverty affects the persons afflicted by it and the society in which it occurs, on the development of self-awareness, have all been tentative, usually isolated and uncertain. It has become, however, at least academically respectable, if not yet fashionable, to find in the vast body of literature evidence or suggestions for formulations that concern other than strictly formalistic "literary" inquiries. Literature must after all be regarded as a most serious and lasting record of human experience in spite of the fact that it may not always be statistically accurate and refined. It has apparently been a mistake, for example, to conclude on the basis of the evidence in *Romeo and Juliet* that marriages in Elizabethan England took place at an early age.

The writings of Homer, Shakespeare, Moliere, Dostoyevski, Ibsen, Strindberg, Joyce, and Eliot, reveal to us the character of living in particular places at particular times under particular pressures, the responses made to these pressures, and the ways developed for coping with life itself. We may not yet be able to perceive the evidence sharply.

That is, we are still involved in trying to determine the full meaning of the text. To this end, history and biography and the broader efforts of literary study all contribute to our understanding of the quality and character of a literary work. For example, when we examine *Paradise Lost*, one of the great records in Western literature describing man's attempt to deal with mortality, it is valuable to understand the poem in relation not only to Milton's own life but also to the political and social events preceding and surrounding the work. The study of the agonizing record of the passage to self-awareness and self-acceptance of a Raskolnikov cannot be adequately carried through without knowing at least something of Dostoyevski's own life and of the history in which it was set. We may make very similar comments about the works of virtually every other writer.

One of the most compelling of literary subjects in the landscape of human experience has been that of grief. Especially in older literatures and those of cultures in which the exhibition of grief was not something to be suppressed, as in recent Western civilizations inhibited by puritan pressures of self-control, we find that grief is treated as fully as other human experiences. We find long passages in the *Iliad* dramatically depicting the grief of Achilles over the loss of his companion, Patroclus, and the grief of Priam over the loss of his son, Hector, and indeed, of the two men meeting and understanding one another by reason of their passage through grief. These are important in setting the tone of the heroism, in establishing the depth and texture of the work, in providing us with a sense of what it meant not only to be a Greek or a Trojan, but also of what it means to be a human being, whether hero or merely father.

In a work that stands as one of the monuments of Western dramatic achievements—*King Lear*—the dominant dynamic may be said to be grief—grief as it is energized by an arrogance and an unawareness so regal as to be extrahuman. The grief of Lear transforms him from someone raging against the universe to someone able finally to accept the inevitable fact of his mortality. The evidence for this transformation may be gathered only from the following two passages, the first in which Lear raves against nothing less than nature, and the second, in which he begins the metamorphosis toward accepting, among other things, the facts of old age and of death.

340

Blow, winds, and crack your cheeks. Rage, blow.
You cataracts and hurricanoes, spout
Till you have drenched our steeples, drowned the cocks.
You sulph'rous and thought-executing fires,
Vaunt-couriers to oak-cleaving thunderbolts,
Singe my white head. And thou, all-shaking thunder,
Strike flat the thick rotundity o' th' world,
Crack Nature's moulds, all germains spill at once,
That makes ingrateful man.

               Pray, do not mock me.
I am a very foolish fond old man,
Four score and upward, not an hour more nor less;
And, to deal plainly,
I fear I am not in my perfect mind.
Methinks I should know you, and know this man;
Yet I am doubtful, for I am mainly ignorant
What place is this; and all the skill I have
Remembers not these garments; nor I know not
Where I did lodge last night. Do not laugh at me;
For, as I am a man, I think this lady
To be my child Cordelia.

Grief may indeed range the gamut. It may be shrill and maniacal;
it may be subdued and reflective; it may be philosophical. The recording of grief and of the response to it, of the sadness that is virtually
physiological and is certainly deeply mysterious in its fullest psychological character, serves, as Aristotle and the later students of tragic
catharsis have suggested, as a kind of purgation, as a means of releas-
ing the terrible suppressed tensions, fears, anxieties, deeply fearsome in
their potential for still greater unknown effect. Identifying the full range
and depth of the symptoms must always come first, must be the basis
on which understanding, management, and assimilation of grief into
the totality of living rests.

Since grief has not been examined systematically by literary students, it may be best to begin with a simple description of some of the
significant works in Western literature which have, in one way or another, recorded experiences of grief in various manifestations, or which

have examined ways of responding to and dealing with grief in terms of daily living.

1.) *Homer.* The *Iliad* and *Odyssey* are among the world's fundamental documents recording an enormously wide range of ordinary and extraordinary human activity and emotional experience. The description of Achilles' response to the death of Patroclus, the understanding and response by his fellows, the encounter between Achilles and Priam, their recognition of their mutual agony, their weariness in each other's presence combined with their natural human sympathy (identification), offer, in terms of sheer testimony, as vivid a portrait of the dimensions of grief as any to be found.

2.) *Greek and Roman Tragedy:* Sophocles, Aeschylus, Euripides, Seneca. The classic work, *Oedipus*, records in dramatic detail some of the awful possibilities that are implicit in human living. Ways of dealing with grief, however, are recorded in *Oedipus at Colonus.* Grief and guilt may at first be experienced simultaneously, and may at first be dealt with by self-mutilation; it is the deeper and calmer wisdom, not terror and not the extremes of guilt, which is recorded in the sequel which suggests, perhaps, a riper means of dealing with the basic emotion. Seneca's *Oedipus* is more explicit and extended in its record of ranting, verbal hysteria as a means of handling the overwhelming agony felt by Oedipus on discovering his identity and the nature of his activity. The *Agamemnon* records a sustained yet primitive response to loss —that of a mother whose husband consigns their daughter arbitrarily to a sacrificial death in the services of what seems to her a purely masculine nationalism. Clytemnestra survives, takes a lover, plots the death of her warrior husband on his return, kills him with the aid of her lover, and settles down to defy the forces above and about her. Medea assuages her grief over the loss of her husband by murdering their children.

3.) Christopher Marlowe's *Dr. Faustus* is the record of the grief that comes to ambition that overreaches itself, that fulfills itself by making satanic bargains, that finally must engage with reality when the books are closed by contract. The almost opera-like aria of Faustus's last appeal to avoid keeping his end of the bargain suggests the passion which one can summon to deal with the inevitability of a death that one knows can only include hell. Faustus's "grief" is a concentration of all of the postponed mortal terror that one lives with in attenuated form throughout a lifetime.

4.) *Shakespeare.* Grief—calm and ruminative, bitter-sweet rather than bitter—is recorded by Shakespeare in his sonnets, which record the grief one encounters in the course of love, most of it by now familiar enough. Occasionally, the grief loses its sweetness and self-assuring gentleness and becomes harsh and bitter. In *Hamlet* grief ranges the gamut, from that following Hamlet's loss of his father to that of Horatio's loss of a good friend. Hamlet with calm passion discusses the effect the loss has on him, considers suicide, examines his place in the order of things, and tries to regain a capacity for meaningful action. *Lear,* too, records an anthology of responses to grief—grief caused by irrational expectations of the world and grief caused by the loss of a beloved. Lear's grief, indeed, seems to be one of his means of continuing to cope with life in his late years: he seems almost to establish an occasion for grief in order to stimulate himself to a response. It is appropriate that the work ends with the epigraph to this article, "Our present business/Is General Woe." One can, indeed, make a "business" of grief, as private or public ritual. We need hardly cite others of Shakespeare's works, which, in various ways and in various dimensions, record grief: *Othello,* which examines grief in relation to jealousy; *Richard II,* which is the attenuated and poeticized record of the grief of a poet king; *Anthony and Cleopatra,* the turbulent grief of lovers, great political figures shaping a world; *Measure for Measure,* the grief implicit in black comedy.

5.) *Donne.* The sharp, conversational, ironic, metaphysical poems of Donne explore the various responses to frustrated and disappointed love, from a raging grief through a cool disillusioned cynicism. The revenge, the agony, the sheer hatred are all expressions of coming to terms with grief, of articulating the emotion and placing it in perspective.

6). *Milton. Paradise Lost* records nothing less than the events leading up to man's loss of paradise, the consequent grief, and the reconciliation to living under the conditions known to us. The despair and grief that follow on the eating of the apple by Adam and Eve and alternatives considered by them, ranging from abstinence to suicide, are sustained attempts to deal with the loss of an ideal, of something so perfect its character could not be fully realized until it was lost. By

343

contrast, the grief recorded in *Lycidas* is posed, is affected for the purposes of examining one's place in the world at a moment of one's development. The loss recorded was not personal and immediate as that following the loss of a beloved. Milton assumes a mask in order to establish a means, a dynamic, for dealing with a loss that might by extension include himself. The work is an exercise in how to deal with loss, how to rationalize and convert the emotion to some practical end, especially when one can identify so readily with the lost one. The element of a controlled identification with the lost one who is the occasion of grief is perhaps most important.

7.) *Romanticism*. The sustained grief recorded in a work like Goethe's *Werther* is of the essence of much of romantic poetry, both continental and English, in which grief becomes a landscape to be explored thoroughly in its largest perspectives and in its smallest and blackest corners. Byron, Shelley, and Keats explore the depths of grief and its enormous range of manifestations and intensities. Keats equates the moment of ecstasy with the moment of ultimate grief, death ending pleasure with the climax of extinction. As Mario Praz suggested in his *The Romantic Agony*, grief becomes interrelated with satanism and with sadism. The Marquis de Sade might almost be described as an assembly line manufacturer of "grief," certainly of pain, which is one component of grief. The onanistic component in the more excessively Romantic works must be taken into account in considering the peculiar character of Romantic grief.

8.) *Dostoyevski*. Grief and the sustained philosophical examination of the wide range of its manifestations according to types of persons and circumstances are perhaps nowhere so well recorded as in the gallery of vignettes found in *Crime and Punishment*. Raskolnikov moves in an ambience of grief, his own and so many others.

9.) Strindberg's *Miss Julie* records the almost contrived, conscious development of disaster, of a movement toward suicide by a dislocated, uprooted, unfocused young middle-class lady caught between the old-fashioned world of feminine dependence and the emerging one of feminine equality and even conscious domination. Miss Julie moves from an emotional landscape which is bright and melodic to a small enclosed area, which is bleak, dark, cacophonic, and dominated by shrill feminine hysterics. In the depths of her denial and self deprivation she can only ask to be ordered to destroy herself.

10.) Gerard Manley Hopkins recorded the passionate griefs associated with forms of religious ecstasy and commitment. His so-called "terrible" sonnets are clinically confessional in their candid self-examination of the private agonies of spiritual dedication and self-denial.

11.) Eugene O'Neill's works, with only one or two exceptions, explore grief in a melodramatic, exaggerated manner, enabling one to concentrate on the rhetoric and the grosser gestures. His greatest work, and one of the great dramatic achievements in Western literature, the posthumously published *Long Day's Journey Into Night*, is the record of the communal grief of a family that is doomed to loving while destroying one another.

12.) Grief, grieving, and the incapacity to deal with these except in terms of Sisyphean repetition, may be found in the contemporary theatre-of-the-absurd and in the theatre of violence. Pinter's *The Caretaker*, Ionesco's *Amedee, or How to Get Rid of It*, Camus' *Le Malentendu*, Albee's *Who's Afraid of Virginia Woolf?* and *The Zoo Story*, Pirandello's *It Is So, If You Think It Is So*, Kopit's *Indians*, Genet's *The Blacks*, are a handful of significant works. Critical studies like George Steiner's *The Death of Tragedy* and Lionel Abel's *Metatheatre* and his essay on tragedy in the modern world provide a framework and an idiom for understanding grief in relation to formal art. These dramas do not so much propose a way of dealing with grief as they force us to confront the varieties of grief that are part of any commitment to living fully in the modern world. Grief may be as calm and patient, a sheer awareness, as that to be found in *Waiting for Godot;* it is present in Genet's *The Blacks*, as a kind which moves repeatedly over the brink of control and understanding into the territory of sheer anger and confusion, but at the same time serves in its ritualization as a last desperate way of ordering the landscape of chaos.

Although conventional literary study may offer no ordered way of approaching the various kinds of grief and the various ways which have been developed for dealing with grief and for assimilating it into the totality of continued human experience, it is true that literature does offer abundant raw evidence. From folk songs and commercial ballads to formal drama and poetry, grief is a common ingredient of passionate statement. Grief informs even the newer forms of black comedy, the gallows humor that has become so fashionable in some areas of literary expression today.

345

HUMANISTIC AND BIOLOGIC CONCEPTS

It is perhaps natural that students have preferred to study laughter and wit rather than grief, anguish, and pain. It is paradoxical, however, that Western philosophers and critics have been so much concerned with the formal study of tragedy, which must be underpinned by a sense and an understanding of grief to achieve a full and valid structure. Even this kind of formalistic study may well be a type of evasion: the attention to form obviates in some degree the need to attend to substance. One can only hope that the study of literature will come to include the fundamental subject of grief and the kind of perceptive attention which up to now has gone into establishing means and criteria for literary study in general.

346

23

Notes on the Comparative Psychology of Grief*

Ethel Tobach

When I command my words to tell
the horror pictures of the mind
they turn away and disappear
they have no traffic with my grief . . .
. . . words won't shape and sounds recede
ebb, ebb my silent grief.
                                        Thomas O. Brandt

Alas! that all we loved of him should be,
But for our grief, as if it had not been,
And grief itself be mortal! Woe is me!
                                        XXI of *Adonais*—An Elegy
                                        on the Death of John Keats
                                        by Percy Bysshe Shelley

The desirable contemporary movement of medical science toward an
increased interest in the basic science of comparative psychology, sometimes thought of as animal behavior or ethology (1), has led to the
consideration of many human behavioral patterns, including grief, in

*While this chapter was being written and edited, I experienced
grief when my husband Charles died suddenly on February 19, 1969—this
after my teacher, T. C. Schneirla, died on August 20, 1968. I will not forget
writing this chapter and I hope that others will find it of value.

terms of evolution. This chapter is concerned with the following concepts: 1) to be human implies a relationship to the evolution of all animals; 2) the physiological and behavioral responses to social loss evolved as inherent components of the process of social organization; 3) the physiological and behavioral responses to social loss are unique on the human level because of the specialized and highly plastic human nervous system, the complexity of human social organization and emotional behavior, and the development of speech; 4) on the human level of organization we encounter a behavioral phenomenon which we call grief; 5) human grief subsumes the evolutionarily shared physiology of social loss, which can be communicated when social loss through death is experienced; 6) to grieve is to be human, and in the absence of human beings there is no grief.

To attempt to determine the evolution of the phenomenon of grief some basic assumptions regarding emotions are necessary (2). The view of emotion as a process implies that one can make an analysis of the evolution of such a process and that emotional processes will vary significantly on different phyletic levels.

On infrahuman levels the process of tensional adjustment between the organism and its environment is sufficiently dissimilar from the process on the human level as to warrant the use of the term "emotion" for human beings only. A further implication of this view of emotional behavior is that it varies with the developmental stage, that is, the emotional behavior of an immature organism differs significantly from that of a mature organism.

Both evolutionary and ontogenetic factors are important in the formulation of any behavioral process, including, of course, grief. Just as categorizations of all behavioral phenomena are possible, so are categorizations within a given behavioral process. Accordingly, grief is identifiable as a discriminable emotional process and is defined in terms of its relationship to a particular given sequence of events. For example, the operationally defined occurrence of activation of the tear ducts is classifiable in terms of a behavior pattern only when the preceding stimulus and the responding organism is known: a gust of acrid fumes, or an auditory stimulus communicating a high level of verbal information such as the news that a loved one is dying. It is possible, therefore, operationally to define grief as a behavioral pattern in this way.

In addition, grief is an emotional process which is predominantly related to social processes. Any particular emotional process is to be understood as representative of at least three variables of social processes. First, in terms of the number of individuals involved; for example, frustration or gratification may be individual processes and would therefore be considered low on the scale of social-emotional processes. Second, an emotional process may be understood in terms of its power to maintain or destroy the integrity of the social bond. Dyadic combat in regard to this variable would then be considered a low-level social-emotional process. The third variable refers to the type of social process involved—that is, whether it is a biosocial or psychosocial bond (3). Biosocial bonds are formed as a result of reciprocal stimulation at appropriate stages of development and are relatively temporary in nature. Such social groups are formed between or among animals with a relatively low level of ability to store and integrate past experience, or among animals at very early stages of development. Psychosocial bonds are a more advanced form of social process and reflect a more plastic neural organization capable of storing and integrating past experiences.

Within this context, grief is a high level social-emotional process. It is predicated on the basis of a social bond, and thus necessarily involves more than one individual. In addition, the bond would perforce have to be psychosocial in nature, and indeed, the most advanced level of psychosocial organization. Grief may, then, be subsumed as a category in the evolution of the socialization process, but it is an advanced level of the psychosocial form of social organization.

It is now possible to so define grief as an emotional process generated by the irreversible dissolution of a psychosocial bond of the most evolutionarily advanced type. As long as there is life there is the possibility of reversibility and the cessation of grief, thus "irreversibility" refers to losses through death only.

The first implication of this definition is that the most evolutionarily advanced levels of behavior are evidenced in human beings. Therefore, grief, as such, is restricted to the human level.

Another implication of this definition is that it should be possible to study and trace the evolution of the physiological and behavioral processes involved in the response to the destruction of the social bond on many phyletic levels and at many stages of ontogeny. A critical question would be: What evidence is there for the evolution of a behavioral process generated by the irreversible dissolution of a social bond?

Effects of Disruption of Social Organization

A survey of the effects of social stimulation indicates that on all phyletic levels—for example: bees (4), fish (5), rats (6)—a properly defined amount of social stimulation is essential for proper growth and development. Some of the most profound effects of such stimulation are seen in fundamental behavior patterns, such as sex behavior (7) and learning (8) in the rat, and maternal-young behavior in monkeys (9). The above-mentioned studies indicate some of the effects of social stimulation on the maintenance or destruction of organismic integrity.

The effects of the presence or absence of such stimulation are functions of the stage of development of the individual—in bees (10), in monkeys (11)—and the ontogenetic history of the individual. Disruption of the social bonds of a young member of a species of monkeys in which there is a high degree of interaction among all members of a group is less devastating than for a member of a species in which mother-young bond formation is limited to the biological mother (12, 13, 14). In lower mammals, as well, the disruption of the social bonds formed by mice during the litter period profoundly affects the physiology and behavior of the young after weaning and in adulthood (15).

It is in the profound physiological effects of a lack of social stimulation that we see the evolutionary forerunner of the human behavioral phenomenon of grief. These effects in infrahuman animals are derived chiefly from the biosocial nature of the bonds which are formed in the course of social stimulation. The effects are somewhat reversible and temporary in nature, and do not depend on the individualization of the source of social stimulation. Thus, it is possible to substitute offspring or peers and eliminate the effects of social isolation. There are limits to this procedure, but such limits are more frequently and more quickly found when psychosocial bonds are involved, as in monogamous bird pair formation, or in primate mother-young relationships. Anecdotes have been related in which a postparturient female chimpanzee (usually a primipara) will continue to clasp and manipulate a dead offspring and will not accept an appropriate, viable, nursing young. More data are required for a proper evaluation of such information, and to determine how similar or dissimilar such behavior is to human grief. The dissolution or interruption of a social bond may be temporary and adaptive. Although rejection or separation from the primate group can result in behavioral disorder for a short time, there is evidence that solitary primates (usually males) do not develop abnormal behavior and physiology (16, 17, 18).

Irreversibility of Social Bond Destruction by Death

The responses of infrahuman animals to dead species-mates apparently also vary in accordance with the level of social organization. In most instances in which animals are carnivorous (and in some instances in which they are not) cannibalism results, as in the lowest levels of social organization. Some insects and other invertebrates remove the dead organisms or treat them as they would other forms of exogenous matter, such as sealing dead insects in hive cells or using dead organisms as "nesting" material (19). On higher levels of social organization (primates), there appears to be a strong withdrawal from dead species-mates (20). This pattern has not been sufficiently studied to permit an interpretation of this behavior as a response to "death" as such.

Another type of social bond formation involves the relationships between different species of animals (21). The relationship frequently found between dog and man is an example of this. As Scott (22) has pointed out, the effects of the dog's experience with man are profound. As a result of the high level of organization in the dog, it is capable of individualizing social contacts to a considerable degree. Thus, the behavioral and physiological effects of the disruption of the bond between dog and man can be extensive. It is unfortunate, however, that there is an abundance of anecdotes about such effects but very little substantial data.

— — —

The fundamental process of material existence is that of coming into being as a function of the cessation of being. The evolution of matter and life is based on the disintegration of organisms and the forma-

351

tion of new organisms. This method of maintaining a system is extremely efficient and is evidenced in the evolution of behavioral processes as well. Along with the ubiquitous process of death, there have evolved behavioral patterns which support the efficiency of the dissolution of social bonds in the process of the creation of new social bonds. In the case of monogamous animals which do not subsequently mate when the original partner is removed by death or other causes, this prevention of the formation of the new social bond may be necessary for the survival of the species as such. When a primate female becomes nonreproductive because of the loss of an offspring, this may again be a selective process to remove from the gene pool a predisposition toward inadequate adjustment to intense stimuli. In most instances, with hormonal changes during the next estrous cycle the female again becomes reproductive, despite the earlier behavioral disorder. In the case of the the bird and monkey, however, there is insufficient information to permit more than speculation in this regard.

In summary, there is evidence that the response of an individual to the irreversible destruction of the social bond is related to the type of social bond formation. It appears that the most evolutionarily advanced response is human grief. An important question which follows from these conclusions is: What aspect of grief behavior is adaptive or facilitates the formation of new bonds?

The expression of grief presents a strong attractive stimulus to other individuals. Eliciting such approaches may lead to the formation of new bonds. In this process, as in many others, there is an optimum value to be reached which will guarantee that the presenting stimulus configuration brought about by grief is not so intense as to bring about withdrawal and avoidance on the part of the potential member of the social bond. The optimal development of the process of grief leads to the formation of new social bonds.

REFERENCES

1. E. Tobach, "Comparative Psychology, Psychobiology, Biopsychology, Animal Behavior, Ethology: What's in a Name?" Animal Behavior

Society Symposium, The University of California at Berkeley, 1965. (Unpublished manuscript).

2. E. Tobach (editor), "Experimental Approaches to the Study of Emotional Behavior," *Annals of the New York Academy of Science, 159,* 1969.

3. E. Tobach and T. C. Schneirla, "The Biopsychology of Social Behavior in Animals," in *The Biological Basis of Pediatric Practice,* ed. by R. E. Cooke, New York: McGraw-Hill, 1968.

4. M. Sitbon, "Contribution a l'étude du determinisme de l'effet de groupe chez les Abeilles," *C. R. Acad. Sci., 266*:1305, 1968.

5. H. Kawanabe, "On the Significance of the Social Structure for the Mode of Density Effect in a Salmon-like Fish," *Mem. University of Kyoto, Series B, 25*:171, 1958.

6. L. P. Baenninger, "Comparison of Behavioral Development in Socially Isolated and Grouped Rats," *Animal Behavior, 15*:312, 1967.

7. H. D. Gerall, I. L. Ward, and A. A. Gerall, "Disruption of the Male Rat's Sexual Behavior Induced by Social Isolation," *Animal Behavior: 15*:54, 1967.

8. J. C. Hitt and H. D. Gerall, "Simple and Complex Learning in Rats Reared Socially or in Isolation," *Psychon. Sci., 4*:179, 1966.

9. H. F. Harlow and M. K. Harlow, "The Affectional Systems," in *Behavior of Nonhuman Primates,* ed. by A. M. Schrier, H. F. Harlow, and F. Stollnitz, New York: Academic Press, 1965.

10. M. Sitbon, "Contribution a l'étude du determinisme de l'effet de groupe Chez les Abeilles," *C. R. Acad. Sci., 266*:1305, 1968.

11. G. D. Mitchell et al. "Long-Term Effects of Total Social Isolation Upon Behavior of Rhesus Monkeys," *Psycho. Rep., 18*:567, 1966.

12. I. C. Kaufman, "Some Biological Considerations of Parenthood," in *Parenthood: Its Psychology and Psychopathology,* ed. by E. James, S. Anthony, and T. Benedek, in press.

13. I. C. Kaufman and L. A. Rosenblum, "Effects of Separation from Mother on the Emotional Behavior of Infant Monkeys," *Annals of the New York Academy of Science, 159*:681, 1969.

14. L. A. Rosenblum and I. C. Kaufman, "Variations in Infant Development and Response to Maternal Loss in Monkeys," *American Journal of Orthopsychiatry, 38*:418, 1968.

15. E. Tobach and T. C. Schneirla, "Eliminative Responses in Mice and Rats and the Problem of 'Emotionality,' " in *Roots of Behavior,* ed. by E. L. Bliss, New York: Paul Hoeber, 1962.

16. T. Nishida, "A Sociological Study of Solitary Male Monkeys," *Primates, 7*:141, 1966.

17. C. H. Southwick, *Primate Social Behavior*, Princeton, New Jersey: D. Van Nostrand, 1963.
18. L. Devore, *Primate Behavior*, New York: Holt, Rinehart and Winston, 1965.
19. T. C. Schneirla, "Behavior of Insects," in *Insect Physiology*, ed. by K. D. Roeder, New York: J. Wiley and Sons, Inc., 1953.
20. D. O. Hebb and W. R. Thompson, "The Social Significance of Animal Studies," in *Handbook of Social Psychology*, ed. by G. Lindzey, Cambridge: Addison-Wesley, 1954.
21. E. Tobach, "The Use of Telemetry in the Study of the Social Behavior of Laboratory Animals," in *Bio-Telemetry*, ed. by L. Slater, New York: Pergammon Press, 1963.
22. J. P. Scott, "The Analysis of Social Organization in Animals," *Ecology*, *37*:213, 1956.

24

The Child's Concept of Death

H. Donald Dunton

Although this chapter deals with the child's concept of death as it evolves developmentally, it is important to point out that broad social and cultural attitudes and changes affect the reactions of the individual. Students of this problem have expressed varied and at times contradictory points of view. It is our impression, however, that each investigator probes only one of the many variables in this extremely complex structure.

Fulton (1), for example, states that attitudes toward death have changed dramatically in the past few decades under the impact of war, medical advances, and scientific inventions. Many forces have contributed to the weakening of religious beliefs, and because no ideology has replaced these beliefs, death has become a taboo subject. Borkenau (2) characterizes cultures throughout the ages as "death-defying" or "death-denying" and discusses the implications of these cultural attitudes. On the basis of a survey of the literature, as well as his own clinical observations, Rheingold (3) concludes that the mother-child relationship is the source of the death complex in its catastrophic aspects.

The bearing of interrelated familial, linguistic, social, and religious factors on the intrapsychic development of the notion of death is a complex one. In order to study the child's concept of death we may ask what the child means by "alive." Piaget (4) describes four stages of animism:

1. The child attributes consciousness and life to anything that is active, undamaged, or useful.

2. The child attributes consciousness and life to anything that moves.

3. The child attributes consciousness and life to anything that moves of its own accord.

4. The child restricts his definition to animals or to plants and animals.

Russell's studies (5, 6, 7) appear to bear out Piaget's description. Klingersmith (8) presents data which suggest that when a child states that an inanimate object is alive, particularly an object which evidences activity, he means much less by this term than most adults do, and much less than Piaget seems to have implied the child means. His findings can serve as a note of caution to our suppositions regarding the child's conception of death.

Nagy (9) describes three stages in the child's conception of death. Children under five variously view death as reversible, a departure, a state of sleep, separation, a change of environment, or as a form of limited life. The child from five to nine usually views death as personified and contingent. The child accepts the existence and definitiveness of death, casts it away, makes it remote and therefore not inevitable. The only people who die are those who are caught and do not get away. After the age of nine, the child understands that death is inevitable, is the end of corporeal life, is universal, and is the end result of an internal process.

The following case history will illustrate these conceptual levels:

A typical family with three children aged 11, 9, and 4½ years suffered the sudden death of a beloved pet dog. When informed of the sad event the 11-year-old responded at first by saying nothing. Slowly the tears welled up in his eyes and he began to cry softly. When he regained his composure he said, "It's such a horrible thing—it's all over." The 9-year-old listened quietly to the news and said, "He has gone a long way. We'll have to get another one." The 4½-year-old looked puzzled and said repeatedly, "What happened? Why are you crying? Let's go get him!"

In a study of children's affective responses (galvanic skin responses) Alexander and Adlerstein (10) found a significant response elicited by "death words" in a word association test. They suggest that this may reflect the relative decrease in ego stability elicited by the increase in psychological stress at certain developmental stages. Thass-Thienemann (11) has pointed out that the words for death in most languages reflect man's attempt to avoid the painful insight of the necessity of death. There are two general categories of such linguistic avoidance or explanation: death is caused by some external agent; death is mere departure.

The child has no understanding of the meaning of death until the age of five or six, and then it is usually in illogical terms. By age eight or nine, causal logical thinking is used to some degree by every child, and by roughly age eleven, logical thinking is used. Cousinet (12) outlined three stages: a refusal to accept the idea of death; the substitution of a curable illness for death; and the disappearance of death as a troublesome idea. Partz (13) postulated that before the age of seven, separation anxiety predominates over anxiety related to aggression, but that after seven, the reverse is true.

Schilder and Wechsler (14) found that children were concerned not so much with dying as with being murdered. Moellenhoff (15) concluded that although children have fluctuating and inconsistent notions about death, these have a common element—denial of death.

It is important to note that a child who is excessively angry or guilty may elaborate fantasies about death being a prolonged torture. The word "death" may be used by the child to refer to concepts of being enclosed in a box without air, being slowly eaten by bugs, or as involving slow, painful rotting. These fantasies fulfill the need for punishment and may reflect the spoken or unspoken ideas of the parents.

Anthony (16) concluded that death is related primarily to a fear of retaliation for aggression and that ideas about death parallel the development of other concepts as described by Piaget.

The preceding discussion is concerned primarily with the child's concept of death. It is necessary to examine the general context out of which these concepts evolve. Some families have a very real and vivid belief in life after death and instill this in their children at an early age. Other families are equally firm in their agnostic or atheistic beliefs. In the setting of any belief system the child's fears of being deprived—either in terms of being murdered or separated from his parents—take on a very specific organization and closure. Those families whose ideas and feelings about death are inconsistent, poorly understood, and avoided, create for their children a setting in which the child's unstructured perception of death will find no guidance and in which his tendencies toward fantasy will find support. Defense mechanisms (intellectualization, denial, projection, obsessive rumination, and others) of members of his family will mold and give final form to the rudimentary concepts of the child.

The actual life experiences of the family play a vital role in the child's conceptualization and management of death. Families of low economic and social positions, who experience many births and deaths, much violence, exploitation, hopelessness, and despair, constitute a sharp contrast to affluent families who know such experiences only through newspaper reports or novels. The factor of the age at which death is experienced is also a crucial one. Early and repeated experiences before the child is able to assimilate and accommodate them may produce a permanent incapacity to deal with any kind of loss, or a permanent tendency to avoid situations in which loss is a probable risk. The role of chronic terminal illness in a family is another dimension in the evolution of a child's concept of death. The ever-present reminder of the fact of death forces the family to come to terms with it.

Another factor to be considered may best be called the presence or absence of a "problem-solving attitude" in the family setting. If the family tends to explore alternate solutions, the effect on the child's concepts will be different from those on the child whose family's collective bonds are torn by despair and bitterness. The manner in which the parents deal with separations, with loss of things, friendships, and pets contributes to how the child will manage loss and separation in the traumatic event of the death of a loved one.

The problem of educating a child for the fact of death is a difficult one. Physicians are repeatedly faced with this problem on the wards of general hospitals, psychiatric hospitals, and in private practice. The clinician must come to an understanding of his own feelings and attitudes toward dying and death before he can distinguish and understand his patient's feeling about death. Although the clinician may believe that there is no life after death he must take into account the attitudes of those involved in caring for the child. Each child must be considered individually and the solution arrived at should take into account his psychic and social environment. The following cases are illustrative:

A 6½-year-old boy was admitted to a psychiatric service after a serious suicide attempt. He stated clearly that he wanted to kill himself so that he could join his dead father in heaven. The father had died suddenly of a myocardial infarct a year prior to the boy's admission. The boy presented a graphic description of his fantasied life with his father in Heaven. In essence, it was a fun-filled life, an endless picnic in an eternal park. He kept asking, "How do you know it isn't so?" In spite of thorough discussion, he persisted in his belief—encouraged by his mother who believed the same thing. The conflict was resolved by the child when he announced one day that he had decided that he would wait for God to send him to Heaven since that was His work. Follow-up evaluation four and six years later revealed that he was making an excellent adaptation. He still believed that it would be God's decision but, "The whole thing is in the back of my mind."

An 11-year-old girl was referred to a private psychiatrist after a minor suicidal attempt which followed the divorce of her parents and departure of her father. She said, "I didn't feel like living after he left. I started to poison myself but I didn't have the courage. I got to thinking what happens after you die. I asked my mother and friends—no one was sure. Since no one was sure whether it was good or bad I decided not to take a chance. I thought maybe I'll get used to the divorce." In this instance very little help or education was required from the psychiatrist.

The problem of educating a child about death is incredibly complex. Since the physician must face the management of dying patients he must be prepared to educate them, their family and friends, and, when called upon, to participate in the training of other "educators." It seems obvious that individuals and families who prefer to be educated by others—their parents, clergyman—should be free to pursue their own course.

If a family is receptive to the idea that their physician should help them in this particular life task, when and how should it start? The physician himself must be knowledgeable about the emotional and intellectual development of the child and about the dynamics of the family. Although all physicians must be prepared to understand and manage problems of loss and death, it is the pediatrician who is primarily responsible for the guidance of the child and his family in this area of living. This responsibility should be assumed not only by the physician in private practice but also by the physician in a clinic practice, whether in the hospital or in the community health center.

The following discussion represents a tentative approach to such care, and it assumes an interested family, a concerned and knowledgeable physician, and relative continuity of care.

The physician can begin the young family's education by exploring with them their own attitudes toward death and loss, and the possible meanings of separation and loss to their child. The physician can follow the growing child by exploring with the family general principles of child development as they relate to loss and death. The idea that loss is an integral part of the various stages of life, that death cannot be concealed from the child, and that natural and honest behavior on the part of the parents can contain for the child the impact of loss may be discussed at appropriate times. Such an educational program must be based on the child's development—his questions, his experiences, his fears and anxieties. It is important to realize that at any given stage of development the child "sees death as he sees it." If he insists that someone has gone away and is not dead it does little good to argue the point beyond stating the simple fact it is not so. Thus, the educator and parents can best help by reflecting the simple reality of the situation.

Beyond the world of clinical medicine and psychiatry the penetrating and perceptive work of a true educator is worth reviewing. Parkhurst (17) of the Dalton School in New York City, and the originator of the radio and television program "Child's World," studied 10,000 miles of wire recordings of unrehearsed interviews with children concerning, among other subjects, their problems regarding death. She presented the following conclusions:

The first discussions (of death) should not concern the death of loved ones because of the emotional elements involved. Instead, the conversations should be general, exploring the various connotations of death. Nor should the introductory discussions concerning death concern afterdeath, dogma or beliefs. Getting used to the idea of death should come first. One should proceed slowly, step by step. The approach will vary as much as the parents because of the differences in their personal beliefs. Parents are the only adults whom one can hold responsible for their children! The big need is to give meaning to the concept of death and see that it holds no terror for children. Their simple faith and directness can light the way for grown-ups who, in turn, review their own faith and understanding. In removing the child's fear he will remove his own. Both will be happier and wiser if they look for the answer they seek in the reality of living.

REFERENCES

1. R. Fulton and G. Geis, "Death and Social Values," *Indian Journal of Social Research, 3*:7, 1962.
2. F. Borkenau, "The Concept of Death," *The Twentieth Century*, April, 1966.
3. J. Rheingold, *The Mother, Anxiety, and Death; The Catastrophic Death Complex*, Boston: Little, Brown and Co., 1967.
4. J. Piaget, *The Child's Concept of the World*, New York: Harcourt, Brace, 1929.
5. R. W. Russell, "Studies in Animism: II. The Development of Animism," *Journal of Genetic Psychology, 56*:353, 1940.
6. R. W. Russell, "Studies in Animism: IV. An Investigation of Concepts Allied to Animism," *Journal of Genetic Psychology, 57*:83, 1940.
7. R. W. Russell and W. Dennis, "Studies in Animism: I. A Standardized Procedure for the Investigation of Animism," *Journal of Genetic Psychology, 55*:389, 1939.
8. S. W. Klingensmith, "Child Animism: What the Child Means by 'Alive,' " *Child Development*, 24(1) : March, 1953.
9. M. Nagy, "The Child's View of Death," *The Meaning of Death*, edited by H. Feifel, New York: McGraw-Hill, 1969.
10. A. Adlerstein and I. Alexander, "Afflicting Responses to the Concept of Death in a Population of Children and Early Adolescents," in *Death and Identity*, edited by R. Fulton, New York: J. Wiley and Sons, Inc., 1965.
11. T. Thass-Thienemann, *The Subconscious Language*, New York: Washington Square Press, 1967.
12. R. Cousinet, "L'idee de la mort chez les enfants" (The Idea of Death in Children), *Psychological Abstracts, 14*:499, 1940.
13. A. Partz, "The Meaning of Death to Children," unpublished Ph.D. dissertation, University of Michigan, 1964.
14. P. Schilder and D. Wechsler, "The Attitudes of Children Toward Death," *Journal of Genetic Psychology, 45*:406, 1934.
15. F. Moellenhoff, "Ideas of Children About Death: A Preliminary Report," *Bulletin of the Menninger Clinic, 3*:148, 1939.
16. S. Anthony, *The Child's Discovery of Death*, London: Kegan Paul, Trench, Trubner and Co., Ltd., 1940.
17. H. Parkhurst, *Exploring the Child's World*, New York: Appleton-Century-Crofts, Inc., 1951.

25

The Hospital Chaplain Looks at Grief

Robert B. Reeves, Jr.

The Passing of the Wake

To oversimplify, I would say that the need for psychiatric concern with grief came with the passing of the wake. In most cultures, the management of loss and grief has been one of the main concerns of the rituals of religion. The wake was only one of many exercises by which religion helped people deal with loss. Each step in life that was marked by a rite of passage was in some sense a dying and rebirth, the loss of an old and taking on of a new identity, culminating in the last step of death in this life and rebirth to the next. Much of the ritual apparatus of religion could be seen as a way of managing loss and grief.

At each critical step in life, the individual was sustained in the passage by rituals that performed three functions: 1) support in the expression of grief at the loss; 2) approval of the renunciation of what was lost; 3) guidance in redefinition and reinvestment of self. The wake served, primarily, the first of these functions through socialized rituals of mourning that supported the bereaved in their grieving, and so prepared the way, secondarily, for subsequent renunciation, redefinition, and reinvestment. Movement through the latter stages was contingent upon successful completion of the working through of grief.

With the passing of the wake in modern Western culture, the mourner is often bereft of social support in grieving and feels compelled to "bear up bravely." He often fails to accomplish the necessary grief work, and tries, unsuccessfully, to renounce his loss and redefine his life without getting rid of the grievous hurt. The hurt persists as an underlay, since it is barred from open expression, and eventually it seeps through in one form of illness or another. If the person is tightly organized with strong controls, the illness is likely to be somatic. If he lacks ego strength, it is likely to be psychic. In either case, without the rituals of religion to support him, he is a prime candidate for medical or psychiatric care.

The Villain: Angelism

How this all came about is not entirely clear. I suspect that a large contributing factor is the "angelism" which has plagued the Judeo-Christian tradition ever since the Neo-Platonic revival in the second century, and has become rampant in twentieth-century alienation of thought and feeling. It put religion on the side of the angels, instead of on the side of man, and, among its many sad effects, made man ashamed to grieve. Religion became so civilized that it forgot that human beings are creatures, and that "when a critter hurts, he has to holler." In the cool, dispassionate intellectualism of the modern religious climate, the wake would be most embarrassing.

"Angelism" refers to the dualistic view in Judeo-Christian thought, in which human nature is regarded as a combination of two entities, "soul" and "body." The soul is believed to be transcendent and eternal, while the body is fated to corruption and decay. Man's life is split into "higher" and "lower" levels, and the goal of his striving must be to win deliverance of his higher life from bondage to the lower. The angel must be liberated from the beast, pure spirit must be redeemed from captivity to "the world, the flesh, and the devil." And an essential part of this liberation is to learn to "rise above" the loss and sorrow attendant upon bodily existence. A true believer does not grieve.

This view, however, is not confined to believers. It is also characteristic of nonreligious rationalists and intellectuals, who substitute "mind" for "soul" and seek deliverance by reason from captivity to feeling. To the degree that intellectuals set the tone, this is characteristic of the culture as a whole. The periods in western history when the rationalistic accent has been the strongest (such as during the Age of

363

Reason) have tended to be the times when the wake was in disfavor, while the least rationalistic periods (such as the Elizabethan) have been the times when the wake flourished.

Under either heading, angelism or rationalism, emotional display is seen as a manifestation of man's lower nature. Where man's higher nature is in control, there should be no fear, anger, or sorrow, let alone unseemly outbursts of such feelings. If the feelings cannot be contained or denied, it is a mark of reproach: one has failed in the exercise of his higher powers—his *faith* if he be religious, his *reason* if he be intellectual. The dualistic view of human nature approves only of unutterable nobility in the management of loss of any kind, whether by accident, misfortune, surgery, or death.

Illustrations in the Hospital

To the academician such a description may appear a simplistic caricature, but in a clinical setting, such as in a hospital, it is vividly illustrated every day. The deceptions and disguises by which people try to disown or keep feelings of grief to themselves are often rudely penetrated by the life-and-death thrust of crisis in a hospital. A chaplain is likely to see in a raw state the things that people usually deal with only under wraps. Patients, their families, and members of hospital staff alike, tend to feel embarrassed by grief, and the more religious they suppose themselves to be the guiltier they become. Even the nonreligious tend to be embarrassed and apologetic. Maintaining control seems to be an obsession.

Instances are encountered daily. Members of a dying patient's family gathered at his bedside and in spite of themselves broke down in anguish. Immediately, nurses in ill-concealed annoyance rushed to herd them into the visitors' room, and with a resentful sigh the doctor ordered medication to quiet the prospective widow. Granted, a hospital corridor is not the ideal place to hold a wake, and an outburst of this sort does present a problem in management, yet the staff disapproval seemed far beyond the requirements for maintaining decency and order.

A nurse who cried at the death of a patient she had served faithfully for weeks was told coldly by her supervisor that she should not have let herself become "involved." Granted, a professional should maintain a degree of objectivity, yet does this require the nurse to deny that she is human and that she can be hurt?

An amputee, who had gone through the whole process of diagnosis, surgery, and postoperative period without complaint was admired by all for his cheerfulness and bravery. When he suddenly became withdrawn and depressed, his family and staff became alarmed and angrily reproached him, failing to see that if he could not grieve, he had no alternative but to internalize the hurt. Sometimes in their exasperation with the patient, hospital staff call upon the chaplain to "snap him out of it"—and they do mean "snap!"

Anticipatory Grief

At all stages of people's experiences with loss—before, during, and after —the chaplain is likely to encounter an inhibition of, or apology for, grief. When loss impends or death threatens, and a patient begins to grieve in advance, the feelings involved—fear, anger, guilt, sorrow— are often denied or consciously held in check. Anticipatory mourning is regarded by the patient as a betrayal of his faith. He gets little support from family or staff at this point since their tendency is to reinforce his denial, keep the lid on tight, avoid emotional upset before surgery or what they fear would be collapse at any hint of approaching death. Family and staff have enough trouble holding their own feelings down, without letting the patient lift the lid.

Frequently, these anticipatory grief feelings find other outlets through complaints about such matters as food, nursing care, side effects of medication, noise, etc. If these complaints are heard out, the patient may begin to realize that he can trust the listener and allow his true thoughts and feelings to be known. When this occurs, it is almost always with apology, frequently with a deep sense of failure and guilt.

Hints of anticipatory grief may appear in the form of bewilderment at what is happening to him. He may say to the chaplain, "I can't understand why . . . ." "I have faith, but sometimes I wonder . . . ." Or, in answer to inquiry of how things are going, he may say, "Oh . . . . they say I'm doing fine . . . ." Such hints are a thin disguise for feelings about impending death. If one continues listening, the feelings are likely

365

to well up and spill over, usually with tears and almost always with self-reproach.

Sometimes, however, the patient's denial seems so complete that one might assume he was going to a picnic instead of to the operating room or the grave. It is often maintained that to break down the denial in such a "brittle" patient would result in his falling apart. I have often taken that risk when there was enough time to help the patient work through his grief, and irreparable damage has never resulted. The confession of failure and guilt for "lack of faith" has sometimes been tortuous, but it usually allows the alleviation of the intense inner pressure of grief.

In some patients this anticipatory grief work goes nearly to the point of acceptance of impending death or loss. The patient is, to some extent, then able to renounce life or limb, and begin to redefine and reinvest. When loss of organ, limb, or function is involved, the patient may want to discuss the readjustments he will have to make. When death is imminent, he may, although it is increasingly rare these days, wish to talk about the life hereafter.

More likely, he may want to discuss the particulars of his postoperative care or the arrangements to be made at his death. In a patient who has worked through his grief to this point, it is no longer so much the anticipation of loss or of death itself that is dismaying as it is the anxiety about leaving things undone, breaking off with loose ends hanging, or losing control over self and possessions. It is of utmost importance for him to know how things are going to be, or to arrange for a tidy disposition of his affairs. Having worked through his grief to this extent, he may be dismayed if he cannot redefine his expectations by putting everything in order, and reinvest himself in the provision for the future of his loved ones. If out of fear his family or the hospital staff avoid the patient's discussion of such arrangements, they do him a great disservice: in effect, they bottle him up in his dismay.

To Tell or Withhold the Truth?

The reluctance of family and staff to let a patient grieve in advance is one of the factors that underlie their reluctance also to tell him the truth about his fatal illness. They are likely to engage in all kinds of apparently protective maneuvers ostensibly in the interests of the patient; but all too often, and for the most part unconsciously, this is done to protect themselves from exposure to his grief.

In itself, the fact whether or not a patient has been told is rarely of much significance. Most people know when they are about to die, and even those for whom death is still not imminent have a way of "putting two-and-two together." I have rarely met a terminally ill patient who did not intimate in some way that he knew, in spite of his own overt denial and the protective fictions spun by staff and family. The question is hardly ever, "should he be told?" but rather, "how shall we deal with what we must assume he knows?"

In the course of a patient's experience with those who attend him, more often than not a moment comes, when all the test results are in, all the circumlocutions have been exhausted, and the truth is *there* as a third party or silent partner. The patient and those who attend him "know," at a level either of rational awareness or of intuition, and are aware that the other knows. At that moment, the truth can be either acknowledged or denied. Which it will be depends very largely on whether or not the patient and those attending him are prepared to face the grief that may be expected to come with acknowledgment.

If, on the other hand, it is of compelling importance to them both to behave well, maintain control, keep up a good front, then the truth will probably be denied. One or the other of them will turn away from it, and the other party will take the cue and appear to ignore it, too. Each picks up the other's signals and with almost instant complicity plays out the part required of him. The presence of the third party, "Mr. Truth," is simply ignored. The tentative moment of truth will come and quickly go, obscured at once by evasive cheer, hopeful make-believe, double-talk, sometimes outright falsehood. For many people—patients, family, staff, alike—this is the only way they know to avoid what they feel would be an intolerable experience of grief.

If, on the other hand, both the patient and the person attending him are prepared to grieve, they will both probably be able to acknowledge it when the moment of truth arrives. The acknowledgment is rarely very dramatic. It is usually subdued, .somber, often dismayed and tearful, sometimes wry or even flippant. It "gives pause," and it is usually followed by several painful days in which the patient experiences many of the steps of mourning. With the support of family and staff, the patient can work his way to an acceptance of death, redefine what remains to him of life, and reinvest himself in closing-out activities and in providing for final arrangements.

Sometimes, when this process has been accomplished, it may appear as if it had not taken place. The patient emerges from his grief acting as if he did not know or were no longer concerned. Sometimes he may begin to spin a fiction of "getting better," as if to protect his family and friends from worry, and to spare the feelings of doctor and nurse. In many cases, a patient can with relative comfort maintain a fiction with everyone else so long as there is some one person with whom he can share his grief—doctor, nurse, pastor. I have been that person for many patients, and have watched in amazement sometimes how beautifully they succeeded in keeping everyone else happy. Occasionally, with me, too, after they have worked through their grief, they blithely close off all further reference to it and seem to go on as if nothing had happened.

If a patient is not prepared to grieve and so does not want to hear the truth, he has many ways to barricade it from awareness. Rarely is a patient damaged from having been told the truth. If "he has not ears to hear, he will not hear." But patients are damaged by the withholding of the truth when they are ready to hear it. If the doctor, family, or pastor evades, double-talks, or lies, when the patient hints that he sees the truth, then the patient's journey from that point on is usually one of increasing fretfulness and misery—a misery far deeper than that which accompanies open grief. The patient may appear to accept the denial, and because he is dependent on the people who attend him, go along with the fiction they present to him. But little by little, as his condition gets worse, the discrepancy grows between what he is told and what he feels, and the suspected truth looms over him like a tormenting ghost. The worse he becomes, the more intolerable the fictions he is told, yet he dare not grieve, for fear of alienating those on whom he depends.

But the alienation has already taken place, for in being denied the truth about himself, *he* is in effect being denied, dishonored, and abandoned. Because he has no one he can trust, he is likely to become bitter, to wallow in self-pity and complaint, demand ever more frequent and stronger medication to control pain and induce sleep, and have trouble eating and moving his bowels. Eventually, in order to be managed by the staff, he will be slugged with drugs into stupefaction.

Many more patients than are permitted could die in peace instead of misery, if those who attended them were less afraid of grief and so were free to acknowledge the truth and stand by their patients in their mourning.

When Loss Comes Suddenly

When death or other loss comes without warning and there has been no opportunity for anticipatory grief, the constraints imposed on the bereaved by angelistic piety or intellectualism are likely to compound the problem. Patients who as a result of accident or emergency surgery wake up to find themselves bereft of arm or leg, eye or breast are typical examples. This is true even when there has been adequate warning, but anticipatory grief has been suppressed, as may be observed among family members—especially parents of young children, who have refused to accept the fact that their child's illness might be fatal. They appear tight, taut, frozen, paralyzed—if only they could cry! Those who do break out of the initial shock and cry openly and unashamedly can usually continue to express grief. But most of the people so bereaved are under constraint not to grieve, and after the initial shock become hostile or depressed. Hostility is expressed through anger at the staff, the institution, fate, God—or the chaplain as His representative! Depression is usually related to feelings of guilt for indifference or neglect and real or imagined wrongs.

When people are seen under these conditions, the less said of religious preachment or reassurance, the better. In this period of anger or guilt, it is most inappropriate to talk of "the will of God," let alone His love. Much later on, perhaps, when controls have loosened enough to allow the expression of grief, such talk may bring comfort, but not when the grief is being held in check.

It makes one cringe to hear the sentiments so many well-meaning friends and clergymen try to impose upon the bereaved. "It is all for the best," they may say, or "It is in the hands of God," or "You should not grieve, your child is with the Lord now," or "Your husband is not really gone, he has just passed over on the other side." These things may be true, but in the face of sudden loss they are often heard as a mockery, and serve only to squelch the expression of feelings that the

369

would-be consoler finds too oppressive to deal with. Instead of supporting the bereaved, the consoler protects himself.

The person who cannot grieve, but can only become angry or depressed instead, above all else needs someone who will listen as he pours out the bitterest of his feelings, who will let him say the most hateful things about himself or God, without feeling compelled either to make excuses for the bereaved or to defend the good name of the Lord. Too many people, including clergymen, find this intolerable, and so they try to talk the bereaved out of his feelings, clamp down on him the platitudes of piety, smother his anger, or cheer away his guilt. Often they succeed and the anger or the guilt, apparently dispelled, is instead turned inward where it works havoc that may last for years, and sometimes for a lifetime.

Whether a person can cry out his grief or must contain it and become angry or depressed instead, the only way to help him is to *listen him out,* and by accepting and trying to understand his feelings encourage him to expel them until quietness comes. Then, and then only, is it appropriate to help him assimilate his loss into his world of meanings, and begin to explore with him how it fits into his faith. It may be too soon to start suggesting answers, unless he asks. The bereaved must be given room for doubts and relapses into grief and should not be urged to "have faith." He must be allowed to *find* his faith again, and he will do so only if those who minister to him have faith enough in him to honor his grieving doubt.

If a person's religious faith can be freed from the constraints of angelistic piety, it can, and should, help him to be honest about his feelings. He needs to see that it is no mark of faith to stifle grief, but rather that the highest faith permits a person to fling the bitterest accusations against himself or God without reproach in the certainty that even this the Lord will accept and understand. The bereaved will see this only as he experiences it in the acceptance and understanding of the chaplain, or whoever comes to him in ministry.

Somaticized Grief

When grief remains repressed before, during, or soon after an experience of loss, it may be expressed through sickness. The high frequency with which people who have suffered loss subsequently have to be hospitalized supports this contention. The recently bereft, the divorced, those who have lost job, fortune, or reputation, those who have lost a cause they had been fighting for, or have lost a following, enter the hospital daily. Because of our preoccupation with physiology, we often fail to relate their symptoms to their loss. Inquiry almost always discloses that at a conscious level they had dealt with their loss successfully, in that they had not broken down or ceased functioning. Unable to grieve in any other way, their only course was to work out the loss through illness.

This most frequently occurs in those whose ego structure and controls are too strong to permit a "nervous breakdown." They can develop numerous physiological diseases whereby the disease functions as a substitute for grief.

In spite of their tight control they send out signals which can be detected either in the history or in "listening" conversation. When indications of recent loss are known, one should look for signs of inhibited or unsuccessful grief. And the signs that turn out to be the surest signals are such as these:

1) Failure to acknowledge anxiety or fear that would be appropriate to the threat implicit in the illness;

2) tendencies to control the conversation in ways that allow the individual to shut-out emotionally laden topics;

3) casual reference, if there is any reference at all, to the loss, with no opportunity given for expression of sympathy or concern;

4) in spite of known or acknowledged church activity, no request, or even hint made for prayer;

5) acknowledgment with very unconvincing reasons for withdrawal from life-time church activity;

6) at the conclusion of an easy, pleasant chat, when the chaplain gets up to leave and says, "God bless you," a sudden welling of tears to the patient's eyes;

7) nonverbal cues, such as white knuckles, shredded kleenex, taut cords in the neck, and a brittle-bright smile.

Such signals are indications to stop by again and gently convey with open-ended questions that the world does not have to be all sunshine and roses. More often than not, the buried hurt eventually breaks through, tears come, and in a surprisingly short period of time the pent-up grief is spent. Just a few moments of complete emotional honesty have an almost miraculous effect in reducing the stress of unresolved grief. Much more remains to be done before healthy redefinition can be achieved, but feeling can be expressed and often the physical disorder begins at once to show improvement.

Psychiatry and Religion

Because of the repressive force of angelism in our religious culture, it is often impossible for a clergyman to rid himself and others of the need to apologize for grief. The passing of the wake and its emotional equivalents in other kinds of loss tends severely to handicap both pastor and people in dealing with life's crises. Religious ministration, which historically has been the most effective means of dealing with loss and grief, now serves usually to compound the problem.

Here is where psychiatrists have effectively come to the rescue. Psychiatry is owed a tremendous debt for the reinstatement of the unitary wholeness of man, and for providing the means by which we can accept ourselves and honor our emotions. In the psychiatric treatment of a religious person who has trouble grieving, the patient should be directed toward the rediscovery of himself as a child of God. The psychiatrist should have a list of clergymen to whom he can with confidence make referrals at the appropriate time, pastors who can work with their people to recover what the wake stands for in human self-acceptance. There never will be enough psychiatrists to handle the problem unless the grip of angelism is broken and religion is freed again to honor grief.

Loss and Grief:
A Selected Bibliography

Richard A. Kalish

Aldrich, C. K. "The dying patient's grief." *Journal of the American Medical Association, 184*:329, 1963.

Critical of the traditionally accepted determinants of a person's ability to accept death, the author describes the psychology of the dying patient from the perspective that loss of personal interrelations is more important than fear of dying. The implications of this approach are explored with respect to who should be told of impending death; the resulting interface with grief of others for the dying patient; the denial-acceptance spectrum; and the role of the doctor.

Alvarez, W. C. "Care of the dying." *Journal of the American Medical Association, 150*:86, 1952.

A physician relates from his own experience techniques in dealing with the dying patient and the family. Frankness, honesty, kindness, compassion, and comfort are the keys to easing the suffering of these patients as well as encouraging them to make the most of the time left to them.

Anderson, B. G. "Bereavement as a subject of cross-cultural inquiry: An American sample." *Anthropological Quarterly, 33*:181, 1965.

Anderson, C. "Aspects of pathological grief and mourning." *International Journal of Psychoanalysis, 30*:48, 1949.

In this article, a survey of a group of selected adult cases shows how certain neurotic responses are attempts to manage and resolve profound states of depression resulting from grief and mourning. There appears to be a repetition of an earlier pattern of successful or unsuccessful working through of an anxiety state which in turn is a repetition of the manner in which the infant has dealt with its primary loss.

Anthony, S. *The Child's Discovery of Death, A Study in Child Psychology.* New York: Harcourt, Brace, 1940.

A study of death imagery in children as expressed in conscious thought and fantasy. The author treats death as an isolated external reality, knowledge of which must be acquired by the child as an intellectual process. She then postulates that death, experienced between the ages of four and eight years, becomes associated with unconscious anxiety and with aggressive impulses. She gives little consideration to the trauma of object loss, first felt in the early months of life and often repeated, of which the loss of a loved person by death is but a later example.

Barnacle, C. H. "Grief reactions and their treatment." *Diseases of the Nervous System, 10*:173, 1949.

This article deals with pathological grief reactions, and presents several cases which required psychiatric treatment before satisfactory adjustment could be made. The methods of psychiatric therapy ranged from office interviews to the use of sodium pentathol and electro-shock treatments. The method of choice in therapy is dependent upon the individual grief reaction.

Becker, H. "The sorrow of bereavement." *Journal of Abnormal and Social Psychology, 27*:391, 1933.

Exposition of the theories and empirical principles of sorrow, with illustrations drawn from case studies made by the writer. The variety of expression described includes the type that gives free vent to its violence in outward behavior; the type that is tearless and mute; the type that sinks under the sense of weakness and discouragement; and the type that engages in activity approaching frenzy.

Bergler, E. "Psychopathology and duration of mourning in neurotics." *Journal of Clinical Psychopathology, 9*:478, 1948.

Because everyone unconsciously harbors traces of the infantile fantasy of "omnipotence of thoughts," a mourner may regard himself as if he were a murderer. Unconscious self-reproach for the alleged "murder in thoughts" is the basis of pathological or exaggerated mourning. These observations of Freud, made thirty years ago, were clinically tested time and again, and confirmed by different investigators. Two cases are described in which the exaggerations of mourning are found to be a reflection of the individual's neurosis. The author suggests that every exaggeration of mourning is most likely due to some form of psychopathology.

Bowlby, J. "Separation anxiety." *International Journal of Psychoanalysis,* *41*:89, 1960.

Because of their survival value, instincts such as crying, smiling, sucking, clinging, to which the mother responds, foster mother-child ties. When the mother is not available, protest behavior and separation anxiety result. Separation anxiety, grief, and mourning are intrinsically related because they are the result of the temporary or permanent loss of the mother-figure. Lability of feeling, separation anxiety, and grief are the unavoidable risks of attachment to a loved object.

————. "Grief and mourning in infancy and early childhood." *Psychoanalytical Study of the Child, 15*:9, 1960.

This article demonstrates the intensity and duration of grief; the psychological processes of mourning in very young children from six months of age onward; and the intimate relationship that grief has to separation anxiety. Bowlby questions the common assumption that, of losses affecting later object relationships, the loss of the breast at weaning is the most significant one sustained by the infant and young child. The role of weaning needs to be evaluated afresh in the light of more systematic evidence and should not be allowed to obscure the significance of loss of the mother-figure during the early years.

————. "Separation anxiety: A critical review of the literature." *Journal of Child Psychology, Psychiatry and Allied Disciplines, 1*:251, 1960-1961.

An examination of the literature shows that there are, at present, six main theories to account for separation anxiety. These are the theories of Transformed Libido, Birth Trauma, Signal Anxiety, Depressive Anxiety, Persecutory Anxiety, and Primary Anxiety. Whereas three of them (Birth Trauma, Signal Anxiety, and Primary Anxiety) were developed explicitly to account for the observation that young children are anxious when their mothers leave them, the other three had different origins and only later came to be applied to the data regarding separation anxiety.

————. "Childhood mourning and its implications for psychiatry." *American Journal of Psychiatry*, *118*:481, 1961.

This article examines psychological and psychopathological processes that commonly result from loss of mother (and, to a lesser extent, father) in infancy and early childhood. The reactions—the sequence of protest, despair, and detachment—of children so deprived are characteristic of all forms of mourning. It is concluded that loss of a mother in early childhood (before the fifth year) is generally more traumatic than such a loss at a later period in the child's life.

————. "Process of mourning." *International Journal of Psychoanalysis*, *42*:317, 1961.

Grief and separation anxiety are intimately related. The basic psychological processes of mourning are described in terms of three phases: urge to recover lost object; disorganization; subsequent reorganization. Similar mourning responses of animals indicate that primitive biological processes are at work in human beings; other features are specific only to human beings. Pathological mourning has as its main feature the persistent seeking of reunion with a permanently lost object. Infants who lose mothers show symptoms typical of pathological mourning. Thus, they are more apt to develop personality disturbances.

————. "Pathological mourning and childhood mourning." *Journal of the American Psychoanalytic Association*, *11*:500, 1963.

Fifth in a series of exploring theoretical implications of behavior of young children who have been removed from mother figures, this article puts forth two theses: 1) separation anxiety results, grief and mourning are set in motion; 2) mourning processes in early years often predispose to future psychiatric illness.

Cain, A. C., I. Fast, and M. E. Erickson. "Children's disturbed reactions to the death of a sibling." *American Journal of Orthopsychiatry*, *34*:741, 1964.

The authors explore a relatively neglected area of child development and psychopathology—that of children's reactions to death. Determining factors in disturbed reactions of children to the death of a sibling—guilt. distorted concepts of illness and death, health phobias, etc.—are discussed.

―――. "Children's disturbed reactions to their mothers' miscarriages." *Psychosomatic Medicine, 26*:58, 1964.

This clinical study emphasizes miscarriage as a potentially disruptive psychological event occurring within the complex interpersonal matrix of the family. Case histories of child, adolescent, and adult psychiatric patients are presented.

Chodoff, P., S. Friedman and D. Hamburg. "Stress, defenses and coping behavior: observations in parents of children with malignant disease." *American Journal of Psychiatry, 120*:743, 1964.

This paper describes the adaptational techniques and coping strategies employed by a series of 46 parents of 27 children fatally ill with leukemia and other malignant diseases. Most of these parents were able to function effectively during the period of the illness without being overwhelmed with despair or anxiety, at the same time preserving their personalities, maintaining key relationships and a measure of self-esteem. The various defenses employed are listed and described. The most important of these were isolation of affect, denial, and motor activity.

Cobb, B. "Psychological impact of long illness and death of a child on the family circle." *Journal of Pediatrics, 49*:746, 1956.

Four categories of impact of illness and death of a child are described: 1) impact of prolonged terminal stage of illness characterized by intermittent remissions and regressions, and eventual death of the child; trend showed family grateful for the time with child as long as there was hope and child's suffering could be controlled; 2) impact of enforced separation and disruption of family life on the marriage and on the siblings of the sick child; in a good marriage, trend showed stress of situation drawing members closer in fight with common enemy; 3) psychological impact of death on other children in family; trend was that each responded differently, in keeping with individual personality; 4) impact on role of religion in the tolerance and acceptance of the illness and death of the child; trend was expressed in terms of "without religion I would not have had the courage to live on."

A SELECTED BIBLIOGRAPHY

Deutsch, H. "Absence of grief." *Psychoanalytic Quarterly,* 6:12, 1937.

Observations from cases in which the reaction to the loss of a beloved object was a complete absence of the manifestations of mourning. Author believes that death of a beloved person must produce reactive expression of feeling in the normal course of events; that omission of such reactive responses is to be considered just as much a variation from the normal as excess in time or intensity; and that unmanifested grief will be found expressed to the full in some way or another.

Eliot, T. D. "The bereaved family." *Annals of the American Academy of Political and Social Sciences, 160*:184, 1932.

Bereavement is not found in groups which do not exhibit affective attachments, and is typically a family crisis resulting in certain primary and secondary effects. Some primary effects are: sense of unreality, shock, self-injury, grief. Secondary effects include: behavior patterns which take time and social interaction to form, such as escape, compensation, introjective identification. Familial changes resulting from bereavement include: disturbance of family unity, necessitating the reshaping of roles; consensus of family regarding new roles; possible decreased family solidarity; possible increased family solidarity; maturity of children; remembrance of deceased which may activate behavior of family.

————. "War bereavements and their recovery." *Marriage and Family Living, 8*:1, 1946.

Respects in which war bereavements may be harder or easier to accept than others; possibility of being prepared for bereavement; principles to guide those called upon to deal with bereaved families; mental hygiene principles for the bereaved which appear to help in recovery from grief; and criteria to judge recovery from bereavement.

Engel, G. L. "Is grief a disease?" *Psychosomatic Medicine, 23*:18, 1961.

Uncomplicated grief proceeds through three phases: shock and disbelief; awareness of the loss; restitution and recovery. The author reviews various attitudes toward the idea of grief as a disease, stating advantages in such a perspective.

————. *Psychological Development in Health and Disease.* Philadelphia: Saunders, 1962.

This book was writen primarily for medical students and psychiatric

378

residents. It is divided into two parts: the first deals with factors and considerations in the individual's psychological development; the second part demonstrates how these psychological factors operate within the framework of health and disease. One chapter, entitled "Psychological Responses to Major Environmental Stress," is pertinent to this bibliography. A discussion of grief and mourning deals with general responses to loss of objects such as persons, job, valued possessions, home, country. Object loss is "compared to a wound and mourning to wound healing. Like wound healing, pre-existing and previous conditions will influence or change the course of the process and sometimes prevent it altogether." The author outlines the course of normal grief and mourning and describes specific forms of pathological grief and mourning.

———. "Grief and grieving." *American Journal of Nursing,* 64:93, 1964.

The following topics are discussed and suggestions for management are offered: sequence of grief; normal/pathological grief; interplay of social, biological, and psychological factors in grief; factors influencing successful mourning; and practical considerations in communicating the death of a loved one.

Freud, S. "Mourning and melancholia." (1917) *Complete Works,* XIV, Standard Edition. London: Hogarth, 1953.

Correlation of melancholia and mourning is justified by the general picture of the two conditions. Mourning is the reaction to the loss of a loved person or an abstraction which has taken the place of one. As an effect of the same influences, melancholia, instead of grief, may develop. Unlike mourning, melancholia is regarded as a pathological state characterized by an extreme diminution of self-regard. It is postulated that the self-reproaches are reproaches against a loved object which have been displaced to the patient's ego. Melancholia borrows some of its features from mourning, and others from the process of regression from narcissistic object-choice to narcissism. An analytic explanation of melancholia is extended to mania as well.

Friedman, S. B. et al. "Behavioral observations of parents anticipating the death of a child." *Pediatrics, 32*:610, 1963.

Forty-six parents of children with neoplastic disease were studied for adrenal cortical response under conditions of chronic psychological stress. This paper reports on the emotional and behavioral aspects of stress and the implications of these findings for physicians managing the parents of children with these and similar diseases. Optimal medical management depends on the physician's awareness and evaluation of certain aspects of the patient's history. His empathy and understanding are vitally important in caring for the child with a fatal disease and the child's family.

Glaser, B. G., and A. L. Strauss. "The social loss of dying patients." *American Journal of Nursing*, 64:119, 1964.

A social value is inevitably placed on a patient, and that value has much to do with the quality of care he receives. The nurse must be aware of her judgments so that she can modify her behavior accordingly, to the objective needs of the patient.

Gordon, N. B., and B. Kutner. "Long term and fatal illness and the family." *Journal of Health and Human Behavior*, 6:190, 1965.

The effects of chronic and terminal illnesses of children on family-life stability are discussed: the evolution of types of parental behaviors and attitudes, practical consequences, intrafamilial relations. The role of the physician in such cases is outlined—care of initial traumatic reaction and helping the parents to manage their situation. Finally, the determinants of the crisis are suggested, such as the nature of the illness, the conditions of the illness, and the personality of the child.

Greene, W. A. "Role of a vicarious object in the adaptation to object loss: I. Use of a vicarious object as a means of adjustment to separation from a significant person." *Psychosomatic Medicine*, 20:344, 1958.

A group of 150 patients with leukemia and lymphoma were studied to observe adaptation to object loss. Three case studies are presented in illustration. Mechanisms other than those usually described as mourning, melancholia, and hypochondriasis are observed. The individual may preserve his own identity and also assume the role of the lost object and/or he may designate someone in the environment as a vicarious object.

Hamovitch, M. B. *The Parent and the Fatally Ill Child*. Los Angeles: Delmar Publishing, 1964.

This book reports a parent participation project in a hospital pediatrics department. The project, at the City of Hope Medical Center, focused primarily upon situations in which parents were faced with the predicted early death of a child from either leukemia or sarcoma. The project proposed to demonstrate that a hospital program providing for full participation by the parents in the care of these children can mitigate the traumatic effects of such a crisis upon the children and the parents. It was proposed also to demonstrate the feasibility of such a hospital program for full parental participation. The results of the study demonstrated that, in general, this program was successful in mitigating the trauma associated with these illnesses. Hamovitch concludes that this experience can serve as an incentive to other hospitals to modify their program in regard to the role of relatives in the care of patients; the principles discussed are applicable to patients suffering from catastrophic illnesses that strike in any age group.

Hinton, J. M. *Dying.* Baltimore: Penguin Books, 1967.

An overview of medical, sociomedical, psychiatric, and psychological aspects of death and dying. Takes a patient-centered (rather than family-centered, physician-centered, or hospital-centered) point of view.

Kalish, R. A. "Dealing with the grieving family." *R. N.,* 26:81, 1963.

The nurse is likely to be involved with grieving members of the deceased patient's family. "Guideposts" are given to help her deal with and perhaps ease their grief, including: most grief-stricken people need to talk; privacy may be the immediate need; resentment and guilt feelings are common; expression of nurse's emotions may be necessary.

Keeler, W. M. "Children's reaction to the death of a parent." *Depression.* Edited by P. H. Hoch and J. Zubin. New York: Grune and Stratton, 1954.

It is argued that children as well as adults are subject to psychopathological mourning states. Three case studies of children who lost a parent are presented in detail. The symptoms of depression (often masked) include: hoped-for reunion with the dead parent; identification with the deceased parent; suicidal attempts and preoccupations; marked anxiety; aggression; and guilt.

Kraus, A. S., and A. M. Lilienfeld. "Some epidemiological aspects of the high mortality rate in the young widowed group." *Journal of Chronic Diseases,* 10:207, 1959.

A review of the relationship between marital status and mortality based on statistical data published by the National Office of Vital Statistics on deaths and death rates in 1949-1951 by marital status, age, race, and sex. There was a lower death rate in the married group than in the single, widowed, or divorced at every age. An outstanding excess of mortality among the young (under age 35) widowed was noted. Three hypotheses were suggested to explain what appears to be a genuine association between young widowhood and subsequent mortality. These were called the "mutual selection of poor-risk rates," "joint unfavorable environment," and "effect of widowhood" hypotheses. Further studies were suggested to assess these hypotheses.

Krupp, G. R. "The bereavement reaction: A special case of separation anxiety—sociocultural considerations." *Psychoanalytic Study of Society, 2*: 42, 1962.

This article centers on adult bereavement in contemporary America, its symptomatology, pathology, and significance. The individual's reaction is conditioned by early infantile neurosis and by biological adaptive mechanisms as well as by the cultural milieu. The intimate nuclear family, the long dependence of children, emphasis on youth and vitality, and the urbanization characteristic of American culture are factors which may account for extreme bereavement crisis.

Langer, M. *Learning to Live as a Widow*. New York: J. Messner, 1957.

This book deals with a specific form of bereavement, widowhood. Its purpose is to provide women with guidance and assistance in their efforts to master their grief and to find new ways to live a rewarding life. The book is written not only for those who are bereaved, but also for those happily married now who may be urged to think ahead about dealing effectively with widowhood if and when it occurs. A resource appendix provides guidance to various services that may be of help to widows.

Lehrman, S. R. "Reactions to untimely death." *Psychiatric Quarterly, 30*: 564, 1956.

Grief reactions commonly are less extreme when death occurs in an aged person and when it has been expected. Under such circumstances, the work of mourning is accomplished more quickly because it has to some extent preceded the event of death. Pathological reactions to death are more frequent when the death is untimely and sudden. Other conditions and etiological factors also contribute to the formation of pathological reactions. This paper is concerned with some variants of pathological reactions to untimely death, their origin and meaning. The clinical material consists of five case histories. Reactions to untimely death tend to follow the pattern of grief reactions which represent a defense against unbearable, painful affect or a defense against serious internal ego-threat such as suicide.

Lindemann, E. "Symptomatology and management of acute grief." *American Journal of Psychiatry*, *101*:141, 1944.

Observations of 101 recently bereaved patients are presented. The hypothesis that acute grief is a definite syndrome with psychological and somatic symptomatology is presented, and several cases are discussed in this light. Both normal grief and morbid grief reactions are dealt with. It is apparent that realistic acceptance of a new role, coming to grips with guilt feelings, and acceptance of the mourning process are all important aspects of the resolution of grief.

Lindemann, E., and I. M. Greer. "A study of grief: emotional responses to suicide." *Pastoral Psychology*, 4:9, 1953.

The bereaved of a suicide are faced with a triple loss: death, rejection, and disillusionment. All these factors operate to increase the potential of hostility in the mourner and the danger of his turning it upon himself as the only available or most appropriate target.

National Association of Social Workers. *Helping the Dying Patient and His Family.* New York: National Association of Social Workers, 1960.

Parkes, C. M. "Effects of bereavement on physical and mental health—a study of the medical records of widows." *British Medical Journal*, 2:274, 1964.

The effects of bereavement and grief on 44 widows are studied by examination of their medical records. There was an increase in office consultations and in morbidity. An effort was made to isolate that part of the increased morbidity related to *recent* bereavement. The analysis also compared psychiatric and nonpsychiatric complaints; effect of bereavement on widows over 65 and under 65; and effect 6, 12, and 18 months after bereavement.

383

A SELECTED BIBLIOGRAPHY

Parkes, C. M. "Grief as an illness." *New Society,* April 9, 1964, pg. 11.

The symptoms of grief are well known. This, and the fact that its cause is known, makes grief unique among functional mental disorders. It is hoped that the study of grief may throw light on the pathology of less clearcut disorders. Three types of grief are described and the differences illustrated by case histories.

Pollock, G. H. "Mourning and adaptation." *International Journal of Psychoanalysis, 42*:341, 1961.

The function of the mourning process is to restore the ego's equilibrium. The chronic mourning stage consists mainly of object decathexis. In man, the object replacement after death depends upon: the instinctual needs of the mourner, the degree of energy liberation resulting from the mourning process, and the maturity of the ego and superego. The cathexis of new objects is not part of the mourning process per se, but an indicator of the degree of its resolution. The objects newly chosen may be substitutes or replacements but rarely are exact equivalents for the lost object.

Siggins, L. "Mourning: a critical survey of the literature." *International Journal of Psychoanalysis, 47*:14, 1966.

With Freud's model of mourning as a springboard, a model delineating intrapsychic aspects of adult reactions to the death of a loved one is presented. Reactions are distinguished as normal, pathological, and clinically recognizable psychiatric illnesses. Normal mourning reactions include guilt, anger, relief, and internalization of the relationship to the lost one. Reactions reflect positive and negative aspects of the relationship. When the bereaved fails to deal with the reality of death, mourning is pathological. There is a discussion of similarities and differences between adult's and children's reactions to death. A lengthy bibliography is included.

Stern, K., G. M. Williams, and M. Prados. "Grief reactions in later life." *American Journal of Psychiatry, 108*:289, 1951.

Bereavement reactions in later life are studied in 25 subjects, and the tendency toward their displacement in somatic illness is explored. These symptoms often are attended by a relative paucity of overt grief and conscious guilt feelings. The application of psychological dynamics of old age are discussed.

Weston, D. L., and R. C. Irwin. "Preschool child's response to death of infant sibling." *American Journal of Diseases of Children, 106*:564, 1963.

This paper focuses on the response of the preschool child to the experience of loss of an expected or an infant sibling and the help which the pediatrician can offer through his understanding. The pediatrician has the opportunity to help the family in the resolution of their grief and in interpreting the meaning of the loss to the other children. The various factors involved, that is, disruption of old roles and assumption of new roles, parents' grief, sibling rivalry, if the child was instrumental in sibling's death, etc., are discussed.

Young, M., B. Benjamin, and C. Wallis. "The mortality of widowers." *Lancet, 2*:454, 1963.

Previous studies suggest that the shock of widowhood might weaken the resistance to other causes of death. A series of 4,486 widowers 55 years of age and older were observed over a five-year period and all deaths of widowers were recorded. An excess mortality in the first six months of bereavement (an increase of about 40 per cent) was found. This increase was followed by a return to the mortality rate for married men in general. The series is to be re-examined in 1967.

Contributors

Kenneth Altschuler, M.D., Assistant Clinical Professor, Department of Psychiatry, College of Physicians and Surgeons, Columbia University, New York, New York

Richard S. Blacher, M.D., Associate Clinical Professor of Psychiatry, Mount Sinai Hospital of Medicine, New York, New York; Psychiatrist-in-Charge of Liaison Service to Department of Surgery, Mount Sinai Hospital, New York, New York

Alexander R. Broden, M.D., Instructor, Department of Psychiatry, Albert Einstein College of Medicine, New York, New York

Arthur C. Carr, Ph.D., Associate Professor (Medical Psychology), Department of Psychiatry, College of Physicians and Surgeons, Columbia University, New York, New York

H. Donald Dunton, M.D., Director, Children's Service, New York State Psychiatric Institute, New York, New York

Morris Freedman, Ph.D., Professor, Department of English, University of Maryland, College Park, Maryland

Robert A. Furman, M.D., Director, Cleveland Center for Research in Child Development, Cleveland, Ohio

Barney G. Glaser, Ph.D., Research Sociologist, San Francisco Medical Center, San Francisco, California

Thomas A. Gonda, M.D., Associate Dean and Professor of Psychiatry, Stanford University, School of Medicine, Palo Alto, California

Henry J. Heimlich, M.D., Associate Professor of Surgery, University of Cincinnati Medical College; Head of the Esophagus Center and Director of Surgery, The Jewish Hospital, Cincinnati, Ohio

Richard A. Kalish, Ph.D., Associate Professor, School of Public Health, University of California, Los Angeles, California

Lawrence C. Kolb, M.D., Professor and Chairman, Department of Psychiatry, College of Physicians and Surgeons, Columbia University, New York, New York

CONTRIBUTORS

Austin H. Kutscher, D.D.S., Associate Professor, Division of Stomatology, School of Dental and Oral Surgery, Columbia University, New York, New York; President, Foundation of Thanatology, New York, New York

Alexander P. Orfirer, M.D., Senior Instructor, Department of Psychiatry, College of Medicine, Case-Western Reserve University, Cleveland, Ohio

David Peretz, M.D., Associate, Department of Psychiatry, College of Physicians and Surgeons, Columbia University, New York, New York

Robert B. Reeves, Jr., Chaplain, The Presbyterian Hospital in the City of New York, Columbia-Presbyterian Medical Center, New York, New York

Ethel May Romm, M.D., Visiting Lecturer, Department of Psychiatry, College of Physicians and Surgeons, Columbia University, New York, New York; formerly, Training Analyst, Southern California Psychoanalytic Institute

Morris Saffron, M.D., Ph.D., Private Practice, Passaic, New Jersey

Bernard Schoenberg, M.D., Assistant Clinical Professor, Department of Psychiatry, College of Physicians and Surgeons, Columbia University, New York, New York

John E. Schowalter, M.D., Assistant Professor of Pediatrics and Psychiatry, Child Study Center, College of Medicine, Yale University, New Haven, Connecticut

Robert A. Senescu, M.D., Professor and Chairman, Department of Psychiatry, School of Medicine, The University of New Mexico, Albuquerque, New Mexico

Anselm Strauss, Ph.D., Professor of Sociology, University of California Medical Center, San Francisco, California

Ethel Tobach, Ph.D., Curator, The American Museum of Natural History, New York, New York

Jerry Wiener, M.D., Director, Division of Child Psychiatry, St. Luke's Hospital Center, New York, New York; Instructor in Psychiatry, Columbia University, College of Physicians and Surgeons, New York, New York

388

Index

INDEX

398